THE NEW ROMANTICISM

WELLESLEY STUDIES IN CRITICAL THEORY, LITERARY HISTORY
AND CULTURE
VOLUME 26
GARLAND REFERENCE LIBRARY OF THE HUMANITIES
VOLUME 2188

WELLESLEY STUDIES IN CRITICAL THEORY, LITERARY HISTORY, AND CULTURE

WILLIAM E. CAIN, *General Editor*

MAKING FEMINIST HISTORY
*The Literary Scholarship
of Sandra M. Gilbert
and Susan Gubar*
edited by William E. Cain

TEACHING THE CONFLICTS
*Gerald Graff, Curricular
Reform, and the Culture Wars*
edited by William E. Cain

THE CANON IN THE CLASSROOM
*The Pedagogical Implications
of Canon Revision
in American Literature*
edited by John Alberti

REGIONALISM RECONSIDERED
New Approaches to the Field
edited by David M. Jordan

AMERICAN WOMEN
SHORT STORY WRITERS
A Collection of Critical Essays
edited by Julie Brown

LITERARY INFLUENCE AND
AFRICAN-AMERICAN WRITERS
Collected Essays
edited by Tracy Mishkin

MODERNISM, GENDER,
AND CULTURE
A Cultural Studies Approach
edited with an introduction by
Lisa Rado

RECONCEPTUALIZING
AMERICAN LITERARY/
CULTURAL STUDIES
*Rhetoric, History, and Politics
in the Humanities*
edited by William E. Cain

TEXTS AND TEXTUALITY
*Textual Instability, Theory,
and Interpretation*
edited by Philip Cohen

THE NEW NINETEENTH CENTURY
*Feminist Readings of
Underread Victorian Fiction*
edited by Barbara Leah Harman
and Susan Meyer

ETHNICITY AND THE
AMERICAN SHORT STORY
edited by Julie Brown

NEW DEFINITIONS OF LYRIC
Theory, Technology, and Culture
edited by Mark Jeffreys

BLAKE, POLITICS, AND HISTORY
edited by Jackie DiSalvo, G.A. Rosso,
and Christopher Z. Hobson

RACE AND THE PRODUCTION
OF MODERN AMERICAN
NATIONALISM
edited by Reynolds J. Scott-Childress

WOMEN ON THE EDGE
*Ethnicity and Gender in Short Stories
by American Women*
edited by Corinne H. Dale
and J.H.E. Paine

LITERATURE AND THE INTERNET
*A Guide for Students, Teachers, and
Scholars*
by Stephanie Browner, Stephen Puls-
ford, and Richard Sears

BRITISH MARXIST CRITICISM
edited by Victor Paananen

THE NEW ROMANTICISM
A Collection of Critical Essays
eduted by Eberhard Alsen

THE NEW ROMANTICISM
A COLLECTION
OF CRITICAL ESSAYS

EDITED BY
EBERHARD ALSEN

GARLAND PUBLISHING, INC.
A MEMBER OF THE TAYLOR & FRANCIS GROUP
NEW YORK & LONDON
2000

Published in 2000 by
Garland Publishing, Inc.
A Member of the Taylor & Francis Group
29 West 35th Street
New York, NY 10001

10   9   8   7   6   5   4   3   2   1

Library of Congress Cataloging-in-Publication Data
The new romanticism : a collection of critical essays / edited by Eberhard Alsen.
        p. cm. — (Garland reference library of the humanities ; vol. 2188.
Wellesley studies in critical theory, literary history, and culture ; vol. 26)
Includes bibliography references and index.
        ISBN 0-8153-3547-4 (alk. paper)—ISBN 0-8153-3548-2 (pbk. : alk. paper)
        1. American fiction—20th century—History and criticism. Theory, etc. 2.
American fiction—20th century—History and criticism. 3. Romanticism—
United States—History 20th century. 4. American fiction—History and Criti-
cism. I. Alsen, Eberhard. II. Garland reference library of the humanities ; vol.
2188. III. Garland reference library of the the humanities. Wellesley
studies in critical theory, literary history, and culture ; vol. 26.

PS374.R6 N46 2000
813'.509145—dc21   00-026504

Printed on acid-free, 250-year-life paper.
Manufactured in the United States of America

For Frauke and Bengt

Contents

Series Editor's Preface		ix
Acknowledgments		xi
Preface		xiii

Introduction

I.	A Definition of Romanticism, Light and Dark	1
II.	The Resurgence of Romanticism Since the Fifties	9

Part I   **Contemporary Novelists on Romantics and Romanticism**

A World Too Much with Us (1975)	31
Saul Bellow	
Is It O.K. to Be a Luddite? (1984)	41
Thomas Pynchon	
Romancing the Shadow (1992)	51
Toni Morrison	

Part II   **Criticism on Contemporary Novelists**

The Romantic Style of Salinger's "Seymour: An Introduction" (1963)	71
John O. Lyons	
The New Romance [On Thomas Pynchon] (1972)	79
Arthur Mizener	

Lancelot: Percy's Romance (1983) 91
   Mark Johnson

John Gardner's "The King's Indian" and the
Romantic Tradition (1984) 105
   Gregory Morris

Bellow and English Romanticism (1984) 113
   Allan Chavkin

Hawthorne and O'Connor: A Literary Kinship (1989) 127
   Ronald Emerick

The Other Ghost in *Beloved:* The Specter of
The Scarlet Letter (1991) 137
   Jan Stryz

Updike's *Scarlet Letter Trilogy:* Recasting an
American Myth (1992) 159
   James A. Schiff

Ellison's *Invisible Man:* Emersonianism
Revised (1992) 177
   Kun Jong Lee

Nabokov and Poe (1995) 203
   Dale E. Peterson

Part III   **Overviews**

All the New Vibrations: Romanticism in 20th-Century
America (1969) 219
   Ronald L. Davis

The Corpse of the Dragon: Notes on Postromantic
Fiction (1975) 233
   Frank McConnell

Hawthorne and the Sixties: Careening on the Utmost
Verge (1985) 261
   Samuel Coale

Realistic and Romantic Tendencies (1996) 277
   Eberhard Alsen

Part IV   **Bibliography**

I. Contemporary Novelists on Romantics and
Romanticism 305

II. Criticism on Contemporary Novelists 306

III. Overviews 326

Index 329

Series Editor's Preface

The volumes in this series, Wellesley Studies in Critical Theory, Literary History, and Culture, are designed to reflect, develop, and extend important trends and tendencies in contemporary criticism. The careful scrutiny of literary texts in their own right of course remains a crucial part of the work that critics and teachers perform: this traditional task has not been devalued or neglected. But other types of interdisciplinary and contextual work are now being done, in large measure as a result of the emphasis on "theory" that began in the late 1960s and early 1970s and that has accelerated since that time. Critics and teachers now examine texts of all sorts—literary and non-literary alike—and, more generally, have taken the entire complex, multifaceted field of culture as the object for their analytical attention. The discipline of literary studies has radically changed, and the scale and scope of this series is intended to illustrate this challenging fact.

Theory has signified many things, but one of the most crucial has been the insistent questioning of familiar categories and distinctions. As theory has grown in its scope and intensified in importance, it has reoriented the idea of the literary canon: there is no longer a single canon, but many canons. It has also opened up and complicated the meanings of history, and the materials and forms that constitute it. Literary history continues to be vigorously written, but now as a kind of history that intersects with other histories that involve politics, economics, race relations, the role of women in society, and many more. And the breadth of this historical inquiry has impelled many in literary studies to view themselves more as cultural critics and general intellectuals than as literary scholars.

Theory, history, culture: these are the formidable terms around which the volumes in this series have been organized. A number of these volumes will be the product of a single author or editor. But perhaps even more of them will be collaborative ventures, emerging from the joint enterprise of editors, essayists, and respondents or commentators. In each volume, and as a whole, the series will aim to highlight both distinctive contributions to knowledge and a process of exchange, discussion, and debate. It will make available new kinds of work, as well as fresh approaches to criticism's traditional tasks, and indicate new ways through which such work can be done.

William E. Cain
Wellesley College

Acknowledgments

Eberhard Alsen, "Realistic and Romantic Tendencies." From *Romantic Postmodernism in American Fiction.* Amsterdam & Atlanta, GA: Rodopi, 1996: 1–24. Reprinted with permission of Editions Rodopi.

Saul Bellow, "A World Too Much with Us." *Critical Inquiry* 2 (Autumn 1975): 1–9. Reprinted with permission of Saul Bellow.

Allan Chavkin, "Bellow and English Romanticism." *Studies in the Literary Imagination* 17.2 (Fall 1984): 7–18. Reprinted with permission of *Studies in the Literary Imagination.*

Samuel Coale, "Hawthorne and the Sixties: Careening on the Utmost Verge." From *In the Shadow of Hawthorne: American Romance from Melville to Mailer.* Lexington: University Press of Kentucky, 1985. Copyright © 1985. Reprinted with permission of the University Press of Kentucky.

Ronald L. Davis, "*All the New Vibrations:* Romanticism in 20th-Century America." *Southwest Review* 54 (1969): 256–270. Reprinted with permission of Ronald L. Davis.

Ronald Emerick, "Hawthorne and O'Connor: A Literary Kinship." *The Flannery O'Connor Bulletin* 18 (1989): 46–54. Reprinted with permission of *The Flannery O'Connor Bulletin.*

Mark Johnson, "*Lancelot:* Percy's Romance." *Southern Literary Journal* 15.2 (Spring 1983): 19–30. Reprinted with permission of the *Southern Literary Journal.*

Kun Jong Lee. "Ellison's *Invisible Man:* Emersonianism Revisited." *PMLA* 107.2 (March 1992): 331–344. Reprinted with permission of *PMLA.*

John O. Lyons, "The Romantic Style of Salinger's 'Seymour: An Introduction'," *Contemporary Literature* 4.1 (1963): 62–69. Copyright © 1963. Reprinted with permission of the University of Wisconsin Press.

Frank McConnell, "The Corpse of the Dragon: Notes on Postromantic Fiction." *Tri-Quarterly* 33 (Spring 1975): 273–303. Reprinted with permission of Celeste McConnell.

Arthur Mizener, "The New Romance." *Southern Review* 8 (1972): 106–117. Reprinted with permission of Mrs. Rosemary Colt.

Gregory Morris, "John Gardner's 'The King's Indian' and the Romantic Tradition." From *A World of Order and Light: The Fiction of John Gardner.* Athens: University of Georgia Press, 1984: 137–142, 243–244. Reprinted with permission of the University of Georgia Press.

Toni Morrison, "Romancing the Shadow." From *Playing in the Dark: Whiteness and the Literary Imagination.* Cambridge: Harvard University Press, 1992: 29–59. Copyright © 1992 by Toni Morrison. Reprinted with permission of International Creative Management.

Dale E. Peterson. "Nabokov and Poe." From *The Garland Companion to Vladimir Nabokov.* Ed. Vladimir Alexandrov. New York: Garland, 1995: 463–472. Reprinted with permission of Garland Publishing.

Thomas Pynchon, "Is It O.K. To Be a Luddite?" *New York Times Book Review* 28 Oct 84: pp. 1, 40–41. Copyright © 1984 by Thomas Pynchon. Reprinted with permission of the Melanie Jackson Agency, L.L.C.

James Schiff, "Updike's *Scarlet Letter Trilogy:* Recasting an American Myth." *Studies in American Fiction* 20.1 (Spring 1992): 17–31. Reprinted with permission of *Studies in American Fiction.*

Jan Stryz, "The Other Ghost in *Beloved:* The Specter of *The Scarlet Letter.*" *Genre* 24 (Winter 1991): 417–434. Reprinted with permission of *Genre.*

Preface

Since the mid-sixties there have appeared over three hundred journal essays, book chapters, and doctoral dissertations that deal with romantic tendencies in contemporary American fiction. Moreover, a number of contemporary novelists have made public statements that reveal their interest in and their indebtedness to the nineteenth-century romantics. Nevertheless, most scholars who have made generalizations about American fiction from 1950 to 1999 have ignored this trend.

I decided to publish this anthology not only to draw attention to this important trend but also to illustrate the wide range of romantic ideas that can be found in contemporary fiction and the various ways in which twentieth-century authors have created a "new romanticism" by ringing changes on the ideas of their nineteenth-century ancestors.

The first three essays I reprint are by three of the most important novelists of our time: Saul Bellow, Thomas Pynchon, and Toni Morrison. I begin with those essays to prove that the romantic trend in contemporary fiction is not an anachronism but needs to be taken seriously.

In selecting studies on individual novelists and overview essays, I was guided by the desire to represent what I found to be the major trends in the three hundred-plus studies of romantic ideas in contemporary fiction that I was able to find. For example, the essays in the middle section of the book are on the ten novelists who have been most often discussed: Saul Bellow (33), Vladimir Nabokov (27), Thomas Pynchon (20), John Updike (16), Flannery O'Connor (14), Ralph Ellison (12), J. D. Salinger (10), Toni Morrison (10), John Gardner (9), and Walker Percy (7).

I also took care to represent the nineteenth-century writers who have been most frequently linked to contemporary novelists. The name that comes up most often is that of Nathaniel Hawthorne. Over forty studies deal with ways in which contemporary writers have adapted his romance theory to their own work or used ideas from his novels—mostly *The Scarlet Letter.* Hawthorne is followed by Edgar Allan Poe, Herman Melville, and Ralph Waldo Emerson, with over thirty items for each. In addition, there are twenty-seven studies that examine the relationship between contemporary American fiction and various English romantic poets, with Wordsworth and Blake being mentioned most often.

Another trend that I sought to do justice to is the preponderance of studies that focus on the Positive Romanticism of Wordsworth and Emerson, as opposed to the Negative Romanticism of Byron, Poe, and Melville. Here it must be noted that earlier studies have been chiefly interested in finding links between contemporary fiction and Positive Romanticism, while later studies have been more interested in pointing out attitudes that resemble Negative Romanticism.

A trend that my selection of essays does not reflect proportionally is the tendency of most critics to emphasize similarities between the ideas of the contemporary novelists and the nineteenth-century romantics and to downplay differences: Almost 90 percent of all studies on romantic tendencies in postmodernist fiction are influence studies. Since the early 1990s, however, there has been an increasing awareness that novelists often borrow ideas that they do not agree with. Thus we are now getting more studies of ways in which contemporary writers criticize or subvert romantic ideas. I reprint four such essays (Stryz, Schiff, Lee, and Peterson), even though that is a disproportionate number; but an anthology that consists almost entirely of influence studies would be too monotonous.

In selecting the four overview essays, I looked for three criteria: I wanted to include one study from each decade since the 1960s, I wanted to represent the linear as well as the cyclical view of literary history, and I wanted to illustrate the focus on Positive as well as Negative Romanticism.

With this reference to Positive and Negative Romanticism I circle back to the beginning of the book: My introduction begins with a definition of the light and dark sides of Romanticism and then presents a summary of the essays and book chapters reprinted in this collection.

THE NEW
ROMANTICISM

Introduction

I. A DEFINITION OF ROMANTICISM, LIGHT AND DARK

Shifts in Connotation

The word *romantic* did not exist until the middle of the seventeenth century. During the first 150 years that it was used, its connotation changed from negative to positive. The same change occurred in recent history. During the first half of the twentieth century, the word *romantic* had a negative connotation, in both its scholarly and its popular use. After mid-century, it began to acquire a positive connotation.

The adjective *romantic* derives from the noun *romance,* and that noun refers to the tales of chivalry that were popular in the sixteenth and early seventeenth centuries. Mario Praz points out that when the word *romantic* first appeared in western European languages, the major writers of the Age of Reason were condemning the romances of the previous century as unrealistic and irrational, and thus gave the word *romantic* connotations relating to what they perceived as "the falsity, unreality, the fantastic and irrational events and sentiments described in these romances" (12).

But as the eighteenth century drew to a close, the connotations of the word *romantic* changed to "interesting," "charming," and "exciting" (12–13). This development had to do with the gradual shift in the outlook of the major writers. According to Praz, "the subjective element implicit in 'romantic' rendered this word particularly suitable to describe the new kind of literature in which suggestion and aspiration had such a large part" (14). As this new kind of literature—written by the likes of

Rousseau, Goethe, and Wordsworth—began to influence the thinking of the educated public, the word *romantic* came to be associated with "vague longings" and with "the magic of the ineffable" (14–15).

Toward the end of the nineteenth century, the noun *romanticism* and the adjective *romantic* reacquired their original negative connotations, which can be traced back to the hostile reaction toward literary Romanticism on the part of nineteenth-century realists such as Henry James, Dean Howells, and Mark Twain. In their novels and their critical essays, these writers identified the essence of the romantic spirit as an unwillingness to face reality. Similarly, most of the poets who came into prominence just before and after World War I—for instance Carl Sandburg, Vachel Lindsay, and William Carlos Williams—felt compelled to declare their opposition to what they perceived as the overblown emotionalism of romantic poetry. This antipathy toward the romantics on the part of novelists and poets shaped much of the literary criticism of the first half of the twentieth century. Leading critics such as T. S. Eliot, Irving Babbitt, and T. E. Hulme consistently pointed out what they considered to be the defects of romantic literature. Russell Noyes explains this negative attitude as follows:

> The most hostile anti-romantic criticism has come from those who have assumed that modern science has made it rationally impossible to maintain romantic beliefs about man and nature. They have concluded that science has proved nature to be wasteful, cruelly savage, and brutal. They have seen man as the mere product of matter, as prisoner of blind chance without choice and without will in a horrible prison house. In such a world the Romantics appear to be childish dreamers; their picture of natural beauty, mere illusions; their moral values, utter emptiness. (xxxvi)

Modernist novelists such as Sinclair Lewis, Sherwood Anderson, and F. Scott Fitzgerald reinforced the negative connotation of the word *romantic* by creating memorable dreamers who were unwilling to face reality. Perhaps the most famous of these dreamers is Fitzgerald's self-destructive Jay Gatsby. Jay Gatsby, so Fitzgerald tells us, had "an extraordinary gift for hope, a romantic readiness," but this quality of his character ultimately made him pay too high a price "for living too long with a single dream."

The word *romantic* retained its negative connotation until the middle of the twentieth century, when there occurred a slow shift in a positive direction. This revaluation of the word was due to two developments, one in criticism and one in fiction. On the one hand, Arthur Lovejoy (1948), René Wellek (1949), and Morse Peckham (1951) provided new, objective definitions of Romanticism (see Works Cited), and F. O. Matthiessen, Charles Feidelson, and Harry Levin came out with books that celebrated the achievements of American romantic writers (Matthiessen's *American Renaissance* in 1941, Feidelson's *Symbolism and American Literature* in 1953, and Levin's *The Power of Blackness* in 1958). On the other hand, the novelists J. D. Salinger, Jack Kerouac, Norman Mailer, Bernard Malamud, and Saul Bellow published books that depicted the romantic attitudes of their protagonists in a positive light (*The Catcher in the Rye,* 1951; *On the Road,* 1955; *The Deer Park,* 1955; *The Assistant,* 1957; and *Henderson the Rain King,* 1958).

At first, these romantic attitudes were absorbed only by the counter-culture, by the beatniks of the 1950s and the hippies of the 1960s. But then Broadway and Hollywood cashed in on these new attitudes and made them fashionable. Two blockbuster examples stand out. One is the immensely popular Broadway musical *The Man of La Mancha,* a travesty of Cervantes' *Don Quixote* in which the protagonist is not a self-deluded madman but a noble character who worships the ideal, dreams "the impossible dream," and reaches for the "unreachable star." Even more popular was George Lucas' *Star Wars* trilogy of movies (1977, 1980, 1983), in which Ralph Waldo Emerson's "Oversoul" shows up as the mystical "Force," which gives its initiates superhuman powers. Even though the public did not directly associate *The Man of La Mancha* and *Star Wars* with Romanticism, the word *romantic* once again acquired a positive connotation during the second half of the twentieth century.

Positive Romanticism

The ideological core of Positive Romanticism is a worldview that is grounded in philosophical idealism. In his two-part essay "The Concept of 'Romanticism' in Literary History," René Wellek points out that this outlook took shape as a reaction against the rationalism of the Age of Reason:

> This new view emphasizes the totality of man's forces, not reason alone, nor sentiment alone, but rather intuition, "intellectual intuition," imagination. It is a revival of Neoplatonism, a pantheism (whatever its concessions to orthodoxy), a monism which arrived at identification of God and the world, soul and body, subject and object. (150)

According to Wellek, this outlook had three characteristic components that we can find in the work of all major romantics: "imagination for the view of poetry, nature for the view of the world, and symbol and myth for poetic style" (147).

Wellek explains that it was through their imagination that the romantics felt connected to the Creator of the universe, for they saw the imagination not merely as the ability to invent things but as a creative power by which the mind "gains insight into reality, reads nature as a symbol of something behind or within nature [that is] not ordinarily perceived" (159). In short, it is the imagination that reveals to the positive romantics the spiritual world of essences beyond the physical world of appearances.

The view of nature of the romantics differs from the views of the Age of Reason in two ways. For one thing, the romantics objected to the eighteenth century's mechanistic view of the universe. Wellek observes: "All romantic poets conceived of nature as an organic whole, on the analogue of man rather than a concourse of atoms" (161). For another thing, many of the romantics shared the pantheistic outlook of Wordsworth for whom "Nature is animated, alive, filled with God or the Spirit of the World" (162).

These views of the imagination and of nature explain the romantics' fondness for symbol and myth. According to Wellek, "all the great romantic poets are mythopoeic [*sic*], are symbolists whose practice must be understood in terms of their attempt to give a total mythic interpretation of the world to which the poet holds the key" (165).

A definition of romanticism that expands the implications of Wellek's ideas is that of Norman Foerster. In his anthology *American Poetry and Prose,* Foerster makes this statement about the shift in the basic outlook from the Age of Reason to the Age of Romanticism:

> Romanticism provided a new and more relevant set of affirmations which may be summarized as follows: Man is something more than a thinking machine in a machine universe. We cannot be content with ideas clear and consistent at the expense of truth; something is always left out. Reality is too large and diverse, too vital and fluid, to be compassed by cool reason. Nor is common sense sufficient; it may be the way to wealth and easy living, but not to high thinking and deep feeling. The world we live in is not a dead machine, but rather a living, breathing being. God is not outside the universe, forgetting and forgotten, but in it and in us, an immanent presence. Man does not come into

this world as a blank page to be written on, but as a spirit trailing clouds of glory. . . .

The secret of life, in the new outlook, lay not in the head but in the heart. Reality was to be sought not through conscious thought but through immediate intuitive perception: the kingdom of God was within. The head brought only doubt and barrenness; man must trust the heart—feeling—desire—the yearning for fulfillment—the Faustian spirit of aspiration. The human spirit had to be emancipated, freed from the tyranny of everything exterior to itself, whether this was a Calvinist dogma of depravity, or a cramping rationalism, or a common-sense obsession with the pots and pans of practical life. Freed from these it might regain the sense of wonder, the bloom of the world; might dwell on the strange, the mysterious, the miraculous; might hope for a revelation here and now. (257–258)

Neither Wellek nor Foerster takes into consideration that many romantics were unable to accept the neoplatonic views of Wordsworth and Emerson. Some, such as Lord Byron, Edgar Allan Poe, Nathaniel Hawthorne, and Herman Melville, had serious reservations about the central assumptions of Positive Romanticism—the immanence of God in Nature and in Man and the existence of a definite order behind the apparent randomness of the universe.

Negative Romanticism

Mario Praz wrote the first book on what later came to be called *Negative Romanticism.* Entitled *The Romantic Agony,* the book was published in Italy in 1930 but was not translated into English until 1950. In that book, Praz focuses on the "erotic sensibility" of romantic writers "who were tormented by obsessions" (xv). He points out that many romantics were fascinated with "the idea of pain as an integral part of desire" (17), with "horror as a source of delight and beauty" (18), and with "beauty tainted with pain, corruption and death" (45). Praz deals at length with five themes that recur in the literature of negative romanticism, that of the "Fatal Man" or satanic hero; that of the "Fatal Woman" or *"belle dame sans merci";* that of the "persecuted woman"; that of incest; and that of the *"vice Anglais,"* the sadistic pleasure of torturing the innocent.

While Praz is chiefly concerned with the psychological aspects of negative romanticism, he also considers questions of ethics and religion when he deals with the dark romantics' fascination with evil. Praz points out that Lord Byron himself became the prototype of the satanic hero who defies God. Examining biographical information about Byron, including diaries and letters by his wife, Praz points out that Byron challenged God by deliberately committing sins such as incest and by being cruel to those close to him because, as Praz believes, he "wished to experience the feeling of being struck with full force by the vengeance of Heaven" (75). Since Heaven never struck Byron, he began to flirt with atheism and nihilism. And so do many of the antiheroes in works of Negative Romanticism.

The critic who actually coined the term *Negative Romanticism* is Morse Peckham. In his 1951 article "Toward a Theory of Romanticism," Peckham defines negative romanticism as "the expression of the attitudes, feelings, and ideas of a man who has left static mechanism but has not yet arrived at a reintegration of his thought and art in terms of dynamic organicism" (15). Thus the negative romantic experiences "a period of doubt, of despair, of religious and social isolation, of the separation of reason and the creative power" (20). Consequently, the negative romantic is able to see "neither beauty nor goodness in the universe, nor any significance, nor any rationality, nor indeed any order at all, not even an evil order" (20). The doubt and despair of the negative romantics is reflected in the fictional characters they create. As Peckham says:

> The typical symbols of negative romanticism are individuals who are filled with guilt, despair, and cosmic and social alienation. They are often presented, for instance, as having committed some horrible and unmentionable crime in the past. They are outcasts from men and from God, and they are almost always wanderers on the face of the earth. (20)

Comparing Positive and Negative Romanticism, Peckham concludes that Positive Romanticism offers "cosmic explanations," that is, illustrations of a divine or at least spiritual force at work in the universe, while "negative romanticism causes isolation and despair because it offers no cosmic explanation" (20–21).

More recent studies have gone beyond the erotic and religious preoccupations of Mario Praz and Morse Peckham and have added more objective criteria to the definition of Negative Romanticism. Two such studies are those of Robert Hume and G. R. Thompson.

In his essay "Exuberant Gloom, Existential Agony, and Heroic Despair: Three Varieties of Negative Romanticism," Robert Hume provides a summary of the major traits of Negative Romanticism that have been established by previous critics and then points out two new traits. Hume mentions the following criteria that previous critics have proposed: (1) doubt, despair, and personal and religious alienation; (2) the exploration of dilemma, ugliness, and perversion; (3) the fascination with evil and pain; (4) disbelief in love and human compassion. One of the two new ideas that Hume adds is his observation that "the traditional Faust story is strikingly recurrent." Hume therefore considers Faust the "archetypal figure" of Negative Romanticism (112). Hume's second addition to the definition of Negative Romanticism is his notion that the central concern of Negative Romanticism is "an acute perception of evil with little move toward either solution or escape." Hume calls this trait "Existential Agony" (123).

Another valuable contribution to our understanding of Negative Romanticism is G. R. Thompson's essay "Romanticism and the Gothic Tradition." Thompson has much to say about the quest structure which the negative romantics borrow from the tradition of the gothic romance. Thompson mentions Charles Maturin's *Melmoth. the Wanderer* (1820) and Herman Melville's *Moby Dick* (1851) as "embodiments of demonic quest romance, in which a lonely self-divided hero embarks on [an] insane pursuit of the Absolute." This quest is not only "self destructive," but more importantly it is "metaphysical, mythic, and religious" (2). Thompson asserts that the heroes of Negative Romanticism are unable "to fully comprehend the haunting reminders of another, supernatural realm" and that they are in "constant perplexity of inexplicable and vastly metaphysical phenomena" (5). And despite the failures of their quests, so Thompson says, these heroes still achieve "some Sisyphean or Promethean semblance of victory" (6). Thompson concludes: "Dark Romanticism is the drama of the mind engaged in the quest for metaphysical and moral absolutes in a world that offers shadowy semblances of an occult order but withholds final revelation and illumination" (6).

Summary: The Ineffable and The Extraordinary

The core of the romantic worldview is the attitude that life is an ineffable mystery, but that beyond the randomness of the physical world there may lie an ordered metaphysical world and a spiritual force that may be either beneficent or malevolent. Thus we get visions of life that range from pantheistic faith to Manichean doubt. A passage from Ralph Waldo Emerson's *Nature* (1836) illustrates pantheistic faith:

Of that ineffable essence which we call Spirit, he that thinks most, will say the least. We can foresee God in the coarse, and, as it were, distant phenomena of matter, but when we try to define and describe himself [*sic*], both language and thought desert us, and we are as helpless as fools and savages. That essence refuses to be recorded in propositions, but when man has worshipped him intellectually, the noblest ministry of nature is to stand as the apparition of God. It is the organ through which the universal spirit speaks to the individual, and strives to lead back the individual to it. (345)

A speech by Herman Melville's Captain Ahab in *Moby Dick* (1851) illustrates the opposite outlook, Manichean doubt:

"All visible objects, man, are but pasteboard masks. But in each event—in the living act, the undoubted deed—some unknown but still reasoning thing puts forth the mouldings of its features from behind the unreasoning mask. If man will strike, strike through the mask! How can the prisoner reach outside except by thrusting through the wall? To me, the white whale is that wall, shoved near to me. Sometimes I think there's naught beyond." (144)

Ahab entertains the idea that there is "naught beyond" the physical world, but he does not embrace that idea. Likewise, Melville himself never achieved certainty one way or the other. As Nathaniel Hawthorne said about him in the November 20, 1870, entry in his *English Notebooks,* "He can neither believe, nor be comfortable in his unbelief." Like Melville, Lord Byron—who was probably the most desperate negative romantic—continued to be baffled to the end by the ineffable mystery of the world and could never be comfortable with his atheism and nihilism.

Because all romantics had intimations of a metaphysical world beyond the physical world, one of the most important themes in romantic literature is the quest for positive or negative proof of transcendence. As far as the romantic view of man is concerned, the faith of the positive romantics makes them focus on man's positive capability, and the doubt of the negative romantics makes them focus on man's negative capability. But both positive and negative romantics always present us with extraordinary characters in extraordinary situations, because neither the positive nor the negative romantics like to deal with the commonplace or the average. Instead, they like to dwell on the extraordinary, the strange, the mysterious, even the supernatural.

Works Cited

Emerson, Ralph Waldo. "Nature" [1836]. In *The Selected Writings of Ralph Waldo Emerson*. Ed. Brooks Atkinson. New York: Modern Library, 1950: 3–42.

Feidelson, Charles. *Symbolism and American Literature*. Chicago: University of Chicago Press, 1953.

Foerster, Norman. "The Romantic Revolt." In *American Poetry and Prose*. 5th ed. New York: Houghton-Mifflin, 1970: 257–59.

Hawthorne, Nathaniel. *The English Notebooks*. Ed. Randall Stewart. New York: Russell, 1962.

Hume, Robert D. "Exuberant Gloom, Existential Agony, and Heroic Despair: Three Varieties of Negative Romanticism." In *The Gothic Imagination: Essays in Dark Romanticism*. Ed. G. R. Thompson. Pullman, WA: Washington State University Press, 1974: 109–27.

Levin, Harry. *The Power of Blackness*. New York: Knopf, 1958.

Lovejoy, Arthur O. "On the Discrimination of Romanticisms." In *Essays in the History of Ideas*. Baltimore: Johns Hopkins University Press, 1948: 228–237.

Matthiessen, Francis O. *American Renaissance: Art and Expression in the Age of Emerson and Whitman*. New York: Oxford University Press, 1941.

Melville, Herman. *Moby Dick* [1851]. New York: Norton, 1967.

Noyes, Russell. "Introductory Survey." In *English Romantic Poetry and Prose*. New York: Oxford University Press, 1956: i–xxxvi.

Peckham, Morse. "Toward a Theory of Romanticism." *PMLA* 66 (1951): 5–23.

Praz, Mario. *The Romantic Agony*. Trans. Angus Davidson. New York: Oxford University Press, 1970.

Thompson, G.R. "Romanticism and the Gothic Tradition." In *The Gothic Imagination: Essays in Dark Romanticism*. Pullman, WA: Washington State University Press, 1974: 1–10.

Wellek, René. "The Concept of 'Romanticism' in Literary History: II. The Unity of European Romanticism." *Comparative Literature* 1.2 (1949): 147–72.

II. THE RESURGENCE OF ROMANTICISM SINCE THE FIFTIES

During the 1960s, a number of critics discovered romantic traits in the fiction of writers who had come into prominence in the previous decade. Some critics even speculated that there might be a new romantic movement under way. One such critic is Charles Hoyt. In his 1964 essay "Bernard Malamud and the New Romanticism," Hoyt writes:

It is becoming increasingly evident that . . . the athletic fatalism of
Hemingway, the closed "realism" of the Naturalist School, the chipped
classicism of Eliot and T. E. Hulme have engendered their opposites.
Romanticism is now abroad in all its traditional forms and proliferat-
ing: Youth in Revolt (Kerouac and others of the Beat group; England's
Angry Young Men), Glorification of Energy, and Passion Unconfined
(the Picaresque romps of Saul Bellow and J. P. Donleavy), the
Unleashed Imagination (Thomas Pynchon, Joseph Heller), Social
Protest (James Baldwin and others above), and of course, the Cult of
the Self, which so baffles classicist critics (J. D. Salinger has certainly
out-Wordsworthed Wordsworth here, drawing upon himself new Jeffreys, as has to a lesser degree Norman Mailer). To this exuberant ill-
assorted group Malamud stands as philosopher, or deepest thinker,
perhaps. (66)

Hoyt observes that while these writers are not committed to a concerted
program, they "hold certain principles in common." What Hoyt conceives to be the center of these principles is "the fundamental Romantic
Rejection of Objectivity" (66). As I will show, later critics have described a variety of additional common principles in the fiction of those
contemporary novelists who seem to be more in tune with the ideas and
attitudes of nineteenth-century Romanticism than with those of Modernism.

Since the publication of Hoyt's essay, over three hundred articles,
book chapters, and doctoral dissertations have appeared that deal with
romantic tendencies in post-1950 American fiction. Most of these studies
are on individual novelists or individual works, but some of them deal
with groups of novelists and try to define what romantic elements of
form, content, and/or ideology their work has in common. In addition, I
also found sixteen essays in which contemporary novelists discuss nineteenth-century romantic literature.

From among the essays on romantic literature by contemporary writers, I
singled out the ones by Saul Bellow, Thomas Pynchon, and Toni Morrison. I picked these essays not only because of the importance of the three
novelists but also because the essays illustrate major traits that link contemporary fiction to nineteenth-century romanticism.

Saul Bellow's 1975 essay is entitled "A World Too Much with Us."
That title alludes to the sonnet "The World Is Too Much with Us" by the
British romantic poet William Wordsworth. Whereas Wordsworth was

concerned that the materialism of his time estranged man from nature and from himself, Bellow is concerned about more than materialism. He says that in the second half of the twentieth century we have been living in a state of distraction, even frenzy, caused by "terror, crime, the instability of cities, the poisoning of nature, the ultimate weapons."

Bellow wonders what the role of the writer is in such a world as ours. After all, in the latter half of the twentieth century, art and literature do not enjoy as much respect as the natural sciences do, because ours is a "head culture" that instills in us a "tedious kind of rationality" that does not value the imagination. Moreover, the public is no longer looking for "the wonderful" in literature: "Now the wonderful is found in miraculous technology, in modern surgery, in jet propulsion, in computers, in television, and in lunar expeditions. Literature cannot compete with wonderful technology."

But then Bellow asks, "Isn't there a branch of the wonderful into which wonderful technology cannot lead us?" And his answer is that "we shall recognize it at once by its power to liberate us from the tyranny of noise and distraction." To be free from that noise and distraction, so Bellow says, would indeed be wonderful. And then he asserts that writers can free us from this noise and distraction because he believes

> that there is a mode of knowledge different from the ruling mode. That this other mode is continually operative—the imagination assumes that things will deliver something of their essence to the mind that has prepared itself and that knows how to listen. (World 8)

In short, writers can help us to reclaim our true identity and our true relation to Nature, because they have the imagination to penetrate to the essence of the phenomena. Moreover, so Bellow says, writers know how to draw on "an inadmissible resource, something we all hesitate to mention though we all know it intimately—the soul."

The importance of this essay is that it reveals a vision of life that is definitely romantic in its preference of imagination over rationality, in its belief in a world of essences behind the phenomena of the physical world, and in its belief that the human soul harbors spiritual truths that artists can access through their imagination.

The title of Thomas Pynchon's whimsical essay "Is It O.K. to Be a Luddite?" (1984) refers to the sympathy that the romantics felt for the Luddites, an organization that opposed the mechanization of the textile industry at the beginning of the nineteenth century. The Luddites organized violent protests during which textile workers smashed the machinery that was replacing them.

From this discussion of the Luddites, Pynchon goes on to consider the antitechnology and antiscience bias of the early romantics, spending considerable time on Mary Shelley's *Frankenstein* (1818), which he calls the prototypical Luddite novel. Then he talks about the Luddite impulse in the twentieth century, which he sees typified in the movie *King Kong* (1933).

What Luddite novels and movies have in common, so Pynchon says, is that they use "the miraculous" in order to get their antitechnology message across:

> To insist on the miraculous is to deny the machine at least some of its claims on us, to assert the limited wish that living things, earthly and otherwise, may . . . take part in transcendent doings. (41)

I reprint this essay not only because it demonstrates Pynchon's sympathy with the antitechnological bias of the early romantics, but more importantly because it suggests that the use of the "miraculous"—by the nineteenth-century romantics as well as contemporary novelists—is an indication of a belief in transcendence.

Toni Morrison's essay "Romancing the Shadow" (1992) illustrates yet another connection between contemporary writers and the nineteenth-century romantics. Although Morrison is chiefly concerned with matters of race, with the shadowy presence of what she calls "Africanist characters" in American fiction from Edgar Allan Poe to Saul Bellow, she also comments at some length on the genre of the nineteenth-century romance.

Morrison says that "the strong affinity between the nineteenth-century American psyche and gothic romance has rightly been much remarked." But she wonders why a new nation such as the United States "should devote its talents to reproducing in its own literature the typology of diabolism it wanted to leave behind?" Her answer is that "one way to benefit from the lessons of earlier mistakes and past misfortunes is to record them so as to prevent their repetition." This is why the form of the romance remained popular in America so much longer than in Europe.

Next, Morrison takes issue with a key idea in previous definitions of the romance and offers a correction. She is probably referring to Richard

Chase's book *The American Novel and Its Tradition* (1957) when she writes:

> It has been suggested that romance is an evasion of history (and thus perhaps attractive to people trying to evade the recent past). But I am more persuaded by arguments that find in it the head-on encounter with very real, pressing historical forces and the contradictions inherent in them as they came to be experienced by writers. . . . Romance offered writers not less but more; not a narrow a-historical canvas but a wide historical one; not escape but entanglement. (36-37)

These comments help us understand why the fiction of some contemporary writers—including Morrison herself—has more in common with the romances of the nineteenth-century romantics than the novels of the twentieth-century modernists.

The main part of this anthology consists of essays on the ten novelists who have been most frequently analyzed in studies of romantic ideas in contemporary fiction. They are Saul Bellow, Vladimir Nabokov, Thomas Pynchon, Flannery O'Connor, John Updike, Ralph Ellison, J. D. Salinger, Toni Morrison, John Gardner, and Walker Percy. I have arranged the ten essays in chronological order to make it apparent in what ways criticism on romantic traits in contemporary fiction has changed in the course of the last four decades.

J. D. Salinger is one of the earliest contemporary authors to have been dubbed a romantic. Henry A. Grunwald, the editor of the 1962 anthology *Salinger: A Critical and Personal Portrait,* was the first critic to do so. A year later, three other critics also talked about romantic traits in Salinger's fiction. Of the ten studies that treat Salinger as a neo-romantic, two relate his ideas to those of Ralph Waldo Emerson. Since I find neither one of those two studies convincing, however, I chose to reprint a more general one, John Lyons' essay "The Romantic Style of Salinger's 'Seymour: An Introduction'" (1963).

At the beginning of that essay, Lyons says that "for more than half a century our literature has been anti-romantic" but that "the style of Salinger's recent work suggests a return to the enthusiasm of the early nineteenth century." Analyzing the novella "Seymour: An Introduction" (1959), Lyons compares Salinger's style to that of nineteenth-century romantics such as Wordsworth, Byron, and Thoreau, whose work he describes as "discursive, organic in form, autobiographical, anti-intellectual, and mystical." But Lyons observes that it is not only the style of "Seymour: An Introduction" that is romantic but also the self-reflexive narrative technique, the fragmented structure, and the idealized character-ization of Seymour Glass. Moreover, so Lyons points out, the novella re-veals a number of romantic beliefs, among them that "man is an extension of organic nature," that there is a "mysterious interrelationship of all things," that there lies a "mystery in spontaneous creation," that we should show "respect for the instincts of a man and reverence for [our] own re-flexes," and that "art *is* life and not manipulated invention."

Twenty critics have pointed out romantic ideas in the fiction of Thomas Pynchon, but no two of them have linked Pynchon to a specific nineteenth-century writer in the way that O'Connor has been linked to Hawthorne and Nabokov to Poe. Instead, critics have pointed out refer-ences and allusions to works of many romantics from Blake, Wordsworth, and Shelley to Cooper, Poe, and Melville. There have been, however, two studies of romance elements in Pynchon's fiction and four studies that have linked his vision of life to romantic idealism. The article I chose to reprint combines these two topics.

Arthur Mizener's essay "The New Romance" (1972) examines Pyn-chon's short story "Entropy" (1963) and his novel *The Crying of Lot 49* (1967). Mizener says that Pynchon and other "twentieth-century roman-tics" are trying "to work out a new form of romance." This new romance shares with its nineteenth-century predecessor a preoccupation with the "transcendent reality lying behind the dull and obvious actual world." While the nineteenth-century romancers did not care to represent physi-cal reality in much detail, however, the writers of the new romance "give their images maximum concreteness and specificity" because "they are anxious to convince the reader that these objects are intensely alive in the transcendent realm." Although Pynchon and other contemporary roman-tics create very precise images, so Mizener says, they seem to believe that not the physical objects themselves but "the metaphysical relations among the images of the mind are the final reality." Thus, in all of his fic-tion, Pynchon "seeks correspondences, the full implications of which he does not—perhaps cannot—always make entirely clear."

The fiction of Walker Percy bears traces of the influence of several nineteenth-century writers. Two critics have related Percy to the British romantics and five to American writers, two each to Hawthorne and Poe, and one to Melville. Three of these critics have commented on Percy's fondness for the nineteenth-century romance, offering various reasons why Percy was attracted to that genre. The article that gives the best explanation is Mark Johnson's "*Lancelot:* Percy's Romance" (1983).

Johnson argues that Percy's *Lancelot* (1977) can only be properly understood when it is read as a romance and not as a novel. He then asserts that "like earlier American romancers, Percy is using the romance to question his contemporaries' materialistic faith in empirical science and capitalism" as well as their "separation of thought from feeling and body from soul." Moreover, *Lancelot* deals with three themes that Johnson says are traditionally associated with the romance: "epistemology, alienation, and the nature of evil." Johnson asserts that while in *Lancelot* "the ostensible subject is infidelity"—that of the protagonist's wife as well as that of his mother—"the real focus is epistemology, the need to know." Comparing Percy's protagonist to a Nathaniel Hawthorne character, Johnson says: "Like Ethan Brand, Lancelot had set out for the embodiment of evil, perversely seeking in unpardonable, uncontaminated evil an implicit proof of good." But unlike Hawthorne's Ethan Brand, Percy's Lancelot cannot recognize his own evil. Therefore, Lancelot comes to the false conclusion that "since he cannot find evil, there is no good." Johnson concludes that despite the different outcomes of the quests of Lancelot and Ethan Brand, Percy's novel still expresses a dualistic vision of life similar to Hawthorne's. And as far as Percy's indebtedness to Hawthorne's theory of the romance is concerned, *Lancelot* demonstrates that "the romance continues to enable our serious writers to ask metaphysical questions without pretending to have pat answers."

Four of the nine critics that have studied the romantic ideas in the fiction of John Gardner have pointed out his familiarity with and fondness for the British romantic poets William Blake, Samuel Taylor Coleridge, and Percy Bysshe Shelley. The other five have commented on his debt to Herman Melville and Edgar Allan Poe. Gardner reveals his interest in the American romantics most clearly in "The King's Indian" (1975). In that novella, he uses ideas and quotations from Melville's *Moby Dick* and *Clarel* and even has the ghost of Melville himself appear on two occasions. Moreover, he also borrows major events, settings, characters, and even names from Edgar Allan Poe's *Narrative of Arthur Gordon Pym*. So far the best analysis of romantic ideas in "The King's Indian" has appeared in a chapter of Gregory Morris' book, *A World of Order and Light: The Fiction of John Gardner* (1984).

Morris points out that in "The King's Indian," Gardner "begins with the standard 'boy at sea' metaphor that worked so well for Melville and for Poe." Because of Gardner's extensive borrowings from Poe, Morris provides us with a thorough inventory of plot elements, characters, settings, and ideas that Gardner took directly from *The Narrative of Arthur Gordon Pym*. More importantly, Morris shows that "The King's Indian" contains philosophical themes that are familiar ones in nineteenth-century romantic fiction. To develop these themes, Gardner created a protagonist, Jonathan Upchurch, who—much like Melville's Ishmael—is on a philosophical quest. He is looking for answers to the questions "Just what is the nature of personal freedom?" and "To what extent can one exercise one's freedom." In developing this quest, so Morris says, "Gardner pursues the same intellectual quarry as his nineteenth-century predecessors." Other romantic themes in "The King's Indian" are that of "the distinction between appearance and reality" and that of "the powers of the imagination." But what best shows the similarity between Gardner's vision of life and that of Edgar Allan Poe is the theme of man trying to usurp the role of the Creator by manipulating Nature. Says Morris: "It is that blasphemous and ignorant grasping for godhood that both [Poe and Gardner] deplore, the belief that man can create a nature that, in its intricate and ingenious mechanics, outdoes the original."

Saul Bellow has been linked to the nineteenth-century romantics more often than any other contemporary novelist (thirty-three articles and book chapters). This is because he has revealed his romantic leanings more clearly than anyone else, especially in his essay "A World Too Much with Us," in the 1975 speech he gave upon accepting the Nobel Prize in Literature, and in the three novels that start with the letter "H": *Henderson the Rain King* (1958), *Herzog* (1963) and *Humboldt's Gift* (1975). These three novels contain more allusions to and quotations from the nineteenth-century romantics than any of his other work. Almost all of the studies of romantic ideas in Bellow's work deal with these three novels, and many relate Bellow's ideas to those of Ralph Waldo Emerson. There are, however, almost as many studies that explore Bellow's relationship to the British romantic poets. So it was a toss-up which type of essay I would reprint. I decided on Allan Chavkin's "Bellow and English Romanticism" (1984).

Chavkin establishes Saul Bellow's affinity with the English romantics by quoting from a number of Bellow's essays, including "A World Too Much with Us," which is reprinted in this anthology. He says that "Bellow's outlook can be best described as a romantic outlook that is strongly colored by his unique sardonic comedy." Chavkin traces the origins of Bellow's interest in romantic thought by pointing out that when

Bellow wrote his first two novels, *Dangling Man* (1944) and *The Victim* (1947), he was still very much "under the domination of what he later called 'the Wasteland Outlook'." Bellow began to shed that outlook in *The Adventures of Augie March* (1953) and *Seize the Day* (1956) but did not develop his own brand of romanticism until *Henderson the Rain King* (1958).

Beginning with *Henderson the Rain King,* Chavkin then presents thematic analyses of five major novels (*Herzog* 1963, *Mr. Sammler's Planet* 1969, *Humboldt's Gift* 1975, and *The Dean's December* 1982), pointing out such typically romantic themes as the quest for spiritual rebirth, the desire to achieve a marriage of mind and nature, and the search for transcendent reality and for assurances of immortality. While all five novels contain references to such British romantic poets as Blake, Coleridge, Shelley, and Keats, Chavkin establishes the special significance that William Wordsworth's ideas have in Bellow's work. In particular, he points out the role that Wordsworth's "Ode: Intimations of Immortality" plays in *Henderson the Rain King* and in *Humboldt's Gift.*

Although Bellow believes, according to Chavkin "that romanticism must be modified and made tough minded enough to prevail in the modern wasteland," he also holds out "a qualified hope that man will redeem himself and his world by the powers of the imagination." Chavkin concludes: "Like Wordsworth and most of the other nineteenth-century English romantics, Bellow calls for the liberation of the mind from the mortmain of custom and the slavery of routine perception."

Flannery O'Connor is one of the two contemporary novelist who have been most frequently compared to Nathaniel Hawthorne (the other one is John Updike). Eight of the fourteen studies of romantic tendencies in O'Connor's fiction examine the influence of Hawthorne. The remaining six discuss echoes of ideas from various other nineteenth-century romantics such as Poe, Melville, and Goethe. The article I decided to reprint is Ronald Emerick's "Hawthorne and O'Connor: A Literary Kinship" (1989).

Emerick comments on several essays by Flannery O'Connor in which she reveals her extensive knowledge of Hawthorne's work. He also quotes a number of statements that she made in letters and interviews in which she acknowledged Hawthorne's influence on her. The most telling one is the admission: "I feel more of a kinship with Hawthorne than with any other writer." In another statement, O'Connor declared that she was writing romances and not novels. Emerick lists three traits of the kind of romance that O'Connor had in mind. One is that "like Hawthorne, O'Connor conceives of the romance as a border-land between two worlds, the natural and the supernatural." Another trait of O'Connor's brand of romance is "the concept of mystery, her term for the deeper realism and essential truths that the romance writer seeks to portray." And the third trait is that "like Hawthorne, O'Connor builds poetic and symbolic tales on broadly allegorical frameworks." In addition to following Hawthorne's definition of the romance, so Emerick asserts, O'Connor shares some of Hawthorne's most typical concerns, themes that have to do with "innocence, original sin, the devil [and] man's fallen state." Then Emerick points out what he sees as the most important theme in Hawthorne's and O'Connor's fiction: "Both concern themselves primarily with sinners . . . men and women who, because of pride or excessive rationality, separate themselves from their fellow man and attempt to play god-like roles."

Our other Nobel Laureate among contemporary novelists, Toni Morrison, has made it her habit to avoid alluding to great writers of the past in her fiction because most of those writers were white, and such allusions would work against her desire to create a literature that is, in her own words, "irrevocably, indisputably black." Despite these efforts on Morrison's part, six studies note similar motifs and ideas in Morrison's most celebrated novel *Beloved* (1987) and in Nathaniel Hawthorne's *The Scarlet Letter.* Moreover, three of these studies point out that in both *Beloved* and the earlier *Song of Solomon* (1977), Morrison employs narrative strategies that are similar to those of the nineteenth-century romance as Hawthorne defined it. Every one of these studies is careful to note the differences as well as the similarities between Morrison's and Hawthorne's use of similar motifs and ideas, and two have suggested Morrison only appropriates Hawthorne's ideas in order to criticize and transform them. One of these essays is Jan Stryz's "The Other Ghost in *Beloved:* The Specter of *The Scarlet Letter*" (1991).

In the first half of her essay, Stryz deals with the relationship between African American women authors and the American literary tradition that was largely forged by White males. She quotes Morrison's protest against literary criticism that "justifies itself by identifying black writers with some already accepted white writer" and she cites Morrison's "deliberate avoidance of literary references" in her novels because they are "inappropriate to the kind of literature [she wishes] to write." To avoid being lumped in with contemporary White novelists, so Stryz asserts, Morrison turned to the form of the romance. She argues that Morrison was attracted to the form of the romance because "romance elements can redefine space and time and our most basic perceptions, hence serving to articulate a particular aesthetic—in this case an African-American aesthetic." Stryz also observes, however, that this strategy, which was meant to release Morrison's works from contemporary White literary tradition, also draws them back into the tradition of nineteenth-century American Romance. In analyzing Morrison's attitude toward the tradition of the romance in general and Nathaniel Hawthorne's *Scarlet Letter* in particular, Stryz observes that Morrison challenges the nature of the authority of the White romance tradition, even while reminding us of it.

In analyzing *Beloved* and its relationship to *The Scarlet Letter,* Stryz points out that Hester Prynne is the "literary prototype for the female pariah figure who derives her identity from the community . . . and who is so central to Morrison's work." She also notes that Morrison's "Sethe enacts what Hester in her seemingly most unstable moments merely imagines," namely infanticide. But while the similarities between the two texts reflect common human concerns, so Stryz says, they also point out "social and cultural differences that lie between the particulars of the situation confronting the black characters in one text and the white characters in the other."

Morrison stresses these differences in what Stryz calls "an improvisation on *The Scarlet Letter,*" the fairy tale–like episode in which the runaway White servant girl Amy tells Sethe the story of her life. while helping her give birth to a baby girl. The story of Amy, who is "a fusion of Hester and Pearl," playfully incorporates fragments from *The Scarlet Letter* such as her obsession with red velvet cloth and her desire to return to Boston (the setting of the *Scarlet Letter*) where her mother died. Stryz concludes that "while escaping the written tradition that lies behind her, Morrison also follows it" because eisode involving Amy takes place within what Hawthorne christened "a neutral territory, somewhere between the real world and fairy land, where the Actual and Imaginary may meet." Ultimately, therefore, *Beloved* "makes an 'original' contribution to the very tradition it denies, is enriched by the tradition it denies, and is enriched by that very denial."

John Updike has been linked to Nathaniel Hawthorne even more often than has Flannery O'Connor. In my bibliography I list sixteen studies that deal with romantic ideas in Updike's work, and eight of them compare Updike's ideas to those of Hawthorne. Unlike O'Connor, however, Updike does not share Hawthorne's religious creed. Nevertheless, Updike wrote three novels for which he borrowed characters and plot motifs from *The Scarlet Letter.* The three novels are *A Month of Sundays*

(1975), *Roger's Version* (1986), and *S.* (1988). The protagonists in these three novels are twentieth-century versions of Hawthorne's Arthur Dimmesdale, Roger Chillingworth, and Hester Prynne. Updike's ambivalent fascination with Hawthorne is most fully explored in James Schiff's essay "Updike's *Scarlet Letter* Trilogy: Recasting an American Myth" (1992).

Aware that Updike's vision of life is very different from Hawthorne's, James Schiff wonders why Updike was so interested in *The Scarlet Letter.* Schiff offers three explanations. The first is that Hawthorne's stories and novels develop some of the same themes and conflicts as Updike's, "the conflict between matter and spirit; a fascination with community and communal experiments; the anxiety and fear of moral damnation; the relationship between sex and religion; an interest in . . . adultery and its effects on the community; and the use of ambivalent symbolism." A second reason for Updike's decision to write his *Scarlet Letter* trilogy, so Schiff suggests, might have been his desire to "deromanticize" Hawthorne's text by "calling into question its authority and moral stance." In this respect, so Schiff suggests, Updike is following in the footsteps of D. H. Lawrence who, as early as 1929, had asked us to "re-examine Hawthorne's characters, particularly in regard to what has been repressed or disguised." A third reason that Schiff sees for Updike's desire to rewrite *The Scarlet Letter* is that "Updike attempts to undo the traditional body-soul division in Hawthorne and to assert the significance of human flesh." Schiff therefore comes to the conclusion that Updike departs from Hawthorne in "affirming the corporal impulse" that has been denied since Puritan times. Accordingly, Schiff believes that one of the messages of Updike's *Scarlet Letter* trilogy is this: "Through acceptance of the body and its needs, the American self can rise from its bourgeois malaise, taste the exhilaration of freedom, and experience faith in the divine."

Few readers of Ralph Ellison's know that his middle name is Waldo and that his father named him after Ralph Waldo Emerson. As Ellison grew up, he became annoyed at the name. He first shortened "Waldo" to the mere initial "W" and later dropped it altogether. Although Ellison did not want to be connected with Emerson, he eventually admitted: "I cannot escape the obligation of attempting to achieve some of the things which [Emerson] asked of the American writer." It is therefore not surprising that seven of the twelve critics who have studied romantic ideas in Ellison's *Invisible Man* (1952) have compared Ellison's ideas to those of his transcendentalist namesake. The other five link Ellison either with

Melville, with Poe, or with Whitman. The essay I have chosen to include in this collection is Kun Jong Lee's "Ellison's *Invisible Man:* Emersonianism Revised" (1992).

At the outset of his essay, Lee reviews the critical controversy concerning Ellison's relationship to Emerson. While some critics focus only on the ideas shared by the two and thus imply that Ellison is deeply indebted to Emerson, others emphasize the differences to the extent of suggesting that Ellison uses Emerson's ideas only to satirize them. Lee tries to resolve the controversy by suggesting that "Ellison affirms the basic ideas of Emersonianism while neutralizing its negative aspects." The most negative of these aspects, according to Lee, is Emerson's racism. He supports this assertion with shockingly racist passages from Emerson's journals, and he also presents evidence showing that Emerson's support of the abolitionists' cause was at best half-hearted. Lee claims that Ellison was aware of this aspect of Emersonianism and that "racism is at the heart of Ellison's critique of Emerson." Lee therefore asserts that Ellison did not believe that Emerson's ideas could work for African Americans. This is why Ellison modified, extended, and enriched those ideas. For instance, "when he revises the Emersonian doctrine of self-reliance, representativess, and social organicism, [Ellison] endows his operative concept of race with positive and liberating connotations that diametrically oppose it to Emerson's." In this way, so Lee says, "Ellison at once criticizes and claims an Emersonian heritage."

Vladimir Nabokov began his career by writing in his native language and by responding to his Russian literary ancestors. Moreover, even after he became an American citizen, he continued to study the work of one of the giants of Russian Romanticism, Alexander Pushkin, and produced what is arguably the best translation of Pushkin's novel in verse, *Eugene Onegin.* Eight of the twenty-seven critics who have dealt with romantic ideas in Nabokov's work have therefore studied his indebtedness to Pushkin. Other European romantics to whom Nabokov has been linked are Goethe, Kleist, Byron, and Keats. As far as Nabokov's connection with American romantic writers is concerned, the name that is mentioned most frequently is that of Edgar Allan Poe (ten items). This is chiefly due to the many references to Poe by the narrator-protagonist of Nabokov's infamous novel *Lolita* (1953). Nabokov's fiction has therefore been combed for elements of plot and characterization that he might have borrowed from Poe. Some critics have commented, however, on more than superficial borrowings. One such critic is Dale Peterson. In his essay "Nabokov and Poe" (1995), he expands an analysis of the Poe influence into a consideration of the romantic aspects Nabokov's "poe-etics."

Nabokov admitted his youthful infatuation with the writings of Edgar Allan Poe, but insisted that Poe did not influence his mature work. Peterson points out, however, that Nabokov kept including parodies of and allusions to Poe's poetry and fiction in his writings throughout his career and that his view of art also resembles that of Poe. As Peterson says, "there are larger affinities with Poe than the obvious play with allusions would suggest."

Peterson first summarizes what previous criticism has established about ideas that Nabokov borrowed from Poe for *Lolita,* and he concludes that "*Lolita* could not have existed without a love for elaborate parody of Edgar Allan Poe." In particular, he points out that "the quest to repossess a vanished eidolon (Lolita) and the pursuit of a hallucinated, hidden double (Quilty)" are themes which Nabokov borrowed from Poe's poem "Annabel Lee" and from Poe's short story "William Wilson."

In the most important part of his essay, however, Peterson considers Poe's and Nabokov's views of art. He begins by pointing out striking similarities between Poe's poem "Al Aaraaf" and a poem that the young Nabokov wrote in his native Russian, "Enclosed in a crystal globe we were." In that poem, "the lovelorn speaker . . . is a fallen angel who openly acknowledges the catastrophe of differentiation that replaces a perfect celestial harmony." Peterson sees in this poem the same shades of Platonic Idealism that he sees in Poe's "Al Aaraaf." Moreover, Peterson also suggests that Nabokov must have been familiar with Poe's schizophrenic essays "The Philosophy of Composition" and "The Poetic Principle," one of which rejects inspiration as a source of art, while the other one embraces that idea.

Peterson believes that Nabokov was similarly torn between two "poe-etics," a cerebral one in which the artists controls all aspects of his composition and an intuitive one in which the artist follows his irrational hunches. Peterson concludes that both Poe and Nabokov "composed texts that deliberately exposed the transference and the transport, the genuine otherworldliness, that could be achieved by an inspired and well-regulated manipulation of the sensation-creating medium of language."

The overview essays that try to define the romantic trend in contemporary American fiction fall into two categories: One group explains this trend in terms of a linear view of literary history and the other in terms of a cyclical one. One group believes that the realist movement of the 1860s and 1870s did not succeed in killing off Romanticism, but that romantic ideas have continued to influence American fiction throughout all subsequent literary periods up to the present day. The other group sees the history of literature as evolving cyclically and in terms of each major period arising in opposition to the outlook of the previous period. Both groups are represented in the four articles I have chosen to reprint.

Ronald Davis' essay "*All the New Vibrations:* Romanticism in 20th Century America" (1969) is important as an early attempt to provide an historical explanation for the resurgence of Romanticism since the 1950s. Davis does not see this trend as a new phenomenon, because he believes that romantic "vibrations" have been growing since the beginning of the twentieth century. But, as Davis also points out, the American public did not accept the romantic outlook until after World War II. The atrocities of that war and the development of nuclear weapons that can annihilate whole cities and perhaps the whole planet made artists begin to search for values that can restore meaning in a world gone mad. In that search they followed the example of the nineteenth-century romantics and turned inward.

Because Davis discusses contemporary Romanticism in various manifestations, including painting, rock music, Broadway musicals, and cartoons, he does not say much about fiction. The two representative novels he discusses are J. D. Salinger's *The Catcher in the Rye* (1951) and Joseph Heller's *Catch-22* (1961). The romantic traits that Davis sees in these two novels are the beliefs that "man in society is more corrupt than man alone" and that society is "bent on his emotional destruction." Thus the new romantics "willingly cut themselves off from society" in order to "search for a more relevant set of values" and "to recapture man's true individuality."

In his essay "The Corpse of the Dragon: Notes on Postromantic Fiction" (1975), Frank McConnell says that the outlook of contemporary American writers is more closely related to the "visions of the great romantics" than "the countervisions of the moderns." Unlike Ronald Davis, McConnell does not see the romantic tendencies in contemporary fiction as a continuation of an unbroken linear trend, but rather as a reaction against the rationalist outlook of Modernism.

McConnell's view also differs from that of Davis in terms of what he takes to be the nature of the romantic ideas and attitudes in contemporary literature. McConnell writes that "there can be no doubt that our own best writing, as inheritor of certain crucial romantic dilemmas, has become increasingly to resemble the 'negative' side of the romantic vision." Following the revisionist criticism of Geoffrey Hartman and Harold Bloom, McConnell says that "the most efficient use we can make of the poetry and fiction of the last two decades is in terms of a revision of our ideas of romanticism." In particular, we must to go beyond "antiquated antinomies" and realize that romanticism can be better understood "in terms of its fundamental union of contraries, rather than as a mere set of mental-physical, spiritual-mechanistic antitheses." Such an approach to Romanticism, so McConnell asserts, will reveal a fundamental skepticism both on the part of the nineteenth-century romantics and their twentieth-century descendants, a skepticism that extends to the meaning of words themselves. And McConnell concludes this part of his argument by saying: "The disappearance of the noumenal, the thing grasped in itself, of the *idea* of essence; this is surely the fate of words from Shelley to Barthelme" (280).

According to McConnell, one of the key similarities between the negative romanticism in the work of the nineteenth and the twentieth-century writers is their use of the dragon slayer myth. McConnell explains that the dragon of this myth is "the oldest *other.*" We confront this dragon, so McConnell explains, when we have a serious car accident or when someone we love dies. McConnell sees a preoccupation with this myth in the poetry of the British romantics Blake, Coleridge, and Shelley, and he cites the figures of Blake's Urizen, Coleridge's vampire Christabel, and Shelley's Demogorgon as symbolic versions of the dragon. In the fiction of the American postmodernists, we get such symbolic monster figures in the title characters of John Barth's *Chimera* and John Gardner's *Grendel,* while in Thomas Pynchon's *Gravity's Rainbow* it is the V-2 rocket that assumes the role of the dragon, and in Saul Bellow's *Herzog* it is "the void" that is the monstrous adversary, "the void" being the metaphor for the protagonist's fear that there is no transcendence,

Like Frank McConnell, Samuel Coale is chiefly concerned with the influence of "negative romanticism" on contemporary American fiction. Unlike McConnell, however, Coale sees romantic tendencies in American fiction throughout the twentieth century. In his book *In Hawthorne's Shadow: American Romance from Melville to Mailer* (1985), Coale studies the influence of Hawthorne on the naturalist writer Harold Frederic and the modernist William Faulkner before he deals with American fiction in the second half of the twentieth century.

Coale offers a two-part explanation for the romantic tendencies we find in the work of contemporary novelists. One part is that many of them write romances rather than novels and that, in so doing, they follow the lead of Nathaniel Hawthorne because "Hawthorne's explanation of the romance, his description of his own techniques and the forms he chose to use, laid the groundwork for the American romance that was to follow." The second part of Coale's explanation concerns Hawthorne's dualistic vision of life, which Coale terms Manichean: "Others since Hawthorne have grappled with the self-same Manichean polarities discovering fleeting reconciliations but more often starker, irreconcilable contradictions. From Melville to Didion, this pattern reasserts itself over and over again." Then Coale analyzes the work of ten contemporary novelists: Carson McCullers, Flannery O'Connor, William Styron, Norman Mailer, John Cheever, John Updike, John Gardner, Joyce Carol Oates, Joan Didion, and Paul Theroux.

In the concluding chapter of the book, "Hawthorne and the Sixties: Careening on the Utmost Verge," Coale notes that there are two major camps of writers in contemporary American fiction, those who are working in Hawthorne's shadow and those who are not. Coale clarifies the typical traits of the fiction of Hawthorne's followers by contrasting them with the traits of the fiction of experimental writers such as John Barth, Donald Barthelme, Robert Coover, and Thomas Pynchon. Coale finds that this experimental fiction creates characters that appear little more than "cartoon folk" who are "victimized by their environment, produced by savage historical forces bearing down upon them." Moreover, so Coale says, the "emphasis on fragmentation of form" in this kind of fiction suggests the belief that we are living in "a primal chaos, an open-ended arbitrary universe in which nearly every value is upended and sabotaged." By contrast, the contemporary romances of such writers as John Cheever and Paul Theroux "use fairly straightforward historical and chronological narrative structures" and their characterization aims at "psychological complexity"; these writers often weave a "mesmeric spell" by grounding their narratives in "exotic settings in unusual and remote places"; they create "intimations of allegorical or at least symmetrical structures in regard to characters and situations"; and one of their recurring themes is a "continuing moral quest amidst fierce polarities that will not cohere."

Like Samuel Coale, Eberhard Alsen also compares two major trends in contemporary American fiction. In his book *Romantic Postmodernism in American Fiction* (1996), he labels these trends "neo-modernist" and "neo-romantic." Unlike Coale, however, Alsen sees the romantic traits in postmodernist fiction as signs of a reaction against Modernism and not as the manifestation of a persistent romantic strain in American literature. Alsen makes this point in his opening chapter "Realistic and Romantic Tendencies," in which he discusses the oscillation theory of the linguist Roman Jakobson and its modification by the historian Hayden White. According to that theory, successive literary periods are alternately dominated by a romantic or a realistic outlook. Alsen concludes that Modernism was essentially a realistic age and that the dominant outlook of the age of Postmodernism is a romantic one.

Having analyzed romantic traits in representative novels of twelve authors, Alsen develops a ten-point working definition of neo-romantic fiction. The heart of that definition is that "the vision of life in works of romantic Postmodernism is grounded in philosophical idealism, in the belief that spirit and not matter is the ultimate reality." From this ideological core, so Alsen maintains, grow the other traits that distinguish works of romantic Postmodernism, the view of art, the content, and the form.

Aside from the crucial point about the idealist vision of life, the most important parts of Alsen's definition are that the new romantics espouse an organic view of art and a belief in inspiration, that their major themes are philosophical or even religious ones (the most typical being "the quest for proofs of transcendence"), and that these novelists employ modes of storytelling that are reminiscent of the romances of Hawthorne, Poe, and Melville, because they combine "the plausible and the fantastic" and because they use "bizarre characters, unusual locations, and supernatural incidents." Alsen bases his conclusions on analyses of novels by Saul Bellow, J. D. Salinger, Norman Mailer, Flannery O'Connor, Kurt Vonnegut, Philip Roth, John Barth, Thomas Pynchon, Toni Morrison, Alice Walker, William Kennedy, and Paul Auster.

If we pull together the romantic traits in postmodernist fiction that the authors of the four overview essays and the authors of the ten essays on individual novelists have pointed out, we will find quite a bit of agreement on matters of form and content, but also some disagreements as far as the ideology or vision of life of the contemporary novelists is concerned. Having read close to three hundred articles and book chapters on connections between postmodernist and romantic fiction, I can report that no matter how many studies we examine, we will still find the same agreements on matters of form and content and the same disagreements on matters of ideology.

In the twenty-six studies of romance elements in contemporary fiction, there is considerable agreement (I reprinted three such studies in this volume: Mizener, Johnson, and Coale). The romance elements that are most frequently mentioned by these critics are straightforward narrative structures, subjective narrative perspectives, a mixture of natural and supernatural events, and heavy use of symbolism, often shading into allegory and myth. Moreover, a number of critics have noted that despite the tendency to mix the actual and the imaginary, the contemporary romantics tend to present images that are very sharply defined and solidly rooted in physical reality. The only disagreement I found concerns characterization. While most critics agree that characters in nineteenth- and twentieth-century romances are often larger than life, some believe that this means their characterization must necessarily be idealized and two-dimensional, while others believe that although characters in neoromantic fiction are often larger than life, they are still developed as complex and multidimensional personalities.

By far the largest number of critics who have studied connections between nineteenth-century and contemporary fiction have dealt with matters of theme. In the great variety of themes that have been discussed, a few stand out, because so many critics have dealt with them. These themes are the conflict between matter and spirit, man's attempts to manipulate Nature and play God, the nature of evil, the denunciation of materialism, attacks on science and technology, assertions of the transforming power of the imagination, and, above all, what Thomas Pynchon has called "the hunger for evidence of God and afterlife."

And with the latter theme, I come to the question of the ideological similarities between the nineteenth century romantics and their late twentieth century descendants. Surprisingly, more than twice as many critics have dealt with this issue than with matters of narrative form. Most of the critics who have analyzed romantic ideas in works of contemporary fiction have interpreted the vision of life in those works as a kind of neo-transcendentalism similar to the optimistic outlook of Wordsworth and Emerson. This includes a number of studies of the influence of Hawthorne on contemporary fiction, because quite a few critics treat Hawthorne as a Christian moralist or as a reluctant disciple of Emerson rather than as the writer in whose work Herman Melville saw a "blackness, ten times black." During the last ten years or so, however, there has been increased interest in the influence of "negative Romanticism" on contemporary fiction, with critics pointing out parallels between Poe's, Hawthorne's, and Melville's doubts about transcendence and similar doubts in the work of contemporary novelists (see McConnell and Coale in this collection).

In short, it is in respect to ideology that we get the greatest disagreements among the critics who have studied romantic tendencies in contemporary fiction. But despite such differences of opinion—which are ultimately due to the critics' own visions of life—there is widespread agreement that there has indeed been a resurgence of Romanticism in American fiction during the second half of the twentieth century.

Works Cited

Chase, Richard. "Novel vs. Romance." In *The American Novel and Its Tradition.* Garden City, NY: Doubleday, 1957: 12–13.

Grunwald, Henry Anatole. "Introduction." In *Salinger: A Critical and Personal Portrait.* New York: Harper, 1962: ix–xxviii.

Hoyt, Charles A. "Bernard Malamud and the New Romanticism." In *Contemporary American Novelists.* Ed. Harry T. Moore. Carbondale, IL: Southern Illinois University Press, 1964: 65–79.

PART I

Contemporary Novelists on Romantics and Romanticism

A World Too Much with Us (1975)

SAUL BELLOW

Wordsworth in 1807 warned that the world was too much with us, that getting and spending we laid waste our powers, that we were giving our hearts away, and that we saw less and less in the external world, in nature, that the heart could respond to.

In our modern jargon we call this "alienation." That was the word by which Marx described the condition of the common man under Capitalism, alienated in his work. But for Marx, as Harold Rosenberg has pointed out,

> it is the factory worker, the businessman, the professional who is alienated in his work through being hurled into the fetish-world of the market. The artist is the only figure in this society who is able not to be alienated, because he works directly with the materials of his own experience and transforms them. Marx therefore conceives the artist as the model man of the future. But when critics influenced by Marxist terminology talk of alienation they mean something directly contrary to Marx's philosophical and revolutionary conception. They mean not the tragic separation of the human individual from himself, but the failure of certain sensitive spirits (themselves) to participate emotionally and intellectually in the fictions and conventions of mass culture. And this removal from popular hallucination and inertia they conceive as a form of pathos. Nothing could be more vulgar in the literal meaning of the word than whining about separation from the mass. That being oneself and not others should be deplored as a condition of misery is the most unambiguous sign of the triumph in the individual of the

ideology of mass culture over spiritual independence. It is a renuncia-
tion of everything that has been gained during the past centuries
through the liberation of mankind from the authoritarian community.

Thus Rosenberg. And why do I associate him with Wordsworth? Simply
because we have now a class of people who cannot bear that the world
should not be more with them. Incidentally, the amusing title of Mr.
Rosenberg's essay is "The Herd of Independent Minds."

I have two more quotations to offer. The first is from a recent statement by Soviet President Nikolai Podgorny. He warns Russian writers
that any deviation from the principles of Socialist Realism is inadmissible and he says, "At a time when ideological struggle between socialism
and capitalism is becoming sharper, our art is called upon to constantly
raise its ideological arsenal, its irreconcilability to manifestations of
alien views, to combine the assertion of the Soviet way of life with the
deflation of apolitical consumer psychology."

Since Mr. Podgorny speaks of "our art," I shall claim the same privilege. In the West *our* art is far from apolitical, if you allow me to give the
word "politics" my own definition. When I say "political" I mean that the
world is very much with us. The world is more populous, more penetrating, more problematical, more menacing than it was in 1807. We can no
longer think of it in contrast to Nature as Wordsworth did. This is an all
made, rather than a naturally created world, a world of artifacts, products
of the mind. This world lives so much in us and upon us, so greatly affects our thoughts and our souls that I can't help thinking of it as having a
political character. "Either too much is happening too quickly, or it is
simply much more visible and audible than it was in earlier centuries.
Society has become more alive," writes Edward Shils. "The populace
[Professor Shils is speaking of the West] has become more demanding of
services, benefits, attention and a share of authority. This adds to the visibility and audibility. . . . The exhilaration, titillation and agitation have
become a continuing feature of our societies." I am inclined to go beyond
this. We are in a state of radical distraction; we are often in a frenzy.
When Baudelaire spoke of a *frénésie journalière,* he was like
Wordsworth and his all-too-present world, describing the condition in its
earlier states. The frenzy has accelerated unbearably in our time. We
have been, as it were, appropriated mind and soul by our history. We are
often cautioned not to exaggerate, not to see our own as the worst or most
trying of historical periods. Every generation has assailed itself in this
way and cried out against its pains and burdens. But things have hap-

pened in the twentieth century for which words like "war," "revolution," even "holocaust" are plainly inadequate. Without exaggeration, we can speak of the history of this century of ours as an unbroken series of crises. Not everyone of course responds to crisis with the same intensity, and some of us are more convulsed by events than others. Some take it with existentialist anguish and feel obliged, they say, to suffer through it as nakedly and acutely as possible. Others are more tough minded or better armored or simply disinclined to give up their lives to an interpretation of history—or to surrender their imaginations, since historical interpretations of this sort deprive the imagination of its ability to make independent judgments. But I don't see how we can be blind to the political character of our so-called "consumer" societies. Each of us stands in the middle of things exposed to the great public noise. This is not the materialism against which Wordsworth warned us. It goes much much deeper. All minds are preoccupied with terror, crime, the instability of cities, the future of nations, crumbling empires, foundering currencies, the poisoning of nature, the ultimate weapons. To recite the list is itself unsettling. The late John Berryman once told me that T. S. Eliot could no longer read the daily paper. "It was too *exciting,*" he said. A poet is of course more liable to be unbearably excited, in his tendermindedness, than a Kansas manufacturer or a Harvard economist. In any case, it is business and economics that most people are thinking about. Their minds are turned towards social problems. They are not thinking much of the time about painting or narrative poetry or Platonism or tragedy. They are far too extensively politicalized for that. I am not sure that I want to deplore this and complain, Victorian style, of the gross insensitivity, even of intellectuals, to art. I simply note, as one who has lived among serious people and knows something about American intellectuals that they can't be said to take literature very seriously. It's simply not important to them. It is not a power in life. Power lies in science, technology, government, business, in institutions, politics, the mass media, the life of nations. It is not in novels and poems. Few people, very few, will be considering, as Henry James did, that art gives meaning to existence or wondering whether they can afford to neglect the faith of Joseph Conrad. He believed that to understand a human event, to see the color of experience, to grasp it morally, to feel its subtleties we must have novels—the temperament of a reader must immerse itself in that of a writer. Not even novelists and poets now share this faith. Men like Osip Mandelstam, who believed that there were in Russia only two real powers, the power of Stalin and the power of the truth manifesting itself in poetry, are very rare

indeed. The artist must evidently find in his own spirit the strength to resist the principal alienating power of our time, and this alienating power
comes, not from the factory or "the fetish world of the market," but from
politics. Marx's "model man of the future" apparently appeared prematurely in Russia.

The man whom I wish to contrast with Podgorny is Goethe. His
view of the writer's social duty is very different. He said in 1830, "I have
never bothered to ask in what way I was useful in society as a whole. I
contented myself with what I recognized as good or true. That has certainly been useful in a wide circle, but that was not the aim."

Nations and societies torn by conflict, enduring famine, beset by
deadly enemies, fighting to survive, may not feel kindly towards
Olympian, contemplative Goethe. Russia during the Civil War, and again
when Hitler invaded it, was such a nation. That, however, was thirty-five
years ago. But we are all familiar with the tycoon who weeps about his
poor childhood and justifies his vices and villainies by telling us how un-
derprivileged he was. Israel is at this moment a country in great peril but
it refrains from ordering writers to enter the struggle. It does not deprive
them of the right to make the Goethean choice. The creators and rulers of
prison states, dictators and oligarchs, terrorists and their intellectual
strategists, the cruelest, most deformed part of our species force politics
upon us and then tell us what "our art" is called upon to do.

In the privileged democracies we find people who force politics
upon themselves. I think, for instance, of a Jean Paul Sartre who expresses his commitment to justice by demanding "action," that is, terror
and murder. He tells us in his introduction to Franz Fanon's *The Damned*
that the Third World finds manhood by its burning ever-present hatred
and its desire to kill us. Us? By us he means guilty and hateful Europe,
and "that super-European monstrosity North America." Sartre explains,

> The native cures himself of colonial neurosis by thrusting out the set-
> tler through force of arms. When his rage boils over, he rediscovers his
> lost innocence and he comes to know himself in that he creates him-
> self. . . . Once begun, it is a war that gives no quarter. You may fear or
> be feared, that is to say, to abandon yourself to the dissociations of a
> sham existence or conquer your birthright of unity. When the peasant
> takes a gun in his hands the old myths grow dim and the prohibitions
> are one by one forgotten. The rebel's weapon is the proof of his man-
> hood. For in the first days of the revolt you must kill: to shoot down a
> European is to kill two birds with one stone, to destroy an oppressor

and the man he oppresses at the same time. There remain a dead man, and a free man, the survivor, for the first time, feels a national soil under his foot.

Sartre reminds us not altogether unjustly of our "ideology of lies," our "strip tease of humanism," and of "the fat pale narcissism of Europe." All that is fair enough. But can we take him seriously when he insists that the oppressed must redeem themselves by violence? I have already suggested that the imagination is being given up by writers. Embracing causes, they have contracted all kinds of political, sexual, ideological diseases; their teeth chatter and their brains are filled with feverish fantasies of purgation and liberation by murder.

Suppose that Sartre had written a novel about the damned. He is not a good novelist but the art itself would have obliged him to deal with real, or approximately real, human beings, not the zombies of a pamphleteer. Suppose the white imperialist killed in a revolt had been a real person. Would Sartre then have been able to show the slave who had butchered his master redeemed by violence? Would it be certain that he was at last a free man? I strongly suspect that the banality of this would have sickened the author of *La Nausée*. War certainly filled Tolstoi with fury, but everything in *War and Peace* is humanly tested in full detail, page by page. The novel is for Tolstoi a method of dealing justly. He subjects his own beliefs and passions to the imaginative test and accepts the verdict of an artistic method. His novel shows human beings rooted in reality, and it shows that their need for truth is a vital need, like the need to breathe. Swift's Platonist horses in *Gulliver's Travels* spoke of a falsehood as the thing that is not. By truth I mean simply what is. "Truth, Clearness, and Beauty naturally are public matters," writes Wyndham Lewis. "Truth or Beauty are as much public concerns as the water supply." The imagination I take to be indispensable to truth, so defined. *It* is the prior necessity, not the desire or the duty to perform a liberating action. Sartre declares that in the eighteenth century a work of the mind was "doubly an act since it produced ideas which were to lead to social upheavals and since it exposed its author to danger. And this act, whatever the book we may be considering, was always defined in the same way; it was a *liberator.* And doubtless, in the 17th century too, literature had a liberating function. . . ."

It is not inconceivable that a man might find freedom and identity by killing his oppressor. But as a Chicagoan, I am rather skeptical about this. Murderers are not improved by murdering. Unchecked, they murder

more and become more brutish. Perhaps fertilizers and modern methods
of agriculture would benefit the peasantry of a famished world more than
the melodrama of rebirth through bloodshed. It may do more for manhood to feed one's hungry children than to make corpses.

It is true that the writer no longer holds the important position he
held in the eighteenth and nineteenth centuries. He has lost out. He is not
at the center of things. The bullying idea that he has a social responsibil-
ity, that he must cause upheavals, and that in the service of justice he
must thrust himself into danger is the result of a certain sense of diminished importance, as well as a boyish nostalgia for eighteenth century
roles. A work of art has many other ways to attain social meaning. The
writer whose imagination is passionately moved by political questions
and who follows his deepest convictions will write political novels worth
reading. But the ideological package, complete with historical interpretations, has no value. I have the greatest admiration for the courage of
writers who, having had politics thrust upon them by the ruling brutes of
their respective countries, honorably stood their ground. I have great
sympathy for them as well. They had no choice but to write as opposi-
tionists. From their side, looking at us in the West, they must be struck by
our innocence, our apparent ignorance of the main facts, our self-indulgent playing about with ideological toys, our reckless rocking of the
boat. They must often wonder as well at the dull refractory minds, the
sleepiness of many of us. For one part of mankind is in prison; another is
starving to death; and those of us who are free and fed are not awake.
What will it take to rouse us?

I said earlier that we lived in a state of distraction, even of frenzy,
and I called this unavoidable immersion in the life of society political. I
said also that intellectuals in America did not really take literature seriously, but were professionally preoccupied with various scientific, technological, or social questions. They were told at their universities that art
is very important and are quite willing to believe it; they are prepared to
accept and even to respect those who are described (quite often by themselves alone) as artists. But that is as far as it goes.

Experts know certain things well. What sort of knowledge have
writers got? By expert standards they are entirely ignorant. But expertise
itself produces ignorance. How scientific can the world picture of an expert be? The deeper his specialization, the more he is obliged to save the
appearances. To express his faith in scientific method he supplies what is
lacking from a stock of collective fictions about Nature or the history of
Nature. As for the rest of us, the so-called educated public, the appropri-

ate collective representations have been pointed out to us, and we have stocked our heads with pictures from introductory physics, astronomy, and biology courses. We do not, of course see what is, but rather what we have been directed or trained to see. No individual penetration of the phenomena can occur in this way. Two centuries ago, the early romantic poets assumed that their minds were free, that they could know the good, that they could independently interpret and judge the entire creation, but those who still believe that the imagination has such powers to penetrate and to know keep their belief to themselves. As we now understand knowledge, does imagination *know* anything? At the moment the educated world does not think so. But things have become dreary and humankind tired of itself because the collective fictions of alleged knowledge are used up. We now bore ourselves by what we think we know. Either life has already given up its deepest secrets to our rational penetration and become tedious or we have developed a tedious sort of rationality by ruling that certain kinds of knowledge are illegitimate. I am inclined to argue that the tedious rationality of our educated heads is a great breeder of boredom and of other miseries. Our head culture inordinately respects the collective powers of mind and the technical developments that have produced the most visible achievements of this civilization; it takes little stock in the imagination or in individual talent. It greatly esteems action. It seems to believe that artists should be harnessed to the social system as intellectual workers.

The Western world does not compel the writer to be an intellectual worker, or functionary. But, feeling no power in the imagination and needing to attach himself to power, under innumerable social pressures and politicized by crisis, the writer begins to think he too must be an activist and exert influence. He must do something, make himself available, be heard in just causes. We are, however, in a position to review the achievements of writers in politics. These are not especially breathtaking. The Tolstois, the Zolas, yes, those were great. But what of the Célines, the Ezra Pounds, the Louis Aragons, the hundreds who supported Stalinism? And what after all, can be said for the view that it is the writer's duty to cause social upheavals? How many of these upheavals have not brought to birth a police state? And if one yearns to live dangerously, is it not as dangerous to persist in the truth as to rush to the barricades? But then it is always more agreeable to play the role of a writer than to be a writer. A writer's life is solitary, often bitter. How pleasant it is to come out of one's room, to fly about the world, make speeches, and cut a swath.

For a very long time the world found the wonderful in tales and poems, in painting, and in musical performances. Now the wonderful is found in miraculous technology, in modern surgery, in jet propulsion, in computers, in television, and in lunar expeditions. Literature cannot compete with wonderful technology. Writers, trying to keep the attention of the public, have turned to methods of shock, to obscenity and super sensationalism, adding their clamor to the great noise now threatening the sanity of civilized nations.

But isn't there a branch of the wonderful into which wonderful technology cannot lead us? If there is, how shall we know it? Why, we shall recognize it at once by its power to liberate us from the tyranny of noise and distraction. Since 1914, in all spheres of life, crisis has ruled over us, survival anxiety has become permanent with us, and public unrest has been set into our souls. To be free from this would indeed be wonderful. It would mean nothing less than the restoration or recreation of culture. Indispensable to such a restoration is the recovery of significant space by the individual, the re-establishment of a region about every person through which events must make their approach, a space in which they can be received on decent terms, intelligently, comprehensively, and contemplatively. At a time when we are wildly distracted and asking ourselves what will happen when the end will come, how long we can bear it, why we should bear it, these notions of culture and significant space may seem hopelessly naive. But for art and literature there is no choice. If there is no significant space, there is no judgment, no freedom, we determine nothing for ourselves individually. The destruction of significant space, the destruction of the individual, for that is what it amounts to, leaves us helplessly in the public sphere. Then to say that the world is too much with us is meaningless for there is no longer any us. The world is everything. But it is apparently in the nature of the creature to resist the world's triumph. It is from this resistance that we infer truth to be one of his vital needs. And he has many ways of knowing the truth. If not all of these ways can be certified by our present methods, so much the worst [sic] for those present methods of certification.

The German philosopher Joseph Pieper speaks in one of his essays *(Leisure, the Basis of Culture)* of a purely receptive attitude of mind in which we become aware of immaterial reality. "Is there," asks Pieper, "such a thing as intellectual contemplation? . . . in antiquity the answer given was always yes; in modern philosophy, for the most part, the answer is no."

According to Kant, Pieper continues, knowledge is exclusively discursive, the opposite of receptive and contemplative. To Kant knowledge was an activity. Any other claim to know was not genuine because it involved no work. In Pieper's own words, "The Greeks—Aristotle no less than Plato—as well as the great medieval thinkers, held that not only physical, sensuous perception but equally man's spiritual and intellectual knowledge included an element of pure receptive contemplation or, as Heraclitus says, of listening to the 'essence of things'." Am I proposing, then, that we should take refuge from crisis and noise in a contemplative life? Such a thing is unthinkable. I am saying, rather, that there is a mode of knowledge different from the ruling mode. That this other mode is continually operative—the imagination assumes that things will deliver something of their essence to the mind that has prepared itself and that knows how to listen. I am saying also that full immersion in the great noise will kill us. Perpetual crisis will tear our souls from us. Indeed this tearing sensation is experienced daily by many people. What can art and poetry do with this great threat to Life? Has the crisis grown too vast—is it now unmanageable? Only the imagination, by its acts, can answer such questions.

Just now writers are asking themselves how can they be interesting, and why should they be taken seriously. Interest follows power, and they do not appear to command the sort of power that is now valued by most of mankind—the power of states or institutions, the power of money or resources, the power of politics, of science and technology, the power that once belonged to religion, the power of ideas, etc. What can make a writer truly interesting is an inadmissible resource, something we all hesitate to mention though we all know it intimately—the soul. I don't know what else can possibly obtain and hold the attention of the modern reader who has already become peculiarly difficult to reach. Granted that his tolerance level is low. Bad and boring novels have made him impatient. But he tends to resist all literary influences especially if he is, or considers himself to be, an intellectual.

Coming from me this may sound a bit odd for I am thought in America to be something of a highbrow. But it should be noted that the character of the public has changed, that it has become more intellectual, that writers themselves have more intellectual interests, and that they have become as concerned to analyze, to investigate problems, or to consider ideological questions as to tell stories. The attitude of intellectuals toward literature has become a "serious" one (the quotation marks are heavy). They see in novels, poems, or plays a creative contribution often unconsciously made to the study of society, or psychology, or religion.

The plots of Dickens are psychoanalytically investigated; *Moby Dick* supplies Marxists with material for the study of the factory system. Books are strongly shaken to see what usable things will fall out of them to strengthen a theory or support some system of ideas. The poet becomes a sort of truffle hound who brings marvelous delicacies from the forest. The writer himself begins to accept this truffle-hound role, acknowledging the superior value, the greater dignity of ideas and explanations over fancy, play, verve—over imagination. The intellectual makes discourse—a plethora of talk. The novelist and even the painter and musician now imitate him and before long become themselves intellectual workers, discourse makers, serious persons, and even functionaries. Obsessive or even monomaniacal professionals do not make wonderful readers. The world is very much with them, and their hearts are difficult to reach. One might even call it a political feat to reach their hearts, to penetrate their preoccupied minds, and to interest them in a story.

The general view now seems to be that the writer's true province is the unconscious. It is from the unconscious that he brings in his truffles. No one can doubt the existence of the unconscious. It is there all right. The question is what it contains. Is it only the seat of animal nature, of instinct, the libidinal forces, or does it also contain elements of higher life? Does the human need for truth, for instance, also have roots in the unconscious? Why, since the unconscious is by definition what we do not know, should we not expect to find in it traces of the soul as well as of aggression? In any case, the unconscious is today the sole source of impulse and freedom that one branch of science has reserved for art.

What I am saying is that the accounts of human existence given by the modern intelligence are very shallow by comparison with those that the imagination is capable of giving, and that we should by no means agree to limit imagination by committing ourselves to the formulae of modern intelligence but continue as individuals to make free individual judgments.

Wordsworth warned that we laid waste our powers by getting and spending. It is more serious than that now. Worse than getting and spending, modern distraction, worldwide irrationality, and madness threaten existence itself. We may not make it. Under the circumstances, I have no advice to offer other writers. I can only say, speaking for myself, that the Heraclitean listening to the essence of things becomes more and more important.

Is It O.K. to Be a Luddite? (1984)

THOMAS PYNCHON

As if being 1984 weren't enough, it's also the 25th anniversary this year of C. P. Snow's famous Rede-Lecture, "The Two Cultures and the Scientific Revolution," notable for its warning that intellectual life in the West was becoming increasingly polarized into "literary" and "scientific" factions, each doomed not to understand or appreciate the other. The lecture was originally meant to address such matters as curriculum reform in the age of Sputnik and the role of technology in the development of what would soon be known as the third world. But it was the two-culture formulation that got people's attention. In fact it kicked up an amazing row in its day. To some already simplified points, further reductions were made, provoking certain remarks, name-calling, even intemperate rejoinders, giving the whole affair, though attenuated by the mists of time, a distinctly cranky look.

Today nobody could get away with making such a distinction. Since 1959, we have come to live among flows of data more vast than anything the world has seen. Demystification is the order of our day, all the cats are jumping out of all the bags and even beginning to mingle. We immediately suspect ego insecurity in people who may still try to hide behind the jargon of a specialty or pretend to some data base forever "beyond" the reach of a layman. Anybody with the time, literacy and access fee these days can get together with just about any piece of specialized knowledge s/he may need. So, to that extent, the two-cultures quarrel can no longer be sustained. As a visit to any local library or magazine rack will easily confirm, there are now so many more than two cultures that the problem has really become how to find the time to read anything outside one's own specialty.

What has persisted, after a long quarter century, is the element of human character. C. P. Snow, with the reflexes of a novelist after all, sought to identify not only two kinds of education but also two kinds of personality. Fragmentary echoes of old disputes, of unforgotten offense taken in the course of long-ago high-table chitchat, may have helped from the subtext for Snow's immoderate, and thus celebrated assertion, "If we forget the scientific culture, then the rest of intellectuals have never tried, wanted, or been able to understand the Industrial Revolution." Such "intellectuals," for the most part "literary," were supposed, by Lord Snow, to be "natural Luddites."

Except maybe for Brainy Smurf, it's hard to imagine anybody these days wanting to be called a literary intellectual, though it doesn't sound so bad if you broaden the labeling to, say, "people who read and think." Being called a Luddite is another matter. It brings up questions such as, Is there something about reading and thinking that would cause or predispose a person to turn Luddite? Is it O.K. to be a Luddite? And come to think of it, what is a Luddite, anyway?

Historically, Luddites flourished in Britain from about 1811 to 1816. They were bands of men, organized, masked, anonymous, whose object was to destroy machinery used mostly in the textile industry. They swore allegiance not to any British king but to their own King Ludd. It isn't clear whether they called themselves Luddites, although they were so termed by both friends and enemies. C. P. Snow's use of the word was clearly polemical, wishing to imply an irrational fear and hatred of science and technology. Luddites had, in this view, come to be imagined as the counterrevolutionaries of that "Industrial Revolution" which their modern versions have "never tried, wanted, or been able to understand."

But the Industrial Revolution was not, like the American and French Revolutions of about the same period, a violent struggle with a beginning, middle and end. It was smoother, less conclusive, more like an accelerated passage in a long evolution. The phrase was first popularized a hundred years ago by the historian Arnold Toynbee, and has had its share of revisionist attention, lately in the July 1984 *Scientific American*. Here, in "Medieval Roots of the Industrial Revolution," Terry S. Reynolds suggests that the early role of the steam engine (1765) may have been overdramatized. Far from being revolutionary, much of the machinery that steam was coming to drive had already long been in place, having in fact been driven by water power since the Middle Ages. Nevertheless, the idea of a technological "revolution," in which the same people came out on top as in France and America, has proven of use to many over the years, not least to those who, like C. P. Snow, have thought that in "Luddite" they have discovered a way to call those with whom they disagree, both politically reactionary and anti-capitalist at the same time.

But the *Oxford English Dictionary* has an interesting tale to tell. In 1779, in a village somewhere in Leicestershire, one Ned Lud broke into a house and "in a fit of insane rage" destroyed two machines used for knitting hosiery. Word got around. Soon, whenever a stocking frame was found sabotaged—this had been going on, sez the *Encyclopedia Britannica,* since about 1710—folks would respond with the catch phrase "Lud must have been here." By the time his name was taken up by the frame-breakers of 1812, historical Ned Lud was well absorbed into the more or less sarcastic nickname "King (or Captain) Ludd," and was now all mystery, resonance and dark fun: a more-than-human presence, out in the night, roaming the hosiery districts of England, possessed by a single comic shtick—every time he spots a stocking-frame he goes crazy and proceeds to trash it.

But it's important to remember that the target even of the original assault of 1779, like many machines of the Industrial Revolution, was not a new piece of technology. The stocking-frame had been around since 1589, when, according to the folklore, it was invented by the Rev. William Lee, out of pure meanness. Seems that Lee was in love with a young woman who was more interested in her knitting than in him. He'd show up at her place. "Sorry, Rev, got some knitting." "What, again?" After a while, unable to deal with this kind of rejection, Lee, not, like Ned Lud, in any fit of insane rage, but let's imagine logically and coolly, vowed to invent a machine that would make the hand-knitting of hosiery obsolete. And he did. According to the encyclopedia, the jilted cleric's frame "was so perfect in its conception that it continued to be the only mechanical means of knitting for hundreds of years."

Now, given that kind of time span, it's just not easy to think of Ned Lud as a technophobic crazy. No doubt what people admired and mythologized him for was the vigor and single-mindedness of his assault. But the words "fit of insane rage" are third-hand and at least 68 years after the event. And Ned Lud's anger was not directed at the machines, not exactly. I like to think of it more as the controlled, martial-arts type anger of the dedicated Badass.

There is a long folk history of this figure, the Badass. He is usually male, and while sometime earning the quizzical tolerance of women, is almost universally admired by men for two basic virtues: he is Bad, and he is Big. Bad meaning not morally evil, necessarily, more like able to work mischief on a large scale. What is important here is the amplifying of scale, the multiplication of effect.

The knitting machines which provoked the first Luddite disturbances had been putting people out of work for well over two centuries. Everybody saw this happening—it became part of daily life. They also saw the machines coming more and more to be the property of men who did not work, only owned and hired. It took no German philosopher, then or later, to point out what this did, had been doing, to wages and jobs. Public feeling about the machines could never have been simple unreasoning horror, but likely something more complex: the love/hate that grows up between humans and machinery—especially when it's been around for a while—not to mention serious resentment toward at least two multiplications of effect that were seen as unfair and threatening. One was the concentration of capital that each machine represented, and the other was the ability of each machine to put a certain number of humans out of work—to be "worth" that many human souls. What gave King Ludd his special Bad charisma, took him from local hero to nation-wide public enemy, was that he went up against these amplified, multiplied, more than human opponents and prevailed. When times are hard, and we feel at the mercy of forces many times more powerful, don't we, in seeking some equalizer, turn, if only in imagination, in wish, to the Badass—the djinn, the golem, the hulk, the superhero—who will resist what otherwise would overwhelm us? Of course, the real or secular frame-bashing was still being done by everyday folks, trade unionists ahead of their time, using the night, and their own solidarity and discipline, to achieve their multiplications of effect.

It was open-eyed class war. The movement had its Parliamentary allies, among them Lord Byron, whose maiden speech in the House of Lords in 1812 compassionately argued against a bill proposing, among other repressive measures, to make frame-breaking punishable by death. "Are you not near the Luddites?" he wrote from Venice to Thomas Moore. "By the Lord! If there's a row, but I'll be among ye! How go on the weavers—the breakers of frames—the Lutherans of politics—the reformers?" He includes an "amiable chanson," which proves to be a Luddite hymn so inflammatory that it wasn't published till after the poet's death. The letter is dated December 1816: Byron had spent the summer previous in Switzerland, cooped up for a while in the Villa Diodati with the Shelleys, watching the rain come down, while they all told each other ghost stories. By that December, as it happened, Mary Shelley was working on Chapter Four of her novel *Frankenstein, or the Modern Prometheus.*

If there were such a genre as the Luddite novel, this one, warning of what can happen when technology, and those who practice it, get out of hand, would be the first and among the best. Victor Frankenstein's creature also, surely, qualifies as a major literary Badass. "I resolved . . . ," Victor tells us, "to make the being of a gigantic stature, that is to say, about eight feet in height, and proportionally large," which takes care of Big. The story of how he got to be so Bad is the heart of the novel, sheltered innermost: told to Victor in the first person by the creature himself, then nested inside of Victor's own narrative, which is nested in its turn in the letters of the arctic explorer Robert Walton. However much of *Frankenstein's* longevity is owing to the undersung genius James Whale, who translated it to film, it remains today more than well worth reading, for all the reasons we read novels, as well as for the much more limited question of its Luddite value: that is, for its attempt, through literary means which are nocturnal and deal in disguise, to *deny the machine.*

Look, for example, at Victor's account of how he assembles and animates his creature. He must, of course, be a little vague about the details, but we're left with a procedure that seems to include surgery, electricity (though nothing like Whale's galvanic extravaganzas), chemistry, even, from dark hints about Paracelsus and Albertus Magnus, the still recently discredited form of magic known as alchemy. What is clear, though, despite the commonly depicted Bolt Through the Neck, is that neither the method nor the creature that results is mechanical.

This is one of several interesting similarities between *Frankenstein* and an earlier tale of the Bad and Big, *The Castle of Otranto* (1765), by Horace Walpole, usually regarded as the first Gothic novel. For one thing, both authors, in presenting their books to the public, used voices not their own. Mary Shelley's preface was written by her husband, Percy, who was pretending to be her. Not till 15 years later did she write an introduction to *Frankenstein* in her own voice. Walpole, on the other hand, gave his book an entire made-up publishing history, claiming it was a translation from medieval Italian. Only in his preface to the second edition did he admit authorship.

The novels are also of strikingly similar nocturnal origin: both resulted from episodes of lucid dreaming. Mary Shelley, that ghost-story summer in Geneva, trying to get to sleep one mid-night, suddenly beheld the creature being brought to life, the images arising in her mind with a vividness far beyond the usual "bounds of reverie." Walpole had awakened from a dream, "of which, all I could remember was, that I had thought myself in an ancient castle . . . and that on the uppermost bannister of a great staircase I saw a gigantic hand in armor."

In Walpole's novel, this hand shows up as the hand of Alfonso the Good, former Prince of Otranto and, despite his epithet, the castle's resident Badass. Alfonso, like Frankenstein's creature, is assembled from pieces—sable-plumed helmet, foot, leg, sword, all of them, like the hand, quite oversized—which fall from the sky or just materialize here and there about the castle grounds, relentless as Freud's slow return of the repressed. The activating agencies, again like those in *Frankenstein,* are non-mechanical. The final assembly of "the form of Alfonso, dilated to an immense magnitude," is achieved through supernatural means: a family curse, and the intercession of Otranto's patron saint.

The craze for Gothic fiction after *The Castle of Otranto* was grounded, I suspect, in deep and religious yearnings for that earlier mythical time which had come to be known as the Age of Miracles. In ways more and less literal, folks in the 18th century believed that once upon a time all kinds of things had been possible which were no longer so. Giants, dragons, spells. The laws of nature had not been so strictly formulated back then. What had once been true working magic had, by the Age of Reason, degenerated into mere machinery. Blake's dark Satanic mills represented an old magic that, like Satan, had fallen from grace. As religion was being more and more secularized into Deism and nonbelief, the abiding human hunger for evidence of God and afterlife, for salvation—bodily resurrection, if possible—remained. The Methodist movement and the American Great Awakening were only two sectors on a broad front of resistance to the Age of Reason, a front which included Radicalism and Freemasonry as well as Luddites and the Gothic novel. Each in its way expressed the same profound unwillingness to give up elements of faith, however "irrational," to an emerging technopolitical order that might or might not know what it was doing. "Gothic" became code for "medieval," and that has remained code for "miraculous," on through Pre-Raphaelites, turn of-the-century tarot cards, space opera in the pulps and the comics, down to *Star Wars* and contemporary tales of sword and sorcery.

To insist on the miraculous is to deny to the machine at least some of its claims on us, to assert the limited wish that living things, earthly and otherwise, may on occasion become Bad and Big enough to take part in transcendent doings. By this theory, for example, *King Kong* (?–1933) becomes your classic Luddite saint. The final dialogue in the movie, you recall, goes: "Well, the airplanes got him." "No . . . it was Beauty killed the Beast." In which again we encounter the same Snovian Disjunction, only different, between the human and the technological.

But if we do insist upon fictional violations of the laws of nature—of space, time, thermodynamics, and the big one, mortality itself—then we risk being judged by the literary mainstream as Insufficiently Serious. Being serious about these matters is one way that adults have tradition-ally defined themselves against the confidently immortal children they must deal with. Looking back on *Frankenstein,* which she wrote when she was 19, Mary Shelley said, "I have an affection for it, for it was the offspring of happy days, when death and grief were but words which found not true echo in my heart." The Gothic attitude in general, because it used images of death and ghostly survival toward no more responsible end than special effects and cheap thrills, was judged not Serious enough and confined to its own part of town. It is not the only neighborhood in the great City of Literature so, let us say, closely defined. In westerns, the good people always win. In romance novels, love conquers all. In who-dunits, murder, being a pretext for a logical puzzle, is hardly ever an irra-tional act. In science fiction, where entire worlds may be generated from simple sets of axioms, the constraints of our own everyday world are rou-tinely transcended. In each of these cases we know better. We say, "But the world isn't like that." These genres, by insisting on what is contrary to fact, fail to be Serious enough, and so they get redlined under the label "escapist fare."

This is especially unfortunate in the case of science fiction, in which the decade after Hiroshima saw one of the most remarkable flowerings of literary talent and, quite often, genius, in our history. It was just as impor-tant as the Beat movement going on at the same time, certainly more im-portant than mainstream fiction, which with only a few exceptions had been paralyzed by the political climate of the cold war and McCarthy years. Besides being a nearly ideal synthesis of the Two Cultures, sci-ence fiction also happens to have been one of the principal refuges, in our time, for those of Luddite persuasion.

By 1945, the factory system—which, more than any piece of ma-chinery, was the real and major result of the Industrial Revolution—had been extended to include the Manhattan Project, the German long-range rocket program and the death camps, such as Auschwitz. It has taken no major gift of prophecy to see how these three curves of development might plausibly converge, and before too long. Since Hiroshima, we have watched nuclear weapons multiply out of control, and delivery systems acquire, for global purposes, unlimited range and accuracy. An unblinking acceptance of a holocaust running to seven- and eight-figure body counts has become—among those who, particularly since 1980, have been guiding our military policies—conventional wisdom.

To people who were writing science fiction in the 50's, none of this was much of a surprise, though modern Luddite imaginations have yet to come up with any countercritter Bad and Big enough, even in the most irresponsible of fictions, to begin to compare with what would happen in a nuclear war. So, in the science fiction of the Atomic Age and the cold war, we see the Luddite impulse to deny the machine taking a different direction. The hardware angle got de-emphasized in favor of more humanistic concerns—exotic cultural evolutions and social scenarios, paradoxes and games with space/time, wild philosophical questions—most of it sharing, as the critical literature has amply discussed, a definition of "human" as particularly distinguished from "machine." Like their earlier counterparts, 20th century Luddites looked back yearningly to another age—curiously, the same Age of Reason which had forced the first Luddites into nostalgia for the Age of Miracles.

But we now live, we are told, in the Computer Age. What is the outlook for Luddite sensibility? Will mainframes attract the same hostile attention as knitting frames once did? I really doubt it. Writers of all descriptions are stampeding to buy word processors. Machines have already become so user-friendly that even the most unreconstructed of Luddites can be charmed into laying down the old sledgehammer and stroking a few keys instead. Beyond this seems to be a growing consensus that knowledge really is power, that there is a pretty straightforward conversion between money and information, and that somehow, if the logistics can be worked out, miracles may yet be possible. If this is so, Luddites may at last have come to stand on common ground with their Snovian adversaries, the cheerful army of technocrats who were supposed to have the "future in their bones." It may be only a new form of the perennial Luddite ambivalence about machines, or it may be that the deepest Luddite hope of miracle has now come to reside in the computer's ability to get the right data to those whom the data will do the most good. With the proper deployment of budget and computer time, we will cure cancer, save ourselves from nuclear extinction, grow food for everybody, detoxify the results of industrial greed gone berserk—realize all the wistful pipe dreams of our days.

The word "Luddite" continues to be applied with contempt to anyone with doubts about technology, especially the nuclear kind. Luddites today are no longer faced with human factory owners and vulnerable machines. As well-known President and unintentional Luddite D. D. Eisenhower prophesied when he left office, there is now a permanent power establishment of admirals, generals and corporate CEO's, up against whom us average poor bastards are completely outclassed, although Ike didn't put it quite that way. We are all supposed to keep tranquil and allow it to go on, even though, because of the data revolution, it becomes every day less possible to fool any of the people any of the time.

If our world survives, the next great challenge to watch out for will come—you heard it here first—when the curves of research and development in artificial intelligence, molecular biology and robotics all converge. Oboy. It will be amazing and unpredictable, and even the biggest of brass, let us devoutly hope, are going to be caught flat-footed. It is certainly something for all good Luddites to look forward to if, God willing, we should live so long. Meantime, as Americans, we can take comfort, however minimal and cold, from Lord Byron's mischievously improvised song, in which he, like other observers of the time, saw clear identification between the first Luddites and our own revolutionary origins. It begins:

> *As the Liberty lads o'er the sea*
> *Bought their freedom, and cheaply, with blood,*
> *So we, boys, we*
> *Will die fighting, or live free,*
> *And down with all kings but King Ludd!*

Romancing the Shadow (1992)

TONI MORRISON

At the end of *The Narrative of Arthur Gordon Pym,* Edgar Allan Poe describes the last two days of an extraordinary journey:

> "*March 21st.*—A sullen darkness now hovered above us but from out the milky depths of the ocean a luminous glare arose, and stole up along the bulwarks of the boat. We were nearly overwhelmed by the white ashy shower which settled upon us and upon the canoe, but melted into the water as it fell. . . .
>
> "*March 22d.*—The darkness had materially in creased, relieved only by the glare of the water thrown back from the white curtain before us. Many gigantic and pallidly white birds flew continuously now from beyond the veil, and their scream was the eternal *Tekeli-li!* as they retreated from our vision. Hereupon Nu-Nu stirred in the bottom of the boat; but upon touching him, we found his spirit departed. And now we rushed into the embraces of the cataract, where a chasm threw itself open to receive us. But there arose in our pathway a shrouded human figure, very far larger in its proportions than any dweller among men. And the hue of the skin of the figure was of the perfect whiteness of the snow."

They have been floating, Pym and Peters and the native, Nu-Nu, on a warm, milk-white sea under a "white ashy shower." The black man dies, and the boat rushes on through the white curtain behind which a white giant rises up. After that, there is nothing. There is no more narrative. Instead there is a scholarly note, explanation, and an anxious, piled-up "conclusion." The latter states that it was *whiteness* that terrified the natives and killed Nu-Nu. The following inscription was carved into the walls of the chasms the travelers passed through: "I have graven it in within the hills, and my vengeance upon the dust within the rock."

No early American writer is more important to the concept of American Africanism than Poe. And no image is more telling than the one just described: the visualized but somehow closed and unknowable white form that rises from the mists at the end of the journey—or, at any rate, at the end of the narration proper. The images of the white curtain and the "shrouded human figure" with skin "the perfect whiteness of the snow" both occur after the narrative has encountered blackness. The first white image seems related to the expiration and erasure of the serviceable and serving black figure, Nu-Nu. Both are figurations of impenetrable whiteness that surface in American literature whenever an Africanist presence is engaged. These closed white images are found frequently, but not always, at the end of the narrative. They appear so often and in such particular circumstances that they give pause. They clamor, it seems, for an attention that would yield the meaning that lies in their positioning, their repetition, and their strong suggestion of paralysis and incoherence; of impasse and non-sequitur.

These images of impenetrable whiteness need contextualizing to explain their extraordinary power, pattern, and consistency. Because they appear almost always in conjunction with representations of black or Africanist people who are dead, impotent, or under complete control, these images of blinding whiteness seem to function as both antidote for and meditation on the shadow that is companion to this whiteness—a dark and abiding presence that moves the hearts and texts of American literature with fear and longing. This haunting, a darkness from which our early literature seemed unable to extricate itself, suggests the complex and contradictory situation in which American writers found themselves during the formative years of the nation's literature.

Young America distinguished itself by, and understood itself to be, pressing toward a future of freedom, a kind of human dignity believed unprecedented in the world. A whole tradition of "universal" yearnings collapsed into that well fondled phrase, "the American Dream." Although this immigrant dream deserves the exhaustive scrutiny it has received in the scholarly disciplines and the arts, it is just as important to know what these people were rushing from as it is to know what they were hastening to. If the New World fed dreams, what was the Old World reality that whetted the appetite for them? And how did that reality caress and grip the shaping of a new one?

The flight from the Old World to the New is generally seen to be a flight from oppression and limitation to freedom and possibility. Although, in fact, the escape was sometimes an escape from license—from a society perceived to be unacceptably permissive, ungodly, and undisciplined—for those fleeing for reasons other than religious ones, constraint and limitation impelled the journey. All the Old World offered these immigrants was poverty, prison, social ostracism, and, not infrequently, death. There was of course a clerical, scholarly group of immigrants who came seeking the adventure possible in founding a colony for, rather than against, one or another mother country or fatherland. And of course there were the merchants, who came for the cash.

Whatever the reasons, the attraction was of the "clean slate" variety, a once-in-a-lifetime opportunity not only to be born again but to be born again in new clothes, as it were. The new setting would provide new raiments of self. This second chance could even benefit from the mistakes of the first. In the New World there was the vision of a limitless future, made more gleaming by the constraint, dissatisfaction, and turmoil left behind. It was a promise genuinely promising. With luck and endurance one could discover freedom; find a way to make God's law manifest; or end up rich as a prince. The desire for freedom is preceded by oppression; a yearning for God's law is born of the detestation of human license and corruption; the glamor of riches is in thrall to poverty, hunger, and debt.

There was very much more in the late seventeenth and eighteenth centuries to make the trip worth the risk. The habit of genuflection would be replaced by the thrill of command. Power—control of one's own destiny—would replace the powerlessness felt before the gates of class, caste, and cunning persecution. One could move from discipline and punishment to disciplining and punishing; from social ostracism to social rank. One could be released from a useless, binding, repulsive past into a kind of history-lessness, a blank page waiting to be inscribed. Much was to be written there: noble impulses were made into law and appropriated for a national tradition; base ones, learned and elaborated in the rejected and rejecting homeland, were also made into law and appropriated for tradition.

The body of literature produced by the young nation is one way it inscribed its transactions with these fears, forces, and hopes. And it is difficult to read the literature of young America without being struck by how antithetical it is to our modern rendition of the American Dream. How pronounced in it is the absence of that term's elusive mixture of hope, realism, materialism, and promise. For a people who made much of their "newness"—their potential, freedom, and innocence—it is striking how dour, how troubled, how frightened and haunted our early and founding literature truly is.

We have words and labels for this haunting—"gothic," "romantic," "sermonic," "Puritan"—whose sources are to be found in the literature of the world these immigrants left. But the strong affinity between the nineteenth-century American psyche and gothic romance has rightly been much remarked. Why should a young country repelled by Europe's moral and social disorder, swooning in a fit of desire and rejection, devote its talents to reproducing in its own literature the typology of diabolism it wanted to leave behind? An answer to that seems fairly obvious: one way to benefit from the lessons of earlier mistakes and past misfortune is to record them so as to prevent their repetition through exposure and inoculation.

Romance was the form in which this uniquely American prophylaxis could be played out. Long after the movement in Europe, romance remained the cherished expression of young America. What was there in American romanticism that made it so attractive to Americans as a battle plain on which to fight, engage, and imagine their demons?

It has been suggested that romance is an evasion of history (and thus perhaps attractive to a people trying to evade the recent past). But I am more persuaded by arguments that find in it the head-on encounter with very real, pressing historical forces and the contradictions inherent in them as they came to be experienced by writers. Romance, an exploration of anxiety imported from the shadows of European culture, made possible the sometimes safe and other times risky embrace of quite specific, understandably human, fears: Americans' fear of being outcast, of failing, of powerlessness; their fear of boundarylessness, of Nature unbridled and crouched for attack; their fear of the absence of so-called civilization; their fear of loneliness, of aggression both external and internal. In short, the terror of human freedom—the thing they coveted most of all. Romance offered writers not less but more; not a narrow ahistorical canvas but a wide historical one; not escape but entanglement. For young America it had everything: nature as subject matter, a system of symbolism, a thematics of the search for self-valorization and validation—above all, the opportunity to conquer fear imaginatively and to quiet deep insecurities. It offered platforms for moralizing and fabulation, and for the imaginative entertainment of violence, sublime incredibility, and terror—and terror's most significant, overweening ingredient: darkness, with all the connotative value it awakened.

There is no romance free of what Herman Melville called "the power of blackness," especially not in a country in which there was a resident population, already black, upon which the imagination could play; through which historical, moral, metaphysical, and social fears, problems, and dichotomies could be articulated. The slave population, it could be and was assumed, offered itself up as surrogate selves for meditation on problems of human freedom, its lure and its elusiveness. This black population was available for meditations on terror—the terror of European outcasts, their dread of failure, powerlessness, Nature without limits, natal loneliness, internal aggression, evil, sin, greed. In other words, this slave population was understood to have offered itself up for reflections on human freedom in terms other than the abstractions of human potential and the rights of man.

The ways in which artists—and the society that bred them—transferred internal conflicts to a "blank darkness," to conveniently bound and violently silenced black bodies, is a major theme in American literature. The rights of man, for example, an organizing principle upon which the nation was founded, was inevitably yoked to Africanism. Its history, its origin is permanently allied with another seductive concept: the hierarchy of race. As the sociologist Orlando Patterson has noted, we should not be surprised that the Enlightenment could accommodate slavery; we should be surprised if it had not. The concept of freedom did not emerge in a vacuum. Nothing highlighted freedom—if it did not in fact create it—like slavery.

Black slavery enriched the country's creative possibilities. For in that construction of blackness *and* enslavement could be found not only the not-free but also, with the dramatic polarity created by skin color, the projection of the not-me. The result was a playground for the imagination. What rose up out of collective needs to allay internal fears and to rationalize external exploitation was an American Africanism—a fabricated brew of darkness, otherness, alarm, and desire that is uniquely American. (There also exists, of course, a European Africanism with a counterpart in colonial literature.)

What I wish to examine is how the image of reined-in, bound, suppressed, and repressed darkness became objectified in American literature as an Africanist persona. I want to show how the duties of that persona—duties of exorcism and reification and mirroring—are on demand and on display throughout much of the literature of the country and helped to form the distinguishing characteristics of a proto-American literature.

Earlier I said that cultural identities are formed and informed by a nation's literature, and that what seemed to be on the "mind" of the literature of the United States was the self-conscious but highly problematic construction of the American as a new white man. Emerson's call for that new man in "The American Scholar" indicates the deliberateness of the construction, the conscious necessity for establishing difference. But the writers who responded to this call, accepting or rejecting it, did not look solely to Europe to establish a reference for difference. There was a very theatrical difference underfoot. Writers were able to celebrate or deplore an identity already existing or rapidly taking a form that was elaborated through racial difference. That difference provided a huge payout of sign, symbol, and agency in the process of organizing, separating, and consolidating identity along culturally valuable lines of interest.

Bernard Bailyn has provided us with an extraordinary investigation of European settlers in the act of becoming Americans. I want to quote a rather long passage from his *Voyagers to the West* because it underscores the salient aspects of the American character I have been describing:

> "William Dunbar, seen through his letters and diary, appears to be more fictional than real—a creature of William Faulkner's imagination, a more cultivated Colonel Sutpen but no less mysterious. He too, like that strange character in *Absalom! Absalom!*, was a man in his early twenties who appeared suddenly in the Mississippi wilderness to stake out a claim to a large parcel of land, then disappeared to the Caribbean, to return leading a battalion of 'wild' slaves with whose labor alone he built an estate where before there had been nothing but trees and uncultivated soil. But he was more complex than Sutpen, if no less driving in his early ambitions, no less a progenitor of a notable southern family, and no less a part of a violent biracial world whose tensions could lead in strange directions. For this wilderness planter was a scientist, who would later correspond with Jefferson on science and exploration, a Mississippi planter whose contributions to the American Philosophical Society (to which Jefferson proposed him for membership) included linguistics, archaeology, hydrostatics, astronomy, and climatology, and whose geographical explorations were reported in widely known publications. Like Sutpen an exotic figure in the plantation world of early Mississippi—known as 'Sir' William just as Sutpen was known as 'Colonel'—he too imported into that raw, half-savage world the niceties of European culture: not chandeliers and

costly rugs, but books, surveyor's equipment of the finest kind, and the latest instruments of science.

"Dunbar was a Scot by birth, the youngest son of Sir Archibald Dunbar of Morayshire. He was educated first by tutors at home, then at the university in Aberdeen, where his interest in mathematics, astronomy, and belles-lettres took mature shape. What happened to him after his return home and later in London, where he circulated with young intellectuals, what propelled, or led, him out of the metropolis on the first leg of his long voyage west is not known. But whatever his motivation may have been, in April 1771, aged only twenty-two, Dunbar appeared in Philadelphia. . . .

"Ever eager for gentility, this well-educated product of the Scottish enlightenment and of London's sophistication—this bookish young *littérateur* and scientist who, only five years earlier, had been corresponding about scientific problems—about 'Dean Swifts beatitudes,' about the 'virtuous and happy life,' and about the Lord's commandment that mankind should 'love one another'—was yet strangely insensitive to the suffering of those who served him. In July 1776 he recorded not the independence of the American colonies from Britain, but the suppression of an alleged conspiracy for freedom by slaves on his own plantation. . . .

"Dunbar, the young *érudit,* the Scottish scientist and man of letters, was no sadist. His plantation regime was, by the standards of the time, mild; he clothed and fed his slaves decently, and frequently relented in his more severe punishments. But 4,000 miles from the sources of culture, alone on the far periphery of British civilization where physical survival was a daily struggle, where ruthless exploitation was a way of life, and where disorder, violence, and human degradation were commonplace, he had triumphed by successful adaptation. Endlessly enterprising and resourceful, his finer sensibilities dulled by the abrasions of frontier life, and feeling within himself a sense of authority and autonomy he had not known before, a force that flowed from his absolute control over the lives of others, he emerged a distinctive new man, a borderland gentleman, a man of property in a raw, half-savage world."[1]

Let me call attention to some elements of this portrait, some pairings and interdependencies that are marked in the story of William Dunbar. First there is the historical connection between the Enlightenment and the institution of slavery—the rights of man and his enslavement. Second, we have the relationship between Dunbar's education and his New

World enterprise. The education he had was exceptional and exception-
ally cultivated: it included the latest thought on theology and science, an
effort perhaps to make them mutually accountable, to make one support
the other. He is not only a "product of the Scottish enlightenment" but a
London intellectual as well. He read Jonathan Swift, discussed the Christian commandment to love one another, and is described as "strangely"
insensitive to the suffering of his slaves. On July 12, 1776, he records
with astonishment and hurt surprise a slave rebellion on his plantation:
"Judge my surprise. . . . Of what avail is kindness & good usage when
rewarded by such ingratitude." "Constantly bewildered," Bailyn goes on,
"by his slaves' behavior . . . [Dunbar] recovered two runaways and 'condemned them to receive 500 lashes each at five different times, and to
carry a chain & log fixt to the ancle'."

I take this to be a succinct portrait of the process by which the American as new, white, and male was constituted. It is a formation with at
least four desirable consequences, all of which are referred to in Bailyn's
summation of Dunbar's character and located in how Dunbar felt "within
himself." Let me repeat: "a sense of authority and autonomy he had not
known before, a force that flowed from his absolute control over the lives
of others, he emerged a distinctive new man, a borderland gentleman, a
man of property in a raw, half-savage world." A power, a sense of freedom, he had not known before. But what had he known before? Fine education, London sophistication, theological and scientific thought. None
of these, one gathers, could provide him with the authority and autonomy
that Mississippi planter life did. Also this sense is understood to be a
force that flows, already present and ready to spill as a result of his "absolute control over the lives of others." This force is not a willed domination, a thought-out, calculated choice, but rather a kind of natural
resource, a Niagara Falls waiting to drench Dunbar as soon as he is in a
position to assume absolute control. Once he has moved into that position, he is resurrected as a new man, a distinctive man—a different man.
And whatever his social status in London, in the New World he is a gentleman. More gentle, more man. The site of his transformation is within
rawness: he is backgrounded by savagery.

I want to suggest that these concerns—autonomy, authority, newness and
difference, absolute power—not only become the major themes and pre-
sumptions of American literature, but that each one is made possible by,
shaped by, activated by a complex awareness and employment of a constituted Africanism. It was this Africanism, deployed as rawness and sav-

agery, that provided the staging ground and arena for the elaboration of the quintessential American identity.

Autonomy is freedom and translates into the much championed and revered "individualism"; newness translates into "innocence"; distinctiveness becomes difference and the erection of strategies for maintaining it; authority and absolute power become a romantic, conquering "heroism," virility, and the problematics of wielding absolute power over the lives of others. All the rest are made possible by this last, it would seem—absolute power called forth and played against and within a natural and mental landscape conceived of as a "raw, half-savage world."

Why is it seen as raw and savage? Because it is peopled by a non-white indigenous population? Perhaps. But certainly because there is ready to hand a bound and unfree, rebellious but serviceable, black population against which Dunbar and all white men are enabled to measure these privileging and privileged differences.

Eventually individualism fuses with the prototype of Americans as solitary, alienated, and malcontent. What, one wants to ask, are Americans alienated from? What are Americans always so insistently innocent of? Different from? As for absolute power, over whom is this power held, from whom withheld, to whom distributed?

Answers to these questions lie in the potent and ego reinforcing presence of an Africanist population. This population is convenient in every way, not the least of which is self-definition. This new white male can now persuade himself that savagery is "out there." The lashes ordered (500 applied five times is 2500) are not one's own savagery; repeated and dangerous breaks for freedom are "puzzling" confirmations of black irrationality; the combination of Dean Swift's beatitudes and a life of regularized violence is civilized; and if the sensibilities are dulled enough, the rawness remains external.

These contradictions slash their way through the pages of American literature. How could it be otherwise? As Dominick LaCapra reminds us, "Classic novels are not only worked over . . . by common contextual forces (such as ideologies) but also rework and at least partially work through those forces in critical and at times potentially transformative fashion."[2]

As for the culture, the imaginative and historical terrain upon which early American writers journeyed is in large measure shaped by the presence of the racial other. Statements to the contrary, insisting on the meaninglessness of race to the American identity, are themselves full of meaning. The world does not become raceless or will not become unracialized by assertion. The act of enforcing racelessness in literary discourse is itself a racial act. Pouring rhetorical acid on the fingers of a black hand may indeed destroy the prints, but not the hand. Besides, what happens in that violent, self serving act of erasure to the hands, the fingers, the finger prints of the one who does the pouring? Do they remain acid-free? The literature itself suggests otherwise.

Explicit or implicit, the Africanist presence informs in compelling and inescapable ways the texture of American literature. It is a dark and abiding presence, there for the literary imagination as both a visible and an invisible mediating force. Even, and especially, when American texts are not "about" Africanist presences or characters or narrative or idiom, the shadow hovers in implication, in sign, in line of demarcation. It is no accident and no mistake that immigrant populations (and much immigrant literature) understood their "Americanness" as an opposition to the resident black population. Race, in fact, now functions as a metaphor so necessary to the construction of Americanness that it rivals the old pseudo-scientific and class-informed racisms whose dynamics we are more used to deciphering.

As a metaphor for transacting the whole process of Americanization, while burying its particular racial ingredients, this Africanist presence may be something the United States cannot do without. Deep within the word "American" is its association with race. To identify someone as a South African is to say very little; we need the adjective "white" or "black" or "colored" to make our meaning clear. In this country it is quite the reverse. American means white, and Africanist people struggle to make the term applicable to themselves with ethnicity and hyphen after hyphen after hyphen. Americans did not have a profligate, predatory nobility from which to wrest an identity of national virtue while continuing to covet aristocratic license and luxury. The American nation negotiated both its disdain and its envy in the same way Dunbar did: through a self-reflexive contemplation of fabricated, mythological Africanism. For the settlers and for American writers generally, this Africanist other became the means of thinking about body, mind, chaos, kindness, and love; provided the occasion for exercises in the absence of restraint, the presence of restraint, the contemplation of freedom and of aggression; permitted opportunities for the exploration of ethics and morality, for meeting the obligations of the social contract, for bearing the cross of religion and following out the ramifications of power.

Reading and charting the emergence of an Africanist persona in the development of a national literature is both a fascinating project and an

urgent one, if the history and criticism of our literature is to become accurate. Emerson's plea for intellectual independence was like the offer of
an empty plate that writers could fill with nourishment from an indigenous menu. The language no doubt had to be English, but the content of
that language, its subject, was to be deliberately, insistently un-English
and anti-European, insofar as it rhetorically repudiated an adoration of
the Old World and defined the past as corrupt and indefensible. In the
scholarship on the formation of an American character and the production of a national literature, a number of items have been catalogued. A
major item to be added to the list must be an Africanist presence—decidedly not American, decidedly other.

The need to establish difference stemmed not only from the Old
World but from a difference in the New. What was distinctive in the New
was, first of all, its claim to freedom and, second, the presence of the unfree within the heart of the democratic experiment—the critical absence
of democracy, its echo, shadow, and silent force in the political and intellectual activity of some not-Americans. The distinguishing features of
the not-Americans were their slave status, their social status—and their
color.

It is conceivable that the first would have self-destructed in a variety
of ways had it not been for the last. These slaves, unlike many others in
the world's history, were visible to a fault. And they had inherited, among
other things, a long history on the meaning of color. It was not simply that
this slave population had a distinctive color; it was that this color "meant"
something. That meaning had been named and deployed by scholars from
at least the moment, in the eighteenth century, when other and sometimes
the same scholars started to investigate both the natural history and the in-
alienable rights of man—that is to say, human freedom.

One supposes that if Africans all had three eyes or one ear, the significance of that difference from the smaller but conquering European in-
vaders would also have been found to have meaning. In any case, the
subjective nature of ascribing value and meaning to color cannot be
questioned this late in the twentieth century. The point for this discussion
is the alliance between visually rendered ideas and linguistic utterances.
And this leads into the social and political nature of received knowledge
as it is revealed in American literature.

Knowledge, however mundane and utilitarian, plays about in linguistic images and forms cultural practice. Responding to culture—clar-
ifying, explicating, valorizing, translating, transforming, criticizing—is
what artists everywhere do, especially writers involved in the founding

of a new nation. Whatever their personal and formally political responses to the inherent contradiction of a free republic deeply committed to slavery, nineteenth-century writers were mindful of the presence of black people. More important, they addressed, in more or less passionate ways, their views on that difficult presence.

The alertness to a slave population did not confine itself to the personal encounters that writers may have had. Slave narratives were a nineteenth-century publication boom. The press, the political campaigns, and the policy of various parties and elected officials were rife with the discourse of slavery and freedom. It would have been an *isolato* indeed who was unaware of the most explosive issue in the nation. How could one speak of profit, economy, labor, progress, suffragism, Christianity, the frontier, the formation of new states, the acquisition of new lands, education, transportation (freight and passengers), neighborhoods, the military—of almost anything a country concerns itself with—without having as a referent, at the heart of the discourse, at the heart of definition, the presence of Africans and their descendants?

It was not possible. And it did not happen. What did happen frequently was an effort to talk about these matters with a vocabulary designed to disguise the subject. It did not always succeed, and in the work of many writers disguise was never intended. But the consequence was a master narrative that spoke *for* Africans and their descendants, or *of* them. The legislator's narrative could not coexist with a response from the Africanist persona. Whatever popularity the slave narratives had— and they influenced abolitionists and converted antiabolitionist—the slave's own narrative, while freeing the narrator in many ways, did not destroy the master narrative. The master narrative could make any number of adjustments to keep itself intact.

Silence from and about the subject was the order of the day. Some of the silences were broken, and some were maintained by authors who lived with and within the policing narrative. What I am interested in are the strategies for maintaining the silence and the strategies for breaking it. How did the founding writers of young America engage, imagine, employ, and create an Africanist presence and persona? In what ways do these strategies explicate a vital part of American literature? How does excavating these pathways lead to fresh and more profound analyses of what they contain and how they contain it?

Let me propose some topics that need critical investigation.

First, the Africanist character as surrogate and enabler. In what ways does the imaginative encounter with Africanism enable white writers to think about themselves? What are the dynamics of Africanism's self-reflexive properties? Note, for instance, the way Africanism is used to conduct a dialogue concerning American space in *The Narrative of Arthur Gordon Pym*. Through the use of Africanism, Poe meditates on place as a means of containing the fear of borderlessness and trespass, but also as a means of releasing and exploring the desire or a limitless empty frontier. Consider the ways that Africanism in other American writers (Mark Twain, Melville, Hawthorne) serves as a vehicle for regulating love and the imagination as defenses against the psychic costs of guilt and despair. Africanism is the vehicle by which the American self knows itself as not enslaved, but free; not repulsive, but desirable; not helpless, but licensed and powerful; not history-less, but historical; not damned, but innocent; not a blind accident of evolution, but a progressive fulfillment of destiny.

A second topic in need of critical attention is the way an Africanist idiom is used to establish difference or, in a later period, to signal modernity. We need to explicate the ways in which specific themes, fears, forms of consciousness, and class relationships are embedded in the use of Africanist idiom: how the dialogue of black characters is construed as an alien, estranging dialect made deliberately unintelligible by spellings contrived to disfamiliarize it; how Africanist language practices are employed to evoke the tension between speech and speechlessness; how it is used to establish a cognitive world split between speech and text, to reinforce class distinctions and otherness as well as to assert privilege and power; how it serves as a marker and vehicle for illegal sexuality, fear of madness, expulsion, self-loathing. Finally, we should look at how a black idiom and the sensibilities it has come to imply are appropriated for the associative value they lend to modernism—to being hip, sophisticated, ultra-urbane.

Third, we need studies of the technical ways in which an Africanist character is used to limn out and enforce the invention and implications of whiteness. We need studies that analyze the strategic use of black characters to define the goals and enhance the qualities of white characters. Such studies will reveal the process of establishing others in order to know them, to display knowledge of the other so as to ease and to order external and internal chaos. Such studies will reveal the process by which it is made possible to explore and penetrate one's own body in the guise of the sexuality, vulnerability, and anarchy of the other—and to control projections of anarchy with the disciplinary apparatus of punishment and largess.

Fourth, we need to analyze the manipulation of the Africanist narrative (that is, the story of a black person, the experience of being bound and/or rejected) as a means of meditation—both safe and risky—on one's own humanity. Such analyses will reveal how the representation and appropriation of that narrative provides opportunities to contemplate limitation, suffering, rebellion, and to speculate on fate and destiny. They will analyze how that narrative is used for discourse on ethics, social and universal codes of behavior, and assertions about and definitions of civilization and reason. Criticism of this type will show how that narrative is used in the construction of a history and a context for whites by positing history-lessness and context-lessness for blacks.

These topics surface endlessly when one begins to look carefully, without restraining, protective agenda beforehand. They seem to me to render the nation's literature a much more complex and rewarding body of knowledge.

Two examples may clarify; one a major American novel that is both a source and a critique of romance as a genre; the other the fulfillment of the promise I made earlier to return to those mute white images of Poe's.

If we supplement our reading of *Huckleberry Finn,* expand it—release it from its clutch of sentimental nostrums about lighting out to the territory, river gods, and the fundamental innocence of Americanness—to incorporate its contestatory, combative critique of ante-bellum America, it seems to be another, fuller novel. It becomes a more beautifully complicated work that sheds much light on some of the problems it has accumulated through traditional readings too shy to linger over the implications of the Africanist presence at its center. We understand that, at a certain level, the critique of class and race is there, although disguised or enhanced by humor and naiveté. Because of the combination of humor, adventure, and the viewpoint of the naif, Mark Twain's readers are free to dismiss the critique, the contestatory qualities, of the novel and focus on its celebration of savvy innocence, at the same time voicing polite embarrassment over the symptomatic racial attitude it enforces. Early criticism (that is, the reappraisals in the 1950s that led to the reification of *Huckleberry Finn* as a great novel) missed or dismissed the social quarrel in that work because it appears to assimilate the ideological assumptions of its society and culture; because it is narrated in the voice and controlled by the gaze of a child-without-status—someone outside, marginal, and already "othered" by the middle-class society he loathes and seems never to envy; and because the novel masks itself in the comic, parodic, and exaggerated tall-tale format.

On this young but street-smart innocent, Huck, who is virginally uncorrupted by bourgeois yearnings, fury, and helplessness, Mark Twain inscribes a critique of slavery and the pretensions of the would-be middle class, a resistance to the loss of Eden and the difficulty of becoming a social individual. The agency, however, for Huck's struggle is the nigger Jim, and it is absolutely necessary (for reasons I tried to illuminate earlier) that the term *nigger* be inextricable from Huck's deliberations about who and what he himself is—or, more precisely, is not. The major controversies about the greatness or near greatness of *Huckleberry Finn* as an American (or even "world") novel exist as controversies because they forgo a close examination of the interdependence of slavery and freedom, of Huck's growth and Jim's service ability within it, and even of Mark Twain's inability to continue, to explore the journey into free territory.

The critical controversy has focused on the collapse of the so-called fatal ending of the novel. It has been suggested that the ending is brilliant finesse that returns Tom Sawyer to the center stage where he should be. Or it is a brilliant play on the dangers and limitations of romance. Or it is a sad and confused ending to the book of an author who, after a long blocked period, lost narrative direction; who changed the serious adult focus back to a child's story out of disgust. Or the ending is a valuable learning experience for Jim and Huck for which we and they should be grateful. What is not stressed is that there is no way, given the confines of the novel, for Huck to mature into a moral human being *in America* without Jim. To let Jim go free, to let him enter the mouth of the Ohio River and pass into free territory, would be to abandon the whole premise of the book. Neither Huck nor Mark Twain can tolerate, in imaginative terms, Jim freed. That would blast the predilection from its mooring.

Thus the fatal ending becomes the elaborate deferment of a necessary and necessarily unfree Africanist character's escape, because freedom has no meaning to Huck or to the text without the specter of enslavement, the anodyne to individualism; the yardstick of absolute power over the life of another; the signed, marked, informing, and mutating presence of a black slave.

The novel addresses at every point in its structural edifice, and lingers over in every fissure, the slave's body and personality: the way it speaks, what passion legal or illicit it is prey to, what pain it can endure, what limits, if any, there are to its suffering, what possibilities there are for forgiveness, compassion, love. Two things strike us in this novel: the apparently limitless store of love and compassion the black man has for his white friend and white masters; and his assumption that the whites are indeed what they say they are, superior and adult. This representation of Jim as the visible other can be read as the yearning of whites for forgiveness and love, but the yearning is made possible only when it is understood that Jim has recognized his inferiority (not as slave, but as black) and despises it. Jim permits his persecutors to torment him, humiliate him, and responds to the torment and humiliation with boundless love. The humiliation that Huck and Tom subject Jim to is baroque, endless, foolish, mind-softening—and it comes *after* we have experienced Jim as an adult, a caring father and a sensitive man. If Jim had been a white ex-convict befriended by Huck, the ending could not have been imagined or written: because it would not have been possible for two children to play so painfully with the life of a white man (regardless of his class, education, or fugitiveness) once he had been revealed to us as a moral adult. Jim's slave status makes play and deferment possible—but it also dramatizes, in style and mode of narration, the connection between slavery and the achievement (in actual and imaginary terms) of freedom. Jim seems unassertive, loving, irrational, passionate, dependent, inarticulate (except for the "talks" he and Huck have, long sweet talks we are not privy to—but what did you talk about, Huck?). It is not what Jim seems that warrants inquiry, but what Mark Twain, Huck, and especially Tom need from him that should solicit our attention. In that sense the book may indeed be "great" because in its structure, in the hell it puts its readers through at the end, the frontal debate it forces, it simulates and describes the parasitical nature of white freedom.

Forty years earlier, in the works of Poe, one sees how the concept of the American self was similarly bound to Africanism, and was similarly covert about its dependency. We can look to "The Gold-Bug" and "How to Write a Blackwood Article" (as well as *Pym*) for samples of the desperate need of this writer with pretensions to the planter class for the literary techniques of "othering" so common to American literature: estranging language, metaphoric condensation, fetishizing strategies, the economy of stereotype, allegorical foreclosure; strategies employed to secure his characters' (and his readers') identity. But there are unmanageable slips. The black slave Jupiter is said to whip his master in "The Gold-Bug"; the black servant Pompey stands mute and judgmental at the antics of his mistress in "A Blackwood Article." And Pym engages in cannibalism *before* he meets the black savages; when he escapes from them and witnesses the death of a black man, he drifts toward the silence of an impenetrable, inarticulate whiteness.

We are reminded of other images at the end of literary journeys into the forbidden space of blackness. Does Faulkner's *Absolom! Absolom!*, after its protracted search for the telling African blood, leave us with just such an image of snow and the eradication of race? Not quite. Shreve sees himself as the inheritor of the blood of African kings; the snow apparently is the wasteland of unmeaning, unfathomable whiteness. Harry's destiny and death dream in Hemingway's Africa is focused on the mountain top "great, high, and unbelievably white in the sun" in "The Snows of Kilimanjaro." *To Have and Have Not* closes with an image of a white boat. William Styron begins and ends Nat Turner's journey with a white, floating marble structure, windowless, doorless, incoherent. In *Henderson the Rain King,* Saul Bellow ends the hero's journey to and from his fantastic Africa on the ice, the white frozen wastes. With an Africanist child in his arms, the soul of the Black King in his baggage, Henderson dances, he shouts, over the frozen whiteness, a new white man in a new found land: "leaping, pounding, and tingling over the pure white lining of the gray Arctic silence."

If we follow through on the self-reflexive nature of these encounters with Africanism, it falls clear: images of blackness can be evil *and* protective, rebellious *and* forgiving, fearful *and* desirable—all of the self-contradictory features of the self. Whiteness, alone, is mute, meaningless, unfathomable, pointless, frozen, veiled, curtained, dreaded, senseless, implacable. Or so our writers seem to say.

NOTES

[1]Bernard Bailyn, *Voyagers to the West: A Passage in the Peopling of America on the Eve of the Revolution* (New York: Knopf, 1986), 488-492.

[2]Dominick LaCapra, *History, Politics and the Novel* (Ithaca: Cornell University Press, 1987), 4.

PART II

Criticism on Contemporary Novelists

The Romantic Style of Salinger's "Seymour: An Introduction" (1963)

JOHN O. LYONS

The rising note of dissen͏ ͏ ͏at can be heard in the criticism of Salinger's recent works is usually   ͏ed on the critics' discomfort at a writer who mysteriously yet conspicu͏u͏sly places himself in the middle of his fiction. At the present time it is evidently disconcerting to have a widely read and generally respected writer who in his work does not keep out of sight, who does not keep his family and prejudices at home, who does not consider brevity to be the essence of fiction, and who does not write in sympathetic harmony with the mythic and symbolic experience of man. This may be stating the case in extreme terms, yet such an astute reader as John Updike (who can himself tease his reader with hoverings and tensions between autobiography and fiction) says in his review of *Franny and Zooey* that

> Salinger loves the Glasses more than God loves them. He loves them too exclusively. Their invention has be come a hermitage for him. He loves them to the detriment of artistic moderation. "Zooey" is just too long; there are too many cigarettes, too many goddams, too much verbal ado about not quite enough.
>
> The author never rests from circling his creations, patting them fondly, slyly applauding. He robs the reader of the initiative upon which love must be given.[1]

Judged against the criteria by which prizes for fiction are now awarded, criteria which have been deduced from the work of Conrad, Joyce, James, Hemingway, and others, the criteria through which we

now even tend to view life itself, Salinger fails. In many of the short stories collected in *Nine Stories* he adheres carefully to the pattern of the
well-made story, but from "Raise High the Roof Beam, Carpenters"
(1955) through his latest published piece, "Seymour: An Introduction"
(1959), the egocentricity and eccentricity have increased. Much of the
anguish on the part of the critics seems to be that Salinger deliberately
flaunts the current academic standards for fiction. A lapse in taste might
be forgiven, but there is general concurrence that Salinger is a painstak-
ing and deliberate writer so that when he deserts the tradition it is a sin of
commission, and apparently a mortal one.

I too agree that Salinger is a deliberate writer, but I suspect that he
knows what he is doing when he turns the current critical canons about
and upon the critics. For more than half a century our literature has been
anti-romantic. The style of Salinger's recent work suggests a return to the
enthusiasms of the early nineteenth century when it was bliss in that
dawn to be alive. Then it was an ecstatic discovery that man was an extension of organic nature. His new found power to form and manipulate
his environment through mechanics and the mind only proved that he
could have mastery over himself and his society. For such as Wordsworth
it was a marvelous mystery that the things of the world flowed through
and were reflected in his being. In such a scheme the writer was appropriately the subject of his art, for to know and expose himself most fully
was the surest way to re create the universe in literature. So Romantic art
tends to be (and ideally is) without form and without fiction; it begins at
the beginning of time with autobiographical babblings, and because it is
as insatiable as life itself it so has no end. Many of the Romantic writers
(Sterne, Wordsworth, Byron, Thoreau), whom I think we must consider
if we are to understand Salinger's style, have been described as discursive, organic in form, autobiographical, anti-intellectual, and mystical.

Under the pressures of science, super-states, and war such Romanticism has long since been crushed or inverted. Conrad, for one, thought
that man would best protect himself from the dangerous ecstasies of self
by the forms of civilization. Joyce, for another, mocked and parodied the
syrupy optimism of Romanticism, replacing it with a sense of the mythic
heroism of man's inevitable defeat by a deterministic world of time and
mind. Now in our inverted Romantic literature the anonymous anti-hero
is a creature of economic, social, and psychological forces beyond his
control. His experience assumes meaning only when the artist imposes
upon it the forms of a myth laced with symbolic statements. More recently the faceless hero in fiction can find salvation by engaging himself

in a worldly cause or by surrendering himself to an otherworldly supernaturalism. If the contemporary writer is an heir to the Naturalistic tradition his hero is often saved by following the existentialist path toward
engagement in art or combat or party. If the writer is an heir to the tradition of psychological realism his hero is often saved by a religious conversion. Both solutions deny the Romantic writer's view of man in that
both solutions dismiss the essential importance and reality of man—if
not of life itself.

In "Seymour: An Introduction"[2] Salinger clearly deserts the inverted
Romantic view of man which has been reiterated in literature for half a
century as though that view were a dead end and returns to the style of
the early Romantics. Much in the style of "Seymour" is latent in
Salinger's earlier works, and I suspect that much of his appeal for the
college audience is based on his perverse, seemingly original joy (to use
the term of Wordsworth and Coleridge) in life. We now have many expert
funny writers (such as Waugh, Amis, DeVries), but Salinger is a rare and
genuine comic writer. Such comedy as his can only be based on the optimistic, indeed ecstatic, Romantic view of man. It is not that he has no objects of satire; by direct assault or implication he attacks formalism and
symbolism in literature, psychiatry and togetherness in the home, and
pompousness and do-goodism in public life. All of these targets deny the
essential mystery (and joy in the mystery) in spontaneous creation and
life.

The quality of "Seymour" (and other recent tales in the Glass saga)
which most disturbs Salinger's commentators is the constant presence of
Buddy Glass, the candid, posturing, erratic, jesting, pretentious narrator.
It is just this narrative technique which also links Salinger to his Romantic mentors. In this day a well-cultured literary taste can only abide the
narrative which is presented as a *fait accompli,* in which the artist stands
above and outside the work, an anonymous manipulator of language and
form. Even, perhaps especially, when modern works are written in the
first person the artist is emotionally dissociated from the narrative by
elaborate disguises. Not so with Salinger and his Romantic forebearers.
Not only is the teller of the story more interesting than the story told, but
he is closely identified with the author, and the reader is frequently reminded of the process of writing as though he were looking over the
shoulder of the writer as he worked, as though neither knows what is
going to happen next. Of course Buddy Glass is not literally Salinger, but
he is a creation which partakes much more of Salinger than most literary
eidolons. Buddy Glass is more than a mere fragment of Salinger, and the

relationship is comparable to that between Tristram Shandy and Sterne or between Childe Harold or Don Juan and Byron. In every case there is a difference between the writer and the narrator or hero, but the reader is constantly teased with the similarities between the historical writer an his professional mask or his hero.

When the reader is frequently reminded that there is an act of composition as well as a finished work of art by being allowed to see the writer suffering the pangs and surprises of creation, the effect is to focus on character instead of on form, on reality instead of art. The aesthetic effect is similar to that of the diary or epistolary novel where the outcome is presumably hidden from everyone. Buddy Glass, in this potpourri of memories of his older brother Seymour, is frequently surprised at his own words. "*His hair jumping in the barbershop.* Jesus God, is that my opening line?" (77) This is the sort of stance that a James or a Joyce would never take. For them selection always precedes composition as though there were an eternal form and order that is separate from the artist's mind and which he must approximate. But for the Romantic Salinger art *is* life and not manipulated invention. "I can usually tell whether a poet or prose writer is drawing from first-, second- or tenth-hand experience or is foisting off on us what he'd like to think is pure invention" (58). For Salinger art is organic or psychological in form because it is written from the heart, not the head (64, 76). There is even supposedly a danger in looking back at what has been written for fear that there would be the temptation to corrupt the initial inspiration with correction (90). How much this sounds like Byron sending his works hot and unblotted to Murray. "Carelessly I Sing" (*DJ* :VIII: 138) says Byron, and although there is much evidence that he was far from careless the pretense that he is asserts the spontaneity of creation. The same effect is achieved by Thoreau who contends that he must follow the bent of his genius. "Which is a very crooked one" (45).[3] In this way the true Romantic writer achieves a double response from his reader; one to the narrative and another to the teller of the narrative. In "Seymour" our interest is drawn as much to Buddy Glass as to his older brother who ostensibly is the subject.

The assertion by the Romantic writer that he is dealing with reality and not fiction is often supported by allusions to specific times and places during the process of composition as well as for the narrative. Like Wordsworth, who pretended to affix specific dates and vales to his poems, or Thoreau, who can write "As I sit at my window . . ." or "Now in the summer of '52 . . ." (94, 151), Buddy Glass present his ruminations on Seymour just as they occur to him. "Between the last paragraph and this just over two and a half months have gone by, Elapsed" (72). His words are written on a specific typewriter, in a specific room at a women's college in upstate New York. The effect of what he says on himself is even recorded, and this can be inspiriting or enervating. "How well do I know the reader? How much can I tell him without unnecessarily embarrassing either of us? I can tell him this: A place has been prepared for each of us in his own mind. Until a minute ago I'd seen mine four times during my life. This is the fifth time. I'm going to stretch out on the floor for a half hour or so. I beg you to excuse me" (104). Such a passage is a half-comic intensification of the relaxed, instinctive, spontaneous approach to composition which the Romantic artist must take according to his doctrine of respect for the instincts of a man and reverence toward his own reflexes.

"Seymour" is "An Introduction." Although the work is half as long as Salinger's only novel, *The Catcher in the Rye,* it is far from finished. There is a venerable Romantic tradition for such incompleteness, and I doubt that we should expect to see "Seymour" finished any more than their contemporaries should have expected Sterne to finish *Tristram Shandy* or Byron *Don Juan.* The overflow of good spirits from which such works spring prohibits a reasoned conclusion an a neat rounding off. If the writer is going to present himself and his subject as both unique and a microcosmos, every distraction is relevant. The result is digression so pervading that it assumes the nature of form. Byron, who says, "I must own,/ If I have any fault, it is digression" (*DJ* :III :96), and calls his muse a butterfly (*DJ* :XIII :89), sets the tone. Buddy Glass says that he is "an ecstatically happy man," and that such a man "can't be moderate or temperate or brief; he loses very nearly all his short paragraphs" (42). And so there is a Shandean joy in a digression, and a puckish joy, too, for Buddy Glass acknowledges that "I'm aware that a good many perfectly intelligent people can't stand parenthetical comments while a story's purportedly being told" (42). And so like a good bad boy of literature, Buddy Glass presents the reader an "unpretentious bouquet of very early-blooming parentheses: (((( ))))" (42). There is deliberately no end to such a work although the writer may soberly pretend he is surprised when he goes on and on. Byron is not serious when he says of Don Juan that he "meant to make this poem short,/ But now I can't tell where it may not run" (*DJ* :XV :22). So Buddy Glass is frequently amazed at how much there is to be said about Seymour.

The Romantic artist is not simply a dedicated one, he is unashamedly candid about his involvement in his material. Thoreau says,

> I wanted to live deep and suck out all the marrow of life, to live so stur-
> dily and Spartan-like as to put to rout all that was not life, to cut a broad
> swath and shave close, to drive life into a corner, and reduce it to its
> lowest terms, and, if it proved to be mean, why then to get the whole
> and genuine meanness of it, and publish its meanness to the world; or if
> it were sublime, to know it by experience, and be able to give a true ac-
> count of it in my next excursion. (74)

How like this is Buddy Glass's program (and I suspect it may be a deliberate echo):

> I want to describe, I want to distribute mementos, amulets, I want to
> break out my wallet and pass around snapshots, I want to follow my
> nose. (45)

It is not only the mood and structure of the two sentences which makes
me suspect the influence of Thoreau here, but later Buddy Glass comments that he feels "just a trifle Thoreauish" (61). It is more than wood-
chopping that may make him feel so, for like that of Thoreau, his prose
often erupts with clichés in surprising places—such as "I want to follow
my nose." He can also turn Pope to his use when he says that his characters "have a rather common flair for rushing in where most damned fools
fear to tread" (47). Indeed, the whole work is full of such verbal quips
and cranks and merry pranks which are difficult to associate with most
modern wit. In "Seymour" the jests operate just as they do in Sterne and
Byron in that they arrest the reader just this side of the sentimental and
momentarily release the author from his involvement in his subject.

Most contemporary fiction attempts to wring profundity from anti-
climax; from the renewed realization of the essential insignificance of
man and his dissociation from society. Romantic art seeks profundity in
the ecstasy of the realization of the mysterious interrelation of all things.
For Wordsworth this mystical relation is often seen as overtaking the
poet by surprise in the most unlikely places and at the most unlikely
times. The apparent rise of a mountain over a lake or a gnarled tree will
create a "spot in time" which will vibrate in sympathy between nature
and the poet all his life. Such spots in time, or epiphanies (to use Joyce's
term), form the loosely jointed backbone of "Seymour." The final and
most impressive memory is the one which prostrates Buddy Glass on the
floor for a half hour or so. It is very Wordsworthian for it takes place on a
cool evening and involves a child's dim recognition of a Truth. The

episode concerns a game of curb marbles between Buddy and a friend when Buddy was eight. He is listlessly using an unconventional method used by Seymour, but although Buddy is losing his marbles steadily at this enchanted hour it makes no difference.

> I was using Seymour's technique, or trying to—his side flick, his way of widely curving his marble at the other guy's—and I was losing steadily. Steadily but painlessly. For it was the time of day when New York City boys are much like Tiffin, Ohio, boys who hear a distant train whistle just as the last cow is being driven into the barn. At that magic quarter hour, if you lose marbles, you lose just marbles. . . . The bulby bright lights had just gone on under the canopy of our house. Seymour was standing on the curb edge before it, facing us, balanced on his arches, his hands in the slash pockets of his sheep-lined coat.

Seymour suddenly suggests to Buddy from across the street that he try not aiming:

> "You'll be *glad* if you hit his marble—Ira's marble—won't you? Won't you be *glad*? And if you're *glad* when you hit somebody's marble, then you sort of secretly didn't expect too much to do it. So there'd have to be some luck in it, there'd have to be slightly quite a lot of accident in it." (103–104)

The rather thin Oriental Truth which Seymour voices here, and which the young Buddy Glass is not willing to acknowledge, seems but a convenient peg on which to hang the enchanted mood of the scene. The real Truth lies in the "time-suspended" quality of the experience and is sustained by such words as "magic," "quietness," "balanced," "shadowed," "dimmed," "spell," and "twilit." This, and a half dozen other such scenes, are effective partly because the details which fill them out are not placed there by the author, but rather seem to place themselves just where they belong—to the surprise of (presumably) both the writer and the reader. The effect of such a passage can only be achieved when the Romantic double aesthetic response has been established, a response from the reader to both the story and the teller of the story, the narration and the narrator.

One of the reiterated qualifications about Salinger's Glass stories is that the Glasses are in no way typical, and so writing the loving accounts of their exploits can only result in un-universal and too precious tales.

But this penchant for the typical is an odd and relatively recent fashion. Certainly Seymour is presented as anything but a typical fellow—but that is Salinger's point. In many ways he is a romantic ideal, perhaps even in his suicide, but Buddy Glass uses him as a fulcrum against which he can get a purchase with his high-spirited prose against the absurdities and pretensions of the world. Salinger measures the world against Seymour and finds it wanting. He is used much as Byron uses Don Juan, or Thoreau uses his life at Walden Pond. In each case the result is satire written from the vantage of good instincts and common sense. The lessons that are drawn from each atypical vantage are much the same. To know Don Juan is to see that "This is the patent age of new inventions/ For killing bodies, and for saving souls" (*DJ* :I :132). To live at Walden Pond is to ask, "And if railroads are not built, how shall we get to Heaven in season?" (75). To understand Seymour is to dismiss "the middle-aged hot-rodders who insist on zooming us to the moon" (42). In each case the observation depends upon the author's jocular, discursive, and unbuttoned style which, however, is also a Romantic affirmation of the worth of man. To be testy about Salinger's evident flaunting of the rules laid down in short story courses is quite mistaken. He resuscitates in "Seymour" an effective literary stance, one which suggests a way to roughen the sheen coating most modern fiction.

NOTES

[1]*New York Times Book Review,* 17 September 1961, p. 52.
[2]*New Yorker,* 6 June 1959, 42–11.
[3]*Walden* (New York and Toronto, 1948). All quotations are from this edition.

The New Romance (1972)

ARTHUR MIZENER

Ordinary fiction operates on the assumption that the objects of perception are real—exist independent of the observer—and that events occur
in space-time in a cause-and-effect, historical pattern for which the ideal
model is a set of equations. Such fictions may introduce characters for
whom none of these things is true, for whom reality is a world of images
in the mind, in which a cloud will shift from camel to weasel to whale according to laws other than nature's. But even such characters are usually
but mad north-north-west; and the voice of the story itself is always
wholly "sane."

For imaginations that do not share the assumptions on which such
fiction is based, its conventions are deeply frustrating. What such imaginations want above everything else is the freedom to represent as reality
the images in their minds and the relations among these images that sat-
isfy them—regardless of what may be "true" in objective reality. Some
established forms of fiction can be adapted to this purpose. Fairy stories
and folk tales can be turned to serious purposes by poets like Coleridge,
as historical romance can be by Scott and Byron. The Gothic romance is
particularly useful for writers who want images of physical violence and
sexual extravagance.

Quite a few such writers—Byron or the Marquis de Sade or their
modern counterparts—try to authenticate their fictions by imitating them
in practice. This kind of authentication may help them to believe that
what they describe in their fiction is not something that exists only in
their minds but a transcendent reality lying behind the dull and obvious
actual world, to which they have penetrated by some special power of

their imaginations. Writers in whom the need to believe that is strong can also often be recognized by the minute and intense—the surreal—verisimilitude of their images. They give their images the maximum concreteness and specificity precisely because, though they scorn ordinary actuality, they are anxious to convince the reader that these objects are intensely alive in the transcendent realm they need to believe in.

But the ordinary forms of romance—at least in their twentieth century guise—never seem quite serious. In spite of their obvious usefulness and in spite of considerable efforts on our part, we do not seem to be able to make what we want out of science fiction, stories of contemporary adventure, or the kind of historical romance that Aldous Huxley, William Golding, and Terry Southern write. The romantic imagination of our time has had to work out a new form of romance, the kind used by writers like Joseph Heller, John Barth, and Donald Barthelme, and, most brilliantly, by Thomas Pynchon. The form of this romance and the reasons for its development show clearly in Pynchon's work, and are particularly evident in his best short story, "Entropy," and his recent novel, *The Crying of Lot 49* (1966) in which the central metaphor of "Entropy" is repeated.

The most striking things about both these works are their precision of observation and their range of perception, and the dazzling virtuosity of their expression. In the very first paragraph of "Entropy," for example, we discover the Duke di Angelis quartet "crouched over a 15 inch speaker which had been bolted to the top of a wastepaper basket, listening to 27 watts' worth of *The Heroes' Gate at Kiev.*" ". . . bolted to the top of a wastepaper basket": it is exactly right. There is the same authenticity about the quartet itself; they know that it was Gerry Mulligan's "Love for Sale" that had no piano, guitar, or accordion to provide "root chords," not "I'll Remember April." They find irresistible (or perhaps Pynchon does) the nostalgic, period charm of popular lyrics (" 'You want me to sing it? A cigarette that bears a lipstick's traces, an airline ticket to romantic places.' Krinkles scratched his head. 'These Foolish Things, you mean' ").

The fullness and precision of details of this kind make innumerable occasions for the kind of historical irony that gives the story's characters the quaint pathos of distance.

> This was in early February of '57 and back then [all of three years before the story was published] there were a lot of American expatriates around Washington, D. C., who would talk, every time they met

you, about how someday they were going over to Europe for real but right now it seemed they were working for the government. Everyone saw a fine irony in this. . . . They would haunt Armenian delicatessens for weeks at a stretch. . . . They would have affairs with sultry girls from Andalucía or the Midi who studied economics at Georgetown.

It sounds like Scott Fitzgerald—except that Pynchon is always putting out signals to show that he knows it sounds like Scott Fitzgerald, that in some way it is parody, as when Callisto remembers "the sad sick dance in Stravinsky's *L'Histoire du Soldat*" and thinks:

> . . . what had tango music been for them after the war, what meanings had he missed in all the stately coupled automatons in the *cafés-dansants*. . . . And how many musicians were left after Passchendaele, after the Marne? . . . Yet with violin and tympani Stravinsky had managed to communicate in that tango the same exhaustion, the same airlessness one saw in the slicked-down youths who were trying to imitate Vernon Castle and their mistresses, who simply did not care. *Ma Maîtresse*. Celeste. Returning to Nice after the second war he found that café replaced by a perfume shop which catered to American tourists. And no secret vestige of her in the cobblestones or in the old pension next door; no perfume to match her breath heavy with the sweet Spanish wine she always drank.

It is wonderfully done—those "automatons in the *cafés-dansants*" that evoke the stiff, doll-like, and romantic figures of the age of Irene and Vernon Castle; that graceful modulation of memory from these people of World War I to "*Ma Maîtresse*. Celeste" of World War II; and how wittily romantic to think that no perfume from the shop that replaced Celeste's café could match her wine-sweet breath. Callisto is composing, as in a poem, images of exhaustion and airlessness—of the void of some cultural equilibrium—from the history of the twentieth century.

What is troubling about Callisto's poem is its air of self-indulgence, of too easy sentiment. Its images are delicately commonplace, consciously literary. It is like an elegant montage of old newsreel clips from both wars. And every so often a sentence or phrase crosses the line into the obvious clichés of such writing ("And how many musicians were left after Passchendaele, after the Marne?" ". . . their mistresses, who simply did not care"). Those cobblestones and that old pension look more like a scene from an early reel of *Casablanca* than like experience. The same air invades the story's account of Callisto's present life. Where is its reality? Are we expected to accept Aubade, that dawn-dream vision of a girl part French, part Annamese, with her exquisitely orderly aesthetic imagination? Or is she a pure image, a figure not in the least probable except as a fancy that satisfies one of man's most persistent longings, real only as a symbol? This is a question that arises about every image in this story, where images appear to have no firm roots in actuality, to exist seriously only as idea—no matter how minutely Pynchon observes the objects that constitute them.

It is as if Pynchon truly felt the Fitzgerald kind of nostalgia but recognized that this is an attitude impossible any more to experience directly, without echoing earlier expressions of it—and perhaps, too, an attitude that hovers on the edge of a special kind of sentimentality. The past was never what nostalgia thinks it until it became the past, the "lost and gone"; nostalgia is not a feeling about what has passed: it is a feeling about the pastness of it. But this feeling is nonetheless very important to Pynchon, for what you might call ontological reasons. It is a way of resisting time's destruction of the meanings and values that accumulate around things people have lived with and through. The "sure obliteration"—the phrase is Wallace Stevens'—of these things is an entropy as frightening as the entropy Gibbs thought must overtake the physical universe. It is not, of course, in any scientifically literal sense, entropy. Pynchon gets from the entropy accumulating in the physical universe to the "entropy" accumulating in individual lives and the lives of cultures by metaphor. Why not? If images in the mind are more reliable, if possibly not more real, than the alleged objects these images stand for, are not correspondences among them—metaphors—more reliable than some set of equations that purport to represent a process linking the alleged objects? Pynchon has noticed that even scientists—or at least mathematicians—have taken to using the idea of entropy metaphorically, in information theory, to describe the meaningless randomness of "noise."

Love and Power, Henry Adams' Virgin and Dynamo, are alike, then, and what makes the nebulae precess and the boccie ball spin makes the world of human experience go round too. If Power is subject to slow decay, an irreversible accumulation of entropy, so too must human experience be. If Clausius is right, "that the entropy of an isolated system always continually increases," then each human being and every culture, as well as each galaxy and every engine, must be moving inexorably from the Condition of the Less to the Condition of the More Probable, declining into a powerless, loveless, indiscriminate chaos. This correspondence is, to be sure, put forward not by the author but by Callisto, who is at the same time described—in a phrase borrowed from the unhealthy sentimentality of Shakespeare's Orsino—as "in the sad dying fall of middle age."

But, as so often in his work, Pynchon seems to be asking himself in this story if the experience of his time does not force one to some such view as Callisto's. Do we not live in an America where everyone dreams of going to Europe "for real," but meanwhile works for the government? Have things, possibly, always been something like this? It is certainly true, at least, that the rich proud cost of felt meanings embodied in things—no matter how indestructibly "brass eternal" they have been—has always been destroyed by time. In an effort they cannot resist making even while they recognize its uselessness, writers like Pynchon struggle to remember, to resurrect in imagination the past, as if by doing so they can stop the process by which entropy accumulates until life—for an age, for an individual—reaches final equilibrium. "Sade, of course. And Temple Drake, gaunt and hopeless in her little park in Paris, at the end of *Sanctuary.* Final equilibrium. Nightwood. And the tango." Again, this is not the author's meditation; it is Callisto's. But Callisto's limiting defects—his inclination to a sophisticated, Wallace Stevens-like sentimentality, to the cultivated man's clichés—are not such as to destroy his point, only such as to allow Pynchon to have his cake and eat it too.

What thus makes it difficult for the reader to know where he is in Pynchon's story is its essential idea, its conviction that the most significant characteristic of life itself—or at least of the consciousness of life—is our uncertainty of where we are. The only things Pynchon is sure of are the images that fill his imagination. These images are therefore for him not perceptions of solid, intractable objects that exist independent of his idea of them. They are final terms; and for him reality is a theory about these images that orders them as ideas and, if possible, makes them interesting, surprising, entertaining. The heroine of Pynchon's *The Crying of Lot 49* tracks down, like some spiritual private eye, what she believes is a secret postal system that has, for centuries, kept communications open among the unofficial undergrounds organized around special perceptions of meaning and value, undergrounds that refuse to conform to the values of established society and therefore dare not keep in touch through its official communications system. But Oedipa is never sure she is not suffering from hallucinations or even a put-on by the enormously rich (and highly symbolic) lover who has died and left her the executor of his will.

> Either way [she thinks], they'll call it paranoia. They. Either you have
> stumbled indeed, without the aid of LSD or other indole alkaloids,
> onto a secret richness and concealed density of dream; onto a network
> by which X number of Americans are truly communicating whilst re-
> serving their lies, recitations of routine, arid betrayals of spiritual
> poverty, for the official government system; maybe onto a real alterna-
> tive to the exitlessness, to the absence of surprise to life, that harrows
> the head of everybody American you know, and you too, sweetie.

She sees very clearly where thinking in this way leaves her:

> . . . there either was some Tristero [the underground she thinks she has
> found] beyond the appearance of the legacy America [her rich lover
> has left her], or there was just America and if there was just America
> then it seemed the only way she could continue, and manage to be at all
> relevant to it, was as an alien, unfurrowed, assumed full circle into
> some paranoia.

The correspondences Oedipa perceives are not among things—at least
she is never sure they exist among things, out there in actuality. All she is
sure of is that they exist among images in her mind, so that for her the operation of the mind is not a process of checking hypotheses by objective
observation of nature; the only positive exercise of the intelligence available to her is a search for correspondences among the images in her
mind, a making of metaphors, an attempt to arrange images in such a
way that they make an imagined—and perhaps also imaginary—world
that can be endured, "some secret richness and concealed density of
dream," not "just America." "The act of metaphor then," Oepida thinks,
"was a thrust at truth or a lie, depending where you were: inside, safe,
outside, lost." Live in the belief that the world actually is what the
metaphor creates and you are "safe"; otherwise, you are "lost," are in
"just America," the present, the obvious, a place so dull and terrible that
any escape—either Oedipa's "orbiting ecstasy of a true paranoia" or her
husband's LSD—is preferable.

What Pynchon does in "Entropy" is to do what Oedipa Maas does in
The Crying of Lot 49, construct a metaphor "of God knows how many
parts." Since the metaphorical relations among the images of the mind
are the final reality, Pynchon's main business as a writer is to remark
them; like Callisto, he seeks correspondences, the full implications of
which he does not—perhaps cannot—always make entirely clear.

The basic correspondence for this story is the one signaled by its epigraph from *Tropic of Cancer,* between the entropy accumulating in the physical universe and the "entropy" accumulating in the consciousness of men. "The weather will continue bad" as the physical universe moves toward a powerless and chaotic equilibrium, and "there will be more death, more despair" as the cultural universe does the same thing. Both Meatball and Callisto—the wholly inelegant hero and the wholly elegant one, who live in flats one above the other but have no contact except random noise (and whose stories come to us in arbitrary alternation)—have lived on Callisto's Machiavellian assumption that *virtù* and *fortuna* are roughly 50/50 and that one therefore has a fighting chance to experience meaningfulness, to live Oedipa Maas's life of otherness, of "the secret richness and concealed density of dream," and perhaps even give it some sort of aesthetic order that will focus its meaning. But this assumption has now been badly skewed, consciously for Callisto by Gibbs's theory, implicitly for Meatball, who discovers that half of what he says to Saul is only noise, not information—"It's a bitch, ain't it," as Saul rightly says—and that the quartet now plays silently. What Gibbs's "spindly maze of equations" suggested, that not only galaxy and engine but human being and culture "evolve spontaneously toward the Condition of the More Probable," has now to be faced by both Callisto and Meatball.

They have worked in opposite ways to live meaningfully, ways determined by their ages or by the generations they belong to, but their objects have been the same. Callisto has built himself an hermetically sealed flat, "a tiny enclave of regularity in the city's chaos, alien to the vagaries of the weather, of national politics, of any civil disorder"; he has perfected its "ecological balance" and "with the help of the girl its artistic harmony." It is alive, this system, but the motions of its life are birdlike and as stylized, as "integral as the rhythms of a perfectly executed mobile." The girl can make it so because she lives in an imagined world of musical order. ". . . [S]he lived on her own curious and lonely planet, where the clouds and the odor of poincianas, the bitterness of wine and the accidental fingers at the small of her back or feathery against her breasts came to her reduced inevitably to the terms of sound: of music which emerged at intervals from a howling darkness of discordancy," exactly as information emerges—if at all, and perhaps only subjectively—from "noise," the random chaos of meaningless sound.

The architectonic purity of her world was constantly threatened by such hints of anarchy: gaps and excrescences and skew lines, and a

shifting or tilting of planes to which she had continually to readjust lest
the whole structure shiver into a disarray of discrete and meaningless
signals. Callisto had described the process once as a kind of "feed-
back": she crawled into dreams each night [like Oedipa Maas of *The
Crying of Lot 49*] with a sense of exhaustion, and a desperate resolve
never to relax that vigilance.

This musical structure in Aubade's mind rises "in a tangled tracery:
arabesques of order competing fugally with the improvised discords of
the party downstairs, which peaked sometimes in cusps and ogees of
noise," Gothic improvisations by life as against the neoclassic order
of Aubade's sleepless imagination, "that precious signal-to-noise ratio
whose delicate balance required every calorie [of heat-energy] of her
strength."

Meatball meets the common problem by opening his door—and
even his windows—wide to all experience of whatever kind until his
party reaches a climax of disorder and non-communication and "the
noise . . . a sustained, ungodly crescendo." Anything alive and moving,
that has a chance of being meaningful, is welcome to Meatball, who is
apparently hopeful of reducing it to some minimal order—"to calm
everybody down, one by one," to keep the "party from deteriorating into
total chaos," final equilibrium—as Callisto, having established perfect
order in his hermetically sealed room, hopes to keep his sick bird alive.
For Meatball, "the day before it had snowed and the day before that there
had been winds of gale force and before that the sun had made the city
glitter bright as April, though the calendar read early February." But for
Callisto, "for three days now, despite the changeful weather, the mercury
had stayed at 37 degrees Fahrenheit"; and when his sick bird dies, he is
convinced that his efforts to communicate life to it, "or a sense of life,"
have failed because the transference of heat-energy has ceased. (This is a
little puzzling: 37 degrees Fahrenheit is a reasonable outside temperature
for Washington in February, but 37 degrees *Centigrade* is bodily heat,
98.6 Fahrenheit. Possibly this play on temperatures is meant to suggest
that human power depends on the gradient between normal bodily and
normal natural winter temperature, and that "the final absence of all motion" will occur when they level off at the normal natural temperature.)

These are the dominant images of "Entropy," but a host of minor images surround and support them with a complication of implications that
appear endless. There is, for example, the story's omnipresent musical

image of the aesthetic order imagination imposes. It creeps in everywhere as verbal figure: the February weather is "a *stretti* passage in the year's fugue"; Callisto and Aubade are "scraps of melody" from an "intricate canon," they move into "series of modulations," and finally resolve into a "tonic of darkness." But this image also sends out branches and capillaries throughout the story in the form of further correspondences (such as the architectural image used to describe the musical structures in Aubade's mind), or as actual events (such as the flicked cigarette ashes that "dance around" in the speaker cone, like molecules moving in thermodynamic order), or as symbolic subplot (such as the actions of the Duke di Angelis quartet).

The quartet's one recording before they took to playing in silence, *Songs from Outer Space,* sounds like a slightly ironic parody of a sophisticated popular song. But there are no songs of outer space; outer space is soundless ("Just listen," as Duke says, "You'll catch on"). "Back to the old drawing board," says Meatball when the quartet gets mixed up in its silent improvisation. "No, man," Duke says, "back to the airless void." The outer spaces of consciousness about which the quartet is making its silent music are where people know Oedipa Maas's "orbiting ecstasy of true paranoia." With this music a man is never sure he is with anyone else, and may discover himself hard at work on "I'll Remember April" when the next man is playing "These Foolish Things."

> "I have this new conception, man," Duke said. "You remember your namesake. You remember Gerry." "No," said Meatball. "I'll remember April, if that's any help." "As a matter of fact," Duke said, "it was Love for Sale."

Duke's new conception "is to think everything. Roots, line, everything." ("Well," he says modestly in a characteristic example of the kind of irony Pynchon directs at himself, "there are a few bugs to work out.") Duke is carrying to its logical limit not only Gerry Mulligan's omission of piano, guitar, or accordion but the earlier reduced instrumentation of Stravinsky's tango ("Almost as if any tiny troupe of saltimbanques had set about conveying the same information as a full pit-orchestra").

Three days earlier—Meatball did remember—"the city glitter[ed] bright as April, though the calendar read early February." But (and here the story makes another of its leaps into the metaphysical reality of correspondence) since the soul *(spiritus, rauch, pneuma)* is nothing, substantially, but air; it is only natural that warpings in the atmosphere should be recapitulated in those who breathe it. So . . . there are private meanderings, linked to the climate as if this spell were a *stretto* passage in the year's fugue . . . months one can easily spend *in* fugue, because oddly enough, later on, winds, rains, passions of February and March are never remembered in that city, it is as if they had never been.

And who knows, perhaps they had not. In any event, Meatball will not remember April, which, "as Sarah Vaughan has put it, . . . will be a little late this year"—delayed, no doubt, about as long as the final equilibrium of perfected entropy can delay it.

Correspondences like these, each with its hint of a meaning, are everywhere in the story. For instance, what Saul's wife Miriam threw at him was a *Handbook of Chemistry and Physics;* when it missed Saul, it broke a window, and Saul "reckon[ed] something in her broke too," and in him, as something broke in Callisto and Aubade and perhaps in the universe itself at the time Aubade broke the window of their flat. Saul has entered Meatball's flat through the window ("Sort of wet out," he says). Saul and Miriam had been quarreling about communication theory, "which of course makes it very hilarious": somehow, the "precious signal-to-noise ratio" has gone awry for Miriam. "She'll be back," Meatball says, and Saul says, "No."

> "Tell a girl: 'I love you.' No trouble with two-thirds of that, it's a closed circuit. Just you and she. But that nasty four-letter word in the middle, *that's* the one you have to look out for. Ambiguity. Redundance. Irrelevance, even. Leakage. All this noise. Noise screws up your signal, makes for disorganization in the circuit . . ."

—the disorganization that information theory calls "entropy." Saul concludes that "successful" marriages are compromises: "You never run at top efficiency." They are, in short, closed circuits in which entropy is steadily increasing and "the secret richness and concealed density of dream" steadily decreasing.

"Entropy" is a dance of metaphors, arabesques of ordering correspondences that have been created, like the architectonically pure world in Aubade's imagination, as a counter-image to that image of man's culture and consciousness gradually sinking into an equilibrium of meaninglessness that is the subject of the story. Though not everyone who writes this form of romance feels precisely the way Pynchon does, all of them share a need to represent as reality the images of the mind and the relations among them that meet the demands of their moral passions. Whatever readers may feel about the implausibility, the psychological danger, even the possible corrupting effect of fictions of this kind (and these charges have been brought against every successful form of romantic fiction), this one has been beautifully designed to serve the needs of these twentieth-century romantics.

Lancelot: Percy's Romance (1983)

MARK JOHNSON

Walker Percy's *Lancelot* has been sharply criticized as an inept novel, but it should be seen as a contemporary romance.[1] As Flannery O'Connor says in "Some Aspects of the Grotesque in Southern Fiction," "Hawthorne knew his own problems and perhaps anticipated ours when he said he did not write novels, he wrote romances. Today many readers and critics have set up for the novel a kind of orthodoxy. They demand a realism of fact which may, in the end, limit rather than broaden the novel's scope." According to O'Connor, the writer's "true country" is "what is eternal and absolute," which she insists "covers considerable territory."[2] While *Lancelot* is not Percy's best book, only reading it properly—as a romance—grants us entry to its true country.

In contrast to the novel, Richard Chase observes, the romance "tends to prefer action to character," presenting two-dimensional characters who tend to be abstract and symbolic and who are frequently in a "deep and narrow, an obsessive, involvement."[3] The first words of *Lancelot* emphasize the narrowness of Lance's obsessions:

> Come into my cell. Make yourself at home. Take the chair; I'll sit on the cot. No? You prefer to stand by the window? I understand. You like my little view. Have you noticed that the narrower the view the more you can see? For the first time I understand how old ladies can sit on their porches for years. (3)

Lance later speaks of his room as "nothing but a small empty space with time running through it and a single tiny opening on the world" (107).

Lance's obsession with his narrow view, while restricting his range of vision, has the virtue of concentrating his perceptions. On one level, the room is a metaphor for the operation of the romance.

While I cannot develop the idea in this essay, certainly the romance has undergone a radical metamorphosis since the nineteenth century. The distinction between novel and romance is still useful, however, and I would direct the reader to Robert Scholes' insightful discussion of Durrell and Fowles as modern romancers in *Fabulation and Metafition.* Citing Borges' statement, "reality is not verbal," Scholes examines the epistemological problems of realism and the consequent return by such authors as Fowles and Barth to the "more fantastic and more philosophical romance." In *The Nature of Narrative,* he and Robert Kellogg are careful to note that "the novel is not the opposite of romance," and they cite Hawthorne as a pivotal figure in the development of the modern romance in his intentional blurring of the distinction between illustrative and representational art. Fifteen years ago, they observed that just as the novel evolved as a synthesis of empirical and fictional impulses, "the grand dialectic is about to begin again, and . . . the novel must yield its place to new forms."[4]

The romance opens up an important avenue for the contemporary writer, notes Chase: "The American imagination, like the New England Puritan mind itself, seems less interested in redemption than in the melodrama of the eternal struggle of good and evil, less interested in incarnation and reconciliation than in alienation and disorder."[5] The Manichaean sensibility which informs the tradition of the American romance is forcefully manifested in Percy's *Lancelot.* Like earlier American romancers, Percy is using the romance to question his contemporaries' materialistic faith in empirical science and capitalism, and to examine his age's abstraction, its separation of thought from feeling and of body from soul.

Lancelot, of course, does not speak for Walker Percy (a mistake made by a few early reviewers and continuing into some later essays),[6] any more than Chillingworth's is the voice of all wronged husbands. While never denying Hester's sin, Hawthorne's harshest judgment falls on Chillingworth. Percy presents us with a first-person account of a Roger Chillingworth, with some of Ethan Brand for good measure. Consequently, the epigraph from Dante could be spoken by Percival:

> *He sank so low that all means*
> *for his salvation were gone,*
> *except for showing him the lost people.*
> *For this I visited the region of the dead. . . .*

While Lancelot does not speak for Percy, he is a useful device for illuminating, if only by moonlight, some of the concerns traditionally associated with the romancer: epistemology, alienation, and the nature of evil.

1.

How do we know what we know? *Lancelot,* like *The Scarlet Letter,* is a tale of infidelity, primarily Lance's discovery of his wife's infidelity but also of his mother's possible infidelity with Harry Wills, a relationship Lance's father understood and accepted. Lance, however, is still driven by questions years later: "Jesus, was I also [Wills'] son" (214). The ostensible subject is infidelity, but the real focus is epistemology, the need to know. The convergence of the two concepts in the one verb is telling. "One has to know. There are worse things than bad news" (131). Lance joins the ranks of such characters as Chillingworth, Robin Molineaux, Ethan Brand, and Goodman Brown in his quest for certainty: "Is all niceness then or is all buggery? . . . How does one know for sure?" (136–37). "Knowing" in both senses is made explicit in the scene in which Lance takes Raine: "What had God in store for us? So it was this. For what comes of being adult was this probing her for her secret, the secret which I wanted to find out and she wanted me to find out. The Jews called it knowing and now I knew why. Every time I went deeper I knew her better" (236). He reduces the act to a struggle of wills: "We were going to know each other but one of us would know first and therefore win. . . . It was a contest. She lost" (236).

But real knowing is harder to come by. Lance interrogates his own need to know on the same page, as he reflects on having spied on his wife and her lover: "I didn't see what I wanted to see after all. What did I want to see? . . . What new sweet-horrid revelation did I expect to gain from witnessing what I already knew? Was it a kind of voyeurism? Or was it a desire to feel the lance strike home to the heart of the abscess and let the pus out? I still don't know. I knew only that it was necessary to know, to know only as the eyes know." Even at the story's end, he says his first act upon his release will be to read the sign only partially visible from his window:

Free &

Ma

B

"At last I shall know what it says" (250). Lancelot, craning his neck and peering around the corner, unable to read the sign, is a forceful type of Percy's idea of man's position in the world, a castaway in search of signs.[7] "Free and maybe" what—an angel, a beast, or a pilgrim? Hawthorne's characters have similar problems interpreting signs, be they pink ribbons or A's in the sky. The narrator of *The Scarlet Letter* discredits the providence in the sky ("it could only be the symptom of a highly disordered mental state") even as he uses it (it "seemed to give another moral interpretation to the things of this world"[8]). Lance turns to videotape for confirmation of his suspicions. Chillingworth has less need of such mundane observations, but Hawthorne sent Ethan Brand around the world in search of his unholy Grail, and Rappaccini and Aylmer destroy that which they love in their failure to find "the perfect future in the present." Lancelot's voyeuristic empiricism is the antithesis of faith.

Percy has frequently distinguished between what science can tell us about—types—and what it cannot tell us about—individuals. His point is not a simple-minded anti-science but a positing of some sort of faith against an age's easy agnosticism. Percy embodies this need for knowledge of the intangible in a poignant aside by Lance as he remembers his plans to discover certainty: "(How happy scientists are! Why didn't we become scientists, Percival? They confront problems which can be solved. We don't know what we confront. Does it have a name?)" (100). But Lancelot's "new order" is certainly mad, naive, murderous itself.

How do we know what we know? In Percy's terms from "The Message in the Bottle," when the bottle washes ashore we must be ready to recognize news and knowledge, and to distinguish between "island news" and "news from across the sea." That Lance does not do so, in spite of his penetrating criticisms of the illusory and real worlds juxtaposed at Belle Isle, prompts us to caution.

In his quest for knowledge, Lance, unlike Hawthorne and Percy, rejects the past as "intolerable, not because it is violent or terrible or doomstruck or any such thing, but just because it is so goddamn banal and feckless and useless" (105). Rather, for Lance, "The mystery lies in the here and now. The mystery is: What is one to do with oneself?" But even this most desperate existentialist recognizes that "there is a clue in the past" (106). If Lancelot is walking away from the past as Margot conceives it, we have to agree with him. He tells us his wife is "a collector, preserver, restorer, transformer" (81). At the very moment he is examining blood types, as "the worm of interest turned" in his spine, he reflects on the pigeon roost she had restored as his workroom: "It took Fluker two weeks to shovel out 150 years of pigeon shit, scrape the walls, and reveal what Margot was after, the slave brick of the walls and the three-inch cypress floor, not only not rotted but preserved, waxed by guano"

(28). "Preserved, waxed by guano" is hardly the way Hawthorne would view the past, and he would have agreed only with the third word of Lance's description of his plan: "Here's my crazy plan for the future. When I leave here, having served my time or been 'cured,' I don't want to go back to Belle Isle. I don't want to go back to any place. The only thing I'm sure of is that the past is absolutely dead. The future must be absolutely new. This is true not only of me but of you and of everyone. A new beginning must be made" (62).

Ethan Brand, of course, did a lot of traveling before realizing the source of his problem. In the words of one of Hawthorne's contemporaries, Lance will be carrying ruins to ruins. Cutting himself off from his past and his place is folly, and at the book's end Percival is rightly aghast when told Lance is being released—"Why do you look at me like that? You don't think they should?" (249–50). Lance comments proudly, "A new life. I began a new life over a year ago when I walked out of that dark parlor after leaving the supper table" (63); but later he is left wondering, "But what went wrong with the other new life last year?" (108). He returns to the plan frequently, at times emphasizing his own sanity as opposed to the world's madness in a manner worthy of Poe:

> It is simply this: a conviction and a freedom. The conviction: I will not tolerate this age. The freedom: the freedom to act on my conviction. And I will act. No one else has both the conviction and the freedom. Many agree with me, have the conviction, but will not act. Some act, assassinate, bomb, burn, etc., but they are the crazies. Crazy acts by crazy people. But what if one, sober, reasonable, and honorable man should act, and act with perfect sobriety, reason, and honor? Then you have the beginning of a new age. We shall start a new order of things. (156)

That Lance "burns" in the manner of the "crazies" he describes is one strong indication of Percy's irony. Lance gets his come-uppance from Anna, the gang rape victim who refuses to go with him. His view of the world as black-and-white, of women as ladies-and-whores, is too simplified, too abstract. Like Brand, Lance has "lost his hold of the magnetic chain of humanity."

2.

Lancelot's problem in his quest for knowledge has been his abstraction an consequent alienation, one of Percy's favorite themes. Separation

from others, of thought from feeling, of body from soul, is not an exclusively modern malady. Lance is a version of the Hawthorne character cut
off from the "magic circle" of humanity, a circle joined by the mutual
recognition not only of the sins of others (Chillingworth, Brown) but of
oneself. So isolated, he has those same "stern and wild teachers" which
taught Hester Prynne "much amiss." This line from Hawthorne's narrator
is as direct a criticism of Hester as we get in *The Scarlet Letter.* Percy's
distance from Lancelot's speculations should similarly be recognized.
Even Lance's discovery of evil is abstract and empty.

> There is a coldness. . . . You know the feeling of numbness and cold-
> ness, no, not a feeling, but a lack of feeling, that I spoke of during the
> events at Belle Isle? I told you it might have been the effect of the hur-
> ricane, the low pressure, methane, whatever. But I still feel it. That is,
> today, I don't feel it. I don't feel anything—except a slight curiosity
> about walking down that street out there. What do you think of it, that
> there is a certain coldness. . . . Do you feel it? (2S3)

Lancelot, after all he has been through and after two hundred and fifty
pages of self-exploration, comes up with even less than Ethan Brand, for
he declares that "there is no answer to the question": "The question?
Very well. The question is: Why did I discover nothing at the heart of
evil? There was no 'secret' after all, no discovery, no flickering of interest, nothing at all, not even any evil. There was no sense of coming close
to the 'answer.'. . . There is no question. There is no unholy grail just as
there is no Holy Grail" (253). Ethan Brand's discovery of the unpardonable sin within his own heart *is,* in its perverse way, a discovery of its opposite by implication, but Lancelot is denied even the questionable
consolation of self-knowledge.

Percival, too, is described as abstracted, not listening to Lance's
monologue, distractedly craning his neck to see further down the street.
Percival, as well as Lance, comes to a sense of how to act, though only by
an implied contrast with Lance. Through most of the book he is a voyeur,
as Lance had been, and as had Roger Chillingworth, Miles Coverdale, or
Nathaniel Hawthorne, and as in fact the reader is. The coldly dispassion-
ate observer troubled Hawthorne, as it should trouble us. Lance, even in
describing his murders, shows no feeling: "What I remember better than
the cutting was the sense I had of casting about for an appropriate feeling
to match the deed . . . and not finding one" (242). He is forever isolated—Anna is certainly right not to go with him—and his dying hour

will be gloom. Note the exchange between the mute Percival and Lance, which again implies an alternative Lance does not accept: "When the truth is, nobody understands anyone else, and nobody is reconciled because nobody knows what there is to be reconciled. . . . Don't you agree? No? Do you really believe people can be reconciled?" (200). Lance violates, and monstrously, the lives of others, however guilty, and he is no less deformed for not having Chillingworth's hump and red eyes. Percival *must* respond at the end, even if only to differ with Lance in monosyllables. To observe without responding to such a plight, to such an examination of evil, would be damning in itself.

Lance's abstraction evidences itself in his tendency to oversimplify matters into polarities of past and present, lady and whore, Louisiana and Los Angeles. Like the world of Hawthorne's romances, that of Lancelot is presented as a series of dualisms, most obviously in the device of the film's artificiality: "Things were split," Lance tells us. "I was physically in Louisiana but spiritually in Los Angeles. The day was split too. One window let onto this kind of October day, blue sky, sun shining. . . . The other window let onto a thunderstorm. My wife's friend's film company had set up a thunderstorm machine in the tourist parking lot" (25). Percy's humor allows Lance to set up some distinctions any reader would accept: "Which is worse, to die with T. J. Jackson at Chancellorsville or live with Johnny Carson in Burbank?" (158). But the dualisms turn sharply serious. Lance predicts that the country "is going to turn into a desert and it won't be a bad thing. Thirst and hunger are better than jungle rot. We will begin in the Wilderness where Lee lost. Deserts are clean places. Corpses turn quickly into simple pure chemicals" (158). Hester Prynne also knew "desert places": "She had wandered, without rule or guidance, in a moral wilderness; as vast; as intricate and shadowy, as the untamed forest. . . . Her intellect and heart had their home, as it were, in desert places, where she roamed as freely as the wild Indian in his woods." Lance's condemnation of his society, like Hester's, has much to recommend it; but what desperate alternatives! This paragraph from Hawthorne's romance ends, "Shame, Despair, Solitude! These had been her teachers,—stern and wild ones,—and they had made her strong, but taught her much amiss." Percy also seems to sympathize with his protagonist's complaints, but both Percy and Hawthorne saw, with Robert Frost, that natures desolation is not ultimate. "I have it in me so much nearer home /To scare myself with my own desert places."

Consequently, we should be distanced, if sympathetic, when Lance discovers his wife's infidelity. His cuckold's sensitivity is so sharp that he believes a character humming "Rudolph the Red-Nosed Reindeer" refers to him, with Rudolph's antlers. Jealousy worms its way into his heart: "How strange it is that a discovery like this, of evil, of a kinsman's dishonesty, a wife's infidelity, can shake you up, knock you out of your rut, be the occasion of a new way of looking at things!" (51). With the subtle double nod to Hawthorne, we should not be surprised nor misled when Lance continues in the "logic" of Ethan Brand:

> Can good come from evil? Have you ever considered the possibility that one might undertake a search not for God but for evil? . . .
>
> But what if you could show me a *sin*? a purely evil deed, an intolerable deed for which there is no explanation? Now there's a mystery. People would sit up and take notice. I would be impressed. You could almost make a believer out of me.
>
> In times when nobody is interested in God, what would happen if you could prove the existence of sin, pure and simple? Wouldn't that be a windfall for you? A new proof of God's existence! If there is such a thing as sin, evil, a living malignant force, there must be a God! (51–52)

Once again, our literature presents us with a perfectly logical lunatic, one whose perverse insights give us real perspective on our own condition whether he gains the same into himself or not. The insights remain, nonetheless, perverse.

3.

Lance's Manichaean view of the world is no novelty for Percy's audience. In *The Last Gentleman* both a stranger and Barrett's girlfriend Kitty make the distinction between ladies and whores; Barrett wants certainty but, to his credit, will not accept such a simple-minded distinction: "But what am I, he wondered: neither Christian nor pagan nor proper lusty gentleman, for I've never really got the straight of this lady-and-whore business. And that is all I want and it does not seem too much to ask: for once and all to get the straight of it." In *Love in the Ruins,* Tom More invented MOQUOL to diagnose and treat an angelism/bestialism syndrome, only to conclude, "Dear God, I can see it now, why can't I see it other times, . . . it is pilgrims we are, wayfarers on a journey, and not pigs, nor angels."[9]

Lancelot continues with such relentless dualisms and such an un-compromising need for certainty that, like Goodman Brown, he is shat-tered when certainty is not forthcoming:

> The innocence of children. Didn't your God say that unless you be-come as innocent as one of those, you shall not enter the kingdom of heaven?
>
> Yes, but what does that mean?
>
> It is obvious he made a mistake or else played a very bad trick on us. . . . Yet God himself so arranged it that you wake up one fine morn-ing with a great thundering hard-on and wanting nothing more in life than a sweet hot cunt to put it in, drive some girl, any girl, into the ground, and where is the innocence of that? Is that part of the inno-cence? If so, he should have said so. From child to assailant through no doing of one's own—is that God's plan for us? Damn you and your God. (176)

Unable to reconcile the ideal with the real, Lancelot finds refuge in evil itself, in violence, in a view of the world which belies its own stated aims. Refusal to accept Sodom does not necessitate going Sodom one better. "God himself so arranged it" echoes Chillingworth's self-defense of a "dark necessity." But we should remember Barrett's characterization of Sutter Vaught: "Where he probably goes wrong . . . is in the extremity of his alternatives: God and not-God, getting under women's dresses and blowing your brains out. Whereas and in fact [the] problem is how to live from one ordinary minute to the next on a Wednesday afternoon" (*LG* 354–55).

Thus, while the characters pursue a cosmic evil, Percy's readers ex-amine it in primarily human terms. Melville said Hawthorne's "power of blackness . . . derives its force from its appeals to that Calvinistic sense of Innate Depravity and Original Sin, from whose visitations, in some shape or other, no deeply thinking mind is always wholly free." For Percy as for Hawthorne, the primary sin is against another human being. In *Love in the Ruins,* Tom More recounts a memorable conversation with his daughter about salvation and a "sin without forgiveness," against which his wife is protected by her "Invincible Ignorance": "Which one is that?" Tom asks. "The sin against grace. If God gives you the grace to be-lieve in him and love him and you refuse, the sin will not be forgiven you" (*LR* 353).

Like Ethan Brand, Lancelot had set out for the embodiment of evil, perversely seeking in unpardonable, uncontaminated evil an implicit proof of good. But Lance is too much of an absolutist: "'Evil' is surely the clue to this age, the only quest appropriate to the age. For everything and everyone's either wonderful or sick and nothing is evil" (138). He comes actually to relish evil, "the sense at last of coming close to it, the sweet secret of evil, the dread exhilaration, the sure slight heart-quickening sense of coming onto something, the dear darling heart of darkness— ah, this was where it was all right" (216). But finally Lance proclaims his search for cosmic evil a failure: "There is no unholy grail just as there was no Holy Grail" (253), concluding in his logic that since he cannot find evil, there is no good. Because he cannot plumb his heart as Brand had, because he cannot recognize his own evil, Lancelot wears the armor of Invincible Ignorance. Percival, with the reader, knows better.

4.

That Percy can speak so unself-consciously of sin, evil, and faith, is testimony to the continuing power of romance. But the indigenous strain of the American romance is viable today because of our writers' willingness to continue asking fundamental questions about the nature of reality, of man and his behavior. "Tell me something," says Lance. "Why did I have to know the truth about Margot and know it with absolute certainty? Or rather why, knowing the truth, did I have to know more, prove more, *see*? Does one need to know more, ever more and more, in order that one put off acting on it or maybe even not act at all?" (89). The piercing nature of Lance's questions belies the unfortunate action he does take. *Lancelot*'s plot is as grotesque as something out of Flannery O'Connor, for Percy too is writing in large and startling figures for the almost blind.

For such metaphysical concerns, nonetheless, our writers have been criticized as "bad novelists," so that Hawthorne and Melville protested that they were writing romances. The problem continues, as in John Gardner's review of *Lancelot:*

> Fiction, at its best, is a means of discovery, a philosophical method. By that standard, Walker Percy is not a very good novelist; in fact *Lancelot,* for all its dramatic and philosophical intensity, is bad art, and what's worse, typical bad art. Like Tom Stoppard's plays, it fools around with philosophy, only in this case not for laughs but for fashionable groans. Art, it seems to me, should be a little less pompous, a

lot more serious. It should stop sniveling and go for answers or else shut up.[10]

At least the intensity of Gardner's response indicates the book's power. Unfortunately Gardner resembles Lancelot in demanding answers, which Percy like Hawthorne is not in the business of providing. O'Connor, speaking of the writer in "the modern romance tradition," notes that "Such a writer will be interested in what we don't understand rather than in what we do."[11]

At the last, however, I must confess to some disappointment with *Lancelot* myself. In *Historicism Once More,* Roy Harvey Pearce identified Hawthorne's major theme as "the discovery and acceptance of guilt (and righteousness too) in the present." Such, it seems to me, is the subject of *Lancelot,* despite the title character's final failure of insight. But Pearce further observed that while "Hawthorne's earlier fictions may serve to indicate the limits to which the romance could be taken and still not lose contact with actuality, so *The Marble Faun* . . . may serve to indicate just where the romance lost such contact, where the form began to lose its cultural strength and significance, where the romantic twilight set in."[12] The intense focus of *Lancelot* similarly removes Percy from the strengths of his earlier novels, notably character and place. It has its advantages as we have seen, but the price is high indeed. We lose the real interaction between the characters so crucial to the earlier books and only implied here. The contact can be tenuous, as in Barrett's joyous bounding toward the waiting Edsel at the end of *The Last Gentleman.* But Percival is at best only a shadow, and his important perspective remains wholly implicit and is consequently unable to maintain the necessary tension to support a credible conflict. As for place, it seems odd to speak of the locale of *Love in the Ruins*—Paradise Estates at "the end of the world," with the ruins of a Howard Johnson motel, a sulphurous golf course, a dilapidated church, Fedville—as an example of a writer's fine sense of place, but I would still argue that place is very well realized in that book and is almost totally absent from *Lancelot.*[13] We have not yet removed to Italy, but the new book is more cerebral than its predecessor and, ironically, seems to be a misguided attempt at universality.

Hawthorne's "The Custom House" locates the romance in "a neutral territory, somewhere between the real world and fairy-land, where the Actual and the Imaginary may meet, and each imbue itself with the nature of the other." So far as Percy loses touch with the actual in his fiction, just so far is his power lessened. Nevertheless, the romance continues to enable our serious writers to ask metaphysical questions without pretending to have pat answers. In a fine touch of dramatic irony, Lance says of Elgin, "Happy the man who can live with problems!" (141). Whether or not Percy, with more questions than answers, should "stop sniveling and shut up," each reader will have to determine for himself by such light as his narrative affords.

NOTES

[1]*Lancelot* (New York: Farrar, Straus, 1977); references to this edition are hereafter made parenthetically.

[2]*Mystery and Manners,* ed. Sally and Robert Fitzgerald (New York: Farrar, Straus, 1969), 38–39, 27.

[3]Richard Chase, *The American Novel and Its Tradition* (Garden City: Doubleday, 1957), 13.

[4]*Fabulation and Metafiction* (Urbana: University of Illinois Press, 1979), 9, 45; *The Nature of Narrative* (New York: Oxford University Press, 1966), 15, 69, 89–90, 99.

[5]Chase, 11.

[6]For instance, Joyce Carol Oates observes that Lance's ideas are "uncomfortably close to ideas Percy has expressed elsewhere" and proceeds to identify the two in her review, *The New Republic,* 5 February 1977, 32–34. John Gardner, to whom I return later, seems to confuse Lance's ideas with Percy's, *New York Times Book Review,* 20 February 1977, 16–20. Certainly, Lance expresses many of Percy's harsh judgments of contemporary America, and Lewis Lawson relates both Lance and Percival to Percy in "The Fall of the House of Lamar," in *The Art of Walker Percy,* ed. Panthea Reid Broughton (Baton Rouge: Louisiana State University Press, 1979), 243. But as Cleanth Brooks observes, "For many readers, the millennium of Lancelot Lamar will be obscured by the fact that his condemnation of the modern world may easily appear to be Walker Percy's own. This may well be. . . . But one can agree with Lance that the world is corrupt without agreeing at all with his single-minded resolution," in "Walker Percy and Modern Gnosticism," *Southern Review,* 13 (1977), 677–87.

[7]See particularly Percy's "The Message in the Bottle" (1959) and "The Man on the Train" (1956), rpt. in his *The Message in the Bottle* (New York: Farrar, Straus, 1975), which inform much of this discussion.

[8]See Robert Shulman, "Hawthorne's Quiet Conflict," *Philological Quarterly,* 47 (April 1968), 216-36.

[9]*The Last Gentleman* (New York: Farrar, Straus, 1966), 100 and 178-80; *Love in the Ruins* (New York: Dell, 1972), 104.

[10]Gardner, 20.

[11]O'Connor, 42.

[12]*Historicism Once More* (Princeton: Princeton University Press, 1969), 153, 176.

[13]See my essay, "The Search for Place in Walker Percy's Novels," *The Southern Literary Journal,* 8 (1975), 55–81. For a very different view of Percival's character, see William J. Dowie's argument that "Percival usurps the novel," in "*Lancelot* and the Search for Sin," *The Art of Walker Percy,* 258.

John Gardner's "The King's Indian" and the Romantic Tradition (1984)

GREGORY MORRIS

In "The King's Indian" Gardner borrows his framework from the masters of the nineteenth century, adopts themes and ideas from the "great tradition," and works out the complexities. He begins with the standard "boy at sea" metaphor that worked so well for Melville and for Poe, and constructs his story line around it. To tell the story he hires a Coleridgian "loon" mariner (the aged Jonathan Upchurch) who spills his tale like an expiation and who keeps his guest awake deep into the morning. There is even a hovering angel who supplies the frowns and smirks and ale, and who lets us know that it is not only the mariner who is telling the tale. It is the artistic triad of artist (Upchurch), critic (guest), and muse (angel), all exemplified and all borne into life.

The young, innocent hero, Jonathan Upchurch, is a lad struggling for an understanding of the ways and the workings of the universe. He leans toward philosophy, a self-conscious intellectual; when he finds himself adrift and hoodwinked (so the symbolism begins), he muses:

> I looked at the name, laid in gold on the bow, the Jolly Independent, and the irony made me burst out laughing. It was a self regarding Byronic laugh, soul-tortured and metaphysical, at first. But even as I laughed a change came over me. Two things came stealing to my mind at once: the sea-dogs had sold me someone else's boat, so it was mine and not-mine, like the whole of Creation—that was one of them—and the other was that, gazing out toward the eastern horizon, feeling the motion of the waves and wind, I wanted to be there, with Plato and Plotinus, despite all my sensible talk about southern Illinois. In land-

lessness alone lies the highest truth, shoreless, indefinite as God!
thought I. Better to perish in that howling infinite than be . . . something or other.[1] (212)

The investigation into metaphysical freedom has begun: Just what is the nature of personal freedom? To what extent can one exercise one's freedom? What are the limits? Gardner pursues the same intellectual quarry as his nineteenth-century predecessors.

He is also concerned, like Poe and Coleridge, with the distinction between appearance and reality and with the powers of the imagination. As a youngster, Upchurch learned dramatically what the imagination can do when pushed far enough, when he witnessed the mesmeric abilities of "the infamous Dr. Flint . . . a great gray craggy Adirondack of a man" (199). Flint takes his daughter Miranda, spellbound, coursing back through time, back to the ancients and the precivilized, and the trip proves nearly too much for young Jonathan:

> I began to feel something going wrong with my vision. I clung to my parents. Great gabbling birds flew all around me, purest white, darting, dipping, plunging, screeching, their wingtips stretching from wall to wall as they warred, all eyes, steel talons, and beaks, with the writhing serpents on the balcony around me. I screamed. I had seen all my life (I was then about nine) queer shadows at the edge of my bad left eye. Fraud though Lord knows he had to be, Flint had made them solidify a little. I was now convinced those shadows were real as the Parthenon, and a man like Flint, if he ever got his claws on me, could populate my world with such creatures. I'd have none of it! . . . I became that instant a desperate man, a fanatic. No mystic voyages for Jonathan Upchurch, says I to myself. No fooling around with those secret realms. (200–01)

Flint's defiance of time and space is horrifying—it is the nightmare, fantasy world that exists at that outermost reach of the imagination. It is all very well that Upchurch pledges himself to pragmatism and common sense, but Fate has already written his ticket. His voyage is to be incontrovertibly mystic and terrifying and perplexing.

The ship that picks up the stranded and unconscious Jonathan, the whaling ship *Jerusalem* (again, Gardner is having his little joke), is a death ship, ill-omened and ill-crewed: "Ye've jined with a company of deadmen, ye see; deadmen pursuing a deadman down into his grave and, could be, through it" (216). The mates are philosophical and suspicious, the Captain (Captain Dirge!) a laconic, gloomy man propped up by the blind lunatic Jeremiah. It is a ship meant to give lessons to a fresh, walleyed boy, and Jonathan learns an important one very early on: "A man mustn't jump to conclusions about what's real in this world and what's mere presentation" (238). What appears to be true is proven false, sham, pretense. The worst thing a man can chase is absolutism, whether it be the absolute faith of Billy More (the Buddian symbol of virtue and personal salvation for Upchurch) or the absolute egotism of Captain Dirge-Flint. The world is too variable and too surprising for certainty.

But Jonathan is after the answer, and he hunts it to its weird and forbidding end. He begins a pessimist and a skeptic, a proper attitude aboard a ship like the *Jerusalem:*

> I began to have an uneasy feeling—residue, perhaps, of my reading of Boethius—that my seeming freedom on the still, dark whaler was a grotesque illusion, that sneaking alone through hostile darkness I was watched by indifferent, dusty eyes, a cosmic checker, a being as mechanical as any automaton displayed in the Boston theaters. . . . Mad as it may sound, I had to concentrate with all my might to resist the temptation to shout or kick something over and force them to reveal themselves. . . . It was that that dizzied me, I told myself—made me populate the ship with a ghostly audience. Adrift in a universe grown wholly unfamiliar, I'd been suddenly ambushed by the dark vastness which suggests to the mind of a healthy man the magnificence of God and of all his Creation but suggested to me, and very powerfully, too, mere pyrotechnic pointlessness. (232–33)

Jonathan is a mind severed from experience and memory. He is afloat on a microcosm that is mad, gone crazy with the force of a lost imagination. On the *Jerusalem,* reality is created and destroyed by Flint (masquerading as the ironically blind Jeremiah), whose mind has been twisted by his creative brilliance; he goes from mere entertainment to crime to Faustian willfulness. He turns the universe into a mechanism, an "automaton" to be manipulated.

In such a world, a person has two choices: if one is dull, he falls back upon intellect (i.e., intellectual metaphysics); if he is imaginative, he relies upon intuition (i.e., emotional metaphysics)—which is what Jonathan does. When the universe becomes inexplicable, says Jonathan, when "there is more in this world than philosophy dreams of," play a hunch:

A hunch is a religious experience, an escape from mere intellect into reality, home of the soul. Put it this way: The mushroom-and-root-eating savages of the South Pacific have queer experiences, learning out of conversation with lizards, or from the scent of wildflowers, answers to questions which couldn't be answered by any means that old scoundrel Locke would countenance. Time and Space become impish, now ingenious and full of wit, like Ariel, now sullen and ill-mannered, like Caliban in a funk.[2] Effect precedes cause, causes and effects which are spatially remote refuse to be sensibly separate in time. The physical world turns crepuscular. . . . All we think and believe, in short, is foolish prejudice, even if some of it happens to be true (which seems to me unlikely). Or to make it all still more altiloquent: Human consciousness, in the ordinary case, is the artificial wall we build of perceptions and *con*ceptions, a hull of words and accepted opinions that keeps out the vast, consuming sea: It shears my self from all outside business, including the body I walk in but muse on the same as I do on a three-legged dog or an axe-handle, a slippery wild Indian or king at his game of chess. A mushroom or one raw emotion (such as love) can blast that wall to smithereens. I become a kind of half-wit, a limitless shadow too stupid to work out a mortgage writ, but I am also the path of the stars, the rightful monarch of Nowhere. I become, that instant, the King's Indian: Nothing is waste, nothing unfecund. The future is the past, the past is present to my senses. I gaze at the dark Satanic mills, the sludge-thick streams. I shake my head. They vanish. (241–42)

This is Gardner's clearest description of the subjective power of his emotional metaphysic. It is also perhaps his most colorful and rhetorical expression of the state of the artistic mind. The artist, overwhelmed by emotion and imagination, becomes the King's Indian, illustrator of the world's mysteries, explicator of the illegible texts.

On one side of that wall are the Wolffs and Wilkinses and Flints of this world, chained securely by their anarchy and existentialism and naturalistic pride. Their laws are crude and clawlike and encourage the animal nature in man:

1. Distrust Reason
2. Deny Equality
3. Succeed by Lies
4. Govern by Violence
5. Oppose All Law but Biological Law (299)

Order (says Wolff) is naturalistic, a Machiavellian dominance by sheer force. Or order may be self-imposed, an anarchical and existential order (as Wilkins proposes): "My acts add up to nothing. No Heaven, no Hell, mere chain of events neither guilty nor glorious. . . . I vow nothing. Nothing. There are no stable principles a man can make vows by, and there are no predictable people, only men like myself. A whole world crammed with cringing half-breeds unfit for the woods or the gabled house" (302–03). The world becomes mere impulse and whim; the distinctions between rape and love, death and creation vanish with the obliteration of the moral tradition. Or order is the quest for individual, "absolute vision," a quest that almost invariably ends in individual and absolute annihilation. Such is the fate of old Flint, spontaneously consumed (like his ancestors in Poe and Melville) in the flames of his own pride and shamelessness, "the daring assertion, always mistaken, that man is God—a high office otherwise left empty" (243). These, Gardner contends, are all the wrong answers to the right questions: "The universe is indifferent. If you decide that the world's a shadow, then you become a pure utilitarian, a pure materialist. If you refuse to play games, you don't say there is a God or there isn't a God, and you leave it all open, and you can't function as a human being without other human beings this is the only security we can reach."[3] Gardner says it another way in "The King's Indian": "What we claim we desire in this vale of tears is resplendent truth, distinct bits of certainty that ring like doubloons, but that very claim is, like everything else in the universe, a skinner, a bamboozle, an ingenious little trick for out-sharping the card-shark gods" (258). It is the Melvillean vision of "God and truth as Confidence Man."

Thus, what survives is love and human interdependence, and the ability to accept a specific amount of lunacy—personal and cosmic. Beauty sometimes turns ugly, but there is always the hope of redemption through love and imagination and art. Everything plummets and perishes but "raw emotion," which rises from the world's iniquity. Miranda and Jonathan-Ferdinand reconstruct their "brave, new world" from the hopes of the old; the birds circle, the wind fills the sails, and Melville's ghost rises once more to lead them on to a different dream. Gardner's metaphorical ship of fools (a metaphor now ragged from use) sails by the barest of luck and good chance, and under the grace of the white-plumed Holy Ghost, who sagely warns: "Hang on thyself, . . . thou fucking lunatic" (323). All one *can* do, indeed, is "hang on," remain humble, and save oneself through an ordained madness. It is the same lesson Gardner teaches in his poetic epic *Jason and Medeia,* in which he seems to anticipate the perfect postscript to his collection of tales and dreams. It comes with the culmination of Jason's pain and terror upon the *Argo,* the world finally comprehended:

> *Or if not the gods, then this:*
> *the power struggling to be born, a creature larger than man,*
> *though made of men; not to be outfoxed, too old for us;*
> *terrible and final, by nature neither just nor unjust,*
> *but wholly demanding, so that no man made any part of that beast*
> *dare think of self, as I did. For if living says anything,*
> *it's this: We sail between nonsense and terrible absurdity—*
> *sail between stiff, coherent system which has nothing to do*
> *with the universe (the stiffness of numbers, grammatical construc-*
> > *tions)*
> *and the universe, which has nothing to do with the names we give*
> *or seize our leverage by. Let man take his reasoning place,*
> *expecting nothing, since man is not the invisible player*
> *but the player's pawn. Seize the whole board, snatch after godhood,*
> *and all turns useless waste. Such is my story.*[4]

It is the world made clear by art through the collaborative effort of reason and imagination. "The King's Indian"—and *The King's Indian*—are delicate reflections of this world in all of its magic and shadow and ambiguity, like a hundred revolving mirrors giving off a blur of the same image: the human being as the King's pawn, the King's Indian.

NOTES

[1]The borrowing of Melville's "howling infinite" is not the last time Gardner makes use of Melville's work. Gardner may be the only novelist ever to quote from Melville's long, philosophical poem, *Clarel.* On page 280, the hoary image of Melville arises from the sea foam and shouts a pair of lines (partly misquoted) from his own poetic work:

> "Even death may prove unreal at last, and stoics be astounded into Heaven." (From *Clarel,* 4.35, "Epilogue")

> "Man, beast, grass, 'tis all one: Bearers of crosses—alike they tend, and follow, slowly follow on!" (From *Clarel,* 4.34, "Via Crucis")

Gardner also takes from *Moby Dick* Melville's question: "Ain't all men slaves, either physical or metaphysical?" (*The Kings Indian,* 198). Beside the straightforward quoting of Melville, Gardner also uses motifs and techniques and characters that Melville exploited so fruitfully; from Melville, Gardner takes his Captain Dirge-Flint (as awesome and foreboding as Melville's Ahab), his Indian harpooner Kiskawah (just the name is enough to remind one of Queequeg), and the notion of the ship as microcosm.

While all of these borrowings are sure evidence of Gardner's attraction to America's genius of the nineteenth century, he is even more liberal in his use of Edgar Allan Poe. His description of Augusta, for instance, is very close (and in some places identical) to Poe's Ligeia. Compare page 252 of "The King's Indian" and this line from "Ligeia": "They were even fuller than the fullest of the gazelle eyes of the tribe of the valley of Nourjahad." Gardner even mentions "Ligeia" on page 310.

Gardner draws most heavily, however, from Poe's only novel, *The Narrative of Arthur Gordon Pym,* which provides Gardner with a good deal of his plot and motivation. What follows is a summary of Gardner's forays into Poe's *Pym.* (The edition referred to is that published by Hill and Wang, 1960.)

A. Both Pym and Upchurch own a sailboat, and both boats are "worth about seventy-five dollars" (*AGP* 5). Pym's is called the *Ariel* and Upchurch's the *Jolly Independent,* and both lie wharfed by the lumberyard of Pankey & Co. Both Pym and Upchurch are washed out to sea by the same hellish storm, and both are picked up by whaling ships (compare the nearly identical descriptions—*AGP* 8–9 and *KI* 212–13).

B. When Pym once more sets out to sea, he sails aboard the *Grampus,* which is the ship which recovers the spurious painting that Flint uses to justify his ghost-voyage (see *KI* 283, 307).

C. Captain Guy of the *Grampus* sets out to look for the Vanishing Isles or Aurora Islands, and he sets his bearings at 52° 37′ 24″ S, 47° 43′ 15″ W. These are the exact headings given by Willkins (*KI* 266) as he traces Captain Dirge's strange tacking pattern. Although Captain Guy does not succeed in finding the Vanishing Isles, Dirge (and Upchurch) do manage to come upon them—or at least they find the proper heading and smell the unaccountable smell of land where there was no land.

D. When the *Jane Grey* explodes in *Pym* (176), savages and birds yell "Tekeli-li! Tekeli-li!" This is the same cry which bursts from the rigging of the *Jerusalem* as it sets out for home (*KI* 323).

E. Jonathan's near-fall from the mast (*KI* 237–38), which has one antecedent in *Moby Dick,* is almost directly taken from Poe's description of Pym's vertigo at the edge of the cliff (*AGP* 185). The lines are, in fact, the same in some places. And the fellow who saves Pym, his good friend Dirk Peters, we are later told now lives in Illinois, where of course both Upchurch and John Gardner have lived.

F. Both Poe and Gardner include mutinies in their tales, and Gardner's description (*KI* 295–96) is a near carbon copy of that written by Poe (*AGP* 41–42). Moreover, in both accounts the black cook is particularly villainous and bloodthirsty.

G. In "The King's Indian" Jeremiah tells us he sailed with "Captain d'O-yarvido on the good ship *Princess* that found out the Vanishing Isles of the South Pacific" (*KI* 234). Poe confirms the factualness of Jeremiah's voyage, writing: "In 1790, Captain Manuel de Oyarvido, in the ship Princess, belonging to the Royal Philippine Company, sailed, as he asserts, directly among the Vanishing Isles" (*AGP* 130–31).

H. Finally, in "The King's Indian," when Wilkins destroys his dumrny and then himself, he lies by the bulkhead upon which sits "the crudely carved but ornate memorial of some mortal presumably dead long since, returned to the universe . . . paroled forever from Discipline, word full of hardness: A. G. P." (*KI* 309–10). It is as if Gardner is adding the final words to a tombstone, echoing Poe's long distrust of man's penchant for invention; as Gardner said in the Lanesboro interview: "Poe hated the idea of slavery to machines." It is that blasphemous and ignorant grasping for godhood that both men deplore, the belief that man can create a nature that, in its intricate and ingenious mechanics, outdoes the original.

[2]The reference to Shakespeare's *Tempest* is only a confirmation of Gardner's intentional use of the play within his tale. By naming his "heroine" Miranda, he makes the connection obvious, and though Flint plays a perverse Prospero, the animalistic Wolff is a fitting counterpart to Shakespeare's Caliban.

[3]Personal interview with John Gardner, Lanesboro, Pennsylvania, 22 February 1979.

[4]John Gardner, *Jason and Medeia* (New York: Knopf, 1973), 269.

Bellow and English Romanticism (1984)

ALLAN CHAVKIN

A prodigious reader who has been intrigued by the work of Rudolf Steiner, Wilhelm Reich, and many other modern thinkers, Saul Bellow is one of the most intellectual authors of the twentieth century, and one can see evidence of numerous philosophical influences on his fiction. Critics have found it difficult to delineate the complex sensibility at the core of his work. A key to this sensibility can be found, however, in his repudiation of what he considers to be "the Wasteland outlook" of modernism and in his allegiance to the older tradition of early nineteenth-century English romanticism.[1] Although critics have often mentioned Bellow's debt to romanticism, no one has discussed in detail this influence on his canon.[2]

Bellow never has explicitly stated that romanticism is a seminal influence on his canon, and it is impossible to argue with certainty that he deliberately adopts this outlook in his fiction. It is likely though that he instinctively turned to romanticism when he became disgusted with the "victim literature" of modernism.[3] The question of certifying direct influence in cases where influence is major, such as in this instance, becomes impossible because an author radically transforms a source, usually beyond recognition, when he makes it his own. Yet one should add that while one can not be certain that Bellow's romantic sensibility is largely a result of his deliberate borrowing from the early nineteenth-century English poets, there is no question that his knowledge of the works of these poets is enormous. In his canon one finds quotations not only from the major works of the romantics but also from their least read works that are seldom referred to by scholars.

In any case, Bellow's outlook can best be described as a romantic outlook that is strongly colored by his unique sardonic comedy. However, this romanticism was not evident at the beginning of his career. At that time, Bellow was very much under the domination of "the Wasteland outlook" and Dostoevsky's fiction, as seen in "Two Morning Monologues" (1941), "The Mexican General" (1942), *Dangling Man* (1944), and *The Victim* (1947). Some time in the late 1940's, he became disgusted with the depressive temperament these works revealed. *The Adventures of Augie March* (1953) and *Seize the Day* (1956), as well as some short works written in the late 1940's and in the next decade, represent his stated repudiation of both Flaubertian pessimism and aestheticism (Harper 12). These works suggest Bellow's deliberate rejection of the highly-wrought, intricate form that he associates with modernism. In contrast to his early works, he now affirmed the worth of the ordinary individual and his everyday life. Like Wordsworth, he had faith in the power of the imagination to liberate the alienated individual shackled by customary perception, distractions of every day life, and the drudgery of the daily routine; thus imagination could expand consciousness and lead toward a spiritual rebirth. In surprising variations, this affirmative romantic theme became the central theme of Bellow's canon.

Bellow turns instinctively to the traditions of comedy and romanticism because of his dislike of what he considers to be the facile pessimism of modern literature, a pessimism which has become, he suggests, a literary convention in itself. According to Bellow, modern literature actually begins with the development of French realism in the middle of the nineteenth century. This realism, which "challenges the human significance of things," becomes the major event of modern literature (Harper 13). In this tradition the romantic concept of the individual and the worth of everyday life become obsolete; in fact, modernism "is not satisfied simply to dismiss a romantic, outmoded conception of the Self. In a spirit of deepest vengefulness it curses it. It hates it. It rends it, annihilates it."[4] Despising the romantic conception of the self, modern literature has, since Flaubert, as Bellow argues, offered in its place a "myth of the diminished man": "Common labor and humble life had their brief decades of glorification at the beginning of the modern era. But after the Cotter and the Leech Gatherer came the Man in the Crowd. In its Western form, realism made the ordinary man extraordinarily limited—weak, sick, paltry, subject to devouring illusion."[5]

Bellow rejects this view of human nature; unlike the modernists, he does not desire to challenge the human significance of things but to affirm it. He believes that they have not really examined the ordinary individual. To probe the "souls" of "the baker's daughters" may allow us to see "revelations and miracles."[6] His intention is to find "the extraordinary in the ordinary," and he thinks that the power that can accomplish this task is the imagination.[7]

Bellow believes that his faith in the imagination is not shared by contemporary society, which is materialistic and hostile to those who suggest ways of knowing that cannot be scientifically explained. The conflict is clearly elucidated in an important article of his published in 1975, aptly entitled "A World Too Much With Us."[8] He suggests that the problem that Wordsworth worried about in 1807, in which man squandered his powers in the dreary routines of daily life, has become much worse now. He implies that the task of the imagination has become much more difficult but all the more necessary. "The imagination I take to be indispensable to truth" (World 5), he announces unequivocally, and he attacks the dominant attitude of contemporary society, which "greatly esteems action" and technical and scientific accomplishment but "takes little stock in the imagination or in individual talent" (World 6).

According to Bellow, by ruling out certain kinds of knowledge and certain ways of knowing as illegitimate, we have created a "tedious rationality" that breeds boredom and other miseries. He recalls with admiration the British romantic poets with their faith in the power of the human mind: "Two centuries ago, the early romantic poets assumed that their minds were free, that they could know the good, that they could independently interpret and judge the entire creation, but those who still believe that the imagination has such powers to penetrate and to know keep their belief to themselves. As we now understand knowledge, does [the] imagination *know* anything? At the moment the educated world does not think so" (World 6). Years earlier, in 1957, he had suggested that while "no one knows what the power of the imagination comes from or how much distraction it can cope with," its task was becoming increasingly difficult.[9] In 1965 he speculated: "I wonder whether there will ever be enough tranquillity under modern circumstances to allow our contemporary Wordsworth to recollect anything" (Harper 14). Bellow finds the task of the imagination becoming increasingly more arduous, and one sees his romanticism becoming increasingly darker during the course of his career, though he does not return to the pessimism of his first two novels.

II

Although one can see the genesis of Bellow's romanticism in *The Adventures of Augie March* (1953) and *Seize the Day* 1956), his romanticism does not flower until *Henderson the Rain King* (1959). The themes of spiritual regeneration and the power of the imagination are treated specifically in romantic terms in this novel, where one finds important allusions to and quotations from the works of Blake, Shelley, Coleridge, and Wordsworth. Jeff Campbell and Daniel Majdiak have shown that the single most important influence on the novel is Wordsworth's "Ode: Intimations of Immortality from Recollections of Early Childhood," for it provides the concept of spiritual growth that the novel adopts.

The novel also alludes to Conrad's *Heart of Darkness,* and Henderson's Conradian quest in the African wasteland is Bellow's version of what one learns from a descent into the nether regions of the soul. On his journey to "burst the spirit's sleep," as Henderson phrases it, borrowing the expression from the third stanza of Shelley's Dedication to *The Revolt of Islam,* he meets a parodic version of Kurtz (*HRK* 160). Although Dahfu undeniably possesses the grandeur of mind that Kurtz is only reputed to possess, he does not resemble Kurtz in his descent into the depths of degradation. When Dahfu becomes Henderson's spiritual mentor, he helps Henderson overcome an excessive anxiety over death. Largely as a result of his meeting Dahfu, Henderson learns that his spiritual rebirth depends upon his recognizing the powers of the imagination, which Dahfu celebrates: "Imagination, imagination, imagination! It converts to actual. It sustains, it alters, it redeems!" (*HRK* 271).

By the end of the novel, Henderson bursts the spirit's sleep and awakens to a universe redeemed by the imagination. The seemingly insatiable voice, "I want, I want," no longer haunts him.[10] He decides that the restless years of wandering are over and that he will enter medical school and acquire a useful profession. He can return to the woman he has abandoned because now he possesses "true feeling" for her, "call it love," though "the word is full of bluff," he says. Most important, Henderson, who was compelled to undertake his quest because of a profound alienation in a meaningless "universe of death," gains self-knowledge and feels reconciled to a world radiant with life and hope.

The ending of the novel deliberately echoes that of Wordsworth's "Immortality Ode." Henderson feels a solidarity with humanity, symbolized by his befriending, on the return home, a Persian orphan: "As for this kid resting against me . . . why, he was still trailing his cloud of glory. God knows, I dragged mine on as long as I could till it got dingy, mere tatters of gray fog. However, I always knew what it was" (*HRK* 339). Henderson reaffirms here the idea of spiritual growth that one finds in the "Ode." Although aging results in the loss of the radiant vision of the child, there are compensations in one's maturity, increased capacity to love, and greater sensitivity to the suffering that is an inextricable part of the human condition. Moreover, the imagination can recapture, at times, the child's radiant perception. In short, the novel ends affirmatively rather than with the bleak vision of man's self-destructive quest for power that one finds in *Heart of Darkness*. On the contrary, Henderson comes to understand "that chaos doesn't run the whole show. That this is not a sick and hasty ride, helpless, through a dream into oblivion" (*HRK* 175). Henderson's journey culminates in his awareness of man's nobility, largeness of heart, and power of mind.

Although one can also see such Wordsworthian humanism in Bellow's next novel, *Herzog* (1964) is a much darker novel than the one published five years earlier. The sardonic humor that somewhat colored the exuberant comedy of *Henderson the Rain King* entirely dominates the comedy of *Herzog*. Bellow's belief that "chaos doesn't run the whole show" is fervidly expressed in Herzog—its fervor is now provoked by a ubiquitous pessimism others feel toward the survival of Western civilization and its humanist values. The romanticism of *Herzog* serves as an antidote to the poison of "the Wasteland outlook," which is so pervasive that even people "who had never even read a book of metaphysics, were touting the Void as if it were so much salable real estate" (*H* 93) Herzog, a professor who teaches a course entitled "The Roots of Romanticism," disdains *"the cheap mental stimulants of Alienation, the cant and rant of pipsqueaks about Inauthenticity and Forlornness"* (*H* 75.).

Herzog has suffered real anguish, and he is rightly suspicious of those who revel in alienation, anguish, and despair. He is disturbed, too, at the bitter rejection and hatred of romantic humanism and warns at one point that one should not "sneer at the term Romantic," for Romanticism preserved "the most generous ideas of mankind, during the greatest and most rapid of transformations, the most accelerated phase of the modern scientific and technical transformation" (*H* 165). The Wastelanders who populate the world of Herzog, however, despise such "sentiments" as these, and their cynical animosity toward romanticism and its adherents is aptly symbolized in the novel by Herzog's discovering "a used sanitary napkin in a covered dish on his desk, where he kept bundles of notes for his Romantic studies" (*H* 489). In short, the malice of the Wastelanders is literally brought home to him.

The problem for Herzog, then, is how to survive in a contemporary wasteland. His idealism has formerly proved disastrous, and with his private life as well as his career in disarray, he is on the verge of a mental breakdown. The relevance of his romantic humanist values in a society that finds them obsolete is not only a philosophical issue but one that also bears upon his daily life. The novel is, in fact, an elaborate meditation in which the professor probes the depths of his psyche, examines his past in intimate detail, and struggles, under much anxiety, to forge the disparate recollected fragments of his grim past into some kind of coherent whole. Like Wordsworth's *The Prelude,* the novel reveals the vicissitudes of the protagonist's mental state.

Fortunately, as Herzog recollects and reconstructs his past, it becomes clear that his beliefs do not have to be completely abandoned, only modified. Herzog's description of his proposed book on romanticism reveals the kind of modified romanticism in which Bellow believes and which he intends to express in the novel: "his study was supposed to have ended with a new angle on the modem condition, showing how life could be lived by renewing universal connections; overturning the last of the Romantic errors about the uniqueness of the Self; revising the old Western, Faustian ideology; investigating the social meaning of Nothingness" (*H* 39). Herzog never does write this book, but he does reveal in this description the relevance of romanticism to modern life. He suggests that mankind can overcome its excessive self-consciousness by achieving a marriage of mind and nature; can affirm the worth of the individual but avoid Faustian glorification of the self; and can establish a society based on brotherhood in place of the Hobbesian jungle that exists in contemporary society.

Bellow's belief that romanticism must be modified and made tough minded enough to prevail in the modem wasteland becomes evident in Herzog's reflection on T. E. Hulme's attack on romanticism. Essentially, Herzog sympathizes with Hulme's dislike of a romanticism that is vague, escapist, ethereal, utopian, excessively emotional, and soft-minded. Yet he also disapproves of Hulme's "narrow repressiveness," his modernist view of man as an extraordinarily limited animal. Hulme's view of romanticism is a reductive view, for while it applies to second-rate works, such as Keats's *Endymion,* it does not accurately describe first-rate works such as Keats's odes or Wordsworth's "Immortality Ode," "Tintern Abbey," and "Resolution and Independence."

By the end of the novel, Herzog has achieved a tough-minded romantic sensibility that will enable him to survive in a harsh predatory society. He has abandoned his past idealism that made him vulnerable to exploitation, but he has also completely repudiated the Wastelanders' brutal "realism." His mental voyage has brought him to a Wordsworthian conclusion that everyday life itself is the highest good, and Bellow himself has said: "I think a good deal of *Herzog* can be explained simply by the implicit assumption that existence, quite apart from any of our judgments, has value" (Harper 15).

In Bellow's next novel, *Mr. Sammler's Planet,* the romantic humanist is a septuagenarian who is often pompous, self-righteous, and posturing. Artur Sammler is Bellow's crankiest humanist; his remarks occasionally verge on misogyny and misanthropy. A survivor of the Holocaust, he finds himself engulfed in the distractions of New York City, as he waits, full of anxiety, for the imminent death of his benefactor, Dr. Elya Gruner.

The romanticism of *Mr. Sammler's Planet* is somewhat different from that of *Herzog* and the preceding works, for the protagonist has strong intimations of eternity and confesses at one point that only the Bible and the thirteenth-century German mystic writers are interesting reading for him. This mystical inclination, which is to become even more pronounced in Bellow's next novel, was not of major significance previously. Yet the romanticism of this novel is not actually mystical, and despite Sammler's reading preferences, the book does not focus upon his mystical proclivity.

In fact, once again one finds a variation of the basic situation of *Herzog* and *Henderson the Rain King.* An alienated and death-haunted romantic humanist who is anxious that his values may make him vulnerable in a nihilistic wasteland, Sammler meditates upon the immediate past as well as the more distant past as he tries to create some kind of order out of chaos. The novel is a version of the characteristic genre of the English romantics—the discursive meditation. The real focus, as in so many romantic poems, is on capturing the process of the mind seeking to come to terms with its anxiety as it recollects, ponders, and endows the past with order and meaning. Two critics have acknowledged the novel's affinity with romantic theme and style. Contrasting *Mr. Sammler's Planet* and Norman Mailer's *An American Dream,* Susan Glickman has said that "if Mailer's God is energy and his experience of God orgasm, Bellow's divinity is Mind, and his experience of it, thought." Irvin Stock writes: "Bellow has a gift, reminiscent of Wordsworth, for evoking in his very sentence rhythms, as well as in his words, the experience of thought, the drama of its emergence out of the life of the whole man."[11]

Both Glickman and Stock associate the romanticism of this novel with the earth-bound romanticism of Wordsworth rather than with a visionary or apocalyptic romanticism. Sammler himself suggests that part of the reason for the decline of Western society is in its false or escapist romanticism. The pioneering walk on the moon becomes a metaphor for contemporary man's escape from the problems of the age. When Gruner's irresponsible son, a cold-hearted "high-IQ moron" (*MSP* 177), tells Sammler that he has a reservation with the airlines for a future excursion to the moon, he is surprised at Sammler's lack of interest. Sammler explains: "I seem to be a depth man rather than a height man. I do not personally care for the illimitable. . . . I am content to sit here on the West Side, and watch, and admire these gorgeous Faustian departures for the other worlds" (*MSP* 183–84). While he is impressed by the moonwalk, he remains dedicated to "this death-burdened, rotting, spoiled, sullied, exasperating, sinful earth" (*MSP* 278).

The difference between Sammler's affirmation of the common life on "this death-burdened" earth and the public's rejection of it becomes clear when he observes the Manhattan crowd on the street. "The conviction transmitted by this crowd seemed to be that reality was a terrible thing, and that the final truth about mankind was overwhelming and crushing" (*MSP* 280). For Sammler, this conviction is especially evident in modern man's penchant for role-playing. Sammler sees this role-playing, especially extreme in the youth cult, as a pernicious and perverse distortion of the function of the imagination.

The histrionic bent of the mob not only symbolizes the rejection of humanism and the acceptance of nihilism but also represents for Sammler a kind of madness. One sees almost all of the characters that Sammler is associated with in the novel as engaging in role-playing, including the licentious Angela, the irresponsible Wallace, and the eccentric Shula. No doubt the best example of the insane destructiveness of role-playing, Sammler implies, is that of Rumkowski, "the mad Jewish King of Lodz" (*MSP* 230). His "play-acting" resulted in the murder of half a million people during World War II, when he helped the Nazis exterminate the Jews of Lodz.

At the end of the novel, Sammler prays for the soul of Elya Gruner, a man who did not engage in this "theatre of the soul" but who remained true to traditional humanist values as much as one possibly can in the spiritual chaos of modern society. It is these values, the great romantic positives, to which man must be true if his life is to be purposeful, Sammler implies. Yet, in the final lines of the work, he also suggests that each individual, by virtue of being human, has an intuitive awareness of transcendent reality. Even though some are not loyal to this reality, it exists. "For that is the truth of it—that we all know, God, that we know, that we know, we know, we know," Sammler says in his prayer that concludes the novel (*MSP* 313).

The intimations of immortality that intrigue Artur Sammler increase in intensity in Bellow's next novel, *Humboldt's Gift* (1975). In fact, the protagonist Charlie Citrine spends much time pondering the anthroposophy of Rudolf Steiner. Some critics have argued that it is Steiner's anthroposophy that is the primary influence on the novel,[12] but such a conclusion is not justified by the text. While Citrine is exuberant at times over the transcendentalism of Steiner, he also mocks this nineteenth-century writer for some of his farfetched ideas. Moreover, it is important to recognize that Steiner's anthroposophy has its roots in English romanticism, and Owen Barfield, Steiner's apologist, whom Bellow interviewed while writing the novel, "repeatedly and consistently" associated Steiner's ideas with those of the romantic poets.[13] In short, the underlying sensibility of the novel and the source not only of the vatic poet Humboldt but also the ironic romantic writer Citrine, owe their primary debt to English romanticism.

As in Bellow's other works, it is a mistake to see any one ideology as providing the foundation upon which this novel is constructed. Yet having made the qualification, one can assert that the sensibility that pervades the work is essentially romantic. In various parts of the novel, Bellow quotes from or alludes to works of Wordsworth, Blake, Coleridge, Shelley, and Keats to suggest that a romantic sensibility is preferable to the gloomy modernist sensibility of contemporary society. Wordsworth's romanticism is of special importance in the novel, and John J. Clayton's claim that the "Ode: Intimations of Immortality from Recollections of Early Childhood" must have been very much in Bellow's mind as he wrote *Humboldt's Gift* helps one to understand the nature of the romanticism in the novel.[14] Bellow depicts the spiritual regeneration of Citrine in terms similar to those of Wordsworth's poem, and in fact *Humboldt's Gift* echoes the "Immortality Ode" at crucial points. The novel is a desultory meditation upon both the perplexing

reality of death and the reasssuring possibility of immortality that underlie the "Immortality Ode." At the core of this novel is a Wordsworthian
faith in the power of the imagination to regenerate the death-haunted individual who has lost the "visionary gleam."

Citrine's meditation upon death and immortality is prompted by his
anguish over the premature death of his friend and mentor Von Humboldt
Fleisher, a poet of immense promise. Both Humboldt's failure and Citrine's failure seem to support the view of the ubiquitous, Machiavellian
"reality instructors" who argue that romantic poets are not "tough
enough" to prevail in a harsh society. Like Herzog, Citrine finds the cynical materialism of contemporary society unacceptable, yet he wonders
if one can adhere to the higher values of the romantic poet in which
Humboldt passionately believed.

The character of Humboldt somewhat resembles Bellow's personal
friends John Berryman and Isaac Rosenfeld but is large modelled on another friend of his, Delmore Schwartz, a poet who attempted to live up to
the higher values of the romantic poet but failed to do so. James Atlas' biography of Schwartz reveals that the poet believed at times that art was
not meant to provide a means to transcend reality but instead promised
salvation in the everyday world. His Wordsworthian goal, which Bellow
eventually embraced, "was to transmute the ordinary into something lu-
minous and enduring"; yet, at other times, Schwartz succumbed to the
notion that "the self immolating powers of the imagination would lead
him to some purer realm."[15] Eventually, he went mad and died prematurely.

Citrine's pondering of Humboldt's life and values enables him to attain a new awareness. Horrified by the "metaphysical assumptions about
death everyone in the world has apparently reached, everyone would be
snatched, ravished by death, throttled, smothered" (*HG* 263), Citrine receives spiritual and moral guidance from Humboldt by means of a
posthumously delivered letter. This posthumously delivered letter can be
considered to be the turning point of the novel because it provides the
impetus for his eventual decision to repudiate the materialism of "the re-
ality-instructors" and to begin a new spiritual life. Bolstered and clarified
by allusions to and quotations from Coleridge, Blake, and Keats, the letter warns Charlie not to succumb to a materialistic existence but to lead
the life of the imagination. This message is stressed by Humboldt's quoting a passage from Blake's August 23, 1799, letter to the Reverend Dr.
John Trusler, which contains the sentence: "And I know that This World
Is a World of Imagination & Vision" (*HG* 347).[16]

Dissatisfied with the current ideological package of "one-shot mortality," Charlie is intrigued with the idealism of Humboldt; he does realize, however, that he must retain a sense of irony or become self-destructive, as Humboldt did when he immersed himself in his idealism to an absurd point. Humboldt's idealism has its source in Wordsworth's "Immortality Ode," and Citrine decides to carry on this idealism but in modified form.

Charlie's spiritual crisis is prompted by an obsession over death, one which results in his disenchantment with the external world. In the course of the novel, he struggles to acquire a new consciousness and thereby gain "the faith that looks through death." His goal is to recover the child's immortal soul within him and thereby perceive the world with a child's sense of awe and enchantment as well as with the inner light which illuminates a dark world. At the opening of the work, he suggests that the process of regeneration is beginning: "I don't know how the child's soul had gotten back, but it was back" (*HG* 3). The process of regeneration is not a smooth path, however, and the inner light that Charlie needs to recover fades when an acute awareness of mortality manifests itself. Wordsworth suggests in the "Immortality Ode" that the inner light that the child possesses dissipates as one grows older, but the imagination can enable one to recapture the child's soul within him, triumph over the anxiety of mortality, and view the world in all its radiance. Bellow's work reveals the same affirmative view.

At the end of the novel, Bellow implies that Citrine is on the correct road to achieving "the faith that looks through death." Reminiscent of the "Immortality Ode," the final sentence of the work invokes, with its symbolic flower, the possibility of spiritual rebirth. Although Citrine can never again perceive the world in the permanent "celestial light" of the child, the child's soul does survive within him, and Bellow implies that his protagonist is readying himself to blow the "imagination's trumpet" and "look again with open eyes upon the whole shining earth" (*HG* 396).

III

Bellow's most recent novel, *The Dean's December* (1982), differs from his previous work in its preoccupation with social problems. Yet even here his romanticism is evident. Albert Corde, the protagonist of the novel, states that in the current moral crisis "the first act of morality was to disinter the reality, retrieve reality . . . represent it anew as art would represent it" (*DD* 123). Bellow suggests that the imagination is the only force that can redeem reality from the "false consciousness" which has enveloped it and show man the way out of the contemporary morass (*DD* 123). Occasionally alluding to and quoting from Blake, Shelley, Keats, and various heirs to English romantic tradition, Corde urges man to acquire a new kind of perception so that he can liberate himself from the mind-forged manacles that enslave him.

Corde's radicalism is implicit throughout Bellow's canon. Like Wordsworth, Bellow abandoned the role of political radical for the role of poetic radical with the goal of subverting false values. M. H. Abrams succinctly describes Wordsworth's task as one requiring the "absolute redemption" of his readers by liberating their sensibilities from bondage to unnatural social-aesthetic norms and so opening their eyes to his own imaginative vision of a new world, in which men who are equal in the dignity of their common humanity are at home in a nature which, even in its humblest or most trivial aspect, is instinct with power and grandeur."[17] This description accurately describes Bellow's task as well as Wordsworth's. Like Wordsworth and most of the other nineteenth-century English romantics, Bellow calls for the liberation of the mind from the mortmain of custom and the slavery of routine perception. The individual needs a new kind of imaginative seeing without prejudices, preconceptions, abstract theories, or multitudes of facts. A twentieth-century romantic, Bellow reveals in his canon a qualified hope that man will redeem himself and his world by the powers of the imagination and thus reclaim the great positives of our Western past.

NOTES

[1]Saul Bellow, *Herzog* (New York: Viking, 1964), 75. Subsequent references to *Herzog* and to Bellow's other novels will be given parenthetically in the text with these abbreviations: *Herzog—H; Henderson the Rain King* (New York: Viking, 1959)—*HRK; Mr. Sammler's Planet* (New York: Viking, 1970)—*MSP: Humboldt's Gift* (New York: Viking, 1975)—*HG;* and *The Dean's December* (New York: Harper & Row, 1982)—*DD*.

[2]Four critics examine the influence of romanticism on specific novels. See Daniel Majdiak, "The Romantic Self and Henderson the Rain King," *Bucknell Review,* 19 (Autumn 1971), 125–46; Jeff Campbell, "Bellow's Intimations of Immortality: *Henderson the Rain King,*" *Studies in the Novel,* 1 (Fall 1969), 323–33; Michael G. Yetman, "Who Would not Sing for Humboldt?" *ELH* 48 (Winter 1981), 935–51; and Allan Chavkin, "Bellow's Alternative to the Wasteland: Romantic Theme and Form in *Herzog,*" *Studies in the Novel* 11 (Fall 1979),

326–37, and his *"Humboldt's Gift* and the Romantic Imagination," *Philological Quarterly,* 62 (Winter 1983), 1–19.

³Gordon Lloyd Harper, "Saul Bellow: An Interview," in *Saul Bellow: A Collection of Critical Essays,* ed. Earl Rovit (Englewood Cliffs, N.J.: Prentice Hall, 1975), 12. Originally published in *Paris Review,* 9 (Winter 1965), 49–73. Since the late 1940's, Bellow has repeatedly criticized modernism for its "Wasteland outlook" and its "victim literature." Even his earliest fiction (his "victim literature") contains criticism of this tradition.

⁴Saul Bellow, *Recent American Literature* (Washington: Library of Congress 1963), 10.

⁵Saul Bellow, "A Comment on 'Form and Despair'," *Location,* 1 (Summer 1964), 12, rpt. in *Herzog: Text and Criticism,* ed. Irving Howe (New York: Viking; 1967), 386–88.

⁶"Where Do We Go From Here: The Future of Fiction," in *Saul Bellow and the Critics,* ed. Irving Malin (New York: New York University Press, 1967), 219. Originally published in *Michigan Quarterly Review,* 1 (Winter 1962), 27–33.

⁷Joseph Epstein, "A Talk with Saul Bellow," *New York Times Book Review,* 5 December 1976, p. 93.

⁸Saul Bellow, "A World Too Much With Us," *Critical Inquiry,* 2.1 (Autumn 1975), 1–9.

⁹Saul Bellow, "Distractions of a Fiction Writer," in *The Living Novel: A Symposium,* ed Granville Hicks (New York: Macmillan, 1957), 6.

¹⁰The phrase, "I want, I want," which is repeated a number of times in the *Henderson the Rain King,* has its source in Blake's caption for the ninth plate of *For the Sexes: The Gates of Paradise.* See *The Poetry and Prose of William Blake,* ed. David V. Erdman (Garden City, N.Y.: Doubleday, 1970), 261.

¹¹Susan Glickman, "The World as Will and Idea: A Comparative Study of *An American Dream* and *Mr. Sammler's Planet,*" *Modern Fiction Studies,* 28 (Winter 1982–83), 577; Irvin Stock, "Man in Culture," *Commentary,* May 1970, 93.

¹²See, for example, Herbert J. Smith, *"Humboldt's Gift* and Rudolf Steiner," *Centennial Review,* 22 (Fall 1978), 479–89. Bellow reveals a vatic impulse throughout his canon, though it is most pronounced in the fiction after *Mr. Sammler's Planet.* Nevertheless, this impulse is tempered by a strong skepticism and ultimately subsumed by a non-transcendental imagination that is anchored in the everyday world. Bellow describes this imagination as "a primitive prompter or commentator . . . telling us what the real world is" (Harper 10).

¹³Michael G. Yetman, "Who Would Not Sing For Humboldt?" 943.

¹⁴John J. Clayton, *Saul Bellow: In Defense of Man.* 2nd ed. (Bloomington: Indiana University Press, 1979), 279.

[15]James Atlas, *Delmore Schwartz: The Life of an American Poet* (New York: Farrar, Straus 1977), 303, 379.

[16]See *The Letters of William Blake,* ed. Geoffrey Keynes (New York: Macmillan, 1956), 35.

[17]Meyer H. Abrams, *Natural Supernaturalism: Tradition and Revolution in Romantic Literature* (New York: Norton, 1971), 392.

Hawthorne and O'Connor: A Literary Kinship (1989)

RONALD EMERICK

Although much attention has been paid to Flannery O'Connor's themes, her vision, and her artistry during the past twenty-five years, the territory of influences upon O'Connor has been insufficiently explored. A survey of criticism reveals passing references and brief comparisons to various authors who have influenced O'Connor; however, few of these comparisons are explored in any depth. O'Connor has been labeled the disciple of such diverse writers as Dostoyevsky and Mark Twain, Edgar Allan Poe and Henry James, Joseph Conrad and Nathanael West. Among the fiction writers that influenced her, O'Connor herself cites Henry James and Joseph Conrad (Feeley, 10). She also states, "Many years ago I read a volume of 'The Humorous Stories of Edgar Allan Poe,' and I think that started me thinking of a writing career. . . . And I'm sure Gogol influenced me" (qtd. in Friedman and Lawson 251). Her close friend Robert Fitzgerald observes that Faulkner's *As I Lay Dying* and Nathanael West's *Miss Lonelyhearts* were of special importance to O'Connor: "These are the only two works of fiction that I can remember her urging on me, and it is pretty clear from her work that they were close to her heart as a writer. So was Lardner" (*Everything That Rises* xv). Although Stanley Edgar Hyman discounts the Faulkner influence, he confirms the importance of Nathanael West, particularly regarding O'Connor's early works. Hyman cites Dostoyevsky as the most important European influence upon O'Connor and Mark Twain as the stylist to whom she is most in debt (43). Leon V. Driskell and Joan T. Brittain, in their more extensive discussion of influences upon O'Connor, emphasize the importance of the novels of François Mauriac and the thought of Teilhard de Chardin, in addition to the works of Hawthorne and West (14). Miles Orvell briefly explores the degree of influence of Hawthorne, Poe, West, and Herman Melville (32–39, 73); and in reference to her mode, the romance, Harold Bloom suggests that O'Connor's line of descent can be traced from Hawthorne through Faulkner, T. S. Eliot, and West (3).

Despite these various claims, most of which are valid, the influence of Nathaniel Hawthorne upon O'Connor is possibly the most pervasive of all. When she lists literary figures whom she admires or to whom she is indebted, O'Connor mentions Hawthorne most often in essays and personal correspondence. Her most extensive reference to Hawthorne, one which reveals O'Connor's deep interest in both his life and his writings, occurs in "Introduction to *A Memoir of Mary Ann*," an essay written in response to a request by Sister Evangelist, the Sister Superior of Our Lady of Perpetual Help Cancer Home in Atlanta, that O'Connor write a story eulogizing a then recently deceased, saintlike cancer patient, twelve-year-old Mary Ann. Although O'Connor declined and suggested that the sisters could write a more authoritative account themselves, she did consent to write a brief introduction for Mary Ann's story. In the essay, O'Connor uses quotations from two of Hawthorne's works—"The Birthmark" and *Our Old Home*—and also reveals her familiarity with Hawthorne's notebooks and the writings of his younger daughter, Rose, the founder of the congregation of nuns who administer the cancer home in Atlanta. O'Connor first compares the child to Georgiana, the ill-fated victim of her husband's scientific experiment in "The Birthmark." The grotesque tumor on Mary Ann's cheek, however, is considerably more shocking and repulsive than the red, hand-shaped mark that mars the cheek of Aylmer's Georgiana. Next, O'Connor recounts from *Our Old Home* the story of a fastidious gentleman who, despite his reserve, caresses and shows affection toward a grotesque child in a Liverpool workhouse. After she quotes a passage praising the gentleman for overcoming a tendency toward "ice in the blood," O'Connor provides a segment from Hawthorne's notebooks revealing that Hawthorne himself was the fastidious gentleman. In the latter part of the essay O'Connor shows how Hawthorne's act of charity, Rose Hawthorne's work with cancer patients, and Mary Ann's piety demonstrate the invisible growth of charity and the Catholic doctrine of the Communion of Saints.

However, O'Connor's debt to Hawthorne is more than just one of extensive familiarity with his writing. In a letter to John Hawkes, O'Connor acknowledges, "I feel more of a kinship with Hawthorne than with any other American writer" (qtd. in Reiter 25). In the same letter she explains more fully the reason for this kinship, a similarity in approach to subject matter: "I think I would admit to writing what Hawthorne called 'romances'" (25). O'Connor reaffirms her debt to Hawthorne's genre in a letter to William Sessions, dated September 13, 1960: "Hawthorne said he didn't write novels, he wrote romances; I am one of his descendants" (qtd. in Friedman and Lawson 223). And in an interview with Gerald E. Sherry, printed in the June/July 1963 issue of *Critic*, O'Connor again emphasizes the similarity between her own approach and Hawthorne's: "I write 'tales' in the sense Hawthorne wrote tales—though I hope with less reliance on allegory" (qtd. in Friedman and Lawson 240). Although O'Connor would disclaim her reliance on allegory, here too she is in debt to Hawthorne. In their continual linking of physical and spiritual worlds, Hawthorne and O'Connor are two of the most consistent allegorists in American literature.

Why is Hawthorne's influence upon O'Connor so extensive? Why is O'Connor attracted to the same genre and technique as a New Englander writing one hundred years before her? Perhaps because upon reading Hawthorne, O'Connor recognized a kindred vision. In the same 1963 interview with Sherry, O'Connor suggests that she and Hawthorne share not just a similarity in approach but in subject matter as well. After explaining that both she and Hawthorne write similar tales, O'Connor continues, "I'm interested in the old Adam. He just talks southern because I do" (qtd. in Friedman and Lawson 240). In Hawthorne, O'Connor finds a concern with "the old Adam" and, therefore, with innocence, original sin, the devil, man's fallen nature—subjects compelling to her as well. Like Hawthorne, she wants to illuminate the many faces of Adam and the reasons for his fallen nature. Because she writes stories that explore similar themes and populates them with characters who embody similar sins, she adopts quite naturally the genre and technique that so effectively convey Hawthorne's vision. Even though O'Connor's vision of man is more consistently theological than Hawthorne's, it is nonetheless a similar and an essentially moral one.

Both Hawthorne and O'Connor extensively define their theories of moral romance. In several critical prefaces Hawthorne defines "romance" and explains why it rather than the novel is better suited to his purposes. In his preface to *The House of the Seven Gables,* Hawthorne points out that the romance need not be a strict imitation of nature. Rather, the writer of this genre may rearrange nature in order to reveal essential truths, to expose "he truth of he human heart." Although the romance writer may sacrifice both probability and surface reality, he gains greater universality and deeper insights about man's essential humanity. Hawthorne also suggests that the romance writer can enrich his tales by using the supernatural in order to create a special atmosphere of ambiguity and indefiniteness. In "The Custom House," the introduction to *The Scarlet Letter,* Hawthorne elaborates upon this special atmosphere, defining romance as the meeting place of the actual and the imaginary. In his preface to *The Snow Image and Other Twice Told Tales,* Hawthorne mentions another essential element, psychological truth. His primary concern is the exploration of character and human nature, more specifically the moral and psychological consequences of guilt and sin. Finally, in his preface to *The Marble Faun,* Hawthorne cites the need for an element of ruin, or mystery, in the romance. He creates mystery in his treatment of nature as both transcendental and sacramental. He views the natural world as a symbol and an embodiment of spiritual reality and thereby suffuses nature with mystery and supernature.

Like Hawthorne, O'Connor conceives of the romance as a borderland between two worlds, the natural and the supernatural, a land suffused with truth and mystery. Also like Hawthorne, O'Connor defines extensively her theory of romance in the essays collected in *Mystery and Manners.* In "Some Aspects of the Grotesque in Southern Fiction," she refers to Hawthorne and echoes his theory that this genre offers a writer greater freedom than the novel. She stresses that the writer must concern himself with "deeper kinds of realism." The romance provides for such realism because it permits the distortion of reality for the purpose of emphasizing essential truths. O'Connor refers to this distortion as the grotesque, but she emphasizes that only external reality may be distorted. Internal reality, the integrity of the human soul, must not be violated and is subject to the strictest demands of realism.

At the core of O'Connor's definition of romance is the concept of mystery, her term for the deeper realism and essential truths that the romance writer seeks to portray. The mysterious is that which lies beneath he surface of reality, the essential nature of reality that cannot always be explained or understood. In the essay "On Her Own Work" O'Connor describes the mysteries that she attempts to reveal as essentially spiritual ones, "the central Christian mysteries." Also, in "Novelist and Believer," she defines mystery in terms both transcendental and sacramental. Nature is holy, and the visible world contains also an invisible world that the romance writer aims to illuminate and make believable for his audience.

Finally, in her essay about the grotesque in fiction, O'Connor associates the role of the romance writer with that of the prophet and the poet, and she associates both roles with Hawthorne:

> The Southern writer is forced from all sides to make his gaze extend beyond the surface, beyond mere problems, until it touches that realm which is the concern of prophets and poets. When Hawthorne said that he wrote romances, he was attempting, in effect, to keep for fiction some of its freedom from social determinism, and to steer it in the direction of poetry. . . . The direction of many of us will be more toward poetry than toward the traditional novel. (*Mystery and Manners* 45–46, 50)

Because the characters and events of the romance often lack verisimilitude and because it seeks to portray essential meanings and spiritual truths, the world of the romance is often a world of symbol and allegory, a fact that is particularly evident in he romances of Hawthorne and O'Connor. By penetrating surface reality and seeking essential truths, Hawthorne and O'Connor reduce the complexities of life to their simplest forms. Life is a struggle between opposing symbolic forces: good and evil, heart and head, country and city. Although these symbolic forces sometimes become complex and ambiguous—a far cry from the neat patterns of traditional allegory—they are, nonetheless, broadly allegorical in the consistent vision they reflect.

Both Hawthorne and O'Connor have been labeled, on one hand, "symbolists" and, on the other, "allegorists." This confusion is understandable because some of their works are clearly symbolic, others are clearly allegorical, and many—occupying a middle ground between the two forms—employ symbolic characters and events within a loosely allegorical framework. Both writers ignore the restrictions of traditional allegory.

Hawthorne's best tales and all of his novels may best be labeled "symbolic allegories," for they exhibit considerable texture, complexity, and, most importantly, ambiguity. In fact, Hawthorne transforms traditional allegory into a symbolic and poetic form. He may have been attracted to this unique genre for several reasons. Arlin Turner attributes Hawthorne's passion for allegory to his passion for moralizing, asserting that Hawthorne values allegory as an effective way of examining moral problems in fiction (123). Richard Harter Fogle, however, attributes Hawthorne's use of allegory to his Puritan heritage, claiming that Puritanism shaped not only Hawthorne's vision but also his aesthetics: "Hawthorne habitually saw things allegorically; perception of he equivalence of object and idea was, in harmony with his Puritan heritage, an organic part of his mental make-up. He could not look at a cloud, a fountain, or a cathedral without simultaneously discerning within its shape the emblem of spiritual reality" (42). Finally, Charles Feidelson claims that the symbolist and allegorist are at war within Hawthorne. Because of its analytic nature and its tendency to preserve order, allegory attracts Hawthorne. On the one hand, the imaginative possibilities of symbolism fascinate him; on the other, however, its threats to reason and order horrify him. The result of this conflict is a sometimes uneasy blend of symbolism and allegory—symbolism expanding the work's meaning, allegory confining it (14–15).

Like Hawthorne, O'Connor builds poetic and symbolic tales upon broadly allegorical frameworks. In *Mystery and Manners,* O'Connor comments in detail about her use of both allegory and symbolism. The writer's task is essentially an allegorical one—to penetrate the surface of he universe and reveal the sacred truths hidden beneath. However, the writer must be not only an allegorist but also a symbolist, exploring a world of maximum possibilities and discovering a multitude of meanings in the universe. O'Connor explains that the writer must have anagogical vision, "the kind of vision that is able to see different levels of reality in one image or one situation" (*Mystery and Manners* 72). A writer who possesses this vision cannot resist writing symbolic allegory, for he discovers spiritual extensions in everything natural. Just as Hawthorne's Puritan heritage influences his use of allegory, so the history of the South and O'Connor's Southern environment explain her use of it. In "The Regional Writer," she claims that every Southern reader holds two histories in common, that of the South and that of the Scriptures, and the Southern writer is able to build upon them imaginatively. Both Southern and Biblical history provide the writer with the concept of a "fall," and O'Connor adopts the fall as a central idea in all of her symbolic allegories. Each story is basically a representation of fallen, sinful man involved in a struggle to obtain salvation and God's grace. In his struggle man is assailed by malevolent forces, most prominently the devil himself, an allegorical figure that appears regularly in O'Connor's tales. As she states, "In my stories a reader will find that the devil accomplishes a good deal of groundwork that seems to be necessary before grace is effective" (*Mystery and Manners* 117).

Both Hawthorne and O'Connor employ symbolic allegory in the service of a similar vision. In the "Introduction to *A Memoir of Mary Ann,*" O'Connor, while discussing the suffering of children and the tendency of our age to use it to discredit the goodness of God, refers specifically to the characteristic Hawthorne sinner: "The Alymers [*sic*] whom Hawthorne saw as a menace have multiplied. Busy cutting down human imperfection, they are making headway also on the raw material of good" (*Mystery and Manners* 227). Here O'Connor reveals the essential kinship between Hawthorne's vision and her own. Both concern themselves primarily with sinners like Aylmer, men and women who, because of pride or excessive rationality, separate themselves from their fellow man and attempt to play godlike roles. Such behavior, which often leads to tampering with the souls of other human beings, is the main target for moral condemnation in Hawthorne and O'Connor. The source of such behavior, of course, is original sin, the pride of Adam inherited by each of his descendants; and both writers employ the concept of original sin in their tales. As Edward Kessler observes, O'Connor is "obsessively aware of sin," and, like Hawthorne, she is fascinated with characters "who proceed beyond the boundaries of conventional 'good behavior'" (65). These writers, therefore, in their emphasis upon original sin and the multitude of related sins that it has spawned in modern man, are writing from a broadly moral and theological framework rather than from a narrow or limiting one. Although elements of Calvinism and Catholicism appear in the work of both, their basic vision is broadly Christian. When dealing with sinners and resolving the plots of her tales, however, O'Connor stresses the role of grace in man's salvation. For this reason her stories have a stronger religious element than Hawthorne's. Whereas Hawthorne's sinners must solve their own dilemmas and seek salvation by their own efforts, O'Connor's sinners can rely upon God's grace and mercy to guide them. Because man has greater access to salvation in O'Connor's stories, her vision is essentially more optimistic than Hawthorne's. As Samuel Chase Coale explains, both Hawthorne and O'Connor "[quarrel] with paradox, [wrestle] with dark designs and even darker necessities"; O'Connor, however, sees the power of Christian faith as "a liberating vision" (91).

At the core of Hawthorne's definition of sin is the sin of Adam—pride, both intellectual and spiritual. Hawthorne's proud sinners voluntarily separate them selves from God and from their fellow man. Most susceptible to the detachment that pride produces are Hawthorne's artists and scientists, characters with superior sensitivity and intelligence. Hawthorne's scientists—men like Aylmer, Rappaccini, Roger Chillingworth, and Ethan Brand—sacrifice their own humanity in their obsessive pursuit of knowledge, their psychological probing, and their scientific experiments. Hawthorne also portrays artists—men like Owen Warland, Holgrave, and Miles Coverdale—as detached observers who are in danger of succumbing to what Hawthorne himself feared most: having "ice in one's blood." Although Hawthorne portrays a bleak world with his continual emphasis upon man's susceptibility to pride and dehumanization, his vision is not totally pessimistic; he never denies man the possibility of salvation. In order to gain it, however, man must recognize his sinfulness and mend his ways. He must divest himself of pride and restore his proper relationship with his fellow man and with the universe. Because he believes that man's regeneration is not an easy matter, Hawthorne is not an optimist. But neither is he a naturalist or a pessimist, for he holds that man can, through his own efforts, attain regeneration and ultimate salvation.

O'Connor, too, creates characters like Ethan Brand, men of excessive pride whose relationship with God, nature, and their fellow man is inharmonious; she, too, is concerned with sin and immorality. Although O'Connor sometimes employs doctrines of the Catholic Church, as well as elements of Protestant Fundamentalism, in her fiction, her vision focuses upon God, Christ, sin, and redemption and is broadly Christian in nature. At the core of her vision is the fundamentalist doctrine of original sin, and in her stories pride is the most common manifestation of it. O'Connor's characters succumb to pride, assert their own self-sufficiency, and thereby alienate themselves from God and their fellow man. Rather than seek salvation in spiritual ways, her characters seek salvation through material gain or put their faith in humanitarianism or rationality. Epitomizing such sinners are O'Connor's humanists and intellectuals, who put their faith in science, technology, and modern social theory. Like Rayber and Sheppard, they are advocates of modern psychology and believe in the perfectibility of man by his own efforts. Like her humanists, O'Connor's intellectuals, who lack Christian faith, put their faith in the power of the human mind. A college education converts them to a philosophy of nihilism or existentialism; and like Joy-Hulga, Julian, and Asbury, they believe that man can save himself through his own intellectual efforts. Finally, O'Connor's materialistic and self-righteous matrons put their faith in hard work, material gain, and property. Refusing to take God or religion seriously, characters like Mrs. Cope, Mrs. McIntyre, and Mrs. May believe they can save themselves by devoting themselves to their land and worshipping their property as if it were a god; others, like Mrs. Shortley and Mrs. Turpin, who are smug and convinced of their own virtues, believe they can impose their own religious terms upon God.

Although portraying a world inhabited by such sinners, O'Connor, like Hawthorne, never denies them the opportunity for salvation. But to accept grace and obtain salvation, man must seek self-knowledge, forego pride, accept Christ, and recognize his total dependence upon divine love and mercy. O'Connor, though sometimes labeled a naturalist and a pessimist, has an essential vision that is optimistic. She never abandons hope that her characters will choose the way of salvation, and she constantly emphasizes man's capacity for free will. Her vision of man includes his capacity for sin and his capacity for self-awareness.

Writing about Hawthorne's basic assumptions, Leslie A. Fiedler says Hawthorne believes that "the writer's duty is to say 'Nay!', to deny the easy affirmations by which most men live, and to expose the blackness of life most men try deliberately to ignore." The function of the writer's art, Fiedler continues, is "to disturb by telling a truth which is always unwelcome" (432). Perhaps better than any other quotation, these words explain the influence of Hawthorne on O'Connor, the reason why she frequently asserts her kinship with her literary predecessor. Like Hawthorne, O'Connor has disturbing truths to tell, a vision that her audience is not likely to accept with enthusiasm—indeed, a vision hat a large part of her audience is apt to ignore or even reject. This similarity of purpose, as well as a similarity in basic vision, seems to explain why O'Connor chooses romance and allegory, the tools of her predecessor, to convey her disturbing truths. To Hawthorne's tools she adds her own: a simple and concrete style; a masterly control of language that can produce passages as lyrical as a poem or as brutal as a slap in the face; and a rollicking sense of humor that, at times, relieves her relentless vision but, more often, subtly reinforces it. Including these elements with Hawthorne's, O'Connor achieves her own distinct and powerful style. As a result, she becomes more than just a disciple of the master. She becomes a master in her own right.

WORKS CITED

Bloom, Harold, ed. *Flannery O'Connor.* New York: Chelsea, 1986.

Coale, Samuel Chase. *In Hawthorne's Shadow: American Romance from Melville to Mailer.* Lexington: University Press of Kentucky, 1985.

Driskell, Leon D., and Joan T. Brittain. *The Eternal Crossroads: The Art of Flannery O'Connor.* Lexington: University Press of Kentucky, 1971.

Feeley, Sister Kathleen. *Flannery O'Connor: Voice of the Peacock.* New Brunswick, NJ: Rutgers University Press, 1972.

Feidelson, Charles, Jr. *Symbolism and American Literature.* Chicago: University of Chicago Press, 1953.

Fiedler, Leslie A. *Love and Death in the American Novel.* Rev. ed. New York: Stein, 1966.

Fogle, Richard Harter. *Hawthorne's Fiction: The Light and the Dark.* Rev. ed. Norman: University of Oklahoma Press, 1964.

Friedman, Melvin J., and Lewis A. Lawson, eds. *The Added Dimension: The Art and Mind of Flannery O'Connor.* New York: Fordham University Press, 1966.

Hyman, Stanley Edgar. *Flannery O'Connor.* Minneapolis: University of Minnesota Press, 1966.

Kessler, Edward. *Flannery O'Connor and the Language of Apocalypse.* Princeton: Princeton University Press, 1986.

O'Connor, Flannery. *Everything That Rises Must Converge.* New York: Farrar Straus, 1965.

———. *Mystery and Manners: Occasional Prose.* Ed. Sally and Robert Fitzgerald. New York: Farrar Straus, 1970.

Orvell, Miles. *Invisible Parade: The Fiction of Flannery O'Connor.* Philadelphia: Temple University Press, 1972.

Reiter, Robert E., ed. *Flannery O'Connor.* St. Louis: Herder, 1968.

Turner, Arlin. *Nathaniel Hawthorne: An Introduction and Interpretation.* New York: Barnes, 1961.

The Other Ghost in *Beloved:* The Specter of *The Scarlet Letter* (1991)

JAN STRYZ

The literary critical establishment has awarded Toni Morrison a place not only in the canon of literature by African-American women, but of "American literature." However, dangers attend such a gesture. What relationship between the previously sanctified texts and the body of Morrison's work is implied by this placement? As Brooks Thomas points out, "the West legitimated its imperialistic domination. . . . most effectively by constructing narratives of inclusion rather than exclusion. Today the most powerful version of control through inclusion is pluralism. . . . whose official voice . . . domesticates subversive voices by appropria-[tion]" (59). Within this context, Henry Louis Gates's carefully balanced comments in "Canon Formation and African-American Tradition" sound even more clearly: "There can be no doubt that white texts inform and influence black texts (and vice versa). . . . But the attempts of scholars . . . to define a black American canon, and to pursue literary interpretation from within this canon, are not meant to refute the soundness of these gestures of integration. . . . Just as we can and must cite a black text within the larger American tradition, we can and must cite it within its own tradition . . ." (35). Morrison's own stance towards an institutionalized literary tradition further problematizes her placement within a widely inclusive canon. She does, indeed, affirm that, "I, at least, do not intend to live without Aeschylus or William Shakespeare, or James or Twain or Hawthorne, or Melville, etc., etc., etc." ("Unspeakable Things Unspoken" 5). But she protests against literary criticism that "justifies itself by identifying black writers with some already accepted white writer. If someone says I write like Joyce, that's giving me a kind

137

of credibility I find offensive. . . . [T]he comparison has to do with nothing out of which I write" ("A Conversation" 121–22). It is not out of the authorization bestowed by a white male literary ancestry that black women take up the pen, and the difference in the content of their works reflects the difference in their source of authority. Gloria Naylor's account of her own journey to becoming a writer illustrates this. Though acknowledging that the writers she had been "taught to love"—all "either male or white"—"were and are . . . masters," the "faintest whisper" of protest found a voice within her at that time: "Was there no one telling my story?" It was "a long road" from the act of writing to "gathering the authority within myself to believe that I could actually be a writer" ("A Conversation" 567).

Placement of African-American (or other marginalized) literature within the established literary canon invites, if it is not in fact preceded by, the placement of the literary canon in African-American works by the literary critical establishment. Whether the "marginalized" work in question, intentionally or not, actually does cite a canonized work, the critic's citation of the established literary masterpiece is a gesture that can too easily lead to colonization of the work, to a reading of the work within the framework of a previously established tradition, and a silencing of the work's unique voice.

Hence, "[t]he deliberate avoidance of literary references has become a firm if boring habit with me," Morrison says, "not only because I refuse the credentials they bestow, but also because they are inappropriate to the kind of literature I wish to write . . . ."

> I want my fiction to urge the reader into active participation in the non-narrative, nonliterary experience of the text. . . . I sometimes think how glorious it must have been to have written drama in sixteenth century England, or poetry in ancient Greece, or religious narrative in the Middle Ages, when literature was needed and did not have a critical history to constrain or diminish the writer's imagination. How magnificent not to have to depend on the reader's literary associations—his literary experience—which can be as much an impoverishment of the reader's imagination as it is of a writer's. ("Memory" 387–89)

Her means of negotiating these literary obstacles is to "translate . . . into print" the characteristics of African-American art forms. "Working within those rules, the text, if it is to take improvisation and audience participation into account, cannot be the authority—it should be the map" ("Memory" 389).

Such a statement implies that to be true to an African-American aesthetic involves a repudiation of the authority that we traditionally conceive of as informing the notion of authorship and the very nature of writing. The act of writing itself then demands that Morrison approach the nature of her own relation to her written texts in such a way as to redefine the notion of "author." This project has confronted African-American authors, especially women, throughout the course of their collective literary careers. Much of the significant criticism devoted to black women writers addresses the issue of what makes their works their own: Hazel Carby, for instance, gives a "literary history of the emergence of black women as novelists," exploring "how black women intellectuals reconstructed the sexual ideologies of the nineteenth century to produce an alternative discourse of black womanhood" and also "confronting [the] history of difference" between black and white women (Carby 6–7). Marjorie Pryse introduces the anthology *Conjuring: Black Women, Fiction, and Literary Tradition* by noting how Alice Walker "implicitly disclaims genius" and hence originality for writing *The Color Purple* by naming herself a "medium"; in so doing, Walker participates in literate black women's shared search for their own literary "mother's gardens" (1–3). In the same anthology, Hortense Spillers affirms the existence and common spirit of a black women's writing community which participates in a redefined "tradition": "an active verb, rather than a retired nominative. . . . the language of learning woven into the tongue of the mother . . . a rare union of bliss toward which African-American experience has compelled us all along" (260). At the same time, she says, "Reading against the canon, intruding into it a configuration of symbolic values with which critics and audiences must contend, the work of black women's writing community not only redefines tradition, but also disarms it by suggesting that the term itself is a critical fable intended to encode and circumscribe an inner and licit circle of empowered texts" (251). Thus, Spillers claims, the African-American woman writer's own tradition is characterized by "discontinuities" and "ruptures"—a nonlinear, many-voiced tradition.

It is not only the existence of an established canon which denies an African American identity and establishes a need to create a written self-definition for the black writer; the culturally defined nature of writing itself historically has posed an obstacle for the African-American who takes on the role of author. From the poetry of Phillis Wheatley on, African-American literature has been faced with allegations of derivation and imitation; in fact, Henry Louis Gates says that "it is fair to describe the subtext of the history of black letters as this urge to refute the claim that because blacks had no written traditions they were bearers of an inferior culture" (*Figures in Black* 26). There is a continued tendency to read "writing" as something defined by the dominant culture as a white male activity, part of an already established domain where the authority of tradition claims any entity that enters as its subject. African-American authors have found means of dismantling the traditional authority of the written word, however. Pryse notes, for example, how Zora Neale Hurston claimed the power of the written word for herself and those who followed her by "writing down the old 'lies'" and "creat[ing] a bridge between the 'primitive' authority of folk life and the literary power of written texts. . . . thereby breaking the mystique of connection between literary authority and patriarchal power" (11–12).

While Hurston was an anthropologist who later drew upon the oral narratives and folk ways with which her work brought her into contact to provide her with materials for her writing, Morrison never had this comparative freedom from the literary text. She came to her craft with a formal education in literature that concentrated on canonical texts, included a minor in classics, and culminated in a master's thesis on Faulkner and Woolf. In such circumstances, conscious avoidance of literary references does not guarantee their absence from a work.

For Morrison, the "lore . . . gossip . . . magic . . . [and] sentiment" which we might regard as embodiments of imagination are used in her work to "centralize and animate information discredited by the West . . ." ("Memory" 388). This accords with Jane Campbell's observation that since the nineteenth century, black authors have found the literary domain of Romance useful in "transform[ing] history and culture as whites have presented them into history and culture as blacks envision them" (xi). But besides merely serving to dismantle and reconstruct social definitions, Romance elements can redefine space and time and our most basic perceptions, hence serving to articulate a particular aesthetic—in this case an African American aesthetic.[1] But those works of Morrison's which most extensively interweave Romance elements, *Song of Solomon* and *Beloved,* are also those which incorporate images from *The Scarlet Letter*—so that through its association with a previous text the technique meant to release her works from literary tradition draws them into the tradition of American Romance. The relation between her own work and that of her predecessor cannot be defined in terms of the general concept of "influence," however—as the above comment by Spillers regarding "reading against the canon" and "redefining tradition" might indicate.[2] However, the question remains: what specific literary strategies does Morrison employ in order to define the borders and preserve the artistic integrity of her own works? The particular forms of authorial identity figured within her texts—author as father, as mother, or simply the absence of "authority"—contribute to the nature of the intertextual relation discussed here. But equally important is the style of handling these figures as well as the manner in which she presents images from *The Scarlet Letter.* Given that the voice of the dominant culture cannot be eliminated, its masterful tone still can be silenced by making it into a representation—breaking it into images that share the field of the text with a host of other images. Where images are what is expressed, and where the image seems to speak itself, the authority of the isolated voice does not operate. The identity of such a voice depends on a linear continuity, its own connected version of history, and cannot sustain the presence of fragmented, apparently self-present (in the sense that they are not dependent on some authorized version of history to express themselves) images.

Gates's explanation of "Signifyin(g)" as a literary device is useful to keep in mind when examining the ways that Morrison's work comments on its own textuality, establishes a multi-voicedness, and also succeeds in taking a turn on images from literature and images of literary authority. Briefly, "Signifyin(g)" is a rhetorical strategy characterizing African American oral and written texts, "allowing . . . the black person to move freely between two discursive universes. . . . that exist side by side in a homonymic relation signified by the very concept of Signification" (*Signifying Monkey* 75–76). The presence of this highly adaptable strategy within a text permits a tropological analysis which can reveal the subtle ties of an intertextual relationship.[3] In *Beloved,* "Signifyin(g)" allows for no resolution of the tensions between the two discursive universes of culturally authorized and unauthorized expression; there is no transcendent space where the contradictions of being a black woman author can be put aside or escaped, any more than the painful experiences to which the text directly refers can be written away. What the text does accomplish is to create from these very contradictions a unique artistic expression in the dance of Signification that both transgresses boundaries and records violations in tropological form.

Before examining the role of *The Scarlet Letter* in Morrison's work it is first necessary to trace the appearances of other predecessors in her texts. Morrison has given written acknowledgment to "actual," non-literary (unauthored) sources for *Beloved* which ground the story in historical reality as well as provide imaginative seeds for the plot: a nineteenth-century newspaper clipping about a woman who had, like Sethe, attempted to kill her children to prevent them from living as she had lived, a photograph and attendant story of a murdered eighteen-year-old girl lying in her coffin, who had forgone medical attention to allow her lover who had shot her to escape. Morrison says that she "can't explain" what connects these two fragments for her, except that "in both instances. . . . A woman loved something other than herself so much . . ." (Naylor 583–84).

But *Beloved* also bears a literary influence through its resurrection of pieces from Morrison's own previous works. The issue of the limits of a woman's love, and the relation between self and sacrifice, is first addressed in *Sula* by way of the fierce and potentially destructive love of a mother for her children. There Eva, financially unable to care for her children, disappears and returns with both legs amputated but a source of funds that lasts her lifetime, which according to community gossip comes from an insurance settlement over a self-inflicted railroad accident. Years later she murders one of the children for whom she made the sacrifice, a heroin addict whom she has watched slowly disintegrating. She explains,

> he wanted to crawl back in my womb. . . . Being helpless and thinking
> baby thoughts and dreaming baby dreams and messing up his pants
> again and smiling all the time. I had room enough in my heart, but not
> in my womb, not no more. I birthed him once. I couldn't do it again.
> (*Sula* 71)

The complementary acts—one sacrifice concerned with the protection of the child, the other concerned with protection of the self—are kept separate here, in a simultaneous acknowledgment of the bond and the separation between mother and child. In *Beloved* the separation dissolves and the sacrifices are merged: infanticide becomes a form of suicide while both mother and daughter are threatened by a state of unreality similar to the one in which Eva finds her son.

Beloved also recalls a passage at the end of *The Bluest Eye:* "There is no gift for the beloved. The lover alone possesses his gift of love. The loved one is shorn, frozen in the glare of the lover's inward eye" (159–60). Applied in the more recent text to a mother-daughter love, the beloved who has been shorn of life and frozen in time returns to become the lover, and similarly threaten the new beloved. When Sethe "is anywhere around, Beloved only has eyes for Sethe" (121); in Beloved's dreamy eye, "She smiles at me and it is my own face smiling" (214). In this incarnation as mother and daughter, lover and beloved become mirror images of the same self. The relationship between characters here is a reflection of the relationship which Morrison says that she as author established with her characters in her first work. Writing *The Bluest Eye* was a process of self-reclamation for her, a search for "the dead girl" she had once been, who had given her some identity in the world. She discovered that "all of those people," her characters, "were me," not in a strictly autobiographical sense, but "because of that process of reclamation" (Naylor 576). When she came to write *Beloved,* she was engaged with the question of "what it is that really compels a good woman to displace the self, her self," and so she "projected" that displaced self, " 'the dead girl'," "out into the earth" (Naylor 585). That is to say, into the book. Along with the displaced self, she places the mother and "twin self" of the dead girl, Morrison's own figurative counterpart.

Between texts a sort of familial relationship is established in the repetition of these family bonds and self-reflections. Morrison's own relation as author becomes that of both twin self and mother to the text, while along with the insertion of this relation into the text is inscribed a maternal concern not only for characters or between characters, but for the text. *Beloved* addresses the question of how to protect the text, to keep it within safe bounds without relegating it to a realm of mere imagination or dream, to prevent it from being made into a foreign image by unfriendly eyes.

In an unspoken memory Sethe silently tries to explain her actions to Beloved by recounting how she had overheard schoolteacher instruct one of his pupils, who was "doing" Sethe, to list " 'her human characteristics on the left; her animal ones on the right' " (193). Sethe is not only a part of Morrison's own text but also a figure representing the mother self who generates the "text" (the baby, the story of its murder, and the inscription on the headstone) which becomes the figure of "Beloved." Hence the importance she places on this reduction of her identity through a process of reading and writing reveals the novel's own occupation with textual concerns. Ironically, it is Sethe's fear of Beloved's being violated that leads to Beloved's being made into a written image—Sethe's image in the sense that Beloved is her own imagined self-reflection, and her *written* image in the sense that this image can be seen and read by others within

and outside the story. The scene with the engraver underlines Beloved's
status as a textual entity. Strategically placed at the beginning of the narrative, this scene of writing displaces the "actual" event; Sethe's recurrent memory of the former scene veils her memory of the act which
moves the story, Beloved's murder. The figure of the writer here, it must
be noted, is a white male, the author as father figure who appears along
with his voyeur son, a less than innocent reader. The already crawling
baby girl whose father was Halle no longer exists, and if Beloved has a
father it must be the engraver who provides her with a name, a symbolic
father who brings her into written existence. Though his role may be portrayed here as superficial, and his portrait unflattering, still the author-as-
father is represented. This story of motherhood cannot seem to escape
the issue of patriarchal authority in writing.

This residual authority also enters with that other tale of a mother
and daughter which this text so clearly recalls: if *The Scarlet Letter* is
haunted by a fictional literary father in the figure of Surveyor Pue, then
Beloved appears to repeat that haunting by a literary father through the
recurrence of images from *The Scarlet Letter* in the text. This representation of the other text differs from the direct portrayal of the literary father
in its effects, and in fact, to associate the uses of *The Scarlet Letter* with
the term "literary father" may be misleading. If in certain ways *Beloved*
wages a battle against white patriarchal authority in writing, another
voice within the text invokes *The Scarlet Letter* in a way that displaces
the image of the father altogether. The mother, and the body of the
mother, become more appropriate metaphors.

Beloved does not mark Morrison's first return to that source, however; *Song of Solomon* resembles *The Scarlet Letter* in its use of an an-
cestral text that needs to be re-presented. But while superficially,
Hawthorne's text expresses anxiety about adherence to the skeletal facts
of the "original" text (which is assumed to adhere to the real case), and
identifies the romantic elements he adds in a way that bows to the claims
of reality even as it attempts to authorize the romantic elements, Morrison's text doesn't bear such anxious relation to the truth of the song that
is its fictional "father" text, nor does it attempt to reproduce the structure
of that text. Rather, its accidental reconstruction from fragments comprises a new story.

This structural similarity by itself does not form enough of a basis
on which to claim influence, of course. The account of Pilate's self-
evaluation and subsequent self-fashioning, in which "her mind traveled
crooked streets and aimless goat paths" (149) echoes, but with more opti-

mism, the passage where "Hester Prynne . . . wandered without a clew in the dark labyrinth of mind" (160). Hester, in fact, provides a literary prototype for the female pariah figure who derives her identity from the community and serves a purpose within the community, and who is so central to Morrison's work.

More significantly, *Song of Solomon* at its opening returns to an image from the beginning of *The Scarlet Letter:* the rose outside the prison door, on the "threshold" of Hawthorne's narrative, which is offered to the reader as a symbol of "some sweet moral blossom that may be found along the track" (120). Morrison's rose petals—red velvet ones, products of craftsmanship, not nature—scatter in the snow outside another institution—a hospital. With the rearrangement and diffusion of the image comes another way of signifying. The authority of a valorized nature is absent, and so the traditional symbolic associations of the rose no longer hold. The petals engage the community in the shared task of gathering the scattered fragments for the girls who "had spent hour after hour tracing, cutting and sticking the costly velvet" (149). Here the role given solely to the reader in *The Scarlet Letter* is handed to the characters, while at the same time the reader is faced with a similar task—piecing together the fragments of the unfolding narrative—but not given any gentle authorial injunction to find a moral. In fact, Hawthorne's rose and embroidered letter are fused and multiplied in this image of the velvet petals. Textuality metamorphizes into simple texture, the moral significance of the red is erased, and the petals assert only their sensory qualities. Any further significance they have is through their placement in a metonymic chain. Morrison's image is not so weighted with metaphoric value as Hawthorne's, which acts as a seducer to the interpreting consciousness, holding forth mystery by representing a world from which one is removed, and slyly hinting at discoverable meaning. Consider, for instance, Pilate's earring, made from a small brass snuffbox that belonged to her mother, and containing the only thing her illiterate father had ever "written"—the name "Pilate," which he had painstakingly copied from the Bible, and chosen for the sake of the visual character of the letters. In one sense it is a metaphoric womb/tomb of significance which attains meaning by emblematizing the death of the letter, in that, divorced from its textual origin and written meaning, the name takes on significance with the growth of Pilate's identity. But the earring does not give us undue pause, does not invite us to linger over its image; it achieves a suggestion of multiplicity of meaning by association with various acts in the text. We are conscious of the image's involvement in a chaotic process that emphasizes displacement because we are within the text, dreaming it, so to speak, and not looking at it from a position of authority from where we interpret. In "The Custom House," the specter of authority is handed to the reader by a ghostly author who repeats, in that gesture, the gesture of his spectral predecessor, Surveyor Pue. Morrison succeeds in asserting the differences between *Song of Solomon* and *The Scarlet Letter* by a simultaneous appropriation and reversal of elements that serves to defuse/diffuse this authority.

Both *Song of Solomon* and *Beloved* accept without question the Romance elements they employ, such as Milkman's dream sequences or Beloved's very existence. But *Beloved* bears a much closer relation to *The Scarlet Letter* than Morrison's other text, and must adopt an additional strategy in order to escape the domains of its voice. Sethe enacts what Hester in her seemingly most unstable moments merely imagines: "At times, a fearful doubt strove to possess her soul, whether it were not better to send Pearl at once to heaven . . ." (160). This entry into the imaginary territory of the other tale is precipitated by a state of despair similar to Hester's over being at odds with the law. Both women violently refuse (though Hester only vocally) to relinquish their children to the hands of authority, and also like Hester, Sethe experiences alienation from the community as a result of her child, the crime of giving birth and that of infanticide oddly serving as mirror images here. Hence when midway through the novel the narrative reveals the incident it had hitherto veiled, we find ourselves at the opening scene of *The Scarlet Letter,* where Hester emerges from prison clutching Pearl, with "a haughty smile, and a glance at would not be abashed" for the gossiping crowd gathered to watch (60). But the scene is reversed: the throng of black faces is silent as Sethe walks past with her yet living daughter, with "head a bit too high" and "back a little too straight" as she climbs into the cart that will take her to the entry of the jail (152).

Throughout *Beloved,* characters slip back into memories which suddenly replace their present moments, as when Sethe notes how much she loved her murdered daughter "and there it was again. The welcoming cool of unchiseled headstones . . ." (4), or when "Easily [Denver] stepped into the told story that lay before her eyes on the path she followed away from the window" (29). These vivid returns, which to a great extent determine the structure of the novel, themselves recall Hester's moments upon the scaffold when "the whole scene" before her "seemed to vanish from her eyes," replaced by scenes from "memory's picture gallery" (64–65). But the text of *Beloved* itself, in re-presenting elements of the other text, plays out a different relation to its written predecessor than that of the embattled one with a patriarchal author suggested by the scene with the engraver. *The Scarlet Letter* becomes a site dissociated from any author, a source of images reproduced in the body of the dream that is the text.

In her recent critical monograph, *Playing in the Dark: Whiteness and the Literary Imagination,* Morrison has called for an examination of the hidden black presence in white American literary texts. While white authors, especially those of the nineteenth century, may seem to have neglected representing Africans and African-Americans in their work, the apparently peripheral "Africanist" presence in various works is significant. She uses the term "Africanist" tropologically, "as a term for the denotative and connotative blackness that African peoples have come to signify, as well as the entire range of views, assumptions, readings, and misreadings that accompany Eurocentric learning about these people" (6–7). When she approached works of American literature as "a writer reading" rather than as a reader reading, she "came to realize the obvious: the subject of the dream is the dreamer. The fabrication of an Africanist persona is reflexive; an extraordinary mediation on the self; a powerful exploration of the fears and desires that reside in the writerly conscious" (17). Applying a similar logic, examination of her own texts for the construction and significance of a metaphoric "literary whiteness" is appropriate.

This is not to suggest that the situation of the white author writing within a culture that imagines whiteness as an "unraced" factor is similar to the situation of the black author, who clearly can not imagine her/his own or another's race to be an insignificant issue. But the black literary artist might also be inclined to trope the figure of "whiteness," and would likely do so with more intricacy and awareness than her/his white counterpart. Such a gesture might accomplish several things. The uses of *The Scarlet Letter* given above employ reversals that illustrate similarities between texts which reflect common human concerns, while also pointing out social and cultural differences that lie between the particulars of the situation confronting the black characters in one text and the white characters in the other. Further, it is important to note Morrison's assertion that she writes for a black audience, not a white one. This, of course, distinguishes her practice from that of nineteenth-century black authors who had to rhetorically construct their narratives to appeal to a white audience. As an escaped slave narrative, *Beloved* represents the freeing of that particular genre from the social constraints imposed by a white

readership. Hence, it enacts a double escape—the story's content reflecting its simultaneous meta-textual move towards literary freedom. (This
act of literary reclamation becomes especially important in light of the
fact that Theodore Parker, in the mid-nineteenth century, proclaimed the
slave narrative the one "wholly indigenous and original . . . portion of
our permanent literature" [Gates, "Canon Formation" 31].) The troping
of literary whiteness thus serves as a form of expression that places black
literary texts within their own tradition—one that includes black readers
as well as writers. Finally, such troping in general calls attention to the
literary elements of the text, and can serve as an instrument to comment
upon those elements.

The central example of such troping in *Beloved* occurs with the incongruous whitegirl, Amy, who wanders into and out of the story. As an
escapee from her own "master," Mr. Buddy, she represents a turn on the
escaped slave narrative. Since the character and her history reconfigure
fragments of *The Scarlet Letter,* she might be considered a runaway from
that text, as well, though the figure Amy's relation to Hawthorne's tale
does not reflect the character Amy's relation to Mr. Buddy. Amy's story
occupies a realm which stands between the two texts, and enacts an improvisation on *The Scarlet Letter* which serves the purposes of *Beloved.*
This interlude comments on the nature of narrative itself—a topic which
obviously joins the two works. Here, a fruitful relation between texts is
represented, and suggestions of literary fatherhood are replaced by
metaphors of motherhood.

Amy's name marks her with the letter "A" in both visual and audi-
tory form, but the "A" has now become an accepted part of the character's identity (A—me) rather than an epithet appended to a character's
identity by the community, as with Hester. A fusion of Hester and Pearl,
Amy is "good with sick things," a daughter uncertain of her paternity.
Possessing the letter without color or texture, she is driven towards
Boston—her dead mother's former home and the vicinity of the site of
what might be called the "original" story—by her desire for the red velvet which she's never seen. The fantasized velvet is inseparable from its
distant place of procurement, that place inseparably associated with her
mother: "velvet is like the world was just born. Clean and new and so
smooth" (33).

Amy's journey is clearly unrealistic, and introduces the danger of
looking back into a fantasy realm. She seeks a utopia where mother is
represented and fulfillment of desire is attained, and she hasn't even the
means to get to the real Boston, or any notion of its distance. Read as a

figurative journey to the site of the earlier story, return is rendered doubly impossible. If desire for the mother is over-determined in this book, however, the version presented in Amy's story at least varies from Beloved's. Regressive desire for her own dead mother or for the fictional womb of *The Scarlet Letter* is unconscious, unintentionally inscribed in Amy's goal, and in fact animates her movement forward.

Amy is a figure for narrative itself, compelled to move towards her destination, her vision of the red velvet: "She raised her eyes to the sky and then, as though she had wasted enough time away from Boston, she moved off saying, 'I gotta go' " (33). Staying to help Sethe constitutes a digression within her own enacted narrative, but with her physical progress curtailed, she seems compelled to erupt into a stream of words with the presence of an audience, that is as innocent and unselfconscious as the journey to Boston it temporarily replaces: "Talked so much it wasn't clear how she could breathe at the same time. . . . Sethe didn't know if it was the voice, or Boston or velvet, but while the whitegirl talked, the baby slept. Not one butt or kick, so she guessed her luck had turned" (32–33). Amy's oral performance soothes like the cradle song she later sings which her mother taught her, and must have sung to her when she was an infant. Unlike the lyrics which proclaim a gentle end to the day and announce the coming of "Lady Button Eyes," a motherly spirit who seduces a child to sleep in what seems like a death masquerade, Amy's story, frenetically told, throws off the past even as it repeats it, and moves towards an imagined future. The tale itself, like her journey, comprises an attempt to fashion a self for herself—a self fashioned by being made fashionable, which incorporates yet departs from her past with Mr. Buddy, and ends in a vision of herself draped in red velvet: "Be so pretty on me" (33). Obviously, this vision radically departs from the function of the scarlet cloth in Hawthorne's text, though Hester's badge does shape her character.

Narrative here reveals how its internally inscribed progress (sometimes inscribed under the guise of regression) can encourage in its audience a forgetfulness through displacement of the past and present. Amy's story, as well as her ministrations, enables Sethe to get through her ordeal. But we must also take note of the strains, or rather the images, of the lullaby that accompanies Amy's narrative. The lyrics represent the scene of a lullaby and its intended effects on its audience; the lullaby is thus marked by a self-reflexiveness. The child we presume is listening (and still awake) finds herself represented in the lyrics as "weary," on the threshold of sleep, and is promised sleep by the image of a spirit who "smooths the eyelids down/Over those two eyes of brown" (81). But while the images suggest a sleep that is oblivion, the narrative form of the lullaby stops at the threshold of oblivion, and turns away. The song draws the listening child into its fictional borders by representing her; yet in representing her as being on the edge of sleep, it fictionally produces the very scene it proposes to create in reality, and masquerades as fictional reproduction of that created scene. This self-reflection contains the child in an image of sleep that is an endless regress over the threshold of yet another dream of sleep. The "clock's dull monotone" that "Telleth of the day that's done" suggests a more final end. But representation defers that end, and in associating the gentle ministrations of a Lady fairy with it, confers a motherly reassurance regarding the dissolution of self that accompanies sleep.

The progress of Amy's narrative and the scene that arrests one in the state of dream portray two possible effects of fiction. At the juncture where Amy sings the lullaby to Sethe, after tending to her flayed back, these alternatives are brought into relief:

> Amy sat quietly after her song, then repeated the last line before she stood, left the lean-to and walked off a little ways to lean against a young ash. When she came back the sun was in the valley below and they were way above it in blue Kentucky light.
>
> "You ain't dead yet, Lu? Lu?"
>
> "Not yet."
>
> "Make you a bet. You make it through the night, you make it all the way." (82)

The idyllic evening setting mirrors the enchanting aspects of the lullaby, though some more sinister aspects to enchantment can be read in the fairies' "haunted green" which "Lady Button Eyes" leaves to travel "through the muck and mist and gloam/To our quiet cozy home." The veiled threat of the lyrics is realized here in the acknowledgment that sleep may mean death. But though Amy occupies the place of the mother in singing the song, she is not the counterpart of "Lady Button Eyes" or of Sethe. Instead of luring (or unceremoniously dispatching) the figure of the child to a place of arrest, Amy issues Sethe a challenge to awaken. She administers painful massage to Sethe's swollen feet and legs, assuring her "Anything dead coming back to life hurts" (35). The following morning, "when [Sethe] felt toes prodding her hip it took a while to come out of a sleep she thought was death" (82). Amy prods Sethe to carry on with her own journey, and acts not just as midwife in the literal sense but midwife to the story as well. She exits this imaginary territory to pursue her own story, and thus the interlude occupies a space at the intersection of two narratives.

The site of the intertextual relation is represented here as a birth-place, and the narrative movement animating the image of the other text (concealed in the character Amy) the enabling factor in the forward motion of the new one. This crossing weaves an arrest that is restful; it creates a fictional space that rather than trapping the figure of charac-ter/author/reader in a fixed moment of self-reflection, opens a field of possibilities. The text becomes a site of pictures that exist independently of their written incarnation, like the pictures of things that happened that exist independently of the subject to whom they occurred: as Sethe notes, "even if I die, the picture of what I did, or knew, or saw is still out there. Right in the place where it happened" (36). With the imaginative erasure of the subject comes an erasure of the author. In this realm definitions blur and texts become permeable to each other; here also regression can become both arrest and progress, and the other text can function as both site and narrative. All of these characteristics describe a language of the novel similar to the language of dreams. As Freud says, "Sleep signifies an end to the authority of the self" and "Dreams . . . think predominantly in visual images" (83, 82).

In this way, *The Scarlet Letter* participates in the attempt at self ar-ticulation inscribed by Morrison's own body of related texts. Though the relation of this other text to the textual field of *Beloved* is harmonious, *Beloved's* own permeable field allows desire, and therefore narrative as well as violence, to enter. There is danger here where the construction of the self is diffused throughout the text and subject to dissolution, where the identity of one feminine self can so easily be come another. Yet in this process of engenderment it is the incorporation of violence into the tex-tual body that comprises identity, the marks of violence on the body of the text. These marks appear at times as writing, such as with school teacher's notes or the headstone's engraving. But more generally, they are translated to a visual realm, as with the tree of scars left on Sethe's back, which transforms writing to an image on the body. The ultimate vi-olation within this visual realm is to be transformed by a look into the look, to be "shorn, neutralized, frozen in the glare of [an] inward eye" whether it is the lover's eye or any other's. In a world composed of muta-ble images, such a gaze fixes the image and imposes identity from with-out.

This way of seeing defines just one form of identity, however. The relation between seeing and a particular form of reproduction does not allow one to reproduce what one sees, or vice versa. Morrison notes being "startled by the ability—even the desire—to 'use' acquaintances or friends or enemies as fictional characters. There is no yeast for [her] in a real-life person, or else there is so much it is not useful—it is done-bread, already baked" ("Memory" 386). Re-production of what one has seen must always be partly invisible for it to become production and appear as original. No longer seeing—that is, then, forgetting—becomes part of the conditions of production. Uniting oneself with the seen enables one unconsciously to re-generate it, and avoid the mere copying that can result from the conscious separation between the self and the seen. To become what has been seen is the project of the text: Amy, as synecdoche for this project, no longer wears the "A" but is the "A" in her written incarnation. The novel replaces being seen with a form of being that is an unfolding scene which can only be written or watched through participation. *Beloved* portrays this type of production in terms of a maternal metaphor that not only repeats itself within the text's images, but incorporates into the maternal bounds of the text elements which comprise a matriarchal line. At the same time, this materialism generates its own narrative by seeking to escape authority, and so is in part produced by means of that very authority by which it is also marked.

Thus while escaping the written tradition that lies behind her, Morrison also follows it. *Beloved* takes place within what Hawthorne christened "a neutral territory, somewhere between the real world and fairy-land, where the Actual and the Imaginary may meet," and fits, with some adaptations for her particular endeavor, within critical definitions of that territory and of American literary myth making. So, for instance, Richard Poirier emphasizes how the stylistic shaping of space and time in writing displaces the "actual" world and creates an environment of which "style is its only authority" (17)—a gesture which places authority within the imaginary domain of the text and notes how an original self is thus shaped within and through the style of the text. (For Morrison, of course, we would need to qualify the notion of authority existing within the text even as we acknowledge its displacement outside authority.) Most recently, and more significantly for this argument, Edgar Dryden has finely traced the way in which

> the American tradition in fiction . . . disturbs and blurs the distinction
> between creative and interpretive acts and raises the question of its

> own relation to history and tradition. By figuring themselves as read-
> ers, the writers . . . seek to maintain their priority and authority by ab-
> sorbing and interpreting fragments that have been broken off from a
> prior and more complete utterance. They sense that for readers the
> question of chronological priority is a matter of perspective since the
> text in hand always echoes, repeats, and displaces others. Hence all
> texts seem linked together in a conceptual space . . . where each can
> claim equal originality. (213)

The a-chronological conceptual space of the Romance provides an environment where African-American writers can re-write the traditional
versions of history, a point Campbell makes which I noted earlier. But if
African-American novelists must creatively contend with everything
ranging from the enactment of history upon the body of their race to the
history of the novel, their efforts must somehow also touch upon the critical fictions the novel has generated. This is particularly true if the writer
is also a woman.

Nina Baym has rightly pointed out how theories of American literature tend to present a myth of exclusively male artistic creation, following a Bloomian line of thought which, she says, is founded on a "facile
translation of the verb 'to author' into the verb 'to father'" (138). However, this critical fiction needn't be "read as a factual system" like
Barthes' "myth" which sets up an illusory causal relation between signifier and signified. Treated as mutable metaphor, it can always be given
one more turn. Thus Morrison's work can fictionally appropriate as well
as disrupt the narrative line of this authorial metaphor which serves so
well to illustrate the drama of male identity for male writers. The concern
with identity and its relations to history, origins and writing which can be
seen as characterizing the canon of works placed within the American
Romance tradition are not essentially masculine, as the easy adoption of
Beloved and *Song of Solomon* into that tradition attests. Though it is necessary for the texts to deal with a history of an oppressive social authority
that is interwoven with the authority of writing, *Beloved* begins to articulate some of "the complexities and pitfalls of maternal experience" and
thus begins to fill the space where "Freud offers only a massive
nothing . . ." (Kristeva 179). Weaving this theme into the form of the
work itself, Morrison also contributes to the displacement of a sovereign
male authorial metaphor. Viewed from outside of the conceptual space
where fragments from prior works can be broken off and incorporated,
while their sources are forgotten, *Beloved,* this best of Morrison's works,

makes an "original" contribution to the very tradition it denies, is enriched by the tradition it denies, and enriched by that very denial.

POSTSCRIPT

A figure wanders through the last several of Morrison's novels: that of the postman who doesn't appear. The presence of this absence is suggested in *Song of Solomon* as soon as the second paragraph, in a digression concerning how the post office did not recognize the name local residents had given their street, "Not Doctor Street," a variation on the earlier "Doctor Street" which they had named it, and which the post office had also not recognized, so that letters addressed there were returned to the sender or "passed . . . on to the Dead Letter Office" (3–4). In *Tar Baby,* the figure appears in connection with Valerian, a wealthy, elderly white man named after a little known and insignificant Roman emperor. (He is at one point mistaken for having been named after a candy, though he is quick to point out the name's correct genealogy: "The candy was named after me. I was named after an emperor" [126].) He is obsessed with waiting for a message which he would then deliver to the world (45). But "the postman passed him by" and he thinks "Perhaps . . . he had never received the message he'd been waiting for" because "his innocence made him unworthy of it." Kings feel the need to slay messengers because a worthy messenger "is corrupted by the message he brings" (209). This figurative (still absent) postman finally is delivered a figurative death in *Beloved* in a discussion between Paul D. and Stamp Paid of Sethe's attempted attack with an ice pick upon Edward Bodwin:

> "Every time a whiteman come to the door she got to kill somebody?"
> "For all she know, the man could be coming for the rent."
> "Good thing they don't deliver mail out that way."
> "Wouldn't nobody get no letter."
> "Except the postman."
> "Be a mighty hard message."
> "And his last." (265)

Moving from this authorized figure's sabotage of a message sent from one's own people, to a representation of the desire for authority that the desire to be both receiver and bearer of the official message represents, the narrative thread settles on the assertion of a textual innocence through the rejection of both official message and messenger. This last scene suggests a reversal of the scene where "Hawthorne" imagines Surveyor Pue hands him "the scarlet symbol, and the little roll of explanatory script" and "exhorted me, on the sacred consideration of my filial duty and reverence towards him—who might reasonably regard himself as my official ancestor—to bring his mouldy and moth-eaten lucubrations before the public" to which he dutifully responds "'I will'!" (42–43). Morrison's text, in refusing to accept the figure wearing the mask of postman, refuses to remember the figure of the author who is her literary predecessor, refuses participation in a genealogical line in which a succession of texts evidence their successive authors, refuses to engender authority by refusing to reflect the author. But in still imagining this disguised figure of the author, it contains the patriarchal authority it can not escape, safely keeps it within the bounds of the text, represented as an absence, a mere ghost, haunting the margins.

NOTES

[1]See Molly Hite for a reading of how in *The Color Purple* Alice Walker "completely inverts the emphasis" of the Shakespearean romance, "unsettl[ing] this structural paradigm in the process of applying it."

[2]The notion of "literary influence" can hardly be invoked without either an explicit or implied reference to Bloomian "anxiety of influence." Mae Gwendolyn Henderson, in her article, "Speaking in Tongues," points out the inappropriateness of this model in application to black women writers. Though this "model configuring a white male poetic tradition shaped by an adversarial dialogue between literary fathers and sons" has been appropriated and applied to black male writers, and Gilbert and Gubar present their own "anxiety of authorship" model in application to white women writers, black women writers follow a tradition "generated less by neurotic anxiety or dis-ease than by an emancipatory impulse which freely engages both hegemonic and ambiguously (non)hegemonic discourse." She cites Andrea Stuart's paraphrase of Toni Morrison that "Only black women writers were not interested in writing about white men and therefore they freed literature to take on other concerns" to illustrate this idea (in *Reading Black, Reading Feminist,* 138). I would agree concerning the inappropriateness of applying this model as a way of explaining how Morrison's text was shaped. But as my reading here points out, the figure of the "literary father" is nonetheless present in *Beloved.*

In his "Review of Harold Bloom's *Anxiety of Influence,*" Paul DeMan, while highly praising the work in certain respects, says that "In some respects" the book represents "a step backward" because Bloom's "theoretical concerns are now displaced into a symbolic narrative recentered in a subject," which represents "a relapse into a psychological naturalism" (271–72). While my argument does not embrace the oedipal paradigm, as becomes clear later, I might also be accused, with Bloom, of lapsing into a type of "psychological naturalism" in my use of metaphors of the self here. I would maintain that self and language are inextricable; hence the extension of metaphors of an authorial drama into the very fabric of the fiction's language itself is appropriate.

[3]Gates explains that the theory of Signifyin(g) "is fundamentally related to Bakhtin's definitions of parody and hidden polemic," which maintains that

> the other speech act remains outside the bounds of the author's speech, but is implied or alluded to in that speech. The other speech act is not reproduced with a new intention, but shapes the author's speech while remaining outside its boundaries. . . . In hidden polemic the author's discourse is oriented toward its referential object, as is any other discourse, but at the same time each assertion about that object is constructed in such a way that, besides its referential meaning, the author's discourse brings a polemical attack to bear against another speech act, another assertion, on the same topic. Here one utterance focused on its referential object clashes with an other utterance on the grounds of the referent itself. That other utterance is not reproduced; it is understood only in its import. (Bakhtin, as quoted in *The Signifying Monkey,* 111)

Morrison's texts do not "clash with" the canonical texts which they recall, but do contend with the nature of their authority in recalling them, while at the same time asserting the relationship of black literature to the other "Literature."

WORKS CITED

Baym, Nina, "Melodramas of Beset Manhood: How Theories of American Fiction Exclude Women Authors," *American Quarterly,* 33 (Summer 1981): 123–39.

Campbell, Jane, *Mythic Black Fiction.* Knoxville: The University of Tennessee Press, 1986.

Carby, Hazel, *Reconstructing Womanhood: The Emergence of the African American Woman Novelist.* New York: Oxford University Press, 1987.

DeMan, Paul, *Blindness and Insight.* Minneapolis: University of Minnesota Press, 1983.

Dryden, Edgar A., *The Form of American Romance.* Baltimore: Johns Hopkins University Press, 1988.

Freud, Sigmund, *The Interpretation of Dreams,* trans. James Strachey. New York: Avon Books, 1965.

Gates, Henry Louis. Jr., "Canon-Formation, Literary History, and the African-American Tradition: From the Seen to the Told." In *Afro-American Literary Study in the 1990's.* Ed. Houston A. Baker, Jr., and Patricia Redmond. Chicago: University of Chicago Press, 1989, 14–50.

———. *Figures in Black.* New York: Oxford University Press, 1987.

———. *The Signifying Monkey.* New York: Oxford University Press, 1988.

Hawthorne, Nathaniel, *The Scarlet Letter.* Vol. 1 of *The Centenary Edition of the Works of Nathaniel Hawthorne.* Ed. Donald Crowley. Columbus: Ohio State University Press, 1962.

Henderson, Mae Gwendolyn, "Speaking in Tongues: Dialogics, Dialectics, and the Black Woman Writer's Literary Tradition," in *Reading Black, Reading Feminist.* Ed. Henry Louis Gates, Jr. New York: Meridian, 1990, 91–115.

Hite, Molly, "Romance, Marginality and Matrilineage: *The Color Purple* and *Their Eyes Were Watching God,*" in *Reading Black, Reading Feminist,* 431–53.

Kristeva, Julia, "Stabat Mater," in *The Kristeva Reader.* Ed. Toril Moi. New York: Columbia University Press, 1986, 160–86.

Morrison, Toni, *Beloved.* New York: Knopf, 1987.

———. *The Bluest Eye.* New York: Washington Square Press, 1970.

———. "Memory, Creation, and Writing," *Thought,* 59 (December 1984): 385–90.

———. *Playing in the Dark: Whiteness and the Literary Imagination.* Cambridge: Harvard University Press, 1992.

———. *Song of Solomon.* New York: New American Library, 1977.

———. *Sula.* New York: Knopf, 1974.

———. *Tar Baby.* New York: New American Library, 1981.

———. "Unspeakable Things Unspoken: The African-American Presence in American Literature," *Michigan Quarterly Review,* 28 (Winter 1989): 1–34.

Naylor, Gloria and Toni Morrison, "A Conversation," *The Southern Review,* 21 (Summer 1985): 567–93.

Poirier, Richard, *A World Elsewhere: The Place of Style in American Literature.* New York: Oxford University Press, 1966.

Pryse, Marjorie, "Zora Neale Hurston, Alice Walker, and the 'Ancient Power' of Black Women," in *Conjuring: Back Women, Fiction, and Literary Tradition.* Eds. Marjorie Pryse and Hortense Spillers. Bloomington: Indiana University Press, 1985, 1–24.

Spillers, Hortense, "Cross Currents, Discontinuities: Black Women's Fiction." In *Conjuring: Black Women, Fiction, and Literary Tradition,* 249–61.

Thomas, Brooks, *The New Historicism and Other Old-Fashioned Topics.* Princeton: Princeton University Press, 1991.

Updike's *Scarlet Letter Trilogy:* Recasting an American Myth (1992)

JAMES A. SCHIFF

Though many readers are aware of how John Updike has chronicled America of the 1950s, 1960s, 1970s, and 1980s in his Rabbit tetralogy, few have paid close attention to his other multivolume work concerning America (and a canonical American text), namely *The Scarlet Letter* trilogy. In 1975 Updike published *A Month of Sundays,* a novel in diary form in which a spiritually tormented and adulterous minister from Massachusetts is ordered to an Arizona motel for ministers-gone-astray; there he is urged to wrestle with his perverse soul and rub out his "stain."[1] Updike later referred to that novel as "Dimmesdale's version" of *The Scarlet Letter.*[2] In 1986 Updike published *Roger's Version,* an unreliable first-person narrative in which a Harvard professor, a crusty old doctor of divinity named Roger, manipulates and feeds upon the life of a youthful, pious computer science graduate student named Dale. Most recently, in 1988, Updike published the epistolary *S.,* in which an angry North Shore house wife, with a strong predilection for Vitamin A, rebels against her Puritan heritage and patriarchal society by traveling to a desert ashram in Arizona. In these three novels, each told from the perspective of one of Hawthorne's three protagonists, Updike has expanded, updated, satirized, and rewritten Hawthorne's text.

That such a bold and intriguing project should go largely unrecognized by the critical community is surprising.[3] Though these novels, with the notable exception of *Roger's Version,* are lighter fare and less substantial than the best of Updike (the Rabbit books, *The Centaur, The Coup*), the project is significant. Any reconsideration of a canonical text by a major literary figure should warrant attention, particularly in light of the contemporary interest in intertextuality. In addition, the project is significant in that it reveals a more experimental and postmodern Updike, one who shares Nabokov's sense of word play and games.

Two questions persist in regard to Updike's project: Why should a prominent novelist explicitly rewrite a story which has already been told so successfully? And why Hawthorne? In answer to the former, Updike has long relied upon the successful work of previous writers.[4] His first novel, *The Poorhouse Fair* (1958), was a futuristic retelling of the story of St. Stephen. *Rabbit, Run* (1960) sprang from Jack Kerouac's *On the Road,* Arthurian grail legend, and Peter Rabbit. *The Centaur* (1963) updated and interlaced a variety of Greek myths, so many in fact that Updike compiled a mythological index as an appendix. The mythic mode, in which a writer appropriates and retells an earlier story or tale which has achieved mythic dimensions, has long been salient in Updike's fiction, though critics have failed to recognize its importance except in *The Centaur.* And according to Updike, the mythic mode is attractive not only because-it offers "a counterpoint of ideality to the drab real level" and provides "an excuse for a number of jokes," but because it demonstrates the "sensation that the people we meet are guises, do conceal something mythic, perhaps prototypes or longings in our minds."[5]

In answer to the latter question—why Hawthorne?—one discovers in Hawthorne many of the same themes and conflicts inherent in Updike's own writing: the conflict between matter and spirit; a fascination with community and communal experiments; the anxiety and fear of moral damnation; the relationship between sex and religion; an interest in what Tony Tanner calls the "unstable triangularity of adultery" and its effect upon a community; and the use of ambivalent symbolism.[6] The link between the two writers is strengthened by the fact that both have lived most of their lives on the same approximate patch of ground near Boston: Hawthorne in Salem and Concord, and Updike in Ipswich, Georgetown, and Beverly Farms. Hawthorne has become more than just a literary antecedent for Updike; he is a figure embedded in the history and myth of Updike's chosen community, a writer whose town Updike must pass every time he goes to and from Boston.[7]

Yet in appropriating Hawthorne's text, Updike presumably was driven by more than just similarities between his work and that of Hawthorne; he must have hoped to gain some benefit. Though enormously successful in both critical and popular circles, Updike has been rather viciously attacked by a small group of critics for lacking depth, for capturing "only the outside of things, the shell of the corporate experience we all have in being twentieth-century Americans."[8] These critics tend to view him as a writer who is all style and little content: "Updike, out of kindness or acedia, has very little to say. And no one writing in America says it better."[9] In light of Updike's often eager responsiveness to address his critics,[10] it seems likely, as Denis Donoghue suggests, that by rewriting *The Scarlet Letter,* Updike expresses "his middle-aged determination to give his art a metaphysical darkening."[11] And in recent novels—*The Witches of Eastwick* (1984), *Roger's Version* (1986), and *Rabbit at Rest* (1990)—there is a darker resonance, a more sustained reflection upon death and solitude, and a growing interest in voyeurism and vicariously experienced life.

Updike becomes the latest apprentice in what Richard Brodhead refers to as "The School of Hawthorne." According to Brodhead, Hawthorne, unlike Whitman or Emerson, was so uncommunicative and gave such little guidance to his followers that they "have been free to put him to any purpose they have required."[12] Writers from Melville, James, and Howells to the present have been able to reinvent Hawthorne so as to suit their own personal needs, creating or aligning themselves with "the Hawthorne tradition" and appropriating the authority and success that are conferred by such a tradition. In turning to Hawthorne, Updike carves out an emotional stance for himself which expresses a mixture of devotion and aggression toward his predecessor.[13] Through his intertextual echoings, Updike works to maintain and confirm a connection with the past, offering homage to an earlier writer and text. The author of a series of essays on writers whom he refers to as "American Masters" (Melville, Hawthorne, Whitman, Emerson, Howells, Franklin), Updike has long expressed his awareness and reverence for such writers and for the hierarchy which confirms such a status.[14] In his utilization of Hawthorne, Updike endeavors to absorb some degree of his predecessor's genius and align himself with a tradition of American "masters," in hopes no doubt that his work at some point will be pondered in relation to Hawthorne. Yet that is only part of the picture. Updike also parodies and de-romanticizes Hawthorne's text, calling into question its authority and moral stance. With his clinical frankness and post-Freudian desire to verbalize, Updike rejects the warfare between body and soul which is so central to Hawthorne, and he satirizes Hawthorne's protagonists for their fragility, prudishness, and self-deception. Updike's stance toward Hawthorne is complex; he pays homage to the past "master" and yet questions and satirizes the master's moral tenets.

In attempting to transform Hawthorne's text, Updike is seeking to alter an American myth. Explaining his project, Updike states: "*The Scarlet Letter* is not merely a piece of fiction, it is a myth by now, and it was an updating of the myth, the triangle as redefined by D. H. Lawrence, that interested me."[15] By referring to Hawthorne's novel as a myth, Updike appears to use the term not primarily in the sense of indicating a primitive pattern of behavior, such as Mircea Eliade, Joseph Campbell, Northop Frye, C. G. Jung, and others might suggest, but more specifically as a story or a pattern of behavior "linked with a particular culture and dealing with named characters and locations" as generated in a work of literature.[16] René Wellek and Austin Warren point to the social elements inherent in myth, defining the term as "the explanation a society offers its young of why the world is and why we do as we do."[17] As witnessed in high-school English curricula across the nation, Hawthorne's novel of adulterous love, perhaps more than any other text, is what America offers its young, both as literature and as history.

At its core a myth expresses, as Denis de Rougemont points out, "*the rules of conduct* of a given social or religious group," and it exposes how the individuals of that historical group relate to one another.[18] In Hawthorne's text, characters remain largely isolated from one another, residing in separate "spheres" and rarely touching. Human contact, in particular coitus between Hester and Dimmesdale, is a legal and moral violation. According to Updike, "Hawthorne's instinctive tenet [is] that matter and spirit are inevitably at war," and in the course of this battle, "matter verges upon being evil; virtue, upon being insubstantial."[19] Hawthorne's characters are literally divided between public and private self, interior and exterior world, body and soul. And as seen in Dimmesdale's dramatic death upon the scaffold, the soul, apparently with Hawthorne's approval, is victorious over the transgressions of the body. In his trilogy, Updike endeavors to transform *The Scarlet Letter* myth by affirming corporeal impulse, and thus reconciling body and soul.

Updike's revision of *The Scarlet Letter* appropriates and builds upon two concepts outlined in Lawrence's *Studies in Classic American Literature:* Hawthorne's duplicity and the American quest for renewal. According to Lawrence, the primary impulse in Hawthorne is toward subversion and deception: "that blue-eyed darling Nathaniel knew disagreeable things in his inner soul. He was careful to send them out in disguise."[20] In recasting Hester, Chillingworth, and Dimmesdale, Updike, like Lawrence before him, compels the reader to reexamine Hawthorne's characters, particularly in regard to what has been repressed or disguised. In addition, Lawrence speaks of the self's ability for "shedding skins," a term which Updike appropriates. Lawrence explains the founding of America as arising not from a desire by the "Pilgrim Fathers" for freedom, but as a desire "largely to get away. . . . To get away from everything they are and have been."[21] The objective was to slough off the old European skin and grow a new American one. Updike's characters, in America of the 1970s and 1980s, find themselves in a rather similar situation, though it is no longer a European skin which must be sloughed off. Bored and oppressed by their own predictable lives and by a repressive middle class Protestantism (handed down from Hawthorne's characters), Updike's characters are in need of passionate experience, what de Rougemont refers to as a "transfiguring force."[22] And so they follow the same spirit of quest which once lured Hawthorne's characters across the Atlantic. In his three novels, *A Month of Sundays, Roger's Version,* and *S.,* Updike recasts Hawthorne's three "divided" protagonists and demonstrates how the "mythic" American situation persists: that of individuals struggling within themselves and against their communities in an effort to shake off the past and reinvent the world.

Updike's first attempt at rewriting *The Scarlet Letter* was *A Month of Sundays,* or Dimmesdale's version. Though the novel has been accurately criticized as excessive and self-indulgent, it is nonetheless more self-consciously clever and complex, more reflexively postmodern, than Updike's earlier productions. Delivered in the form of a diary, *A Month of Sundays* is the Reverend Thomas Marshfield's account of the infidelities and transgressions which landed him in exile at a motel for ministers-gone-astray in Arizona. Like Dimmesdale, Marshfield is an anxious and confused Protestant minister from Massachusetts who has become entangled in adultery with his parishioners. From his desert exile, Marshfield explains how his marriage to Jane Chillingworth, a woman of "goodness" and a model of Christian ethics, had become stale and unsatisfactory. He then describes how he fell passionately into an affair with his parish organist, Alicia Crick, which "opened the floodgates" and "slashed the walls of my prison." Soon he finds himself administering to the sexual needs of a large number of his female parishioners: "there was a smell about me now. Women sensed it. They flocked to be counselled" (*MS* 32).[23] Marshfield is Dimmesdale with a hint of Don Juan, reminding us of the strong attraction which Hawthorne's preacher had upon his female parishioners: "the virgins of his church grew pale around him, victims of a passion so imbued with religious sentiment that they imagined it to be all religion" (*SL* 142). *A Month of Sundays* is Marshfield's account of himself and his over active libido, recorded as he struggles with his inner being and under goes self-therapy to return home after his month in desert exile.

In his revision Updike reminds us of just how significant the act of verbalization (speaking, writing) is to the character of Dimmesdale, and how Dimmesdale's duplicitous and clever speech serves as a metaphor for his divided and conflicted self. Repeatedly in *The Scarlet Letter* Dimmesdale finds himself in pulpits and on balconies and scaffolds, speaking and preaching to the people of Boston. In his initial appearance Dimmesdale is called upon by his superiors to rectify an element of so-cial disorder, Hester's adultery, by acting in the capacity for which he is best suited: speaking to the public. It is an ironic moment as Dimmesdale employs clever language and veiled speech, representative of his divided self:

> "Hester Prynne, . . . thou hearest what this good man says, and seest the accountability under which I labor. If thou feelest it to be for thy soul's peace. . . . I charge thee to speak out the name of thy fellow-sin-ner and fellow-sufferer!" (*SL* 67).

Speech is a crucial act for Dimmesdale not only because he is a minister, an occupation which almost exclusively relies upon verbal communica-tion, but more importantly because he is guilty of an act that he feels de-mands public disclosure through speech. Tempted and yet fearful of speaking truthfully, Dimmesdale divides and tortures himself, employ-ing a language of double-speak.

Updike appropriates this speech metaphor for Marshfield in *A Month of Sundays*. Like Dimmesdale, Marshfield has been asked by his superiors to address, with words, a social wrong: "my keepers have set before me a sheaf of blank sheets—a month's worth, in their estimation. Sullying them is to be my sole therapy" (*MS* 3). Employing significant rhetorical skills, Marshfield, too, proves to be a clever and deceptive speaker with his own "tongue of flame." Yet, where Dimmesdale strives to repress dangerous thoughts and words, Marshfield endeavors to ex-press everything; Dimmesdale's retention is replaced by Marshfield's volubility. Holding his secret and passion within, Dimmesdale allows his Calvinistic soul to devour his body. But Marshfield, with a clinical frank-ness and a post-Freudian desire to be expressive, attempts to restore him-self by reconciling body and soul.

In *A Month of Sundays,* there is undoubtedly a strong relationship between writing and adultery. As John Matthews suggests, Marshfield comes to understand that writing repeats adultery as it tries to cure it.[24] Writing allows another form for Marshfield's seductive and desirous inclinations. Tony Tanner points out that the chaos of adultery can be related to the chaos of language, suggesting that "puns and ambiguities are to common language what adultery and perversion are to 'chaste'. . . sexual relations."[25] Marshfield's narrative—loose, comic, colloquial, sexually explicit, and playful—adopts a singular form of speech which creatively breaks away from conventional language. In addition, just as adultery undermines social order, law, and authority, Marshfield's writing questions and subverts the authority of the text itself and creates a level of uncertainty and ambiguity: "or perhaps these words were never spoken, I made them up, to relieve and rebuke the silence of this officiously chaste room" (*MS* 33). Much like adultery, writing creates an awakening of energy which can lead to the forging of a new kind of expression, yet it may also pose a threat to the social order, as we see in Hawthorne's discussion of his own authorship in "The Custom-House."

Updike's Marshfield stands in direct contrast to Michael Davitt Bell's contention that if *The Scarlet Letter* were told from Dimmesdale's point of view it might sound like a tale by Poe.[26] Marshfield's diary is parodic and humorous, filled with word play and silly puns. The solemn and highly proper Dimmesdale is replaced by the witty and radically improper Marshfield. By recasting Dimmesdale as a prankster and a clown, Updike of course parodies Hawthorne's preacher and demonstrates how sexual attitudes have changed drastically since 1850 (and 1640); yet there is more. Through the voice of Marshfield, Updike is attempting to revise America's understanding of Christianity. As he stated in an interview, Updike is not at all pleased with the contemporary critical perspective on Christianity:

> People nowadays, at least liberal literary, assume that the Christian religion is primarily a system for enforcing ethics. It is not. It is an organization for distributing the good news of Jesus Christ.[27]

Like so many of Updike's protagonists, Marshfield is a disciple of Karl Barth, the neo-orthodox Swiss theologian who depreciates ethics because it is solely an affair of the lowly human element, having nothing to do with the Divine. For Marshfield a vital belief in the Incarnation of Christ, not good ethical behavior, is central to Christianity. Though much of Marshfield's discourse is comic (he suggests the commandment, "Be fruitful and multiply," is meant to encourage adultery), he does warn his readers to resist Christian ethical humanism and its intolerance of the corporeal: "we and our bodies are one . . . [and] we should not heretically . . . castigate the body and its dark promptings" (*MS* 44, 135).

According to Marshfield, the American self has been deprived since the early seventeenth century because of "lost baggage" which was apparently left behind in England:

> Somewhere . . . an American mystery was circumscribed, having to do with knowing, with acceptance of body by soul, with recovery of some baggage lost in the Atlantic crossing, with some viral thrill at the indignity of incarnation, with some monstrous and gorgeous otherness the female and male genitals meet in one another (*MS* 134–5).

Marshfield reinterprets corporeal impulse affirmatively, arguing that America has been physically handicapped for too long and must recover its wholeness by reconciling body and soul. The endings of the two novels, both triumphant, highlight how Updike and Hawthorne respond differently to the urgings of the body. Dimmesdale, in confessing publicly, allows his soul to triumph over his body; by escaping into death, he terminates corporeal anxiety and torture. Marshfield, on the other hand, proves successful in at last seducing the motel manageress, a certain Ms. Prynne, and their bodies, wrapped in ecstatic coitus, experience an altogether different form of death, and one which exalts in the mutual pleasures of the flesh.

Updike's second attempt at rewriting Hawthorne was *Roger's Version,* which refers to Roger Chillingworth's version of events. Chillingworth, the learned and bookish doctor, finds a contemporary counterpart in Updike's Roger Lambert, an equally bookish doctor of divinity and professor at what appears to be Harvard. Dressed in his academic "armor of amiable tweed," Lambert, like Chillingworth before him, is resistant to any type of passionate engagement with others. Yet along comes Dale Kohler, whose first name refers to Hawthorne's minister and whose last alludes to Kaufmann Kohler, an influential theologian of Reform Judaism who tried, much as Dale shall, to reconcile traditional faith with modern knowledge. Young, tall, pale, and pious, Dale is a computer science graduate student in search of a grant. Possessing a born-again Christian's zeal for prayer and biblical quotation, he hopes to use his knowledge of computers and science to find God, literally to see Him appear on a computer screen. Imagining God to be that "purposeful Intelligence" who "fine tuned the physical constants and the initial conditions,"

Dale determines "to demonstrate from existing physical and biological data, through the use of models and manipulations on the electronic digital computer, the existence of God" (*RV* 75–6). In a novel largely concerned with visualization, Dale is determined literally to see that which is unseeable, to shine a light on that which has no understand able physical essence. "God can't hide any more," Dale declares, expressing his hope that he can show the people of the world, who have been intimidated into not believing in God by the atheistic science community, that God can be proven. If successful, Dale would become a contemporary savior.

Roger Lambert, Updike's recurring Barthian who envisions God as "Wholly Other," finds Dale's project "aesthetically and ethically repulsive. Aesthetically because it describes a God Who lets Himself be intellectually trapped, and ethically because it eliminates faith from religion" (*RV* 24). Annoyed not only by an attempted heresy, Dale's technological pursuit of God, but also by Dale's youthful self-confidence and piety, Roger, the curmudgeon and symbol of old male authority and intellect, responds aggressively, locking the younger man in an intellectual struggle designed to ruin him and his precious faith. The situation ultimately becomes ironic: the scientist is "intent on proving God's existence," while the theologian "rejects the possibility of such a proof."[28] Although Dale receives the grant and momentarily sees the outline of a face and hand on the computer screen, the impossibility of his project eventually overwhelms him. In addition, the affair which he has been carrying on with Roger's young wife Esther has drained him physically and emotionally.

Roger's Version addresses many of the same themes and concerns from *A Month of Sundays*—reparation of the split between body and soul, adultery as a transfiguring experience—yet there is a new focus and controlling metaphor: the act of seeing. Like Chillingworth, whose eyes were said to possess a "strange, penetrating power," Roger Lambert (who takes his last name from the eighteenth-century German physicist Johann Heinrich Lambert, known for a variety of inventions in the study of light) is proud of "the keenness of my eyesight." Updike's Lambert is less a participant and more an observer, witness, and manipulator of others. With his expert vision, Roger is unusually perceptive of how light is continually transforming vision. In virtually every scene in the novel we are made aware of the type of light being generated: "gray, autumnal light," "double-barrelled light," "hospital light," "islands of light in a jagged arboeal ocean." We are also alerted to the direction from which the light arrives ("behind me," "overhead"), and light is continually transforming objects and people: "[Dale's] easy tallness, which in the slant chapel light of my office he quickly folded into the university chair opposite my desk, here in my front hall loomed, all suited and combed, as a costume of grace, a form of potency" (*RV* 95).

Obsessed with the youthful Dale, who himself is attempting literally to see God, Roger endeavors to see into the eyes and mind of the young man so as to reach his soul. Like Chillingworth (and Miles Coverdale from *The Blithedale Romance*), Roger Lambert delights in seeing into and through the eyes of others, and in the process, manipulating those lives. *Roger's Version* is largely a series of visions, fantasies, and day-dreams in which Roger telepathically follows the movements of Dale Kohler. Longing to escape his dull, middle-aged existence, Roger is simultaneously attracted and repulsed by Dale, yet he experiences "a grateful inkling that [Dale] was injecting a new element into [his] life" (*RV* 90). In sharing Dale's "field of vision," Roger temporarily sheds his gray skin and is able to see anew. His wife Esther, who has ceased as a stimulating presence, becomes transformed when seen through Dale's eyes:

> I saw her through his eyes, my little wife, her tense and tidy figure fore-shortened even more from his angle than from mine. . . . Esther had put on a glint, an alertness, an older woman's assured and ironic potential playfulness. (*RV* 96)

Updike follows the lead of both Hawthorne and James, not only in his concern with voyeurism, but also in what Brodhead refers to as "literature's essential vicariousness": "the need to remedy a felt life deficiency not by living one's own life more fully but by appropriating life in simulated or surrogate forms."[29]

Dale is used as a pawn by the Lamberts in an effort to improve their conjugality (D. H. Lawrence reads *The Scarlet Letter* as an attempt by Hester and Chillingworth, accomplices tied by marriage, to subdue the pure spiritual man). Through Dale, each attempts to annoy, hurt, frustrate, reawaken, and anger the other. And by the end of the novel Dale has become so disillusioned and abused by the people of the East that he returns, like Nick Carraway of *The Great Gatsby*, to his roots in the Midwest. Yet just as *The Scarlet Letter* concludes with Dimmesdale's "triumph," *Roger's Version* ends with a triumph of sort for Dale Kohler. He not only has escaped Roger's visionary grasp (by leaving Boston), but much to Roger's annoyance he has impregnated Roger's wife and inspired her to attend church.

The epistolary novel *S.*, or Hester's version, is Updike's most recent addition to the trilogy, and it forms the final side of the *Scarlet Letter* triangle. The volume most interested in the American experiment of dissent, separation, and heroic struggle to rebuild the world, *S.* arises not only from *The Scarlet Letter,* but also from *The Blithedale Romance,* Frances FitzGerald's 1986 *Cities on a Hill,* and Hawthorne's letters from Brook Farm. From Hawthorne's Brook Farm letters to Sophia, Updike appropriates a vehicle and genre for telling his story, namely the epistolary, and the seeds for a character type: a less-than-committed pilgrim adventurer who has an obsessive need to possess and control the lives of those residing back in the world left behind. In this respect, Updike is satirizing Hawthorne the pilgrim and letter writer. *The Blithedale Romance,* echoing strongly throughout *S.,* provides for Updike the backdrop of social duplicity, in which a society not only "repeats" and "intensifies" the features of the society it has rejected, but also indulges its own personal desires under the guise of communal reform.[30] Finally, from *Cities on a Hill,* Updike utilizes a real-life blue print—the guru-inspired, Rolls Royce-outfitted Rajneeshpuram in Oregon—and appropriates its philosophy, organization, and dynamics for his own fictional Ashram Arhat.[31]

The American experiment of dissent, separation and heroic struggle to rebuild the world is the focus of all of the above texts, and in each, individual selves attempt to shed old skins in an effort toward self-transformation. Implicit, of course, in any such experiment is the question of whether the self can indeed be altered. In *S.* Sarah Worth, the contemporary Hester Prynne, is a pilgrim on a quest to change herself and the world. She informs her husband: "I will change my name. I will change my being. The woman you 'knew' and 'possessed' is no more. I am destroying her. . . . I shed you as I would shed a skin" (*S.* 12). Frustrated by her husband's infidelity and trapped by a Puritan heritage, Sarah leaves her safe suburban Massachusetts home and travels to the wilderness, here a desert ashram in Arizona (the desert in Updike's trilogy is the topos of temptation, instruction, enlightenment, and redemption). At the ashram, she seeks to realize her spiritual and physical potential, practicing yoga to awaken the kundalini, or "coiled up" female energy lying dormant at the base of her spine.

More than the other two novels in the trilogy, *S.* most consciously and playfully alludes to *The Scarlet Letter.* Sarah is continually pushing

Vitamin A on her mother for her eyes, skin, and thyroid. Sarah's female lover Alinga is addressed as "Dearest A," and together they live in an "A-frame." Instead of displaying a scarlet A on her breast as a sign of her adultery, Sarah conceals a mini-tape recorder in her bra in order to document the actual moment of adultery. And in the town of Forrest, a day's drive from Hawthorne, California, Sarah stays at the Babbling Brook Motor Lodge, whose stationery portrays a child dabbling in the brook while dark ominous trees surround.

Yet in spite of its comic and playful nature, *S.* challenges and attempts to revise significantly our understanding of *The Scarlet Letter,* offering a reconsideration of both Hester Prynne and the American quest for spiritual rebirth. For many readers Hester has evolved into a feminist heroine of literature, a sacred sister, a model of dignified defiance. Mark Van Doren refers to her as New England's "most heroic creature," a heroine who is "almost a goddess."[32] More recently Nina Auerbach has spoken of Hester as "a solitary icon," "a feminist saint, the vehicle for 'a new truth' of empowered and transfigured womanhood."[33] In *S.* Updike deromanticizes Hester, challenging feminist readings which confer sainthood upon her. Updike's Sarah Worth resists Hester's stoicism, releasing a torrent of anger and bitterness directed mostly at the male species: "Shams. That's what men are. Liars. Hollow frauds and liars" (*S.* 229). Though some critics have argued, with cries of sexism and misogyny, that Updike has reduced Hester to "a wholly hateful woman," Updike suggests rather that Hester is far more complex, conflicted, defiant, and self deceptive than is commonly imagined.[34] Updike is following Hawthorne's lead:

> The world's law was no law for her mind. . . . She assumed a freedom
> of speculation, then common enough on the other side of the Atlantic,
> but which our forefathers, had they known of it, would have held to be
> a deadlier crime than that stigmatized by the scarlet letter (*SL* 164).

However, where the shadowy Hawthorne resists explicitly exposing the interior Hester, Updike takes us beneath the textual surface to reveal an angry and defiant woman.[35]

Updike's purpose in *S.* is largely satirical, as he exposes the duplicity, hypocrisy, and folly of the spiritual community and quest. Supposedly based upon antimaterialism, the Ashram Arhat boasts of its own shopping mall which sells Arhat t-shirts and tapes, and the Arhat can be spotted wearing large diamonds and being driven about in expensive automobiles. Ma Prapti, the ashram administrator, is ultimately arrested for having sprinkled drugs into the vegetarian curry so as to keep the pilgrims passive. And the Arhat himself, the Supreme Meditator, turns out to be not an Indian guru but rather a Jewish dropout named Art Steinmetz from Watertown, Massachusetts. As the Dimmesdale figure in the novel (Art, Arthur, Arhat), the guru is another example of the fraudulent holy man, whose fictional predecessors include Dimmesdale and Sinclair Lewis' Elmer Gantry, and whose real-life counterparts are such figures as Jim Baker, Jimmy Swaggart, and the Bhagwan Shree Rajneesh. The Arhat is a prime example of that uniquely American mode of thinking in which one believes that one can transform oneself into anything one chooses. Steinmetz is the Jay Gatsby of religion.

No one, however, is more hypocritical or duplicitous than Updike's Hester, Sarah Worth. For a woman who has recently freed herself from material concerns, Sarah inventories family possessions like an accountant and hoards them like a miser. And she has deceived herself into believing that her quest is centered upon spirituality and love, rather than revenge and hatred. Sarah is not unlike a comic Shakespearean heroine who fails to see her own hypocrisy and hidden motives. Like Hester, Sarah too fails to become he "destined prophetess" for womankind. Her quest for a new identity, intimately associated with the dream of America, fails largely as she discovers that her old self cannot be fully shed: "We shed our skins but something naked and white and amara slithers out and is always the same" (*S.* 262).

In his *Scarlet Letter Trilogy* Updike has retold an earlier story which concerns America, its history, and as Lawrence would say, its very "spirit." The story concerns the American self as it is isolated from others and imprisoned by its own oppressiveness. Though contemporary America is no longer beleaguered by the gray, iron men of Hawthorne's sensibility, there is nevertheless a new beast that menaces the land: an "ease and comfort," a "milky human kindness," a yawning boredom (*MS* 50, 59). Without the rigid restraints of Puritanism (as Sarah Worth puts it, "Puritanism in my parents had dwindled to a sort of housekeeping"), Updike is suggesting that America has mellowed and lost its passion. Updike's characters have become stifled, bored, and oppressed by their predictable lives, and, like Hawthorne's characters, they are in need of a transfiguring passionate experience. Once again, geographical movement offers the remedy: as Hawthorne's Puritans crossed the Atlantic in their quest for renewal, Updike's contemporary pilgrims leave familiar communities (Marshfield and Worth travel to Arizona, and Lambert to the projects of Boston and to the interior of Dale's mind) in hopes of escaping past identities.

Updike's America is vastly different from Hawthorne's; it has been released not only from the constraints of Puritanism, but also from the claims of tragedy. The torment that Updike's characters experience is comic. In upper-middle class America, life and death struggles against primitive forces have become less visible; a more trivial and darkly comic existence is mandated. Hawthorne's America, supernaturally marked by primitive forests, ghostly images, and divine celestial messages, is transformed by Updike into the locus of quotidian concerns, domestic squabbles, and bourgeois angst. And Updike's America is no longer one in which we can catch only shadowy glimpses of Hester and Dimmesdale together; Updike offers lengthy and graphic scenes in which the Hester and Dimmesdale figures are intimately wrapped in coitus. Updike attempts to undo the traditional body-soul division in Hawthorne. Following Tertullian and Barth, Updike's Roger Lambert argues for the significance of human flesh, blasting those "who make an outcry against the flesh . . . who accuse it of being unclean . . . infirm, guilty . . . burdensome, troublesome" (*RV* 152). Updike departs from Hawthorne in refusing to punish immoral behavior. Affirming corporeal impulse, Updike argues that America has been physically handicapped for too long and must recover its wholeness. Through acceptance of the body and its needs, the American self can rise from its bourgeois malaise, taste the exhilaration of freedom, and experience faith in the divine.

NOTES

[1]In his essay "Hawthorne's Creed," Updike states: "Where the two incompatible realms of Hawthorne's universe impinge, something leaks through; there is a stain. . . . The stain, this sinister spillage from another world, can take the form of poison, of a potion . . . of over-insistent symbols like the scarlet letter." See *Hugging the Shore* (New York: Knopf, 1983), 77.

[2]Updike, "A Special Message for the First Edition," *Roger's Version* (Franklin Center: Franklin Library, 1986), iii.

[3]Most critics and reviewers have not yet acknowledged the depth and extent of Hawthorne's significance in Updike's trilogy. There are, however, several notable exceptions, including Donald Greiner, "Body and Soul: John Updike and *The Scarlet Letter*," *Journal of Modern Literature* 15 (1989), 475–95; Raymond Wilson III, "*Roger's Version*: Updike's Negative-Solid Model of *The Scarlet Letter*," *Modern Fiction Studies* 35 (1989), 241–50; and John N. Duvall, "The Plea-

sure of Textual/Sexual Wrestling: Pornography and Heresy in *Roger's Version,*" *Modern Fiction Studies* 37 (1991), 81–95. See also my forthcoming book, *Updike's Version: Rewriting Hawthorne's The Scarlet Letter* (Columbia: University of Missouri Press, 1993). For other studies of Hawthorne and Updike which consider Updike novels not in the trilogy, see Samuel Chase Coale, *In Hawthorne's Shadow* (Lexington: University Press of Kentucky, 1985), and Donald Greiner, *Adultery in the American Novel: Updike, James, and Hawthorne* (Columbia: University of South Carolina Press, 1985).

[4]Updike speaks at length about the sources of his fictions in "One Big Interview," in *Picked-Up Pieces* (New York: Knopf, 1975), 491–519.

[5]Updike, interview with Charles Thomas Samuels, in: *Writers at Work/The Paris Review Interviews/Fourth Series,* ed. George Plimpton (New York: Penguin, 1976), 442.

[6]Tony Tanner, *Adultery in the Novel: Contract and Transgression* (Baltimore: Johns Hopkins University Press, 1979), 12.

[7]When traveling to Boston by rail, Updike writes, he actually passes underneath Salem: "the train takes a dark plunge into the earth beneath Salem. . . . Perhaps the ominous darkness fittingly memorializes Hawthorne." "A Short and Happy Ride," in *Odd Jobs* (New York: Knopf, 1991), 67.

[8]Richard H. Rupp, "John Updike: Style in Search of a Center," in *John Updike,* ed. Harold Bloom (New York: Chelsea House, 1987), 17. For a more recent comprehensive critical analysis of Updike, see Frederick Crews, "Mr. Updike's Planet," *New York Review of Books,* 4 December 1986, pp. 7–14.

[9]Keith Mano, "Doughy Middleness," *National Review,* 30 August 1974, 987.

[10]In an interview with Mervyn Rothstein ("In *S.,* Updike Tries the Woman's Viewpoint." *New York Times,* 2 March 1988, p. C21), Updike says of his portrayal of women that "knowing that there is this reservation out in some quarters about my portraits of women, I'm constantly trying to improve them . . . *The Witches of Eastwick* . . . was one attempt to make things right with my, what shall we call them, feminist detractors, and *S.* is another." The caveat, of course, is Updike's tendency toward irony, particularly since these two novels have most angered feminist critics.

[11]Denis Donoghue, " 'I Have Preened, I Have Lived'," Rev. of *Self-Consciousness. New York Times Book Review,* 5 March 1989, p. 7.

[12]Richard H. Brodhead, *The School of Hawthorne* (New York: Oxford University Press, 1986), 15–16.

[13]Heide Ziegler, "Love's Labours Won: The Erotics of Contemporary Parody," in *Intertextuality and Contemporary American Fiction,* ed. Patrick O'Donnell and Robert Con Davis (Baltimore: Johns Hopkins University Press, 1989), 60.

[14]John Updike, "Three Talks on American Masters," in *Hugging the Shore,* 73–117; "Emersonianism," in *Odd Jobs,* 148–68; "Howells as Anti-Novelist," in *Odd Jobs,* 168–89; and "Many Bens," in *Odd Jobs,* 240–61.

[15]John Updike, letter to the author, 26 January 89.

[16]John J. White, *Mythology in the Modern Novel* (Princeton: Princeton University Press, 1971), 38. See also John B. Vickery, ed., *Myth and Literature* (Lincoln: University of Nebraska Press, 1966); Earl Miner, ed., *Literary Uses of Typology from the Late Middle Ages to the Present* (Princeton: Princeton University Press, 1977).

[17]William Righter, quoting René Wellek and Austin Warren, *Myth and Literature* (London: Routledge and Kegan Paul, 1975), 5.

[18]Denis de Rougemont, *Love in the Western World,* trans. Montgomery Belgion (Princeton: Princeton University Press, 1983), 18.

[19]John Updike, "Hawthorne's Creed," 77.

[20]D. H. Lawrence, *Studies in Classic American Literature* (New York: Penguin, 1977), 89.

[21]Lawrence, 9.

[22]De Rougemont, 16.

[23]John Updike's *A Month of Sundays* (New York: Knopf, 1975); *Roger's Version* (New York: Knopf, 1986), and *S.* (New York: Knopf, 1988) will be cited in the text as *MS,* RV, and *S.* Citations in the text from *The Scarlet Letter (SL)* are from *The Centenary Edition of the Works of Nathaniel Hawthorne,* ed. William Charvat, Roy Harvey Pearce, and Claude M. Simpson (Columbus: Ohio State University Press, 1971), Vol. 1.

[24]John T. Matthews, "The Word as Scandal: Updike's *A Month of Sundays,*" *Arizona Quarterly,* 39 (1983), 351–80; and John T. Matthews, "Intertextuality and Originality: Hawthorne, Faulkner, Updike," in *Intertextuality in Faulkner,* ed. Michel Gresset and Noel Polk (Jackson: University Press of Mississippi, 1985), 144–56.

[25]Tanner, 53.

[26]Michael Davitt Bell, *The Development of American Romance: The Sacrifice of Relation* (Chicago: University of Chicago Press, 1980), 178.

[27]John Updike, interview with Donald J. Greiner, "Updike on Hawthorne," *The Nathaniel Hawthorne Review,* 13 (Spring 1987), 3.

[28]Richard Eder, "Roger's Version" [rev. of *Roger's Version],* Los Angeles *Times Book Review* 14 September 1986, p. 3.

[29]Brodhead, 99.

[30]Richard H. Brodhead, *Hawthorne, Melville, and the Novel* (Chicago: University of Chicago Press, 1986), 150.

[31]Frances FitzGerald, *Cities on a Hill* (New York: Simon Schuster, 1986).

[32]Mark Van Doren, *Nathaniel Hawthorne* (New York: William Sloane, 1949), 151.

[33]Nina Auerbach, *Woman and the Demon* (Cambridge: Harvard University Press, 1982), 166, 176.

[34]For negative critical responses to Updike's depiction of Sarah Worth as a contemporary Hester Prynne, see Alison Lurie, "The Woman Who Rode Away" [rev. of *S.* and *Trust Me*], *New York Review of Books,* 12 May 1988, p. 4; and Michiko Kakutani, "Updike's Struggle to Portray Women," *The New York Times* 5 May 1988, p. C29.

[35]Updike states: "I see Hester, in the context of her time, as tough and defiant and practical as she could be" (letter to the author, January 26, 1989).

Ellison's *Invisible Man:* Emersonianism Revised (1992)

KUN JONG LEE

When the protagonist-narrator of Ralph Ellison's *Invisible Man* tinkers with the electricity of Monopolated Light and Power, he is symbolically tinkering with a powerful source of American cultural vision: Ellison's namesake, Ralph Waldo Emerson. *Light* and *power* are quintessential Emersonian words, those most closely associated with the character of the poet, and Emersonian ideas echo conspicuously throughout the protagonist's meditation on his past and his search for identity. At best, however, the Concord sage is ambivalently represented in Ellison's novel, for not only are Emersonian principles openly appropriated by negative figures such as Bledsoe, Norton, and Jack but, more specifically, the name Emerson is bestowed on a "trustee of consciousness" and his decadent son. The narrator's underground tinkering with Emerson's ideas, then, suggests both an act of subversion and an attempt at appropriation and redirection. Through these complex efforts, Ellison at once criticizes and claims an Emersonian heritage.

Ever since the novel was published in 1952, Ellison's ambivalence has generally eluded the critics, who have tended to emphasize only the views shared by the novelist and the philosopher. This partiality, or neglect, is well attested by the several collections of critical studies on Ellison and his novel: no essay in these anthologies analyzes in detail Ellison's complex relation to Emerson.[1] The few critics who have recognized Ellison's critique of Emerson have not adequately explained its grounds or perceived its centrality to *Invisible Man.* The issue was first raised in 1960, when Earl H. Rovit suggested that "Emerson's work is given short shrift as rhetorical nonsense in *Invisible Man*" (38); then, in

1970, in the only study to take Ellison's treatment of Emerson as its thesis, William W. Nichols interpreted the novel as a satire on Emerson's "American Scholar"; two years later Leonard J. Deutsch criticized both Rovit and Nichols and judged their arguments "certainly wrong" (160). And there the discussion ended until 1988, when Alan Nadel cautiously questioned Deutsch's reading (114). When Ellison's relation to Emerson has been viewed as controversial at all, then, it has constituted a minor problem in Ellison criticism.[2] The reason, I contend, is that studies of Ellison to date have failed to define the heart of his critique of Emerson: the question of race.

Ellison's ambivalent relation to his namesake derives from his recognition that Emersonianism, which claims to be a universal doctrine, is circumscribed by an inherently racist dimension. Ironically, scholars have missed the central locus of race in his critique of Emerson because their readings of *Invisible Man* have been governed by a sort of Emersonian universalism, a tendency to focus on the "universality" (or the "Americanness") of the black protagonist's experience. In other words, the issue has remained invisible by virtue of the fairly consistent inclination—at least in essays that place the novel in a literary historical frame—to transcend or to bleach the protagonist's racial identity. Emerson's transcendentalism and Ellison's critique are, however, steeped in the question of race. Hence, no criticism of the Emerson-Ellison relation can be color-blind.

I

If Ellison's black narrator, as Nadel has observed, is not a member of Emerson's implied audience, we need to identify and analyze the embedded racist dimension in Emersonianism before we study Ellison's strategy to correct and transcend it. Emerson states, in "The American Scholar," that every "man" contains within himself the Universal Soul (*Essays* 57).[3] In Emersonianism, the Universal Soul, or the Universal Mind, is the source of all minds, and runs through nature as well as through humankind. Since everyone is a part of the Universal Mind, each mind is a point to the Universal Mind and a prospective container of it, so that dignity and equality are shared by all. Emerson's egalitarianism presupposes more than anything else that everybody can achieve a fully realized humanity, and this potential echoes in his famous declaration that "America is not civil, whilst Africa is barbarous" (*Works* 11: 145). Such radical egalitarianism, transcending racial and geographical boundaries, could have been a firm basis for an active abolitionism, had Emerson applied it to the social reality of his time.

Emerson's egalitarianism, however, is basically idealistic and abstract: "the *only* equality of all men," he believes, "is the fact that every man has in him the divine Reason" (*Journals* 4: 357; my emphasis). As befits one whose teaching is confined to a single doctrine, "the infinitude of the private man" (*Journals* 7: 342), he thus internalizes and spiritualizes the meaning of the social word *equality* in the same way that he depoliticizes two other political words, *power* and *freedom*. This kind of abstraction is socially useless, since it cannot explain the specific social and historical causes of arbitrary inequality and provide a practical idea to end the slave system, the obvious social touchstone for any egalitarian idea in America during the 1830s and 1840s. Was Emerson blind to social factors in human life because he was wholeheartedly dedicated to the spiritual power and freedom that were contingent on private thought and independent of political meanings?

Although Emerson's privatism was so dominant a voice that it eclipsed the concept of public life, his writings are saturated with social content (Marr 25). One finds there, in particular, his distinct views on human inequality in society. For Emerson, it was nothing more than a "convenient hypothesis" or an "extravagant declamation" to declare that "all men are born equal," for he understood that the reverse was true. He believed that the inequality built into human society indicates "the design of Providence that some should lead and some should serve" (*Journals* 2: 42, 43). This notion, a secularized version of the Calvinistic conception of predestination, is supremely illustrated in American history by John Winthrop's statement on board the *Arbella* in 1630: "God Almightie in his most holy and wise providence hath soe disposed of the Condicion of mankinde, as in all times some must be rich some poore, some highe and eminent in power and dignitie; others meane and in subjeccion" (116–17). The idea of natural inequality was thus an inevitable corollary of the Calvinistic doctrine that "eternal life is foreordained for some, and eternal damnation for others." In fact, Calvin himself, who "tended to stress the Old Testament, with its patriarchal and aristocratic concept of society" (Horton and Edwards 37), adapted the principle of the soul's predestined fate to justify a hierarchical social structure. Naturally leadership in society and prosperity in business were regarded as evidence of God's favor by those self righteous Calvinists who considered themselves among the elect. Predestination, however, is neither a Christian concept unique to Calvinism, since it dates back at least to

Augustine's writings (Horton and Edwards 10), nor even a Christian monopoly: it was also elaborately developed in the caste system of Hinduism and in the metempsychosis doctrine of Buddhism, which holds that one's social position is determined by one's karma. Besides, it was more than a religious idea. Originally a political ideology of primitive societies, it found expression in various versions of the divine origin of royal power. Still, Emerson's understanding of predestination parallels the Calvinistic one. Most significantly, both versions have a double vision of human (in)equality. Many Calvinists made a clear distinction between the spiritual realm, in which human beings could be equal before God, and the temporal realm, in which human inequality was seen as a manifestation of God's judgment (Fredrickson, *White* 140–45). For them, the secular hierarchy was as immutable as the spiritual equality. Thus, they contained the political and social implications of Christianity's potentially revolutionary ideas. If they even considered equality in society, they regarded it at best as what Fredrickson calls "*Herrenvolk* equality"—that is, master-race equality (*White* 154). A similar elitism characterizes Emerson's work, coexisting with an all-embracing egalitarianism. In his ideas on society, equality, race, and history, this elitism circumscribes his otherwise universalistic doctrines.

Emerson regards society as an organic whole comprising mutually dependent classes in a harmonious relationship. In this organic society, everyone has a specific niche. Like most social organicists, Emerson believes that an individual's social position should be "proportioned to his means and power." He finds one merit even in slavery, "the pricing of men," and goes so far as to wish to have an "anthropometer" to determine the proper place for every member of society (*Works* 10: 47, 48–49). True to his elitism, his social organicism is thus hierarchical. He is interested, however, not so much in stratifying social classes in detail as in dichotomizing human beings into leaders and the mass.[4] In Emersonianism, the mass are "rude, lame, unmade, pernicious" and need to "be schooled" by the leaders (*Works* 6: 249). Since the mass cannot attain their full human potential unless they follow the steps of their superiors, the leaders' relationship to the underlings is paternalistic. Emerson's tendency to dichotomize humanity into higher and lower groups inclines him to read all differences as natural hierarchies. The danger of this view is most evident when the generalization is applied to a multiracial society.

Emerson's abstraction of individual differences to define the character of groups becomes more pronounced, and even cruel, in his ideas on race. Because his social organicism sees the existing racial hierarchy as naturally evolved rather than as artificially imposed, it necessitates, by its internal logic, a racist view. Emerson thinks it "fit" for a race to live at the expense of other races, since "eaters and food are in the harmony of nature" (*Journals* 9: 124). While this conclusion might be an objective observation on the cannibalistic dimension of human evolution, it is, in fact, a prejudiced notion concocted to justify the a priori racist idea sanctioning the dominance of the Saxon. According to Emerson, each race grows as its genius determines, some to triumph, some to annihilation. The racial differences are essentially permanent, since each race is assigned a different degree of intellect and the barriers between races are insurmountable (*Journals* 2: 43). It follows that the dominant race has attained its hegemony naturally, thanks to God's selection and its own powerful genius. For Emerson, the Saxon is the master race and its divine mission is to civilize the world. His Saxonism is frankly imperialistic, for he is sure that the Saxon will absorb and dominate "all the blood" and conquer "a hundred Englands, and a hundred Mexicos" (*Essays* 958). All other races are temporary beings destined to serve the Saxon and to lose their lives at the end of their terms: they are inferior races who "have quailed and done obeisance" before "the energy of the Saxon" (*Journals* 12: 152). His xenophobic Saxonism makes the German and Irish immigrants transient beings transported to America only "to ditch and to drudge, to make corn cheap, and to lie down prematurely to make a spot of green grass on the prairie" (*Essays* 950).

Although Emerson's racism was directed indiscriminately at non-Saxon races, it was vented most acrimoniously against blacks.[5] As early as 1822, Emerson wrote in his journal, "I saw, ten, twenty, a hundred large lipped, lowbrowed black men who, except in the mere matter of languages, did not exceed the sagacity of the elephant" (*Journals* 2: 48). These blacks are described in terms similar to those used by racist linguists to support a prognathic hypothesis of black English and are consequently compared to an animal. In 1838, blacks were dubbed "preAdamite" (*Journals* 7: 84). They were sentenced to death in the 1840s: "It is plain that so inferior a race must perish shortly" (*Journals* 7: 393); blacks are destined to "serve & be sold & terminated" (*Journals* 9: 125). Emerson's racism is most clearly expressed in his prescriptive argument, in 1848, for the (merciful) extermination of the black race: "It is better to hold the negro race an inch under water than an inch over" (*Journals* 10: 357). His journal entries of the 1850s continue to record his bias: blacks have "a weakness" and "too much guano" in their race (*Journals* 11: 376); they stand "in nature below the series of thought, &

in the plane of vegetable & animal existence" (*Journals* 13: 35); they are created "on a lower plane than" whites and have "no origination . . . in mental and moral spheres" (*Journals* 13: 198); they are destined "for museums like the Dodo" (*Journals* 13: 286).

Scholars have been embarrassed by the racist motif undercutting the apparently egalitarian doctrines in Emerson's works. The general trend of Emerson criticism has been to explain away the disparity somewhat superficially or to emphasize his abolitionism without taking due notice of the jarring voice. But Emerson's racism is not a marginal element in his writing that can be easily dismissed; neither was Emerson an active abolitionist in the antislavery movement.[6] If one of the criteria differentiating a proslavery apologist from an antislavery crusader was recognition of the black's humanity, Emerson was as limited an abolitionist as he was "a relatively mild racist" (Nicoloff 124), for he was not quite sure on this point. Len Gougeon, an Emerson scholar concentrating on Emerson's abolitionism, emphasizes that Emerson's public pronouncements after 1837 never expressed "his occasional doubts about the Negro's racial equality" and that Emerson denounced "the old indecent nonsense about the nature of the negro" in an address commemorating the West Indies Emancipation (574). Nevertheless, Emerson's lingering skepticism about the blacks' racial equality and even about their human nature continued to surface even after that much acclaimed address. This attitude was inevitable for Emerson, however much he wanted to be clear of historical and social restraints, for he could not help being a member of a society deeply steeped in the myth of white supremacy.

Shaped by the prejudices of his age, Emerson's racial ideas echoed the propaganda of the proslavery apologists. We can find in Emerson most of the important proslavery arguments: polygenesis, biological determinism, pre-Adamitism, survival of the fittest, the blacks' arrested evolution, and the eventual extinction of the black race. Given the social reality, it is not at all surprising that Josiah Nott, a major proslavery theorist, vindicates the peculiar system of racial subordination by resorting to the same logic and terminology that Emerson uses: "Nations and races, like individuals, have each an especial destiny: some are born to rule, and others to be ruled. No two distinctly-marked races can dwell together on equal terms" (468). Nott goes on to say that the Caucasians are destined to conquer and hold "every foot of the globe" and that the blacks will pass away after having fulfilled their destiny. Like Emerson, he regards the black as inferior to the white because the black's "mental and moral" structure is deficient. Nott and Emerson also share a white-racist view of history and celebrate white imperialistic expansion. For both of them, polygenesis is the first step in demoting the black to subhuman status, and the expectation of the black's eventual extermination is the ultimate result of this logic. In between lies the popular teleological racism that views blacks as destined by providence for slavery.

Emerson was not the only abolitionist who echoed his ideological opponents' prejudices against the black. The prejudices were so pervasive that they were expressed explicitly or implicitly in most antislavery speeches and writings, subverting the orators' official ideology. The abolitionists were torn between humanitarianism and racism. It was one thing to write addresses and articles condemning slavery as the worst sin, and it was quite another to accept the supposedly inferior ex-slave as one's equal in society. Consequently, while disowning social egalitarianism, many antislavery crusaders propagated abolitionism abstractly.[7] In fact, as scholars have shown, it was common for white abolitionists to avoid the issue of racism and social transformation altogether by resorting to "abstractions about humanity" to argue their position: "When . . . emancipation . . . was translated to mean only . . . repentance of the sin of slavery, the needs of the human beings who were slaves were ignored" (Pease and Pease 695). In the same manner, Emerson eased the strain of his double vision on abolitionism and blacks by seeing slavery fundamentally as a moral concern for whites, not as a politicosocioeconomic issue of black white relations.

Emerson's moral interpretation of slavery was best expressed in his speech at a meeting of the Massachusetts Anti-Slavery Society in 1861:

> They say that the Asiatic cholera takes the vital principle out of the air by decomposing the air. I think it is the same with the moral pestilence under which the country has suffered so long; it actually decomposes mankind. The institution of slavery is based on a crime of that fatal character that it decomposes men. . . . The moral injury of slavery is infinitely greater than its pecuniary and political injury. ("Ungathered Address" 41)

In this extemporaneous address, Emerson made no mention of "Negroes" and their predicaments, as he had avoided, in earlier abolitionist speeches, referring to the oppressed blacks and had emphasized only slavery's adverse effects on the minds of whites. If he did mention the blacks, he usually depicted them as mere objects by means of which the whites could exercise spiritual transcendence. In other words, Emerson's abolitionism was motivated primarily by his concern for the "corrupting and denaturalizing" ramifications of slavery rather than for the blacks' denied humanity. From this perspective, the West Indies Emancipation interested Emerson mainly as a concession from the whites. He called the event "a moral revolution," since the masters voluntarily gave up their mastery over the slaves (*Works* 11: 140). The blacks were permitted to enter the human family because they had won "the pity and respect" of the whites. Emerson thought that the blacks' liberty was a matter of "concession and protection" from whites (*Journals* 11: 412) and that "the conscience of the white" made emancipation in America inevitable (*Journals* 9: 134). As was usual with abolitionists, Emerson endorsed an abolitionism that was at best tinged with a patronizing paternalism.

Yet, Emerson's failure to recognize blacks as independent subjects having the dignity of human personality is not merely an echo of the racism of his time. As I have argued, it is an integral element of Emersonianism. In other words, Emersonianism includes and perhaps implicitly demands a racist dimension. Although Emerson believes in human potentialities, he is neither naively optimistic about everybody's capacity to develop them nor blind to powerful limitations on the will and capability of an individual. For Emerson race can be such a limitation, perhaps the most significant one, since it is predetermined, immutable, and therefore beyond anybody's control. As Cornel West rightly observes, it is closely associated with Emerson's notions of "circumstances, fate, limits—and, ultimately, history," the adverse forces of "the circumstantial, the conditioned, the fateful." In this connection, Emerson's racial ideas are "neither extraneous nor superfluous in his thought" (31, 34). Given the centrality of race in Emersonianism, it is inevitable that Emerson's principles are racially circumscribed and that the black, whose race is "of appalling importance" (*Essays* 792), cannot draw more than Emerson's condescending attention.

II

Emerson's racism, which complicates, limits, and ultimately undoes his liberationist project, is at the heart of Ellison's critique of Emerson in *Invisible Man*. And this critique, in turn, is central to the novelist's comprehensive reevaluation of "the conscious intentions" of American literature (*Going* 40). Ellison thinks that African Americans are absent or subhuman in American literature simply because the writers *"philosoph-*

ically . . . reject" blacks as Americans (*Going* 47). The American Renaissance writers are no exception to this general judgment. Rather, the racial limitations of Emerson, Whitman, and Melville are the very target of his critique in his novel.[8] This emphasis is inevitable for an African American writer who, while consciously claiming the canonical writers' heritage, cannot ignore the irrefutable fact that he is not an implied reader (let alone a producer) of their discourse. From this perspective, Ellison professes to have felt the need to make "some necessary modification" to their visions in order to find his own voice and to define his true relationship to them (*Shadow* xix). This revisionary stance derives from his understanding that even these democratic writers were not free from the moral compromises and insincerities that he finds typical of the American malaise. Accordingly, Ellison appropriates and redirects their visions in his own work and, in so doing, differentiates their racism from what he terms their "imaginative economy," in which African Americans symbolize the downtrodden (*Shadow* 104). This distinction makes it possible for him, in his novel and essays, both to construct his own "usable past" from the American Renaissance and to denounce the canonical writers' illiberal and undemocratic racial ideas.

Ellison puts Emerson in the American tradition of intellectuals whose racial myopia has compromised their democratic visions. Still, he rarely attacks his namesake's racism openly. His most outspoken criticism in essays takes the form of indirection, as when he mentions, without committing himself, Thoreau's remarks on Emerson's "intellectual evasion" (*Shadow* 36). But this indirection, a mode of signification that he defines as "rhetorical understatement," becomes a powerful trope in his novel. Emersonianism provides Ellison's protagonist with guiding lights in his quest for independence from the dehumanizing institutions in America. What we find in the novel, however, is not Emerson's ideas per se; they are revised à la Ellison, whose tactics are, in his own terms, "identification and rejection": he uses Emersonian concepts "while *rejecting* [Emerson's] beliefs, his prejudices, philosophy, values" (*Shadow* 78; *Going* 278).[9] Ellison, then, resembles the musician in a jam session who improvises on the jazz tradition and asserts individuality "*within* and *against* the group" diachronically as well as synchronically (*Shadow* 234; my emphasis). In short, Ellison's strategy is to deconstruct Emerson on the philosopher's own terms: in the narrative proper, where the protagonist reads Emerson literally, Ellison demonstrates that his namesake's ideas do not work for an African American; then, in the narrator's ex post facto ruminations, he modifies, extends, and enriches those ideas. Finally, when he revises the Emersonian doctrine of self-reliance, representativeness, and social organicism, he endows his operative concept of race with positive and liberating connotations that diametrically oppose it to Emerson's. In this way Ellison "change[s] the joke and slip[s] the yoke" (*Shadow* 45).

Appropriately enough, Ellison first attacks the critical reception of the American Renaissance in the Golden Day episode, which gives the novel an enigmatic aura. Lewis Mumford labeled the period from 1830 to 1860 "the Golden Day" because he saw in the "flood of intellectual and imaginative power" that characterized those years "the climax of American experience" (*Melville* 141; *Golden* 91). In his view the dominant tone of the heyday of American cultural history, led by Emerson, was "one of hope" (*Golden* 88). Contrary to Mumford's rhapsodic style, Ellison's surreal description of the Golden Day portrays the chaotic nadir of American racial experience: the dominant tone of the "sinkhole" is one of despair (135); the intellectual and imaginative power of the black intelligentsia is straitjacketed. An observation by Mumford suggests Ellison's reasons for pushing the question of race to the forefront in his revisionist allusion to Emerson and the American Renaissance: "the blight of Negro slavery awakened [Emerson's] honest anger . . . but even this great issue did not cause him to lose his perspective: he sought to abolish the white slaves who maintained that institution" (101). This passage implies that Emerson, despite his advocacy of universal doctrines, failed to understand the racial limitation of his own perspective. Ellison could not have missed this significant assertion in his reading of *The Golden Day*. Indeed, his clear perception of the centrality of race in Emersonianism is evidenced by his consistent association of veiled or unconscious racism with the Emersonian figures in the novel.

It is Norton who first mentions Emerson in the novel. Norton, "a bearer of the white man's burden" (37), has a self-consciously humanitarian attitude toward the protagonist. Even though Norton, in the final analysis, believes that Negroes must be kept in their "proper" place, he is more than a representative of northern liberal intellectuals with limited views on race relations. By his own admission "a New Englander, like Emerson" (41), Norton ultimately merges with the unseen character "Mr. Emerson" into "one single white figure," who, in his "arrogant absurdity," sees the protagonist simply as "a material, a natural resource to be used" (497). Ellison's identification of the Bostonian with Mr. Emerson reminds one inevitably of the historical Emerson, whose philosophy, as I have shown, sheds its mask of idealistic universalism when measured against the real world and discloses a hierarchical and racist account of society.

Similarly, Norton's philanthropy is built on a hidden, corrupt, and power-inflected desire: incest. When incest is signified in a specific cultural setting, its "symbolic meaning" is at issue (Arens 106). At stake in Ellison's depiction of Norton's incest is, then, not the banker's sexual perversion per se but its sociopolitical implications in the context of American race relations. The northern aristocrat's incest may be compared with royal or aristocratic incest in other societies, which was largely dictated, anthropological studies have shown, by extrasexual reasons, such as "maintenance of rank and conservation of property" (Firth 340).[10] The strategy of committing incest to consolidate power and possessions was not unique to non-Western or ancient societies. Frank Whigham notes that aristocrats in Jacobean England tended to "limit exogamy" when their vested interests in the traditional social hierarchy were being threatened by the rise of the middle class (168). Whigham's interpretation of Ferdinand's incestuous obsession with his sister in *The Duchess of Malfi* is illuminating for our understanding of Norton's incest:

> I conceive Ferdinand as a threatened aristocrat, frightened by the contamination of his ascriptive social rank and obsessively preoccupied with its defense. . . . His categorical pride drives him to a defiant extreme: he narrows his kind from class to family and affirms it as absolutely superior. . . . The duchess then becomes a symbol . . . of his own radical purity. (169)

Ferdinand's class-oriented incest wish can be easily translated into Norton's race-oriented incest desire. As Ferdinand is frightened by the upward mobility of the lower class, so Norton is appalled by the vision of blacks' achieving social mobility by slipping across the color line unnoticed. For Norton, blacks' "passing" can be prevented by incest, the most symbolic act to preclude racial amalgamation, to maintain racial purity, and ultimately to consolidate white supremacy. His incestuous preoccupation with such purity assumes the veneer of philanthropy when he is confronted with blacks. He gives money to the incestuous farmer Trueblood in recognition of Trueblood's part in conserving the purity of each race; he invests in the black college that teaches black students where they belong. Since Trueblood's crime has sociopsychological implications from Norton's perspective, his money in both cases functions to ensure the racial hierarchy and to preclude blacks' upward mobility, social and ontological.[11] The banker admits that the "sacred" reason for his philanthropic investment is to construct a "living" memorial to his daughter (45). His "pure" daughter crossed the snowcapped Alps and traveled in, among other countries, Italy and Germany, where aristocrats had been interested in potentially racist eugenics. She is the most suitable symbol of racial purity, since she is dead, unapproachable by any blacks. Just as Emerson regards blacks as mere vehicles by which whites can achieve spiritual transcendence, so Norton relegates black students to the status of living sacrifices on the altar of a white goddess, which he built to sublimate his incestuous yearning for his otherworldly daughter and, more significantly, to guarantee white supremacy. Consequently Norton's philanthropy, like Emersonianism, dissolves when it is confronted with self-assertive blacks in the real world.

Norton is scathingly satirized in his encounters with Trueblood and, at the Golden Day, with the black ex-physician inmate of the veterans' hospital. While Norton assumes an Emersonian pose toward the protagonist, Trueblood is the real Emersonian poet who sees his own chaotic psyche and reveals to Norton what underlies the banker's seeming philanthropy and altruism. Proclaiming "I ain't nobody but myself" (66), the illiterate black sharecropper finds that what is true for himself is also true for the white community and Norton. If Trueblood is an unconsciously Emersonian poet, the "vet" is a consciously "Representative Man" who professes "to put into words things which most men feel, if only slightly" (152). He paraphrases Emerson's understanding of race in identifying the white with "authorities, the gods, fate, circumstances—the force that pulls your strings until you refuse to be pulled any more" (152). His farewell advice to the protagonist is also Emersonian: "Be your own father" (154). He tries to destroy Norton's self-deceptive fantasies by revealing the real identity of the philanthropist: "confusion" (92). But Norton, unable to "look beneath the surface" (151), judges the vet to be "insane." The irony of these episodes is that the true Emersonian poets, because of their race, are not recognized as such by the Emersonian figure (who advises the narrator to read Emerson) and are despised and rejected by the community. Inevitably, Ellison's irony here is directed not only at Norton, this "New Englander, like Emerson," but at Emerson himself.

The historical Emerson, however, is most deliberately undercut by Ellison's depiction of two Emersons. Young Emerson is a typical northern liberal: while he tries to find a place for the invisible narrator in American society, his prejudices do not admit the possibility of any real sharing with the black man. He is not basically different from those who want to keep the narrator subservient, in spite of his seemingly good intention to "disillusion" the naive protagonist. While his stereotyped rhetoric maintains a friendly egalitarianism, he sees the protagonist not as a unique individual but only as a type. The limitation of this quasiliberalism is well disclosed anticlimactically when young Emerson tries to keep the protagonist as his valet. The attempt, aside from its potentially exploitative undertone, satirizes young Emerson as a decadent hypocrite.

Ellison's portrayal of old Emerson is more complex. Probably Bledsoe's letter provides the best description of Mr. Emerson: he is a rainbow figure who gives the narrator "vain hopes" while actually distancing himself as much as possible. He can exert his power from afar: an unseen trustee of the hero, he is also an absent jailer of his own son. This invisible power reminds one of Alfred Kazin's depiction of the historical Emerson: "Emerson owed much of his influence to his private aura; he impressed by seeming inaccessible" (47). This private aura also characterizes old Emerson in the novel. He is the personification of monologic speech: "No one speaks *to* him. *He* does the speaking" (184). In implying that old Emerson would not accept any dialogic and dialectic relationship with others, Ellison alludes to Emersonian doctrines. Nadel finds "a covert form of literary criticism" in this allusion: "the assertiveness of Emerson, his domination, and his failure to communicate with others" (117). Since old Emerson is self-centered, he is in a sense blind to realities. In this connection, it is a double joke that the invisible hero tries to see the invisible Emerson blindly. Old Emerson's inaccessibility to the narrator suggests symbolically that Emersonianism is not intended for the black. Recognizing this ethnocentrism in Emerson, Ellison questions the applicability of Emersonianism as a universal doctrine.

If Ellison wants to appropriate the positive aspects of Emersonianism, he must first erase the gap between the ideal audience and the actual one. In other words, Ellison's main challenge, in seeking to portray his protagonist as an American self, is to clear up and transcend Emerson's racial prejudice so that the hero can break through the outer surface of racial difference to the inner core of common humanity. And the only way to break this racial barrier is to misread "the Negro" in Emerson. When Ellison says that Emerson saw the Negro as "a symbol of Man" (*Shadow* 32), he hints at his own misreading of "the Negro."[12] The black in Emerson's work, if divested of the contemporary racist assumptions and read in the context of Emerson's democratic vision, might transcend any racial identity and have universal implications: the black can represent "Man," not to mention American, whatever Emerson's intentions might have been. In fact, Emerson's racism stems partially from his hatred of human weakness and impotence, qualities emblematized by the Negro's subjection to slavery. Hence the Negro might symbolize a particular position in a cannibalistic natural order; should that position change, he might be taken to represent some other reality in this system. Anybody, whether white or black, is a Negro, if he is not self-reliant enough to be a master of his own life. However, since this symbolism cannot do more than neutralize a negative aspect of Emersonianism, Ellison goes on to play variations on Emersonian senses of self-reliance, representativeness, and social organicism.

But before modifying Emersonian ideas, Ellison needs to send his invisible man underground. Symbolically, the protagonist's descent under ground is a meditative retreat into a deeper level of his mind in the Emersonian framework. An underground room is a perfect place for meditation, since "there's no place like isolating a man to make him think" (458). Thinking is also an important faculty in Emerson, since it differentiates man from beast. More important, it makes a man an Emersonian poet. According to Emersonianism, it is in a deeper level of one's mind that an individual discovers that his is a part of the universal mind (*Essays* 64). In Emerson, the recognition of this identity of all minds is what gives the scholar self-reliance and individuality, thereby making him "the world's eye," the poet. Without this recognition, no one can be a poet in an Emersonian sense. The narrator's subterranean withdrawal, then, is a symbolic ritual of initiation for an Emersonian poet. But seeing alone—finding a universal significance in one's experience—does not make one a poet. One must express one's vision. The Emersonian poet is both seer and sayer. He is the one who sees through the appearance of the world, "turns the world to glass, and shows us all things in their right series and procession" (*Essays* 456). Similarly, the nameless protagonist of *Invisible Man,* after having set out to effect "a transformation from ranter to writer" (*Shadow* 57), articulates the meaning of his experience by his narrative. He has looked inward and writes his memoir with the belief that what is true for him in his private heart is also true for all: "Who knows but that, on the lower frequencies, I speak for you?" (568).

In this connection, the protagonist's withdrawal underground is a rite the invisible man must go through to gain selfhood and voice, prerequisites for universalizing his experience in an Emersonian framework.

The first thing he does in the dark hole is to burn the accumulated identifications and emblems of his former life. When he burns the paper, he is symbolically burning the illusory roles of his past so that he can be reborn with a new identity. Ellison explains that the narrator's movement is both geographical and intellectual: "his movement vertically downward (not into a 'sewer'. . . but into a coal cellar, a source of heat, light and power and, through association with the character's motivation, self perception) is a process of *rising* to an understanding of his human conditions" (*Shadow* 57). But more important, the movement is social: the invisible man is transformed into a communal being in his underground metamorphosis. His movement can be characterized, in Robert B. Stepto's terms, as "immersion (in group consciousness)" through "ascent (to self-consciousness)" (169).

Here we can find Ellison's reworking of Emerson. As has been noted before, Emerson also plays on the descent-ascent axis: descent into self is ascent to the universal. But there is from the first a signal difference between the Emersonian poet and the narrator. An Emersonian poet voluntarily retreats from society, but Ellison's narrator is "clubbed" underground by reality (559). When the invisible man descends into himself, the self he finds is not a spiritual essence so much as a repository for the deepest cultural values of black experience in America. In other words, the self is not a vague Universal Mind but a distinct communal identity. Thus Ellison redefines the self of Emersonian self-reliance, bridging the gap between the personal and the political, the meditative and the active, in ways Emerson could not. From this perspective the protagonist's underground viewpoint both articulates a black experience and simultaneously defines the American reality. Consequently, by insisting on, and having access to, the very historical and racial identity that Emerson associates with helpless fate, Ellison comes to sustain more effectively the Emersonian dialectic of "local" and "universal." After all, fate and freedom qualify each other in Emerson, since they are reciprocal necessities and different moments of the same identity.

The coal pile is a catalyst that transforms an individual black experience into the corporate American experience. It is no accident that the coal pile is thus endowed with a symbolic meaning, since an underground coal pile is associated with a moment of awakening in Ellison's own life. In his essay "The Little Man at Chehaw Station," Ellison records his encounter with four "uneducated Afro-American workingmen" in the basement of a tenement building in New York. These coal heavers were comparing the artistic performances of two famous Metropolitan Opera divas "behind a coal pile." For Ellison, they were the "little men behind the stove," ideal critics of American arts, who cloak themselves in invisibility.[13] The little man, Ellison states, draws on the uncodified Americanness of his experience—whether of life or of art—as he engages in a silent dialogue with the artist's exposition of forms, offering or rejecting the work of art on the basis of what he feels to be its affirmation or distortion of American experience (*Going* 7). Therefore, his experience is an important touchstone for the artistic representation of American experience.

The little man's function in society is both artistic and cultural. Like the coal heavers who criticize the artistic performances of celebrated opera divas, "the anonymous and the lowly" of the American social hierarchy can judge whether or not the mainstream culture represents the complex vision of American experience truthfully. As a reader-critic of American culture, the little man will ask that the relation between his own condition and the condition of others be recognized, because "he sees his own condition as an inseparable part of a larger truth in which the high and the lowly, the known and the unrecognized, the comic and the tragic are woven into the American skein" (*Going* 14). He understands that the American society is pluralistic and that all its tributary cultures are to participate in a heteroglossic discussion to define the corporate American culture. In the framework of this dialogism, no one tributary culture is to be put in a diglossic situation against another tributary culture. Otherwise, the picture will be rejected as distorted.

In a similar vein, the nameless narrator of *Invisible Man* also emphasizes that American culture is not monolithic: "Whence all this passion toward conformity anyway?—diversity is the word ... America is woven of many strands; I would recognize them and let it so remain. ... Our fate is to become one, and yet many—This is not prophecy, but description" (563–64). What the narrator asks for in this passage is the recognition of America's unity in diversity. Although this passage sounds Emersonian, Emerson's idea of diversity differs significantly from Ellison's: Emerson's proclamation of his own individuality relies basically on his hierarchical social organicism; Ellison's organicism is not vertical but horizontal. Therefore, the narrator in fact collapses Emerson's social dichotomy and hierarchy into the dialogical and dialectical framework of society. The harmonious oneness in manyness of American culture will be possible, then, only when all the constitutive voices are duly recognized as equal members. Hence, Ellison argues, there is the cultural necessity of a little man in every group; if he did not exist, he would have to be invented.

Ellison's little man is his signifying revision of Emerson's poet. In fact, Ellison staged his little man in the *American Scholar* 140 years after Emerson's 1837 address "The American Scholar" declared American literary independence. Ellison argues that the gist of Americanization is the vernacular process that created American English out of King's English and liberated American literature from European influence. From this perspective, the little man embodies the American vernacular spirit and is a figure more American than an Emersonian poet who assumes the authoritative voice. The relation between the Emersonian poet and the Ellisonian little man parallels that between Emerson's "Representative Men" and Ellison's "Renaissance Men." Emerson's Representative Men are all canonical European figures: Plato, Swedenborg, Montaigne, Shakespeare, Napoleon, and Goethe. The list is a rather unexpected one for a man who emphasized the American perspective. The Representative Men were basically *others* whom Emerson tried to surpass as a true genius personifying genuine facts or thoughts. Although Emerson just picked up already canonized figures, Ellison fabricated the notion of the Renaissance Man and became one himself. His roguish Renaissance Man is a vernacular man of versatility and possibility. Ellison mentions specifically that his ideal hero would overcome any limitations imposed on an African American by the racist society (*Shadow* xiv). Rejecting virtually any categorization, the Renaissance Man has the most incongruous characteristics imaginable. He is born out of, to use one of Ellison's favorite terms, the American "vernacular revolt" against "all ideas of social hierarchy and order and all accepted conceptions of the hero handed down by cultural, religious and racist tradition" (xvi). He is representative of certain desirable qualities of

> [g]amblers and scholars, jazz musicians and scientists, Negro cowboys and soldiers . . . movie stars and stunt men, figures from the Italian Renaissance and literature, both classical and popular . . . combined with the special virtues of some local bootlegger, the eloquence of some Negro preacher, the strength and grace of some local athlete, the ruthlessness of some businessman-physician, the elegance in dress and manners of some head waiter or hotel doorman. (xv–xvi)

In the vernacular spirit, which passes through and beyond the Italian Renaissance, the American Renaissance, and the Harlem Renaissance, Ellison may lay claim to Emersonianism as he reclaims his own voice in its full range. It is toward this perspective that Ellison's protagonist moves. But, the epiphany for the invisible man does not come about suddenly without presage. His retrospection reveals that there have been many cues from those he met in his blind days: the vet who advised him to play the game, "but play it your own way" (151); Wheatstraw, who admonished him not to "deny" a soul brother (170); the old man who sold the yams that made him recognize his "birthmark" and proclaim, "I yam what I am!" (260); Tarp, who passed on to him the filed leg chain that had "a heap of signifying" (379). All these cues acquire new meanings in the protagonist's retrospection and help him recognize his need to affirm his African American folk heritage before he asserts his personal identity. In short, he comes to embrace the resilience and wisdom of his culture after he has been boomeranged to his racial and cultural origins. Particularly, the definition of his own voice depends on his return to the rejected legacy of his grandfather.

The grandfather is more a representative voice of the African American experience than a lineal ancestor of the nameless hero, since his seemingly paradoxical deathbed advice encapsulates the gist of the African American vernacular wisdom for "puttin' on massa." His survival strategy is, Ellison explains, "a kind of jiujitsu of the spirit, a denial and rejection through agreement" (*Shadow* 56). In jiujitsu, one of the basic principles is not to be sucked up into the rhythm of the opponent's pace. Hence the importance of maintaining one's own identity in the struggle between cultural forces. The grandfather's injunction, then, may be translated into a warning against "trying to be Paul" (372)—against the double consciousness that will make the hero "keep running." Only at the end of his nightmarish odyssey, however, does the nameless hero learn the significance of his grandfather's advice, although in the narrator's dreams and subconscious his grandfather keeps asking to be read correctly while sardonically watching him run. In fact, the grandfather is an indispensable, though invisible, figure in the development of the narrative: the narrative proper begins with his sphinx-like advice and ends with his grandson's decoding of its message. Thus the plot of the novel evolves around the advice: the protagonist's frightened flight from, blind reading of, and creative acceptance of it. At first, the hero avoids the advice as if it were a "curse" (17). He associates it with something negative and destructive: "the malicious, arguing part; the dissenting voice, my grandfather part; the cynical, disbelieving part—the traitor self that always threatened internal discord" (327). Later, he follows it literally in his anger against the Brotherhood, a strategy that ends in fiasco. The irony of this episode is that his blind yessing comes to choke himself rather than to undermine the brothers. Finally, after recognizing "the hole" he inhabits in America (559), he realizes the absurdity of his own involvement in his society's effort to make him invisible. This realization makes him comprehend why meekness means treachery and how an African American can "find transcendence" in a racist society (561). The invisible protagonist now understands that the cryptic meaning of his grandfather's instruction is in essence to affirm the principle while denouncing its corruptions and corruptors.

The invisible man's interpretation of his grandfather's precept echoes Ellison's persistent argument that the principle of the American "sacred" documents should be respected notwithstanding its past distortions and appropriations. This echo also points toward three other affiliations linking Ellison, his literary namesake, and the key figures in his novel: these mirrorings connect Emerson with the grandfather, Emersonianism with the grandfather's advice, and Ellison with the protagonist. The association of Emerson with the grandfather has been suggested significantly by Ellison himself, who confesses that Emerson is "as difficult to pin down as the narrator's grandfather" (Nadel 159n). Emerson and the grandfather are omnipresent, powerful voices of the past. They are ideological twins in that both celebrate an individual's identity as a revolutionary anchor. But their teachings are ambiguous and apt to be illusory or misleading; both are not universalistic but limited in their applications. One reason for the ambiguity and limitation is a self-deconstructing element in each teaching: racism for Emerson and spite for the grandfather. So both need to be read creatively, in an Emersonian sense.

Ellison's response to Emersonianism enacts a creative reading of the grandfather's advice: Ellison yesses it to death (in an ironic version of the affirmative Emersonian position) until Emersonianism chokes on him. In this way, like the narrator who reclaims his grandfather as his ancestor, Ellison brings Emerson into his own genealogy while subverting and expanding Emersonianism in the process: as the narrator reads his grandfather's advice while negating its (and his) anger and bitterness, so Ellison affirms the basic ideas of Emersonianism while neutralizing its negative aspect, resocializing its spiritualized, abstract premises, and reinterpreting its monologic, dogmatic, and oracular implications. Thus Ellison both accepts and rejects Emersonianism. This stance, paradoxically, makes him a truer American scholar in the Emersonian tradition, which, by its internal logic, asks for critique and reinterpretation in each age.[14]

NOTES

[1]See Benston, *Speaking;* Bloom; *College Language Association Journal* 13.3; Fabre; Gottesman; Harper and Wright; Hersey; O'Meally; Reilly; and Trimmer.

[2]Rovit's seminal opinion is not elaborated in detail, since his main purpose is less to raise the matter for discussion than to point out that in "And Hickman Arrives" Ellison's attitude shifts in favor of Emerson (38). And Nichols is concerned not with examining why Ellison plays variations on Emersonian principles but exclusively with establishing ironic parallels between an Emersonian scholar and the invisible protagonist. In opposition to Rovit and Nichols, Deutsch argues that Ellison does not reject "Emerson's ideals and ideas themselves" (160). This argument is a half-truth, since Ellison's hero simultaneously accepts and rejects Emersonianism. Finally, Nadel recognizes that Emersonian principles are inapplicable to Ellison's narrator since the invisible man is not the ideal audience for Emersonianism (122)—a significant observation that, nonetheless, is left undeveloped.

> Although Benston mentions Ellison's ambivalence toward Emerson, his essay has not contributed to the critical debate on the issue. He argues that African Americans' self-designation by (un)naming reflects their need "to resituate or displace the literal master/father by a literal act of unnaming" ("I Yam" 152) and rightly notes that Ellison's contraction of his middle name to W is a highly self-conscious act symbolizing his proclamation of simultaneous independence from and identification with Emerson. Benston does not explain, however, how *Invisible Man* represents Ellison's ambivalence, still less the reasons for it.

[3]In discussing Emerson and Ellison, I maintain the presumably generic uses of *man* and *he* that are endemic to their writing. The practical reasons for this decision are obvious, but this usage is not intended to endorse language that is now considered discriminatory.

[4]On various occasions Emerson calls the leaders poets, scholars, aristocrats, superior men, model men, representative men, and men of aim or invention.

[5]Following Daniels and Kitano, I am using the word "racism" in the sense of "the belief that one or more races have innate superiority over other races" (2).

[6]Cabot attributes Emerson's ambiguous position as an abolitionist to his reflective temperament and his habit of thinking about what might be said for the other side, here the slave-holders (2: 426); Gougeon notes Emerson's "temperamental and philosophical" disinclination to address specific and controversial so-

cial issues directly (562); Reynolds understands that Emerson responded ambiguously to the spirit of abolitionism since he had "shrewdly perceived the *immorality* and *uncleanness*" of many abolitionist writings (74).

> Emerson himself, however, recognized that he was not suited to the
> role of active abolitionist, and he frankly confessed that the task of
> speaking for the cause was to him "like Hamlet's task imposed on so
> unfit an agent as Hamlet" (qtd. in Rao 82). He also seemed to lack gen-
> uine interest in his abolitionist speeches and to doubt the effectiveness
> of his rhetorical efforts; in his private correspondence, he confided that
> his abolitionist speeches were "an intrusion . . . into another sphere"
> and were made "without hope of effect, but to clear my own skirts"
> (Slater 373, 470).

[7]Many abolitionists disavowed social egalitarianism lest they be criticized
for denying the established social order. As Lydia Maria Child clearly defines the
principles of abolitionism, they intended no "violence to the distinctions of society" and at best advocated keeping the black at the bottom rung of the social hierarchy as an equal to "the lowest and most ignorant white man in America" (qtd.
in Fredrickson, *Black* 37).

[8]The association of white paint with America and money in *Invisible Man*
demonstrates Ellison's critique of the central concerns—economics and white
supremacy—in Whitman's dealing with the future of African Americans in
America; and Ellison's description of the "democratic [trade] union" that expels
the black protagonist is a criticism of Whitman's unionism. For Whitman's concern with whitewashing America, see his *Gathering* 1: 179–228 and *I Sit* 86–91.
Moreover, the Golden Day episode in *Invisible Man* can be read as Ellison's re-
enactment of Melville's *Benito Cereno,* with a significant difference in the portrayal of blacks. Omans was the first to note the similarity between the two.

[9]Here Ellison anticipates Henry Louis Gates, Jr.'s theory of signification. Ellison's simultaneous acceptance and rejection of Emerson is an example par ex-
cellence of what Gates terms "repetition . . . with a signifying black difference"
("Criticism" 3). Gates argues that black writers' revision or rewriting of antecedent canonical white texts is a common strategy in many post-colonial black
cultures. He understands that a black text repeats white texts "to produce *difference*" (10): repetition is not a blind imitation but a means of affirming one's individuality.

[10]These anthropological studies usually cite as examples the royal families
of ancient Egypt, Thailand, Hawaii, Persia, the Incan empire, and some central-
ized African societies, adding passing remarks on the ancient Greek aristocracy

and the more recent European aristocracy. For a summary of sociological interpretations of royal incest, see Arens 102–21.

[11]For the sociopsychological implications of racial amalgamation, see
Fanon 41–82.

[12]By a "misreading" I mean a symbolic reading, but I prefer the word *misreading* in this context, since Emerson usually intended "the Negro" literally, not
symbolically, although he frequently used "a slave" as a symbol. In his essay
"Twentieth Century Fiction and the Black Mask of Humanity," Ellison argues that
this conception of the Negro was "organic" to, among others, Emerson (*Shadow*
32). But R. W. B. Lewis, who is skeptical of Ellison's argument that slavery and
the Negro were central to Emerson's imagination, understands that Ellison's reading of Emerson is "the critical paraphrase by which every authentic writer creates
a new literary tradition for himself, to suit his artistic needs and abilities" (48).

[13]Although "a little man" as a critic also appears in the Bible, the prototype
of Ellison's little man seems to be "a small black man" in the African Cuban folklore (Gates, *Signifyin(g)* 3–22) rather than "the least of these my brethren" (Matt.
25.34–46).

[14]I gratefully acknowledge the helpful comments of Evan Carton, who read
the earlier versions of this essay with interest and dispatch.

WORKS CITED

Arens, W. *The Original Sin: Incest and Its Meaning.* New York: Oxford University Press, 1986.

Benston, Kimberly W. "I Yam What I Am: The Topos of (Un)naming in Afro-
American Literature." Gates, *Black Literature,* 151–72.

———, ed. *Speaking for You: The Vision of Ralph Ellison.* Washington: Howard
University Press, 1987.

Bloom, Harold, ed. *Ralph Ellison.* New York: Chelsea House, 1986.

Cabot, James Eliot. *A Memoir of Ralph Waldo Emerson.* 2 vols. Boston:
Houghton, 1887.

College Language Association Journal 13.3 (1970): 217–334. Spec. issue on Ellison.

Daniels, Roger, and Harry H. L. Kitano. *American Racism: Exploration of the
Nature of Prejudice.* Englewood Cliffs: Prentice, 1970.

Deutsch, Leonard J. "Ralph Waldo Ellison and Ralph Waldo Emerson: A Shared
Moral Vision." *College Language Association Journal* 16 (1972): 159–78.

Ellison, Ralph. Going to the Territory. New York: Vintage-Knopf, 1987.

———. *Invisible Man.* New York: Vintage-Random, 1972.

———. *Shadow and Act.* New York: Vintage-Random, 1972.

Emerson, Ralph Waldo. *The Complete Works of Ralph Waldo Emerson.* Ed. Edward W. Emerson. 12 vols. Boston: Houghton, 1906.

———. *Emerson: Essays and Lectures.* Ed. Joel Porte. New York: Library of America, 1983.

———. *The Journals and Miscellaneous Notebooks of Ralph Waldo Emerson.* Ed. William H. Gailman et al. 16 vols. Cambridge: Harvard University Press, 1960–82.

———. "An Ungathered Emerson Address before the Rowdies at the Anti-Slavery Society in Boston (Jan. 24, 1861)." Ed. Kenneth Walter Cameron *American Transcendental Quarterly Supp. to 36* (1977): 39–42.

Fabre, Michel, ed. *Ralph Ellison.* Spec. issue of *Delta* 18 (1984): 1–131.

Fanon, Franz. *Black Skin, White Masks.* Trans. Charles Lam Markmann. New York: Grove, 1967.

Firth, Raymond. *We, the Tikopia: A Sociological Study of Kinship in Primitive Polynesia.* London: Allen, 1936.

Fredrickson, George M. *The Black Image in the White Mind: The Debate on Afro-American Character and Destiny, 1817–1914.* New York: Harper, 1971.

———. *White Supremacy: A Comparative Study in American and South African History.* New York: Oxford University Press, 1981.

Gates, Henry Louis, Jr., ed. *Black Literature and Literary Theory.* New York: Methuen, 1984.

———. "Criticism in the Jungle." In Gates, *Black Literature and Literary Theory,* 1–24.

———. *The Signifying Monkey: A Theory of Afro-American Literary Criticism.* New York: Oxford University Press, 1988.

Gottesman, Ronald, ed. *The Merrill Studies in Invisible Man.* Columbus: Merrill, 1971.

Gougeon, Len. "Emerson and Abolition: The Silent Years, 1837–1844." *American Literature* 54 (1982): 560–75.

Harper, Michael S., and John Wright, eds. *A Ralph Ellison Festival.* Spec. issue of *Carleton Miscellany* 18.3 (1980): 1–242.

Hersey, John, ed. *Ralph Ellison: A Collection of Critical Essays.* Englewood Cliffs: Prentice, 1974.

Horton, Rod W., and Herbert W. Edwards, eds. *Backgrounds of American Literary Thought.* 3rd ed. Englewood Cliffs: Prentice, 1974.

Kazin, Alfred. *An American Procession.* New York: Vintage/Random, 1985.

Lewis, R. W. B. "Ellison's Essays." In Benston, *Speaking,* 45–48.

Marr, David. *American Worlds since Emerson.* Amherst: University of Massachusetts Press, 1988.

Mumford, Lewis. *The Golden Day: A Study in American Experience and Culture.* New York: Boni, 1926.

————. *Herman Melville.* New York: Harcourt, 1929.

Nadel, Alan. *Invisible Criticism: Ralph Ellison and the American Canon.* Iowa City: University of Iowa Press, 1988.

Nichols, William W. "Ralph Ellison's Black American Scholar." *Phylon* 31 (1970): 70–75.

Nicoloff, Philip L. *Emerson on Race and History.* New York: Columbia University Press, 1961.

Nott, Josiah. "Types of Mankind." *Racial Thought in America.* Ed. Louis Ruchames. Vol. 1. Amherst: University of Massachusetts Press, 1969. 462–69.

Omans, Stuart E. "The Variations on a Masked Leader: A Study on the Literary Relationship of Ralph Ellison and Herman Melville." *South Atlantic Bulletin* 40.2 (1975): 15–23.

O'Meally, Robert, ed. *New Essays on Invisible Man.* Cambridge: Cambridge University Press, 1988.

Pease, William H., and Jane H. Pease. "Antislavery Ambivalence: Immediatism, Expediency, Race." *American Quarterly* 17 (1965): 682–95.

Rao, Adapa Ramakrishna. *Emerson and Social Reform.* New Delhi: Arnold, 1980.

Reilly, John M., ed. *Twentieth Century Interpretations of Invisible Man.* Englewood Cliffs: Prentice, 1970.

Reynolds, David S. *Beneath the American Renaissance: The Subversive Imagination in the Age of Emerson and Melville.* New York: Knopf, 1988.

Rovit, Earl H. "Ralph Ellison and the American Comic Tradition." *Wisconsin Studies in Contemporary Literature* 1.3 (1960): 34–42.

Slater, Joseph, ed. *The Correspondence of Emerson and Carlyle.* New York: Columbia University Press, 1964.

Stepto, Robert B. *From Behind the Veil: A Study of Afro-American Narrative.* Urbana: University of Illinois Press, 1979.

Trimmer, Joseph F., ed. *A Casebook on Ralph Ellison's Invisible Man.* New York: Crowell, 1972.

West, Cornel. *The American Evasion of Philosophy: A Genealogy of Pragmatism.* Madison: University of Wisconsin Press, 1989.

Whigham, Frank. "Sexual and Social Mobility in *The Duchess of Malfi.*" *PMLA* 100 (1985): 167–86.

Whitman, Walt. *The Gathering of the Forces: Editorials, Essays, Literary and Dramatic Reviews, and Other Material Written by Walt Whitman as Editor of the Brooklyn Daily Eagle in 1846 and 1847.* Ed. Cleveland Rodgers and John Black. 2 vols. New York: Putnam's, 1920.

————. *I Sit and Look Out: Editorials from the Brooklyn Daily Times,* ed. Emory Holloway and Vernolian Schwarz. New York: Columbia University Press, 1932.

Winthrop, John. "A Model of Christian Charity." *Colonial American Writing.* Ed. Roy Harvey Pearce. 2nd ed. New York: Holt, 1969, 116–31.

Nabokov and Poe (1995)

DALE E. PETERSON

The pen of Edgar Allan Poe left a ghostly trace in the texts of Vladimir Nabokov, both early and late, in poetry as in prose. As a famous (and famously opinionated) author, Nabokov freely admitted to a boyhood enthusiasm for Poe, but he also claimed in his maturity to have set aside "Edgarpoe" a favorite (*Strong Opinions* 42–43, 64). Such summary dismissals of literary kinfolk typically occurred whenever interviewers pressed Nabokov too hard or too crudely for admissions of influence: "I can always tell when a sentence I compose happens to resemble in cut and intonation that of any of the writers I loved or detested half a century ago; but I do not believe that any particular writer has had any definite influence upon me" (*Strong Opinions* 46). What is most telling about Nabokov's repudiation of so-called literary influences is his assumption that awareness of a stylistic echo removes the spell of an ancestor. It mattered to Nabokov to be clear about matters of apparent sameness; he drew careful distinctions between conscious and unconscious resemblances, between translations and travesties. It follows, then, that Nabokov's pride in his writing's conscious evocation of literary precedent dictated an art of composition that was always close to the wit of parody, inviting a shared enjoyment of decoded references to the features of a precursor. But it so happens that this conception of genuine artistry's appreciation of its own literariness derives in large measure from Poe's own theoretical understanding of the poetic process. It was no accident that parodies of Poe kept recurring throughout the career of the Russian conjuror who specialized in producing verbal mirages of lost love objects. These parodies allowed Nabokov to distance himself from subjection to the "influence" of Poe while consciously (and ironically) continuing to cultivate Poe's poetic principles in a post-Romantic age. There are, in short, larger affinities with Poe than the obvious play with allusions would suggest.

Only recently have literary critics (Maddox 1983, Sweeney 1991) begun to explore the larger effect of Poe's prior texts on Nabokov's poetics, noting the pervasive thematic role of "enchanted hunters" of unpossessed shapes of loveliness and of "purloined letters," cloaked literary thefts, in the poems and narratives of both writers. But scholars have long observed that Nabokov's *Lolita* could not have existed without a love for elaborate parody of Edgar Allan Poe. For understandable reasons, that most notorious and noticed novel has become the focal point for most commentary on the Nabokov-Poe connection. As Alfred Appel Jr. has definitively proven, Poe is the most conspicuous source of allusions in Humbert Humbert's highly literary "confessional" narrative of his romantic quest to possess the essence of "Lolita."[1]

One peculiarity of Lolita's many intertextual references to Poe was already evident to the first explicator (Phillips 1960) who pointed out that Humbert's account of his own romantic affliction drew analogies to Poe's biography as well as to materials from his poetry and fiction. This is important because it highlights the narrator's facile fusion of an artist's life with the artist's texts in stark contrast to the distinction the reader must draw between Nabokov himself and Humbert Humbert. Indeed, one of the permanent challenges faced by critics wishing to account for the exceptional visibility of allusions to Poe in Lolita is how to distinguish between Humbert's invocations and Nabokov's intentions. Humbert is only occasionally aware that the narrative he composes is rehearsing plots that obsessively recur in Poe's writing whereas Nabokov presides in full consciousness over all the allusions that scholars have excavated.[2] The quest to repossess a vanished eidolon (Lolita) and the pursuit of a hallucinated, hidden double (Quilty) replicate central features of Poe's lyrics and detective stories, but Humbert sees an analogous sameness where Nabokov is exposing a parodic difference. Whereas one can appreciate the rhetorical gain Humbert derives from associating his "nympholepsy" with a literary genealogy, the purpose and tone of Nabokov's conspicuous mimicry of Poe remain very much in dispute.

At the outset of his artful confession and seductive narrative, Humbert Humbert speaks a stark truth: "In point of fact there might have been no Lolita at all had I not loved, one summer, a certain initial girl-child. In a princedom by the sea" (*Lolita* 9). The first consequence of this admission is that Humbert himself perceives his Lolita as a spectral love, the phantasmic facsimile of a lost Riviera figure of desire. We learn that his nympholepsy, or condition of being captivated by "nymphets," is a question of focal adjustment: the inner eye of thwarted desire leaps at the chance to impose an archetypal form of loveliness on any semblance that comes along. Visually, then, Humbert's Lolita is presented as a kind of found poem, an involuntary composition, "a little ghost in natural colors" (*Lolita* 11).

But Humbert's Lolita is also simultaneously a made poem, a verbal artifact. As the recuperated image of an initial beauty born in a Poe-etic atmosphere, "a princedom by the sea," Lolita's derivation is as much verbal as optical. She is *consciously* evoked as a reiteration of the already read, as a warmed-over quotation from a haunting literary echo. This Lolita is made of the stuff from which waking daydreams are made—inaccurate translations from poetry into life. As is appropriate to a dealer in Anglo-French poetry manuals for lazy students, Humbert Humbert has conceived a passion for a tawdry American translation of a Continental original who was herself conjured from a sonorous resemblance to Poe's "immemorial" lost love "Annabel Lee." Humbert's narrative reveals a character in whom nympholepsy and literacy have combined to create an endless imprisonment in the zoo of words. In believing that he can reincarnate an unattainable original, Humbert is in the unenviable position of being an unwitting parodist who "relates to" his own invention.

Fortunately, the author who designed Humbert's performed narrative has arranged for his readers to share, yet be liberated from the narrator's captivity. We can see that Nabokov has selected Poe texts as pretexts for visible parody, yet we have also been implicated in envisaging Humbert's Lolita. A lesser artist might well have employed parody, like the proverbial ten-foot pole, to establish a safe distance from an alien presence. But in Nabokov's hands parody made visible is not necessarily risible. It is not a simple instrument of satire. To what end has Nabokov practiced the art of parody?

Nabokov consistently held an unconventional attitude toward parody finding in it something rather more interesting and complicated than transparent rejection of a highly stylized content. The standard Formalist (and Marxist) view insisted that parody was the "destructive or depreciative imitation" of a literary model in which a deliberately stylized speech is marked as the satirized voice of an opposite "other."[3] Nabokov, on the contrary, sensed in parody not a "grotesque imitation," but a playful collision of tradition with critical talent, as in his praise of Joycean parody for the "sudden junction of its clichés with the fireworks and tender sky of real poetry" (*Strong Opinions* 75–76). The fact is that parody is always a form of reluctant tribute to the unforgotten appeal of a once-seductive paradigm. Like a game, parody is a time-consuming artifice that entertains even as it announces itself as an autonomous realm of delusion. Thus, the art of parody admits to a penchant for serious play with transparent illusion. As I shall argue, the practice of Nabokovian parody is quite in accord with Poe's explicit understanding of poetic composition. Nabokov's numerous parodies of Poe are literary tributaries that flow from the common source of inspiration—the insight that genuine poetry is inseparable from the spirit of parody.

One deep and lasting affinity between Poe and Nabokov can be measured by their shared challenge to the platitudes of a "humanist" defense of poetry. Well before Vladimir Nabokov had surfaced as the scourge and public scorner of "human interest" criticism and of the "great ideas" approach to literary merit, Poe had scandalized American public opinion (and even given a *frisson* to Baudelaire) by excommunicating from literary criticism "the heresy of *The Didactic*." Edgar Allan Poe stoutly proclaimed that the proper business of poetry was "the poem which is a poem and nothing more"; the authentic domain of the poetry of words, and the source of its poetic effect, was "the Rhythmical creation of Beauty."[4] Yet a surprising paradox followed from Poe's apparently narrow definition of literary power. For Poe, as for Nabokov, genuine art was both a supremely conscious verbal activity and the mysterious utterance of an intuition beyond common sense and common morality.

In "The Philosophy of Composition" (1846), Poe deliberately deglamorized the myth of poetic frenzy, arguing that the effect of art was to convey a unity of impression that could only be achieved by conscious design—"the work proceeded, step by step, to its completion with the precision and rigid consequence of a mathematical problem" (15). Yet in "The Poetic Principle" (1850), Poe acknowledged that the impetus to conceive and utter a patterned textual unity derived from a higher Intuition, a Platonic shade, of Beauty: "We struggle, by multiform combinations among the things and thoughts of Time, to attain a portion of that Loveliness whose very elements, perhaps, appertain to Eternity alone" (77). (In that very Nabokovian formulation perhaps nothing is quite so like the later Nabokov as that agnostic "perhaps"!) Poe-etic composition was, then, a curiously melancholy and unfree exercise of a conscious fluency in making verbal surfaces and sounds imitate an intuited harmony. This splendid substitute universe of verbal manipulation was cause for both celebration and mourning. Aesthetic utterance was indeed a pale fire, the afterglow of a dazzling premonition. Nabokov's own shadow-poet, John Shade, had surely read both his Plato and his Poe very carefully before phrasing his playful conceit: "Maybe my sensual love for the *consonné/D'appui,* Echo's fey child, is based upon/A feeling of fantastically planned,/Richly rhymed life" (*Pale Fire* 68).

Edgar Allan Poe must be taken seriously as both a precursor and mentor to the Russian grand master of aesthetic play. Nabokov's formative Petersburg years coincided with the heyday of Poe's Russian reputation; Konstantin Bal'mont was busily duplicating for Russians Baudelaire's heroic and harrowing image of an unappreciated "Columbus of new regions of the human soul" (Grossman). With the reissue, in 1884, of Baudelaire's translations, *Histoires Extraordinaires,* all of Europe had the French "metaphysical" Poe at its fingertips. And the Russian climate became especially receptive to the new wave of post-Realist aestheticism after 1895. Well before the erudite poet Voloshin introduced Nabokov in the Crimea to Bely's technical analyses of the relationship of rhythm to meter in Russian poetics, the young Nabokov was surely familiar with the volume in the Nabokov family library, *Ballady i Fantazii,* in which Bal'mont compiled his earliest Russian translations from English of the most famous works of the writer he called the "first Symbolist."[5] Either in the English originals or in Bal'mont's later translations of Poe's literary essays (enthusiastically reviewed by Blok), Nabokov surely was also well aware of Poe's announced poetic principles. In any event, Poe's presence as a technician of rhythmical beauty can be clearly felt in the cadences and themes of the young poet who emerged as the legendary Sirin.

Consider, for instance, both the sound and sense of the first and third quatrains of one of the early poems Nabokov chose to reprint in the 1979 Ardis collection of his verse: "V khrustal'nyi shar zakliucheny my byli,/i mimo zvezd leteli my s toboi,/stremitel'no, bezmolvno my skol'zili/iz bleska v blesk blazhenno-goluboi . . . No chei-to vzdokh razbil nash shar khrustal'nyi,/ostanovil nash ognennyi poryv,/i potselui prerval nash beznachal'nyi,/i v plennyi mir nas brosil, razluchiv." ("Enclosed in a crystal globe were we,/and past the stars flew you and I,/swiftly, silently did we glide/from gleam to blissful sky-blue gleam . . . But someone's breath burst our crystal globe,/halted our fiery rush,/and sundered our timeless kiss,/and hurled us, separate, into a captive world.") The lyric was composed in the Crimea in 1918, before Nabokov had gone into permanent exile or begun to conceive *Ada,* his epic romance of the hellish separation of twin-souled lovers. It resonates in perfect harmony with the music and standard libretto of much Poe-etry. Nabokov is here orchestrating an elegy of angelic displacement that bears rather startling resemblance to a description of young Poe by St. Petersburg's best-known commentator on the American genius: "In practically a childhood poem, his 'Al Aaraaf'— he wasn't twenty yet—he had conceived a self-generated Platonic theory of poetry. The Deity says to the angel-like being, Nisace: 'Leave your crystal star [ostav' svoiu khrustal'nuiu zvezdu], spread your splendor to other worlds . . . reveal my secrets'."[6]

Virtually in his own boyhood, Nabokov had composed his rendition of a fall from a world of higher harmony—in this case, housed within "a crystal globe." In a time before time began, in a kind of primordial amniotic sac, two angelic spirits float in a rapturous unity. Nabokov's verse observes the classic decorum of iambic pentameter with a strict caesura at the second foot, yet it also gracefully scuds into fluent, tripping ternary rhythms. And this effect is similar to Poe's characteristic anapestic lilt which he achieves by alternating line lengths and by making free use of spondees and pyrrhics.[7] Even more typically Poe-etic, however, is the rude rhythmic interruption at mid-poem that coincides with a dramatized fall from grace. Both in "Annabel Lee" and in this early Nabokov lyric, a chilling breath bursts the bubble of a lofty bliss. As the twin-souled lovers are catapulted into a world of time and difference, the strict rule of meter suddenly, rigidly replaces the graceful lilting rhythm.

Exiled to the strictly measured confines of earth-bound mortality, it would seem that only in dreams can "the quiver of astral dust and the wondrous din" of celestial harmonies be recovered. Or so Nabokov's penultimate stanza suggests. But then, as in Poe's allegedly morbid love poems, victory is snatched from the maw of defeat by the power of verbal incantation: "Khot' my grustim i raduemsia rozno,/tvoe litso, sred' vsekh prekrasnykh lits,/mogu uznat' po etoi pyli zvednoi,/ostavsheisia na konchikakh resnits. . . . ("Though we grieve and rejoice apart,/your face, 'midst all the beauteous ones,/I can detect by that trace of starry ash,/ left behind on the tips of every lash. . . .") Here, as in so many of Poe's elegiac love lyrics, a survivor's imagination avidly attaches itself to a spectral image, an eidolon. The Poe-etic speaker knows how to rise to ecstasy inside a sonorous structure of rhymed signs that is the verbal figure for solipsistic glee. Poe's unreconciled champions of a lost, pure love typically create for themselves an artificial paradise of euphonious speech and "lie" by it, the verbal epitaph, forever. Given a high enough fidelity to this incantatory music of resonant sound and reiterated image, nothing "can ever dissever my soul from the soul/of the beautiful ANNABEL LEE."

As evidenced by his melodious and witty lyric of 1918, the young Nabokov could readily imitate and emulate the imperfect, substitutionary bliss of truly Poe-etic evocations of remembered raptures. The lovelorn speaker in Nabokov's poem is a fallen angel who openly acknowledges the catastrophe of differentiation that replaces a perfect celestial harmony. But at the same time, the poem's last stanza makes audible the exiled singer's attempted restoration of "timeless" perceptions. The strain of rebuilding paradise from verbal traces is exposed in the cunningly imperfect rhymes of the last quatrain. The penultimate rhyme is the first imprecise euphony in the entire performance (rozno/zvezdnoi) and the final rhyme enacts the willed substitution of a shadowy part for an irrecoverable whole (lits/resnits). It is as if Nabokov already knew that verbal artistry was, at best, a synecdoche for an ineffable entity, an unspeakable intuition.

Edgar Allan Poe's earliest definition of poetry maintained that it was a distinctive use of language having for its immediate object an indefinite pleasure; a poem was a work "presenting perceptible images . . . with indefinite sensations, to which end music is an *essential,* since the comprehension of sweet sound is our most indefinite conception" (*Essays* 11). More recently, critics have noted that Poe's poetry combines an obsessive theme with an obligatory musicality that deliberately obscures referential meaning. A Poe poem, in one influential formulation, is always the metrical account of an archetypal action, a song-narrative relating the strains of a voice "struggling to say what he has seen in a world so unlike ours that he has difficulty using the language of ours to describe it."[8] Another way of putting the same point rightly emphasizes the melancholy core that fuels Poe-etic composition. Always the activity of verbal creation is occasioned by a prior fall from a happy prescience, "leaving the poet with (and within) a medium that only traces, 'in a nebulous light,' the original and unrepeated creative moment."[9] This way of positioning the genesis of Poe's lyrics creates a noteworthy intersection with Nabokov's life-long obsessive reweaving of lost textures of experience. It was no random coincidence that both Poe and Nabokov dramatized verbal creation as an act of refiguring once-enchanting figures. In Poe's poetry, in Humbert's memoir, and in Nabokov's sophisticated parodies, the verbal sign is an image that remarks the absence of an original, unrepeatable form.

Through Poe's poetic and prosaic example, the young Nabokov

encountered an "otherworldly" shade of Platonic Idealism written into dramas of exiled consciousnesses, enthralled and tormented by what they could vaguely bring to mind through frustratingly imprecise words. In an unpublished parable of January 1923, "The Word" ("Slovo"), a dreaming man wakes in a pearl and jasper heaven wishing to articulate the beauty and suffering of his former existence. He finally is understood by one angel, himself not quite detached from earth, who, taking pity, divulges one word that explains the mystery of the two existences. Crying that word aloud, the man awakes again to mortal life with no recollection of the all-explaining word. Boyd rightly acknowledges that this brief tale is "reminiscent of Poe's symbolic tales," and that it presages the obsessive theme in the later Nabokov of an all-resolving secret uttered only at the borderline between death and life."[10] It is also of interest to note that Nabokov's future bride was already in close psychic harmony with her life-companion's cast of mind; on July 29 of that same year Vera Slonim published next to a Sirin poem in the Russian emigré newspaper *Rul'* her own translation of another of Poe's otherworldly parables, "Silence."[11]

Well before and well after the parodic double exposure of Poe and Humbert in *Lolita,* Nabokov's prose works repeatedly rehearsed the thematics and paradigmatic plots of Poe's tales. In "The Return of Chorb" (1925) Nabokov wittily retraced one of Poe's most familiar compositional paths. In relating the tragicomedy of a widower's project of repossessing his virginal bride through a reverse reconstruction of the perfect image he had wed but not taken to bed, Nabokov was recycling one of the trademark Gothic plots of Edgar Allan Poe. In a series of world-famous stories ("Morella," "Berenice," and especially "Ligeia") Poe had made his own a special variant on the theme of metempsychosis; a distraught artist-lover attempts to transcend loss through artful (though often compulsive) restitutions of the obsessively remembered furnishings and features of an idealized lady love. This motif extends far and wide in the prose fiction of Vladimir Nabokov. It is obviously present in the elaborate, ambitious verbal restorations of the "primal scenes" of romantic ecstasy when Mary, or Zina, or Hazel Shade, or Ada first captivated the imagination of a Nabokovian poet-protagonist. It is a theme still very much present in and central to Nabokov's penultimate novel, *Transparent Things*—a work which also manages to retrieve and elaborate upon a rare and ignored genre that Poe had pioneered: the posthumous dialogue among shades.

Informed readers of Poe and Nabokov eventually have had to ask themselves what to make of certain opaque fictions that are transparently about the afterlife. Just as Nabokov's critics are only lately coming to terms with an undeniable "spectral dimension" in a number of ghostly stories, so, too, Poe scholars only belatedly addressed his baffling angelic colloquies.[12] There are some curious resemblances between the narrative frames of Poe's best known posthumous dialogue, "The Conversation of Eiros and Charmion" (1839) and *Transparent Things* (1972); surely one can suspect that Poe provided one source for the odd genre of vaguely allegorical "physics fiction" that Nabokov served up late in his writing career.[13]

In Poe's short colloquy, a veteran of post-mortal existence greets a newcomer at the threshold of a painless, omniscient realm called Aidenn. His words of greeting carry a significant double entendre: "Dreams are with us no more . . . I rejoice to see you looking life-like and rational . . . I will myself induct you into the full joys and wonders of your novel [*sic!*] existence."[14] This hint of a "metafictional" level of meaning is remarkably close to the benevolent coaching of a disembodied voice that greets Hugh Person (you, person) at the entry point of his posthumous existence as a character recently transferred into the apparent transparency of a textual realm of being. And Poe's fable, like Nabokov's short novel, also contains the irony that the all-seeing privilege of an "afterlife" is employed in seeking the words to depict the feel and sensation of a now-departed world. Although all ties to the mortal coil are severed, an adequate language is sought to recollect the familiar feel of a perished existence. Although a transfer into a new reality has in fact occurred, the verbal medium serves as a vehicle of transport back into an obliterated and unrecoverable world. Expressed this way, Poe's cosmological fantasy of the "angelic imagination" reconceiving an exterminated earthly garden is not so far removed from the fantastic perceptions of Nabokov's poetic sleep-walkers who insist upon superimposing one world on another.

Language must deal in artificial likenesses, in approximations that strive to align sound and sense, signifier and signified. The notion that one can literally re-present or re-produce human experience is a figment of some angelic imagination. What we readers commonly accept as renewed contact with significant aspects of our lives is never more than a ghost play with verbal shades and visual shadows. We contemplate a parody of an obscure primary text.

In Nabokov's writings, as in Poe's poetry and prose fantasies, lyrical commemoration of what has been lost cannot be far removed from the spirit of parody. If parody is understood as a transparent mistranslation of an original text that is distorted, but not beyond recognition, then it is a form of utterance that is akin to poetry as understood by Edgar Allan Poe. A Poe poem draws attention to its own substitutionary inadequacy, being in its obvious artificing of sound and image the pale reminder of an absent form it cannot replace. Poe's poetic principles are Platonic since his melancholy singers understand, like Socrates in the *Cratylus* dialogue, that verbal mimesis always marks a loss: "Names rightly given are the likenesses and images of the things which they name."[15] Words knowingly employed are at their beautiful best but replicas and foreshadowings of an intuited Form that has been eroded in the stream of mortal time.

Parodies of Poe and shades of Plato regularly recur within Nabokov's works. It is not very surprising that Nabokov should have paid regular tribute to his fellow poets of the mind's exile in a lapsed world. Although shy of metaphysics and contemptuous of vulgar spiritualism, Nabokov fully appreciated the need for some recourse to alleviate the pain of early dispossession of a world of remembered harmony and grace. But why, then, the evident impulse to parody his strong predecessors?

A certain type of knowing artistry could provide consolation and even some bliss through conscious parodies and admitted simulations of vanished moments of significance. Thus John Shade, Nabokov's poet of combinational delights, could proclaim: "I tore apart the fantasies of Poe,/And dealt with childhood memories of strange/Nacreous gleams beyond the adults' range" (*Pale Fire* 56). Genuine art was the diversionary play of creative memory; it made possible the joy of a figurative restoration of lost experience within the tyranny of the cruel present. Nabokov's survival artist, himself a Shade, was thus a master parodist whose intellect was well aware of how texts translate the irreversible actuality of worldly phenomena into a new dimension of reflected reality.

Nabokov's many conscious parodies of Poe were themselves schooled in Poe's philosophy of composition. Both writers were explicitly aware of that trick of human consciousness that enables the conjuror of words and images to straddle two worlds at once and, as it were, to get away with "two-timing" life. They composed texts that deliberately exposed the transference and the transport, the genuine otherworldliness, that could be achieved by an inspired and well-regulated manipulation of the sensation-creating medium of language. True poetry is composed as a knowingly inaccurate, but necessary translation of an unforgotten, unrecovered source of inspiration. Poe's poetic principles and example had indeed anticipated that much-quoted conundrum from Nabokov's *Gift:* "the spirit of parody always goes along with genuine poetry" (12).

NOTES

[1]Alfred Appel Jr., *The Annotated Lolita,* 328–32.

[2]The most complete discussions, other than Appel's, of the many allusions in Lolita to Poe's poems and stories may be found in Carl Proffer, *Keys to Lolita,* 34–45, and in Lucy Maddox, *Nabokov's Novels in English,* 72–76.

[3]For a valuable survey of historic definitions of parody, see Henryk Markiewicz, "On the Definition of Literary Parody." Some influential Russian definitions are available in English; see Yury Tynyanov, "Dostoevsky and Gogol: Towards a Theory of Parody" and Mikhail Bakhtin, *Problems of Dostoevsky's Poetics,* 93–96.

[4]The particular phrasings are from "The Poetic Principle" in Poe, *Essays and Reviews,* 75–76.

[5]On the subject of Nabokov's analytic appreciation of Russian verse, see Brian Boyd, *Vladimir Nabokov; The Russian Years,*149–52, and especially G. S. Smith, "Nabokov and Russian Verse Form." In Konstantin Bal'mont, *Edgar Po: Ballady i fantazii,* one finds important early Russian versions of "The Raven," "Annabel Lee," "The Fall of the House of Usher," "Ligeia," and of "Shadow" and "Silence"—those metaphysical parables in a literary form Bal'mont labels in his introduction as unique to Poe, "fantasias that can be called philosophical tales."

[6]Evgeny Anichkov, "Bodler i Edgar Po," 249—a reprinting of his influential article of 1909, "Baudelaire and Edgar Poe." On the importance of Anichkov among educated St. Petersburg readers, see Joan Delaney Grossman, *Edgar Allan Poe in Russia,* 163.

[7]In *Keys to Lolita,* 36, Carl R. Proffer speaks specifically of the "anapestic lilt" created by the rhythmic phrasings of "Annabel Lee"—"I was a child and she was a child,/In this kingdom by the sea;/But we loved with a love that was more than love—/I and my ANNABEL LEE." Incidentally, Smith's statistically based study, of Nabokov's metrics, "Nabokov and Russian Verse Form," displays a clear-cut preference for iambic and anapestic groups, a strong proclivity for exact rhymes and quatrains, and he rather significantly concludes that Bal'mont was probably "his chief mentor in his earlier work" (301–02).

[8]Daniel Hoffman, *Poe Poe Poe Poe Poe Poe Poe,* 59.

[9]Joseph Riddel, 121.

[10]Brian Boyd, *The Russian Years,* 203.

[11]Brian Boyd, *The Russian Years,* 210.

[12]For an early (and literal-minded) pursuit of the supernatural in Nabokov, see William Woodin Rowe, *Nabokov's Spectral Dimension;* the most complete explication of the "metaphysical" dimension apparently signaled within Nabokov's aesthetic is Vladimir Alexandrov, *Nabokov's Otherworld.* On Poe, see Allen Tate, "The Angelic Imagination," for a sophisticated essay on Poe's otherworldly cosmological fantasies.

[13]A fuller version of a parallel reading of *Transparent Things* and Poe's otherworldly fable is in Dale E. Peterson, "Nabokov and the Poe-etics of Composition," 101–04.

[14]Edgar Allan Poe, *Poetry and Tales,* 358.

[15]Jefferson Humphries, in *Metamorphoses of the Raven,* 18–27, offers an elegant explication of the Platonic epistemology that informs Poe's poetics.

WORKS CITED

Alexandrov, Vladimir. *Nabokov's Otherworld.* Princeton: Princeton University Press, 1991.

Anichkov, Evgeny. "Bodler i Edgar Po." In *Predtechi i sovremenniki I; Na zapade.* St. Petersburg: Osvobozhenie, 1911, 213–271.

Appel, Alfred, Jr. *The Annotated Lolita.* rev. ed. New York: Vintage, 1991.

Bahktin, Mikhail. *Problems of Dostoevsky's Poetics.* Ed., trans. Caryl Emerson. Minneapolis: University of Minnesota Press, 1984.

Bal'mont, Konstantin. ed., trans. *Edgar Po: Ballady i fantazii.* Moscow: Izdaniia Bogdanova, 1895.

Boyd, Brian. *Vladimir Nabokov: The Russian Years.* Princeton: Princeton University Press, 1990.

Grossman, Joan Delaney. *Edgar Allan Poe in Russia: A Study in Legend and Literary Influence.* Würzburg: Jal, 1973.

Hoffman, Daniel. *Poe Poe Poe Poe Poe Poe Poe.* New York: Avon, 1978.

Humphries, Jefferson. *Metamorphoses of the Raven: Literary Overdeterminedness in France and the South Since Poe.* Baton Rouge: Louisiana State University Press, 1985.

Maddox, Lucy. *Nabokov's Novels in English.* Athens: University of Georgia Press, 1983.

Markiewicz, Henryk. "On the Definitions of Literary Parody." In *To Honor Roman Jakobson: Essays on the Occasion of His Seventieth Birthday.* Vol II. The Hague: Mouton, 1967, 1264–72.

Nabokov, Vladimir. *Ada, or Ardor: A Family Chronicle* [1969]. New York: Vintage, 1990.

———. *The Gift* [1963]. Trans. Michael Scammell and Vladimir Nabokov. New York: Vintage, 1991.

———. *Lolita* [1955]. New York: Vintage, 1989.

———. *Pale Fire* [1962]. New York: Vintage, 1989.

———. *Strong Opinions* [1973]. New York: Vintage, 1990.

———. *Transparent Things* [1972]. New York: Vintage, 1989.

Peterson, Dale E. "Nabokov and the Poe-etics of Composition." *Slavic and East European Journal* 33.1 (Spring 1989): 95–107.

Phillips, Elizabeth. "The Hocus-Pocus of *Lolita*." *Literature and Psychology* 10 (Summer 1960): 97–101.

Poe, Edgar Allan. *Essays and Reviews*. New York: Viking, 1984.

———. *Poetry and Tales*. New York: Viking 1984.

Proffer, Carl R. *Keys to Lolita*. Bloomington: Indiana University Press, 1968.

Riddel, Joseph N. "The 'Crypt' of Edgar Allan Poe." *Boundary* 27 (1979): 117–44.

Rowe, William Woodin. *Nabokov's Spectral Dimension*. Ann Arbor: Ardis, 1981.

Smith, Gerald S. "Nabokov and Russian Verse Form." *Russian Literature Triquarterly* 24 (1991): 271–305.

Sweeney, Susan Elizabeth. "Purloined Letters: Poe, Doyle, Nabokov." *Russian Literature Triquarterly* 24 (1991): 213–37.

Tate, Allen. "The Angelic Imagination." In *The Man of Letters in the Modern World*. New York: Meridian Books, 1955, 113–31.

Tynyanov, Yury. "Dostoevsky and Gogol: Towards a Theory of Parody." In *Dostoevsky and Gogol: Texts and Criticism*. Ed. Priscilla Meyer and Stephen Rudy. Ann Arbor: Ardis, 1979, 101–17.

PART III

Overviews

All the New Vibrations: Romanticism in 20th-Century America (1969)

RONALD L. DAVIS

Throughout the first three centuries of the development of the United States, the American character was formed into a pragmatic, absolutist, materialist framework. The initial impetus was furnished by the Puritans; then came the frontier experience, and finally the rapid industrialization during the age of Enterprise. Traditionally, Americans have been instinctively realistic and outer-directed, concerned primarily with the physical world they have been so bent on conquering. Although the American intellect theoretically went through a period of romanticism during the first half of the nineteenth century, this romantic experience was always on tentative ground and remained for the most part artificial. Most of the subtleties of European romantic thought were meaningless to America, and this was particularly true of the pessimistic, introspective, brooding strains.

But in the years before World War I, the first discernible cracks began to appear in the materialistic-realistic-pragmatic wall, and the sands of tradition began to shift beneath. By the turn of the century the limitations of an ungainly material system and the complications of industrialized society were becoming apparent to a maturing group of American artists and intellectuals. The rise of Bohemian cults in New York, Chicago, San Francisco, and elsewhere clearly demonstrated a disgust with traditional American values, as did the expatriates of the literary world, most notably T. S. Eliot, Ezra Pound, and Gertrude Stein.

After the war, amid the prosperity of the 1920s, the explosion came, still restricted largely to the intellectual world, but filtering down in perverse forms to the flapper and the raccoon-coat set on college campuses.

Partly as a reaction against the blatant materialism of that decade, partly as a general disillusionment over the war and former ideals, partly as a result of the growing complexity of modern life, Americans began turning away from a physical orientation to become more introspective. As this happened, the American mind, for the first time, began identifying with certain tenets not unlike those of classical nineteenth-century romanticism.

Few intellectual currents are more difficult to establish than that of romanticism. Scholars can be sent into an uproar at the very mention of the term, and graduate seminars have been known to disband without having settled on a definition. The complexity of romantic thought is one of the movement's few consistent characteristics. But some romantic ideals do seem apparent. By and large the romantic has looked at the society in which he lives, analyzed it intellectually, and then alienated himself from this society, finding it mechanical, regimented, chaotic, and incomplete. The true romantic, however, detaches himself from society not to escape reality, but to embrace it more fully by enlarging his definition of truth to include human emotion, illusion, and intuition. To the romantic, the realist (by concentrating on the material, physical, and factual aspects of life) conceives the world in limited terms and fails to see problems in their total complexity. For the romantic, truth is an individual matter and can be discerned only through use of reason, emotion, and passion. The romantic approaches this search for truth with nobility and enthusiasm—borrowing ideas from nature, from simpler societies, from civilizations of the past, and from behavior considered exotic—somberly, even pessimistically, aware that the answers he seeks may never appear.

The romantics, according to Jacques Barzun, "were forced . . . to take stock of the universe anew, like primitives, because the old forms, the old inter-subjective formulas, had failed them." Even before the close of World War I, the United States, along with most of western Europe, found itself uncomfortably being forced to take stock of its universe anew. So convinced were the European Dadaists, in fact, that the old formulas had failed that they actually sought to destroy western civilization through ridicule and laughter. But the optimism in which America had been nurtured was still too ingrained for the extremism of Dada to make much lasting impression here. Instead, the American intelligentsia of the 1920s began broadening their concept of reality to include the widest possible range of sensations, questing less after material progress and more for the sublime emotional and intellectual experience.

Among those who most clearly came to perceive technological advancement as a mirage was Sherwood Anderson. Reared in Ohio, Anderson suddenly walked away from his declining paint factory one day, went to Chicago, and joined the literary rebellion going on there. His most successful novel, *Winesburg, Ohio,* was published in 1919. For Anderson the conventional world was a snare, and life was filled with loneliness, man isolated from man. His characters are involved, usually unconsciously, with breaking away from a materialistic society that for the individual is humiliating, degrading, and stifling. Through Anderson's works walks a procession of deviates—alcoholics, sexual perverts, and the rest—who have become twisted through an inability to find satisfactory outlets for their emotions. His heroes end by escaping from the prison cast by society, progressing toward some obscure horizon, seeking some chance to rekindle their sinking spirits. To Anderson the personal quest is vague, yet for the achievement of individual happiness the "living force within" somehow must find expression. At all costs "poetry and vague thoughts" must not be destroyed by the industrial giant.

With Ernest Hemingway the romantic tendencies of the twenties became more conspicuous, finding almost a classic expression. Hemingway saw the world as chaotic, violent, purposeless, filled with death, disaster, and horror. And yet out of the ashes of futility man could emerge as something beautiful and noble, if the individual could but preserve himself in a decadent society and conduct himself with dignity and valor. The only real virtues to Hemingway were personal virtues, the only immortality a triumph in oneself, preferably in one's art. Amid a web of fatalism, Hemingway's heroes found their brief happiness quietly and apart from society, revealing themselves as monuments of personal courage and displaying nobility in a world that gave little in return. As for the bullfighter or the hunter, death—the great Nada or Nothingness—must be accepted with courage and fortitude, so that even in that moment of final agony, honor and beauty emerge triumphant.

By contrast the tragedy of F. Scott Fitzgerald stems largely from his inability to escape emotionally the society that would eventually destroy him. Although convinced that the values of the older generations were no longer valid, Fitzgerald's preoccupation with contemporary middle-class society was incessant. In many respects the perpetual college sophomore, at least through the 1920s, he never lost his fascination with the American success story, wealth, social glamour, and the tinsel world of the playboy. And yet, underlying all of this was a sense of inherent disaster. In his adolescent wisdom Fitzgerald recognized a need for something more—a philosophical something he was never able to discover. Herein lay the source of his self destruction. Unable either to accept a position of reform realism such as Sinclair Lewis advocated or to adopt the romantic idealism of Hemingway, Fitzgerald was battered from two directions, sensing the limitations of society without being able to change it or leave it. In his obsession with being society's darling, he was forced to remain a part of a weary, superficial world his mind essentially disowned. Thus he became the tragic symbol of a disturbed age, itself "beautiful and damned" and groping between two opposing viewpoints.

With dramatist Eugene O'Neill the dilemma is considerably different, for certainly his intellectual strain is deeper than Fitzgerald's, his detachment from society and his commitment to a romantic view point more complete. O'Neill possesses the brooding inwardness characteristic of romanticism, he sees the anguish of the sensitive individual in twentieth-century society, and his tormented characters seek desperately to know what lies "beyond the horizon," as they struggle to find meaning in a world that seems essentially empty of meaning. Yet for O'Neill success or failure matters little; it is the struggle that is worthwhile. Suffering and the very need to explain suffering are for him the source of man's action and creativity. At the same time, ill-fated though he may be, man is ultimately a free agent, bringing most of his grief upon himself. But when man out of his feeling of "lostness" seeks to belong to humanity, his freedom is lost. By belonging he abdicates his individualism and becomes a passive vegetable at the mercy of forces outside his control. Man's only hope of controlling his destiny lies in remaining existent within himself.

O'Neill sees quite clearly that the individual cannot live without illusions, that these become part of reality, and in this the playwright is comfortably a romantic. His exploration of emotion, such as the terror depicted in *The Emperor Jones,* his use of symbols, his probing of the subconscious, and his attempts at revealing the thoughts of his characters through the use of masks, as in *The Great God Brown,* all make him at home in the romantic scheme. His limitations as a romantic stem mainly from certain naturalistic tendencies, especially his concern for environmental detail and a pessimism so intense that at times O'Neill seems to suggest that life and art may not after all be worth the struggle. The true romantic, despite his melancholia, remains convinced that life and art can be worthy and beautiful if only the nobility of the individual can survive.

Less penetrating was the romantic impulse in the art of the twenties, although a number of painters were at least flirting with romantic concepts. While academic objectivity and an "ashcan" realism of the George Bellows genre continued, a minority, reacting against what they considered misuse of intelligence, dismissed reason by emphasizing primitive, childlike, dreamy qualities in their work, even abandoning at times the consciousness of the real world. The abstraction, expressionism, and cubism of the prewar years continued, but with an additional hedonism and a restless, highly personalized experimentalism. In a decade of abundant prosperity, with no national calamity imminent, the experimentalists felt themselves less an organic part of society than ever before and became unconcerned with combating social evils. For them a pure aestheticism of art for art's sake reigned supreme. This was at least a step in the direction of romanticism. While Dada made only slight impression on American art, its offspring, surrealism, attempted to synthesize inner and outer reality—obviously a broadening of the concept of realism, one in which emotion played a considerable part. In a different way, through form and color, Georgia O'Keeffe achieved an emotional intensity that took her even closer toward romanticism. "In her art," Edgar P. Richardson says, "loneliness, silence, the inner world of contemplation became a new form of poetry of unmistakable eloquence and personal accent."

Still vaguer were romantic tendencies in music, particularly since America's serious composers as late as the twenties were more concerned with musical form than with philosophical orientation, a position which often resulted in a separation of music from life. Young composers like Howard Hanson continued to use a musical idiom that harked directly back to the nineteenth-century European romantic tradition, but this simply reflected a nostalgia for an earlier musical style rather than a discontent with the contemporary world or an effort to broaden the dimensions of artistic creativity. Other composers, like Gershwin, Copland, and Thomson, took a fairly romantic look at folk themes and aspects of the American locale, but in each case the romantic impulse was rather superficial, the breadth and depth of the true romantic never really coming into view. Experimentation, breaking the bonds of tradition, was certainly present in the work of George Antheil, the American *enfant terrible* of the period—his *Ballet Mécanique,* in which he used horns, buzz saws, and airplane propellers, seeming especially revolutionary in its first performance at Carnegie Hall in 1927. But Antheil lacked most of the other ingredients essential for genuine romanticism. His fascination with technological development was obviously more intense than the romantic ideal would normally allow. Carl Ruggles came closer, rugged individualist to the core, separated if not alienated from society, and composing almost exclusively for himself and his own artistic satisfaction. Still, the early jazz of the decade—the improvised, emotional outpourings of Oliver, Armstrong, and Beiderbecke—and the earthy, poignant blues sung by "Ma" Rainey and young Bessie Smith were probably far closer to a true romantic ideal than anything taking place in the art music of the period.

The significance of the 1920s is that a breakthrough was being made toward a redefinition of American values, at least within a limited stratum of the intellectual world. While few out-and-out romantics emerged on the scene, American intellectuals began seriously questioning the traditional materialistic-pragmatic-realistic complex—at the very time when society generally seemed to be lauding these principles as never before. As the intellectual rebellion matured, certain romantic features began to creep in, paralleling the growing alienation from society. The prosperity of the decade and the lack of apparent need for social involvement permitted key thinkers to build for themselves their own world with an individualistic value system and allowed them to expand their concept of reality to include meaningful illusions.

But with the stock market crash of 1929, and the resulting depression, a society in peril began calling her alienated back into the fold. As a social conscience returned, so did most of the traditional American values—most certainly hard work, material concern, practicality, and hard-nosed realism. While Hemingway and a few others might continue to focus on abstractions, and still others resorted to flights of unmitigated escapism, most of the artists of the thirties and early forties became caught up in the immediacy of first the Great Depression and then World War II. Amid calamity of such proportions esoteric romanticism, with its emphasis on the nobility of the isolated individual, had little chance for survival. Instead the social realism of John Steinbeck became more typical, and the pessimistic strains of the neo-romantics were replaced by a determined optimism which indicated that disaster, no matter how grave, could be over come if somehow "the people" could just stick together.

At the same time the Depression and World War II, from the long-range viewpoint, played their part in softening traditional American optimism. Toward the end of the war the grim implications of the atomic bomb became apparent, and the realization dawned that any peace achieved would be an uneasy one. Thrust into the turmoil of the postwar world, Americans for the first time began to seriously question the divinity of technology. The very inventiveness with which Americans had been gifted for so long had finally advanced to the point that a weapon had been devised capable of total destruction. On a lesser scale, but of no less immediate importance, industrial technology had been developed to such proportions that the individual appeared entwined in a mechanistic web over which he had little control. Threatened by personal suffocation on the one hand, by annihilation on the other, mid-twentieth century America, intellectually more mature after two recent disasters, resumed the search for a more meaningful value system. And again, now more definitely than in the 1920s, the path led toward romanticism—a path traveled this time not just by select intellectuals, but by a discernible portion of the general public as well.

Probably at no time since the French Revolution have conditions appeared more chaotic and complex than in the contemporary post-war world. Pessimistic, confused, and downright afraid, Americans have recently entered an exploration of human emotion that is unprecedented in our history. Individualism is being redefined increasingly as a personal matter of the inner self, while the numbers of society's alienated have grown beyond counting. For youth particularly, nothing is more desirable than being permitted the freedom to "do your own thing." In most instances doing one's own thing is an emotional and intellectual experience rather than a physical one. Making a comfortable niche for themselves in society might have been a satisfactory goal for the generation of the thirties and forties; but the present youth, having known nothing but prosperity, are much more concerned with a quest for "something else," an intangible something which they sense is essential if life is to have meaning, before happiness is possible.

Yet underlying this search for a more relevant set of values is a strong sense of tragedy. Existentialism, which both in pure and diluted forms has permeated so much of recent American thought, is bathed in this feeling of despair, emphasizing the evil in man, his irrationality, and the futility of his situation. For most existentialists the only hope for man is to escape from earthly chaos by denying objective reality—a reality which is, after all, merely illusion. Their goal is to recapture man's true individuality, but liberation can be achieved only by recognizing life as absurd. The existentialist hero, such as Yossarian in Joseph Heller's *Catch-22*, is essentially an anti-hero, who accepts living in a world of insignificance and turmoil. On a more popular level motion pictures and television series of late have abounded in nonheroes of the type depicted in *Blow-Up* or on *Have Gun, Will Travel* and *The Man from Uncle*, or portrayed time and again by Steve McQueen and Paul Newman.

Theologians, even during World War II, began stressing man's inherent depravity and the relativity of human values. For Reinhold Niebuhr too much optimism has been man's consistent error, poorly equipping him for the vicissitudes of life. Instead, Niebuhr offers a tragic view of history, based upon a recognition of man's limitations and the impermanence of his accomplishments. In the 1950s Americans were enchanted into a morning ritual of devouring echoes of this theology through Charles Schulz's comic strip *Peanuts*. Reflecting his certainty of man's fundamental evil, Schulz's children are savage in their torment of one another, full of insecurities, colossal in their failures. Only Schroeder, absorbed completely in the art of his toy piano; Linus, bound to his blanket for security; and the dog Snoopy, dwelling in a world of illusions from supper dish to supper dish, approach contentment. Meanwhile, Charlie Brown, the cartoon's anti-hero, is a born loser, bungling his way through life, a bundle of neuroses, with nothing to look forward to but an adulthood that somehow he suspects will be worse.

But for most contemporary writers, man in society is more corrupt than man alone. Certainly this is true of J. D. Salinger, who is vitally concerned with the survival of the sensitive individual in a vicious world. A recluse in his own life, Salinger sees alienation as the only way for the intellectual to exist in a society bent on his emotional destruction. In his early novel *Catcher in the Rye* (1951), sixteen-year-old Holden Caulfield finds the world full of phonies, yet while he is incapable of accepting them, neither is he able to isolate himself. Repulsed by a society he wants desperately to join, he stands in limbo, on the threshold of manhood, already nostalgic for his youth and vanishing innocence, uncertain of his own emotions. His moment of supreme pleasure comes while watching his younger sister, Phoebe, happily riding a carousel:

> I felt so damn happy all of a sudden, the way old Phoebe kept going around and around. I was damn near bawling, I felt so damn happy, if you want to know the truth. I don't know why. It was just that she looked so damn *nice,* the way she kept going around and around, in her blue coat and all. God, I wish you could've been there.

But in the Glass family stories, Salinger's characters have moved a step farther. They willingly cut themselves off from society, even revel in doing so. The Glass children are brilliant (all former Quiz Kids), sensitive, yet emotionally unstable. They have sought refuge by withdrawing into themselves, speaking in symbols that only they understand, believing in a vague mysticism, held together by an idealization of Seymour, their brother who by committing suicide has become the source of the family's moral fiber. Contact with the ordinary world is plainly too much for the Glasses, and they cope with it only in an abstract way. "There isn't anyone anywhere that isn't Seymour's Fat Lady," Zooey tells Franny at the height of her emotional crisis. "Don't you know that god-dam secret yet? And don't you know—*listen* to me, now—*don't you know who that Fat Lady really is*? . . . Ah, buddy. Ah, buddy. It's Christ Himself. Christ Himself, buddy." Along the line Salinger has become a thoroughgoing neoromantic, and his Glass family emerges as something of a summary of inner-directed individualism. Comparing the contemporary romantics with those of the nineteenth century, Henry Grunwald writes, "the romanticism of the present American generation is more private, more limited, more given to introspection than to the dream, marked by the small gesture rather than the large escapade." This is the romanticism which J. D. Salinger epitomizes.

But equally romantic in his specialized way and no less convinced of society's devastating impact on the sensitive individual is Tennessee Williams. Williams's major characters are most often as delicate, as initially innocent, as gentle, as beauty-haunted, and as pure as Salinger's Glass family; the difference is that Williams's anguished lack the ability to break away from society, are unable to barricade themselves from cruelty and pain, and are thus battered and crushed by the soulless brutes around them. In Williams's view, says R. H. Gardner, "Life is a jungle of monstrous beings preying upon one another, in which only the most brutal survive." Unable to deal with the harshness of human existence, Williams's characters struggle with the problems of their nightmare world, resort to fantasy and sensuality for temporary asylum, are plagued by psychic affliction. Yet for Williams these people—sick as they are—are superior, even approach nobility; their very goodness, in its failure to provide a defense against brutality, is responsible for their sickness. And so the tender, the trusting, are destroyed by the vicious, usually through sex. "But, before being devoured," says Gardner, the gentle "must first undergo a weakening ordeal, so that when the time comes they will be too helpless to put up a fight. The weakening process occurs through corruption—which . . . serves to debase the person in his own eyes." Still the pure do not simply join the vile; they become something monstrous.

> Longing for their lost purity and loathing themselves for having lost it, they achieve satisfaction only by twisting the knife in the wound,

weakening themselves through greater and greater excesses, seeking
even more revolting forms of debauchery with which to punish themselves—until, drained of all goodness and flopping helplessly upon exposed sands of ultimate degradation, they are pounced upon by the
brutal forces of nature and devoured.

The world of Tennessee Williams seethes with emotion, most frequently with horror and animal passion, although in the course of his
plays the emotional gamut is fairly well run. The tour with Mrs. Venable
through the prehistoric garden in *Suddenly, Last Summer,* punctuated by
the sounds of wild beasts preying upon one another, illustrates the playwright's penchant for exotic settings, obviously in this case to underline
the mood of terror he is creating. Examples of eroticism abound, but
Stanley in *A Streetcar Named Desire* remains the very embodiment of
raw, animal passion.

Other postwar writers—dramatists, novelists, and poets alike—have
been equally involved in this exploration of emotion. Edward Albee's
Who's Afraid of Virginia Woolf? is nothing if not an emotional experience, while Truman Capote's twisted figures reach an emotional intensity that takes on Gothic proportions. The characters drawn by Jack
Kerouac and James Baldwin in differing ways are frantically searching
for a meaningful experience, which will at least comfort them for the
moment. Kerouac emphasizes the open road, the man who drifts, seeks
human companionship, yet offers no alternatives to a society he rejects.
Baldwin's characters move from hetero to homosexual couplings with
agility and ennui, amid a world in which emotion, human contact—however brief, twistet, unsure—is the only meaning. The poems of e. e. cum-
mings dwell on the moment of a rose, the fragility of a smile; in an
uncertain, chaotic world are there more lasting realities?

Personal emotion has also come to play a principal role in modern
painting, especially for the abstract expressionists. Jackson Pollock, for
example, caught the sense of violence and confusion that has permeated
the postwar world and reflected the doubt that objective reality exists at
all. Vastly withdrawn in his own life, Pollock seemed to retreat into his
art, creating works that were meaningful to him—which captured his
feelings at a given time and not particularly caring whether the public understood or not. His technique was to spread his large canvases over the
floor, then hastily apply pigments to them, sometimes spattering or drip-
ping paint, sometimes pouring it directly from cans. Describing Pollock's initial experiment with this method, Rudi Blesh says, "Hours went

by before the pails were empty and the fury over. Pollock squatted on his heels in a corner, trembling and spent, looking out over the exultant, screaming chaos that lay on the floor." If nothing else, the act of creation had been an intense emotional experience for the artist. While the public at large tended to dismiss these paintings as humbug, more sensitive viewers caught the excitement Pollock created through his spontaneity, his freedom, and his fascinating use of color.

A musical equivalent of Jackson Pollock might be John Cage. Like Pollock's, Cage's work is experimental, abstract, highly personal. He insists that music must not be separated from life and yet stresses the irrationality of a tumultuous world—a world to which he has nothing to say, no message to give, since none is relevant. Meaning seems to exist only in expression. True, Cage lacks the emotional magnitude of Pollock, but other musical idioms equal the painter's intensity or go beyond. Current "soul" music—the type sung by Bobby Blue Bland, Aretha Franklin, and James Brown—is almost pure passion, with both lyrics and vocalism blatant in their sensuality. Human suffering is the most frequent theme of the "soul" singers, and a climactic moment often finds the performer falling on one knee and asking his audience, "Did you evah cry?" Sex is approached with unabashed frankness; James Brown and others intentionally create a mood of sexual excitement by frenzied bodily movements and even by peeling off articles of clothing. The "rock" so popular with the young people is also strongly sensual, particularly in its primitive, driving rhythm, while the accompanying dances are based upon a freedom of expression and a personalized involvement which the Lawrence Welk generation finds difficult to fathom.

But the more advanced "rock" groups reflect contemporary romantic attitudes on a more sophisticated level. Particularly is this true of the Beatles' mature work. To the Beatles—as to hosts of the college-age Americans who now worship them—traditional values at best spell boredom and loneliness. The world, they seem to say, is filled with nameless, faceless people, who are incapable of communicating with one another. In "Eleanor Rigby" they sing of "all the lonely people, where *do* they all come from?" Eleanor herself lived "in a dream," then "died in the Church and was buried along with her name. Nobody came." *The Sergeant Pepper's Lonely Hearts Club Band* album, their best effort to date, obviously repeats the loneliness theme. "She's Leaving Home" tells of an aging girl who runs away from parental comfort to meet a man "after living alone for so many years." When her absence is discovered, the mother incredulously cries, "We gave her everything money could buy," to which the Beatles reply, "Fun is the one thing that money can't buy." Boredom is seen as equally appalling: "Everybody knows there's nothing doing." And in "When I'm Sixty-Four," played in a refined, 1920s jazz beat, the Beatles ask, "Doing the garden, digging the weeds, who could ask for more?" At this point the young musicians conclude, as Eugene O'Neill did years before, that illusion is essential to life. In *Sergeant Pepper* they speak of the illusions of show business, physical love, drugs, and naive optimism. While each plays a part in helping its accepter—not through life, but through another day—love, genuine human caring, the Beatles indicate, is the best answer: "With our love— we could save the world." But the world has grown too hard, too insensitive to embrace its salvation, and so illusion remains a necessary rallying point for existence. In probably their finest song, "A Day in the Life," objective reality and illusion are placed side by side, almost interwoven. The routine ("Woke up, fell out of bed, dragged a comb across my head") is suddenly interrupted by reference to a drug-induced "trip" ("I'd love to turn you on"). And at the end a dissonant, almost unbearably sustained orchestral chord seems to portend nothing but continued chaos, if not actual destruction.

On the Broadway musical stage the profoundest expression of neoromanticism to date is the smash success *Man of La Mancha*. Based on the Don Quixote theme, the musical, like the Beatles, superimposes illusion upon objective reality. Don Quixote, as knight errant, views a "bleak and unbearable world," as "base and debauched as can be." Determined that goodness and courage shall survive, he sets off on his quest for the "impossible dream"—striving "to fight the unbeatable foe," "to right the unrightable wrong," "to reach the unreachable stars." By contrast Aldonza, the arch-realist, understands nothing of Quixote's mission— "Why do you give when it's natural to take?" Attempting in vain to convince the Don that she is not his Lady Dulcinea, she pleads with him to take the clouds from his eyes and see her as she really is: "Born on a dung heap, to die on a dung heap, a strumpet men use and forget." But in the end Aldonza has decided that the illusion of Dulcinea is preferable to the reality of Aldonza, and she appears at Don Quixote's deathbed to beg him to resume the quest and to "bring back the dream of Dulcinea." The drama concludes on a note of unmitigated romanticism. Quixote dies, but Aldonza, having caught the romantic vision, refuses to recognize his death. When questioned by Sancho, she replies, "My name is Dulcinea." Quixote, by seeing her throughout as an individual of depth and value, has in reality transformed her.

Nor have these romantic overtones been limited to the arts, for in at least two instances since World War II they have taken on the semblance of a mass movement. Certainly the beatniks of the 1950s were estranged by the sad state of traditional society, particularly the materialistic aspects. Reverting to a more primitive behavior pattern, the beats emphasized quiet noninvolvement. If life did indeed have meaning, this meaning could best be approached through emotional experience and personal camaraderie. Sitting around a coffeehouse, talking and listening to cool jazz, became one of the ideals of the beats. Much more active in their protest and positive in their thinking are the hippies of the sixties. Equally "turned off" by straight society, the hippies, unlike the beats, offer alternatives—not for conventionalists, but for those who are willing to "drop out." Love, human compassion, and gentleness are their key answers to the problems of a decaying world. Most hippies (in contrast with the "yippies") see hope not in political involvement but in personal example; their major request of society is to be left alone. Idealizing a simpler way of life, they esteem the natural (bare feet, long hair, beards), human communication (love, assisting one another, even communal living), emotional catharsis (sex, drugs, psychedelic impressions), peaceful demonstration (the sit-in), the wisdom of other cultures (the Orient and American Indians, especially the Hopi), and beauty (flowers, color, nobility of character, art). While the number of hippies has remained relatively small, their impact, particularly on the younger people, has been substantial. "There's a whole generation with a new explanation," we are told in a recent popular song, "All across the nation, such a strong vibration."

In truth the vibrations have been growing since before World War I, for the intellectual rebellion crystallizing around 1913 set Americans on the path toward reorientation. In the 1920s the neo-romantic tremors became solidified, at least in the minds of select intellectuals. But not until after World War II could Americans in a more general way accept a romantic leaning. The atrocities of that war, the development of weapons capable of destroying not only an enemy but the world itself, the assassination of a young, dynamic President who seemed to offer hope, the increasing complexity and regimentation of urban living, the bitterness and chaos that have grown out of the civil rights movement, and the questionable involvement in Vietnam all combine to convince Americans that absolutes are dead. As our traditional optimism declines, new attitudes emerge—attitudes which carried to their logical extremes have produced a negativist, existential, nihilistic viewpoint which has long been current in Europe, but which until recently was inconsistent with the American mood and character. When not pushed to such an extreme, however, the new attitudes have resulted in a search, the romantic quest for something—anything—which will give meaning to a world that may already be lost.

In a world grown corrupt, where rational forces appear bent upon irrational ends, a total reorientation seems the only hope. Convinced that society has failed, the romantic sees only one alternative: the individual must reassert himself—not to conquer society as the nineteenth-century industrialists did, but to separate himself from society, redefining for himself what values are relevant. Rejecting a world that has ceased to communicate, a society he cannot imagine reforming, the romantic individualist seeks answers which to him personally make sense. For him this search and the integrity of adhering to his own ideals constitute the only reality.

The Corpse of the Dragon: Notes on Postromantic Fiction (1975)

FRANK McCONNELL

> *I must create a system or be enslaved by an-*
> *other man's.*
>
> —WILLIAM BLAKE

I want to take Blake's manifesto as seriously as possible in this essay, both as an important text in the history of modern writing and as a counsel to critics hoping to make some general sense of that writing. It seems to me one of those statements which not only make, but include, their own intellectual history: a summary and transformation of movements in thought and imagination preceding it, and a prophecy (though an ironic one) of the future it helps generate. Centrally romantic in its assertion, it is also centrally modern, postromantic in its implicit negations.

Those negations, of course, are more murderously conscious, operative for us than they were for most of Blake's contemporaries. Whatever the justice or accuracy of Arthur O. Lovejoy's famous discrimination of romanticisms as "positive" and "negative," there can be little doubt that our own best writing, as inheritor of certain crucial romantic dilemmas, has come increasingly to resemble the "negative" side of the romantic vision. And, indeed, the "romanticism" our critics and scholars have been rediscovering for some years now—after an age of disfavor under the reign of the New Criticism—is a peculiarly negative, dark version of the movement. Byron, for example, that darkest and most problematic of all romantic poets, has recently attained a prominence in the canon which had been denied him almost since his death in 1824. And the Wordsworth discussed by such brilliant commentators as Geoffrey Hartman and Harold Bloom—obsessive, wrestling with deep psychic evasions which at once create and occlude his poetic genius bears little if any resemblance to the Wordsworth who, for John Stuart Mill and Matthew Arnold, seemed to offer a radiant possibility of sanity and peace amid the bewildering antitheses of nineteenth-century thought. Coleridge, at the conclusion of *The Eolian Harp,* speaks to his beloved Sara Hutchinson of the God

> *Who with his saving mercies healed me,*
> *A sinful and most miserable man,*
> *Wilder'd and dark and gave me to possess*
> *Peace, and this Cot, and thee, heart-honour'd Maid!*

I think it is fair to say that, while an earlier reader of these lines would have been most moved by the characteristically romantic conclusion, the collapse of the incomprehensible God into the quotidian manifestations of a peaceful day with mild Sara, we—veterans of fiction since Joyce and of poetry since Eliot and Pound—are much more struck by another tone: the words "Wilder'd and dark," which resonate through that peaceful conclusion as a reminder of how desperately Coleridge—*our* Coleridge—needed and failed to construct such an elegantly humble sanity. To alter Wilde's famous epigram about Caliban and mirrors: the poet as monster not only desires to see his own face in the mirror of the past, but forces the critic (an Ariel of uncertain loyalties) to forge that mirror, even if it means introducing bubbles and distortions into the surface of the glass.

  I do not mean that an attempt to read modern writing as post-romantic is *simply* a distortion or caricature of the impulses of romanticism. Rather, I am suggesting that the most efficient sense we can make of poetry and fiction of the last two decades is in terms of a revision of our ideas of romanticism and of the history of thought which itself produced the romantic movement. My point is that distortion, though inevitable, is sometimes a way to the truth—and to a truth which "accurate" interpretation could not attain. I return to Blake's manifesto. If the terms of existence are, as he suggests, total freedom—creation—or total loss of freedom—*enslavement by another man's system*—then any attempt to explain, either by poet or by critic, is foredoomed to the antinomies of capriciousness and imitativeness, must locate itself on a spectrum ranging from absolutely perverse originality to absolutely uninformative faithfulness to the History of All Previous Thought. Thus this essay is that oldest and most idiosyncratic of literary forms, an anatomy. It is, literally, a sketch of the origins and continuity of romanticism: one which tries to map the relationship between the romantic movement and that contemporary fiction which it is my main purpose to examine. In imitation and perhaps parody of Blake, I have tried to "create" a system which allows me to make sense of Saul Bellow, Thomas Pynchon, John Barth, and John Gardner in continuity with the history of language and fiction in the last three hundred years, rather than in distinction from that history. But the system I have invented is a parallel to the problems faced by post-romantic systematizers like Bellow or Barth, and is caught on the same polarities of self-consciousness described by Blake's statement itself. That is, if all men are faced with the necessity of creating systems for themselves, as a pledge of their authenticity, then we shall have a great deal of difficulty trying to connect one system with another, trying to constitute out of that romantic universe of autonomous individuals a polity, or a society of individuals who can talk to one another.

"Would to God that all the Lord's people were Prophets," quotes Blake at the beginning of *Milton*. The irony of the romantic prophecy is that its wishes, at least in literature, are granted. For if all the Lord's people do become prophets—i.e., romantic poets—then it becomes nearly impossible to identify a "people" at all, in the sense of a shared community of belief—or even information—within which the poetic word can realize its efficacy. A brilliant young critic, Robert D. Hume, has suggested that romanticism is important for modern writing not in its temporary solutions, but only in the problems it has bequeathed us. I should like to extend that insight even more generally to suggest that romanticism—the only romanticism we can turn to human use—is primarily the discovery of a self-consciousness, an historical neurosis even, from which we cannot, and cannot desire to, escape. Man must "create a system," a language and an idiosyncratic rationality for controlling the world: trying not to do so is like trying to make up a series of absolutely random numbers, or like trying to kill yourself by holding your breath. But now—unlike, perhaps, Aquinas or Chaucer—we are aware of the impossibility. And since we are aware of it, our writing and thinking take on the form of a struggle against it, a struggle to assert, in the face of the artificiality and facticity of all thought, an authentically human voice, a civilizing idea. *"Pereant qui ante nos nostra dixerunt"* Berryman entitles one of his *Dream Songs* (#225); may they perish who have written our poems, thought our thoughts before us:

> *Madness & booze, madness & booze.*
> *Which'll can tell who preceded whose?*
> *What chicken walked out on what egg?*

This is not simply the fear of "unoriginality" but, rather, a terrified sense that "originality" itself, the ideal of the originating Word, may be only the behavioristic illusion of a predestinarian universe. It is one of the grimmest parallels I know to the thesis of Harold Bloom's study of the modern tradition, *The Anxiety of Influence,* in which Bloom describes the obsessive concern of the modern writer that his own imaginative life is threatened, impinged upon by those very figures who are his strongest source of inspiration. The modern writer who, like Berryman, directs his energies—in a profoundly romantic experiment—toward the invention of a *voice* which may distinctively carry his vision is caught by the discovery that that *invention* of a voice implies, also, the fictiveness, the artificiality, of all speaking voices. Until finally, that "vision" becomes an obsessive concentration upon the velleities and possibilities of the articulating voice itself: Nabokov's ape tracing, again and again, the bars of its cage.

I hope the reader shares my slight embarrassment at the word "inspiration" in the last paragraph: it is an important feature of exactly the history I am trying to describe. "Inspiration" is an old-fashioned, somehow excessive word for our sense of literary relationships. And it is the romantic movement, in its concentration upon the personality of the inspired poet and the process of poetic inspiration, which paradoxically empties the word of any real usefulness for our own speaking about literature. Romanticism, that is, like modernism is quintessentially a self-*un*fulfilling prophecy, a mythmaking shot through with a tragi-comic distrust of myth itself.

Concerns of myth and language, moreover, are obviously central to my own scheme for describing the permutations of the modernist imagination. Of all the characteristics that have been identified, in one way or another, as crucial to the *postmodernist* tradition in writing—free play, "writing degree zero," the escape from (or the end of) history, etc.—the one truly consistent and creative difficulty of that writing seems to remain the basically romantic (post-Cartesian) problem of the nature and status of language as (a) an accurate reflection of the universe man confronts and (b) an incarnation, indeed the first and necessary incarnation, of human freedom. Problems (a) and (b) are, to be sure, indistinguishable from each other at the deepest level of their urgency—the level at which, speaking at once about the nature of the outside and the nature of the inside the universe and our position as secondary creators of that universe, we approach the status of mythological, cosmogonic thought. Thus, in this introductory cartoon of romantic history—and in the discussion to follow—I begin with Descartes and Milton, the two seventeenth-century writers who most firmly establish the new ambiguities of language and mythmaking. The *Discourse on Method,* after all, may be viewed as a heroic attempt to reconstitute the ideas of matter and consciousness, *res extensa* and *res cogitans,* within the lost paradise of Descartes' own urbanized, technological imagination. And *Paradise Lost,* on the other hand, is itself a discourse on method: the method whereby the Christian soul cast adrift in the infinite universe of Cartesian mechanics may attempt a re-creation of the myth of the Fall. It is by now conventional wisdom that cosmogony—myths about the origin of the universe is always to some degree confessional autobiography, myths about the origin and importance of the self. Both Milton and Descartes, considered as confessional poets, help us see the connections between the poetic careers of Wordsworth and Byron—two crucially influential romantic language-myths which determine, respectively, the possibilities of poetry as a verbal reintegration of self and world, and the possibilities of poetry as a disintegration of that primal unity which leaves the poet at once denuded of all his fictions and at peace with the resulting void.

The Wordsworthian and Byronic examples are, even in the context of fiction after World War II, extreme: no writers since them have surrendered quite so unremittingly to the alternatives of the Word as repletion or exhaustion of human meaning, human freedom. Blake, alone among the romantics, was able to forge a mythology which could include both those alternatives in a creative, profoundly rational tension with each other. Blake, indeed, may be the first truly *post*romantic writer, precisely because, in his anticipation of the major terms of the nineteenth-century romantic dilemma, he managed to see so far beyond that dilemma into its basic—and therefore contemporary—linguistic manifestation. Saul Bellow's Mr. Sammler muses that the real problem with the barbarism of '70s New York is its total closure as a grammar of pure inanity. Like Marcuse's "happy consciousness," the cosmogony of the Silly City is too yielding, too pluralistic, too comfortable even to admit the possibility of negation:

> The labor of Puritanism now was ending. The dark satanic mills changing into light satanic mills. The reprobates converted into children of joy, the sexual ways of the seraglio and of the Congo bush adopted by the emancipated masses of New York, Amsterdam, London.

But Blake, the inventor of the phrase "dark satanic mills," also anticipates Bellow's refutation of that phrase and that vision. He seems, more and more as his work progresses, to understand that the poet's problem is not so much an escape from the burdens of mechanism, industrialized society, and—their literary analogue—the overwhelming weight of tradition, but rather that the problem is to find a way of creating, of civilizing both language and society *through* the medium of those characteristically contemporary debilities. Blake's apocalypse, finally, is an apocalypse of language in its deepest mythic, cosmogonic implications: language which is at once transparent and opaque, confessional and anti-confessional, manifesting and obliterating the personality of the artist from the structure of his work. And as such, it is not simply an analogue or a progenitor, but a competitor with the intricate fictions of Bellow, Barth, and Gardner.

The point I am trying to make is that the visionary linguistics of contemporary writing, like that of romanticism, must be understood in terms of its fundamental union of contraries, rather than as a mere set of mental-physical, spiritual-mechanistic antitheses. Writers as disparate as William K. Wimsatt, Jr., and Noam Chomsky have been indicating as much for sometime now, of course; but remarkably, the antiquated (Arnoldian? Wildean?) antinomies about romanticism persist in even our most recent attempts at explication.

Wimsatt—by now, I think, obviously the most perspicuous and valuable of the New Critics—is certainly no friend of romantic ideas of selfhood or language. Yet, in *The Verbal Icon,* discussing the evolution of romantic diction out of its eighteenth-century predecessors, he precisely locates that genesis in the philosophical (Cartesian and Lockean) "victory . . . of the phenomenal over the noumenal, of qualities over things." To a mind so ardently Thomistic, of course, the "noumenal" is never very far from the "numinous." And indeed I am not sure that Wimsatt is not, perhaps even unconsciously, punning here between the two terms. But his conclusions about the fate of romantic language, negative though they may be in their implied judgment, are of undeniable value for the kind of argument I wish to pursue:

> When the proper names and essences of things had been deprived of any special dignity, the things themselves easily became less impressive than their definitions, their periphrases, their qualitative connotations.

The disappearance of the noumenal, of the thing grasped in itself, of the *idea* of essence: this is surely the fate of words from Shelley to Barthelme, from the "Wilder'd and dark" Coleridge to Berryman trapped by "Madness & booze." But at the same time that this destiny seems an exile from the world of things into the infinite regressions of the self-beholding mind, it also implies a kind of freedom, a liberation into the radical structuring of periphrasis and definition which is part of what Blake meant by "creating one's own system."

Noam Chomsky, on the other hand, in *Language and Mind,* identifies himself as an enthusiastic participant in the romantic ideal of linguistic originality. There, more explicitly than in any of his other books, he acknowledges the debt of transformational-generative grammar to post-Cartesian ideals of "universal grammar" and a massive, almost vatic humanitarianism. Paraphrasing Schlegel, Chomsky observes:

> The medium of poetry—language—is unique in that language, as an expression of the human mind rather than a product of nature, is boundless in scope and is constructed on the basis of a recursive principle that permits each creation to serve as the basis for a new creative act.

This "recursive principle" of speech, though (which Chomsky elevates to such a dominant position in his own conceptualization of language) may be seen as not only an infinitely creative function of the human Word but also an infinitely uncreative one, the generative vision not of the *Hymn to Intellectual Beauty* and *Ulysses* but of *Mont Blanc* and *Watt.* For Chomsky, though his system does not permit the terms "noumenal" or "numinous" to be used with any efficiency, is describing, no less than Wimsatt, their disappearance from our believable myths of language, and the agonies such disappearance leaves behind it.

I do not, indeed, suggest that the history of imaginative writing since the romantic age is a matter of linguistics; rather, I wish to propose that linguistics itself, perhaps the most characteristically self-conscious of twentieth-century disciplines, is a late product of the romantic sensibility, and therefore a particularly efficient one for describing the evolution of that sensibility. Linguists are fond of speaking in terms of "metalanguages." As I attempt to describe the grammar of a specific language, that is, I produce a description which is in effect a *second* language, a coherent system of verbal norms, whose *subject* is the system of norms, the first language, I set out to describe. And if I try to determine a more general set of rules governing the grammar I have developed, I create another metalanguage, at a yet higher order of abstraction. It is a useful concept for literary history as well as linguistics. For it allows us to talk about the relationship between contemporary fiction and poetry and the achievements of romanticism, not in terms of "influence" or of an inherited set of logical propositions or problems, but as a progressive development, a "meta-myth," which elaborates, renders more complex or more conscious, some of the generative insights of the romantic system of mythology.

Wimsatt and Chomsky help indicate how truly ambiguous the romantic legacy of visionary linguistics is. Far from being a simple warfare of spirit against mechanism, of sublime madness against arthritic rationalism, it is, rather, an attempt to make a civilized peace between those terms. A book like John Vernon's recent *The Garden and the Map: Schizophrenia in Twentieth Century Literature and Culture* can be taken as representative of a great number of apologies for the contemporary (Poirier, Sontag, Stevick) which, by ignoring or simplifying this complex tension, in fact disserve the real profundity of our best writers. Vernon's position, that the value of Barth, Burroughs, Roethke, *et al* is their enthusiastic embrace of irrationalism (the "garden" sensibility) against the three-century narcosis of Cartesian logic (the "map" mind), will not take us very far toward understanding *Naked Lunch* or *Chimera;* moreover, the position itself suffers from a pseudo-Cartesian innocence of categorization. Between the garden and the map is a third term, the city, neither Edenically infantile pastoral nor mathematicized wasteland, at once both and greater than both, the true field of human civilization—just as language itself is both within and outside the mind, the condition of all we can say and the means through which we can escape from conditioned, inauthentic existence. And it is this field, the human city constructed on the foundation of our own fictiveness, which I think the high romantics and the so-called "postmodernists" most seriously explore.

We have spoken of the impingements which the romantic and postromantic writers characteristically feel and which, as a counter force to the expansive imagination, effectively constitute the nature of their art. The question is whether those impingements have not become, for the contemporary writer, insurmountable: whether the creative antagonism between personal system and public structure, solitary voice and common rationality, has not become a murderous, uncreative warfare generating a literature of frivolity and aridity. Two writers with quite different vantages on the romantic spirit have recently suggested that this is so. Gerald Graff, in an essay on "The Myth of the Postmodernist 'Breakthrough'," argues that the practice of what he calls romantic "poetolatry" has produced a tradition of phoney—and, currently, self-deluding—individuality which both hampers real imaginative vitality and subtly enforces political repressiveness. For Graff, that is, creating your own system and being enslaved by another man's are not alternatives but correlatives. And in *The Anxiety of Influence* Harold Bloom makes an even more serious—since more empathetic—case against the modern tradition. For Bloom, the romantic revolution is the "Fall," which constitutes both the consciousness and the guilt of the modern writer. And though that Fall offers us our only chance of a regained innocence, a poetic glory, Bloom argues that it also makes inevitable its own defeat, the exhaustion in our day of its own best promise:

> The death of poetry will not be hastened by any reader's broodings, yet it seems just to assume that poetry in our tradition, when it dies, will be self-slain, murdered by its own past strength. An implied anguish throughout this took is that Romanticism, for all its glories, may have been a vast visionary tragedy, the self-baffled enterprise not of Prometheus but of blinded Oedipus, who did not know that the Sphinx was his Muse.

It is an extraordinarily gloomy vision. The quality of Bloom's intelligence as well as Graff's demands that we take their pessimism seriously. While I do not share that pessimism, it is nonetheless clear that such critics, in their considered nay-saying, perform a better service to the understanding of the modern tradition than many of that tradition's most enthusiastic defenders. They both ask serious questions about the morality—esthetic and political—of writing. And to ask such questions is to assume the intimate, unbreakable connection between writing and political, esthetic morality which is at the heart of the romantic enterprise and, I suggest, of the postmodern or contemporary continuation of romanticism. Such questions are not, cannot be resolved by the vision of modernity presented by writers such as Richard Poirier or Susan Sontag. If we choose to see in the best work of Thomas Pynchon, John Barth, or John Gardner merely another manifestation of the "performing self," or merely alternative "styles of radical will," then we have assimilated those works only by avoiding their most important implications. "Play" and "free fantasy" are terms frequently used—almost as frequently as "irony" and "ambiguity" a decade or so ago—to justify and explain the nature of contemporary fiction. But, as all children know and too many of their parents forget, play is a serious business; and few things are less free, more constrained by social and moral considerations than fantasy.

Bloom, in fact, rather startlingly echoes the voice which, in contemporary fiction, seems to offer the strongest chance for the continuing life of the romantic tradition. The modern writer's dilemma, he says, is involved with the recognition that he is not, after all, Prometheus, titanic archetype of the romantic prophet, but Oedipus, the tragic clown of rationalism and archetypal monster-slayer who learns—too late—that his monster is his Muse.

Is this a vision of the death of the imagination? Thinking about such contemporary retellings of the monster-slayer myth as Burroughs' *Nova Express,* Brock Brower's *The Late Great Creature,* Barth's *Chimera,* or John Gardner's *Grendel* and *Jason and Medeia*—and about the submerged but obsessive importance in Blake, Byron, and Shelley of the monster-slayer motif—one can perceive it, rather, as an insight into the vitality of the imagination, and into its inescapably romantic nature

I return to the image of continuity I have already proposed: that of romantic language and postromantic metalanguage. It should be characteristic of a metalanguage (if our description of it is efficient) that it clarifies the terms of the language upon which it is based. And in the myth of the monster-slayer, I want to argue, we confront one of the central terms in the continuity of the last two hundred years of writing—central not only because it is a link between the visions of the great romantics and the countervisions of the moderns, but also because the real subject of the myth is the efficacy of language itself. Our version of the myth has increasingly, for two centuries, shifted its focus from the freedom of the hero to the gross factuality of the monster he slays—a monster who exists only to be slain by the hero, and is thereby at once the symbol and limit of the hero's heroism, of humankind's most fondly wished humanity. And in so shifting our focus on this oldest, most primal of myths, we have come to rediscover a harsh wisdom older than Judeo-Christian versions of rationality, a wisdom which is radically "postmodern" only because it has been forgotten for so long in our culture: the wisdom at the heart of the corpse of the dragon.

The myth is, of course, well-known to us. We have rediscovered its primacy, thanks to Freud, Jung, Frazer, Lévi-Strauss, and Joseph Campbell—to name only a few of its explorers. But to rediscover its primacy is not to recover its real importance. We are adept by now at finding elements of the dragon myth in works like *The Faerie Queene, Pilgrim's Progress,* and *Frankenstein.* And we have a well-established set of formulae to explain the permanence, even in displaced or mutated form, of the archetype. The dragon and his heroic slayer, our analysts tell us, may represent the organization of chaos into human order, the creation of time out of eternity, even the evolution of the ego out of the id.

The only problem with this knowledge is that we know it too well. Information theorists have established that, for a message to be efficiently transmitted, it must consist of a certain irreducible mixture of real information and redundancy. It is possible, in other words, for a circuit to be too open, to transmit too much information, and thence to become at once significant and meaningless. We know what the myth *means,* I have said. But of course the moment you think you know what a myth *means* you have lost contact with the myth itself. Because a myth, whatever else it might do, does not *mean* in that way. If anything, it is a kind of predisposition toward meaning, a verbal *prima materia* where narrative and order, drama and metaphysics, the aboriginally linguistic and the insuperably unspeakable all dance together in the moment before all other moments of human utterance. Myth is not *about,* it is that precarious energy-exchange between self and other, language and silence, word and world which, in romantic theory at least, is the explosive origin of speech. There is a curious doubling, here, between the problems of our discursive understanding of the *meaning* of myth and the use of myth— or, simply, the sense of language in contemporary fiction. For the visions of Barth, Pynchon, and Gardner involve the struggles of characters to survive in a world which is informationally overdetermined: a world where there are *too many* names, too many systems to explain any given fact, and in which, therefore, the definitively human enterprise of language is thrown back into its primal—its mythic warfare against the namelessly phenomenal, the silent *other.* We may think here of the contradictory, maddening multiple truths which afflict Barth's Ebeneezer Cooke in *The Sot-Weed Factor* or Gardner's *Grendel.* But the most powerful statement of the dilemma—one which, in fact, *reconstitutes* the archaic struggle of language against chaos comes near the center of Pynchon's *Gravity's Rainbow,* as V-2 engineer Horst Achtfaden reflects upon the metaphysics of flight:

> Right here, at the Interface, the air will be rising. You follow the edge
> of the storm, with another sense—the flight-sense, located nowhere,
> filling all your nerves . . . as long as you stay always right at the edge

between fair lowlands and the madness of Donar it does not fail you,
whatever it is that flies, this carrying drive toward—*is* it freedom?
Does no one recognize what enslavement gravity is till he reaches the
interface of the thunder?

"The interface of the thunder": Pynchon's genius for fusing the languages of technology and apocalyptic poetry here gives us the hidden
epigraph to his entire gigantic novel. The interface of the thunder is not
simply the meeting point between the shaping mind and the shapeless,
terrifying phenomenal world: it is the interrealm, the no-man's-land
where the two antagonistic systems, mind and world, simultaneously operate, each in its own terms and each in the other's. On the pathological
level, it is the realm of paranoia and schizophrenia; but on the level of
language and the psychic history of the race, it is precisely the realm we
have already described as that of aboriginal myth.

Martin Heidegger, in one of his late works, *On the Way to Language,*
contrasts the philosophy of language to the technological enterprise,
which in his view contemporary linguistics amounts to. For Heidegger,
philosophy is that mysterious and yet intimately familiar state of attention, that return to the profound simplicities of the pre-Socratic shamans,
which is such an obsessive concern of his own later thought. Linguistics,
on the other hand—the *science* of language is, for him, the soulless discourse, not of men, but of globe-circling satellites, the "language of
rocketry." No reader of Pynchon's book can help but be struck by this
startling anticipation of the brooding, evil, *other* figure of the Rocket in
Gravity's Rainbow, just as no reader of Blake can help but notice the
Blakean overtones of "enslavement"—mental and political—in the passage from Pynchon I have cited. Between the humanistic anguish of Hei-
deggerian philosophy and the killing geometries of Rocketspeech lies
the interface, the realm of fiction and mythmaking in their aspect as the
most urgent acts of human primacy and human risk. The Rocket, avatar
of Gravity, of the world's mute weight, of what Pynchon calls the "irre-
versibility of the Lord of Night," is the Dragon of the archaic myth. And
it is a measure of Pynchon's courage, as well as of his deep indebtedness
to the tradition of romanticism, that he has given us a book which redis-
covers, at the most elemental level, the uncertainty of the struggle between the civilizing, human hero and his Great Adversary.

The energy of romanticism, I suggest—and of its contemporary
progeny—needs to be seen as just such a revision—*re*-vision—of the
implications and problems raised by this oldest of tales. The dragon
myth, until the end of the eighteenth century, is preserved in Western lit-

erature primarily in a displaced forms: variants of the St. George legend, allegorizations of the dragon into Satan, Pride, Lust. The dragon, that is, is seen as a Fall, a possible error or sin which a man might commit, but not as a real force, sufficient unto himself and existing independently in his own universe. He is baptized, defined in terms of a moral and linguistic myth which robs him of his greatest, unbaptized, terribleness. (We may think of St. Augustine here, in his revulsion against Manichaeanism—defining Evil, not as a *principle* but as a *deficiency* of the transcendent, omnipresent Good—as the seminal obscurer of the dragon's meaning.) Frequently in early Western literature, the dragon becomes comical in his immensity and clumsiness. And the focus of dragon slayer tales comes to be on the hero, the knight of holiness, rather than upon the awfulness of the monster he must defeat. With the end of the Renaissance and the beginning of the modern period comes the recognition, by poets and philosophers, of the dragon's perennial, if forgotten, importance.

Who is the dragon? He is the oldest *other.* If the hero, in slaughtering him, affirms the triumph of civilization and reason, he also, through the necessity of slaughtering him, reaffirms the difficulty, permanence, and perhaps final illusoriness of the struggle. He is, at least in one romantic acceptance of his meaning, the baffling, insurmountable fact that *things happen* and that we have no control over their happening. When you make love for the first time, when your car, unbelievably, collides with *that* car you previously accepted as a harmless part of the landscape, when war is declared or someone you love dies, then you are face to face with the dragon in his oldest, most threatening, and most mythic aspect. You do not need a Heidegger or a Pynchon to realize the primacy or the omnipotence of the dragon, as a figure of unwilled impingement upon your illusion of centrality and control. And yet, at least in the history of Western thought, it apparently took the romantic movement to rediscover that impingement. Or, at least, it took the romantics to create the myth of that impingement in its distinctively modern sense. Literary eras are distinguished, not so much by their solutions to existence as by the varieties of existential malaise they discover—a new headache for every age. And with the romantics, the lineaments of the monsters of antiquity and the Renaissance take on the shape of our nightmares. Legions of critics and commentators have argued about the "meaning" of the figure Demogorgon from Shelley's *Prometheus Unbound.* But surely Demogorgon is—like Blake's monster Urizen or Coleridge's seductive vampire Christabel—the consciousness that we are here, things are there, and *they* happen to *us.* Sexual awakening (for Coleridge), the imprisonment of the mind in a self-limiting system (for Blake), or the inhuman dynamics of cosmic history (for Shelley) are all manifestations of the dragon, of the immortality of the monstrous, and—most shatteringly—of the perishability of human names and human explanations in confrontation with that monstrosity.

Great civilizations—though not, until the romantics, our own—have been constructed upon the basis of this inhospitable mythology of the dragon; and to these we might turn to comprehend our own most civilizing fabrications. One of the oldest tales in the world is the Babylonian creation-epic, the *Enuma Elish*. It tells how the primal dragon-goddess Tiamat creates the Babylonian pantheon and how the gods and goddesses of the pantheon rebel against their tyrannical mother. They send Marduk, their strongest and best, to fight against her. Marduk slays her and creates, out of her corpse, the world of men and beasts as well as the new heaven of the gods. As he returns to the other gods from his labor of destruction and creation, they—and the first men he has just created— sing a litany to his beauty, power, and terror.

The *Enuma Elish* is one of the eeriest tales we have, since its latent subject is the origin of writing—the origin, in a way, of itself—out of inarticulate nothingness. As few later versions of the dragon myth can afford to, it takes the primacy of the dragon seriously. Tiamat's preparations for the battle with Marduk are the revelation, in fact, of all that threatens language, civilization, humanity most primally and most intimately. Tiamat's warfare is the creation of the monstrous, the other:

> Now the all gathered around Tiamat,
> and they worked furiously on their plans,
> night and day, they all worked in a great rage,
> they were impatient for the final fight.
> . . . . ,
> Then she made fierce dragons out of fire,
> flaming and hateful, fateful to look upon,
> they flew with shrieks of terror through the air,
> for they were truly strange and dangerous.
> Then she created lions and spiders,
> hornets and scorpions, great angry apes,
> sullen vultures and screaming hyenas,
> with loud howling to pick out their victims.
> Now Tiamat was pleased with these creatures
> for she could see that they were terrible.

We are not surprised to see N. K. Sandars, a contemporary translator and commentator of the *Enuma Elish,* compare Tiamat to the principle of "Entropy"—to universal Gravity, that is, or to the title and subject of Pynchon's first published story. The dragon-goddess is, in this version of the myth, the opponent of all that is rational, organizing, or civilizing in the god—her child—Marduk; we cannot help catching, in lines like "Tiamat was pleased with these creatures/for she could see that they were terrible," the echo and reversal of God's "And He saw that it was good" in *Genesis.* This monster, granddam of Descartes' and Blake's fiercest visions, is the origin of all that is not "good," not civilized and ordered, *tov* in the Hebrew myth. And the *Enuma Elish* is unrelenting in its judgment that such things, since they are not humanly assimilable, are terrible.

The poem is cosmology and logology at once, a story about the creation of the world and the creation of language. But this double genesis is significantly grimmer, more problematic than in its Judeo-Christian version. We are all creatures of a splendidly rational god, but formed from the corpse, the wrecked but still existent body, of an immitigably irrational monster. That is the knowledge, the primacy of the material and its eternal impingement upon language and thought, which the *Enuma Elish* brings. The litany to Marduk with which it concludes, writing on stone in praise of a sky god, catches profoundly the subtlety of the Babylonian literary metaphysics. The poem, graven on earth, *becomes* the Other on the defeat of which (whom?) its grandest assertions are founded.

To comprehend the language-myth, we need only remember its later epochal parody in the first chapter of *Genesis.* The sublime *fiat* of *Genesis* is the perfect contradiction to the story of the *Enuma Elish.* In this myth the word is not posterior to the material universe, arising from it and returning to it: it is the Word, creative, generative, self ratifying, beyond matter and calling matter into existence. We are not children of the monster; we are heirs of the divine language which created and controls the monster.

The triumph of the Judaic over the Babylonian cosmogony may well be the signal, constitutive event in the history of Western rationalism and Western writing. It was with extraordinary insight that the rhetorician Longinus chose *Fiat Lux* as one of his prime examples of the literary sublime. At least, its implicit and powerful assumptions about language, materiality, and the role of reason remain without successful challenge until the re-emergence of the older, dragon-centered myth we have suggested the romantic movement to represent. Two figures, particularly, anticipate and give impetus to the massive shift in thought which was romanticism and is the tradition of the modern: Descartes and Milton.

Descartes' *Discourse on Method* drives a wedge between word and world; a wedge whose magnitude, apparently, we have not even yet finished measuring. Writers as unlike each other as Sartre and Noam Chomsky have located, in Descartes, the originating point of their central concerns: language, freedom, and the possibility of an alliance between language and freedom. The Cartesian opposition between free thought and physical limitation, the dualism of *res cogitans*—what thinks—and *res extensa*—what *is there*—manifests itself in the *Discourse* as more than simply the isolation of mind in infinite space. It is a rediscovery of the monstrous, the other, under its aspect as silence and mechanism. Descartes was fascinated with the problem of automata, in much the same way contemporary linguists are interested in the possibilities of machine translation or talking machines, or writers like Beckett, Burroughs, and Barth are concerned with the media of tape recorder and computer as narrative tools. Can the mind, operating only on its own certainties, construct an efficient replica of reality? Yes, answers the *Discourse:* and metaphysics has already become the supreme fiction of a counterplot to the divine creation. But Descartes goes farther. Can the mind, then, he asks, construct by itself a human being? Can it *become* God, finally bridge the gulf between its aspirations and its involvement in the physical, the phenomenal, the other? No, answers Descartes: for, however convincing and accurate might be the automaton constructed by such a hypothetically omnipotent human mind, the robot would still lack the power of speech, of *language,* that God-given power which is the sure sign of our humanity and of our ultimate deliverance from the world of *res extensa.* Later writers and thinkers have had the sorry task of discovering just how gratuitous Descartes' confidence really is. But the terms of the debate remain his. Language, after the Cartesian revolution, must be viewed as either our ultimate liberation from, or our ultimate bondage to, our own materiality.

So Milton, in *Paradise Lost,* makes the myth of the Fall a parable, among other things, of his own ferociously Christian confrontation with the terrors of the Cartesian universe. His primal serpent is at once the most heroic and most pitiable character in the epic, for he alone, of all the protagonists of *Paradise Lost,* wanders through an infinite Cartesian space. His exile and fall, in fact, are, precisely, his exile into that space— the space of the modern mind. Early in the poem, Satan utters what was to become, in many ways, the romantic manifesto of consciousness: "The mind is its own place." But that manifesto, as Milton knew and the romantics experienced, is an admission, finally, that the mind cannot be any *other* place but its own—that the world of matter has resumed its original identity as threat and limit to the soul. Milton's Satan does not *want* to be the serpent. He wants to exist in the freedom of his own vitality; but the poem will not let him, as the new physics of Milton's and our era will not let us. Satan is exiled, in a sense, into the world his rebellious Cartesian mind has created, just as Adam and Eve, who create history through their sin, are punished for their sin by being driven from the prehistorical state into the history they have generated. *Paradise Lost,* in other words, is not only a poem about the Fall; it contains a recapitulation of the Fall in a more bitter—and more modern—formulation. Consciousness, fallen consciousness, is no longer an exile from the Garden, but an exile into the Garden in its altered existence as temporal, material universe. But the romantics—who were called, among other things, "Satanists" by their contemporaries—were to accept the exile which Milton denied, to acknowledge their parentage from the ruined Garden and the monster's corpse as a precondition, rather than an annihilation, of their own attempts at prophetic speech.

Two modern poets beautifully catch the conjunction of Cartesian and Miltonic obsessions in the formation of our own visionary obsessions. Yeats writes, in "Fragments":

> *Locke sank into a swoon;*
> *The Garden died;*
> *God took the spinning-jenny*
> *Out of his side.*

Locke's swoon—Blake frequently spoke of it as "Newton's sleep"—is the ungenerative trance of the new, phenomenological Adam: a counter-creation which, since it emphasizes the alienness of the "garden" in which we are born, in effect kills the Garden. The new Eve of this anti-Genesis is the spinning jenny, the machine with a grimly punning woman's name, a delusive promise of peace with the universe which we can now call, also, gravity's rainbow. Wallace Stevens, in *Notes Toward a Supreme Fiction,* is even more explicit:

> *The first Idea was not our own. Adam*
> *In Eden was the father of Descartes*
> *And Eve made air the mirror of herself. . . .*

The pre-existence of the Cartesian universe—not as phenomenal fact, but as myth—confutes ideas of the creative possibilities of language. Our words are all quotations upon the surface of impenetrable matter which we inhabit: the first idea was not, nor could have been, our own.

"Paradise lost" is a slogan of epochal irony for the poem behind so much of romanticism. For under the new dispensation the paradise of Judeo-Christian myth is, indeed, lost, supplanted by the more problematic myth of the Garden as monstrous corpse *(res extensa),* and the mind as inescapably secondary, inauthentic in the face of that otherness *(res cogitans).* This is the vision, preeminently, of the prophet of Leviathan, Blake himself. The dragon Tiamat had been a female; and Cartesian space, whether as passive or as "swallowing," has often been mythicized as a female principle. Blake, in his own revision of the Miltonic persona, *Milton,* describes the Satanic or female space of the fallen world:

> The nature of a Female Space is this: it shrinks the Organs
> Of Life till they become Finite & Itself seems Infinite.

> And Satan vibrated in the Immensity of the Space, Limited
> To those without, but Infinite to those within: It fell down
> Became Canaan, closing Los from Eternity In Albion's Cliffs.
> A mighty Fiend against the Divine Humanity, must'ring to War.

Blake's enterprise is an exploration of the hemmed-in universe bequeathed us by Descartes, and a nervous experimentation with possible modes of liberation from its trap. His language is a language, not of mysticism or "vision," but crushing physicality. And as such, it is one of the first appearances of the modern fictive voice, a speech whose "substance" is precisely the difficulty of *using* words to clear a space for consciousness in the world of things.

But Blake can still employ the language of prophecy, one which—though parodistically—invokes the tradition of the creative Word whose demise is his subject. William Burroughs, in *Nova Express,* describes a universe where even that option is no longer possible. For Burroughs, *all* language has become entrapment, addiction and bondage to the entropic powers he visualizes as the galactic gangsters of the "Nova Mob":

> Bring together state of news—Inquire onward from state to doer—
> Who monopolized Cosmic Consciousness? Who monopolized Love
> Sex and Dream? Who monopolized Life Time and Fortune? Who took
> from you what is yours? Now they will give it all back? Did they ever
> give anything away for nothing? Did they ever give any more than they
> had to give? Did they not always take back what they gave when possi-
> ble and it always was? Listen: their Garden of Delights is a terminal
> sewer.

If we regard postmodern writing as a metalanguage of romanticism, Burroughs represents perhaps the most extreme elaboration of that metalanguage on the matter of writing itself. If "Life Time and Fortune" have been monopolized, turned into junk (addictive *res extensa*), then the only hope for the writer—indeed, for the man—is a literature which somehow does away with words altogether, which obliterates the writer as conscious creator, freeing the man inside the writer from "other men's systems" in a liberation so austere that it threatens to obliterate his humanity itself.

There are many good reasons why our examination should take us from Blake to Burroughs, from an English romantic poet to a distinctively American antinovelist. Leslie Fiedler once called America a land doomed to play out the imaginary childhood of Europe—the childhood, that is, of Rousseau's noble savage, Chateaubriand's metaphysical Indians, Schiller's "naive" poet or Wordsworth's infantile "mighty prophet, seer blest." But then America, as projection and living quotation of European romanticism, is also a land doomed to live out the attendant nightmare of that fantastic childhood: a civilization condemned to invent its possibilities within the very landscape of the Garden as Dragon's Corpse. This is partly what Gertrude Stein meant when, in *The Autobiography of Alice B. Toklas,* she called America the most modern country in the world because of its "abstract disembodied" quality. But Claude Lévi-Strauss puts it more precisely in his own discovery of America, *Tristes Tropiques,* when he comments on the "naturalness" of American cities. The found land of European mythological yearnings is a cartoon, a caricature, of the romantic sublime:

> Our [European] judgments are . . . permeated and deformed by this difference of scale. Those who call New York ugly, for instance, have simply failed to make the necessary change of registration. Objectively, no doubt, New York is a city, and can be judged as one; but the spectacle which it offers to a European sensibility is of a different order of magnitude: that of European landscape; whereas American landscape offers us, in turn, an altogether more monumental scheme of things, and one for which we have no equivalent.

"No equivalent," that is, save in the infinite and terrifying prospects of Goethe's *Faust,* Byron's *Cain,* or the vertiginous, seductive and dangerous foliage of Chateaubriand's *Atala.* Lévi-Strauss's own Rousseauistic vision is, in fact, perhaps the last historic instance of Europe's psychic imperialism over its most interesting colony. For he insists upon having discovered the key to all mythologies among the not-quite-noble savages of Brazil at the very moment—the eve of World War II—when American writing, like American civilization, was to assume the full mantle of its heritage of romantic self-consciousness: its immitigable exile into what Robert Lowell called at that time the Land of Unlikeness, its double bondage to the conviction of its own fictiveness and the pressure of the world's mute weight.

Nuclear fission and information theory, the two great American artifacts spawned by the War, are terminal versions of *res extensa* and *res cogitans* in their mutual closure. Norman Mailer's prophetic analysis of the modern American psyche works not only as a description of the problems of the writer, but also as a description of the agonies of most of our populace. We are caught in a civilization which, while owing a great debt to eighteenth-century myths of liberation and of the imperial self, nevertheless increasingly manifests its own plastic, preproduced unreality and the corresponding impossibility of real communication within our gigantic information network. The solipsistic games played by the heroes of Burroughs' novels—and the heroes of Mailer's *Why Are We in Vietnam?*, Pynchon's *The Crying of Lot 49*, or Robert Coover's *The Universal Baseball Association*—are in one sense archetypal games of antiprophecy, elegant graffiti which announce the death of the realistic, sacramental Word unendingly, since there is nothing else to announce, no other message which does not compound the already overfull network of "facts" which is smothering us.

To say this much is to reiterate the now familiar attitude toward current fiction as the "literature of silence" or the self-reductive "Pythagorean genre" celebrated by George Steiner. But this attitude, as I have suggested, actually distorts the tradition of the "postmodern." The invocation of the Babylonian creation story helps us see the *creative* aspect of the materialistic counter-genesis discovered by the romantics. For if the dragon's corpse spells the end of one kind of civilizing myth—and one idea, perhaps, of the civilizing power of language it is also the originating point of another. It is in American writing—especially the work of Malcolm Lowry, Saul Bellow, John Barth, and John Gardner—that the fiction of the New Foundation and the return of the myths, though radically inverted from their "classical" form, frequently achieves its greatest complexity and power.

Lowry's *Under the Volcano,* published in 1947, is to postmodernist fiction what *Ulysses* was to its predecessor: indeed, Lowry's novel, patterned self-consciously on aspects of *Ulysses,* is a "metalinguistic" transformation of that source, and of the nineteenth-century literary history which *Ulysses* itself implicates. Both books involve the action of a single, cataclysmic day in the lives of their central characters; both are set on the eves of the two great Wars which were to initiate their respective fictional eras; and both are written by and about exiles—Joyce in Trieste on the Irish Jew, Lowry in British Columbia on the English consul in Mexico—men for whom the "quoted" life is not only imaginatively, but politically and demographically, central to their experience.

Lowry's private demons did not allow him to complete the series of books whose center *Under the Volcano* was to have been. But in an important way the series is implicit, and splendidly complete, in that single book. Dana Hilliott, the hero of Lowry's first novel, *Ultramarine,* describes himself as living a life "in inverted commas, " a terrified sense of inauthenticity which reduces Hilliott's life to the level of helpless fantasy. It is this apprehension of quotedness, of the inadequacy of consciousness to make meaningful order out of the riot of the world, which generates the creative warfare of *Under the Volcano.*

Geoffrey Firmin, the alcoholic consul who is the Faustian center of the book, lives out his last day in a drunken haze of regret, hallucination, fear, and ferocious pride. At the heart of his frenzied life is the terror of the world, of history, and of his own inability to control it. He is an alchemist, an adept of the cabala: a familiar of the monsters of history and his own delirium tremens, and of their "official" ancestors in the ancient magic. And he is an immensely civilized man whose speeches and nightmares are packed with allusions, with drunkenly askew quotations from Jacobean tragedians and romantic poets.

His civilization, indeed, is the point of his tragedy. For the consul is not only a witness to his own damnation, he is also its critic. In him we recognize the father of so many of our central characters, damned and laughing at their fall. For he understands soberly, at every point, the full silliness of his self-indulgence and self-destruction. Addiction to alcohol, the absurd dependence of consciousness upon things, is the book's key icon. The consul is both himself and Other, poet and addict, creator and monster. At an important point in the novel, Firmin talks with his friend, film-maker Jacques Laruelle, about a film the latter had planned to make of Shelley's *Alastor.* But if the poet in *Alastor,* archetypal romantic quester, was destroyed by mistakenly seeking a beauty in the outer world that existed only in his own projective imagination, the consul's doom is even more frightening: he must follow the same quest while realizing, from the beginning, its innate delusion. He must attempt to make the *process* of the quest real even though he understands the fictitiousness of its goal. His battle, in other words, is a battle for a revived myth, for a vision of adequate humanity which his own humanity will not betray.

The consul himself observes his deep bondage to the myth we have been tracing, the myth of the ruined, monstrous garden:

> "I've often wondered whether there isn't more in the old legend of the Garden of Eden, and so on, than meets the eye. What if Adam wasn't really banished from the place at all? That is, in the sense we used to understand it. . . . What if his punishment really consisted," the Consul continued with warmth, "In his having to go on living there, alone, of course, unseen, cut off from God. . . ?"

The consul, as Lowry observes in one of his letters, "has turned into a man that is all destruction—in fact he has almost ceased to be a man altogether, and his human feelings merely make matters more agonizing for him, but don't alter things in the least: he is in hell." This hell is also the inversion of the creative *fiat,* the undermining of the logos by a world where accidentally encountered signs, posters, and snatches of verse take on a preternatural weight of doom, where "other words," "other systems," are the only words a man can use, and are never enough. The brilliant stylistic web of Lowry's narration is an equivalent icon of the consul's situation, a tapestry of quotations duplicating Firmin's own paralyzed self-consciousness. For, of course, Firmin is also the projection, the monster, of Lowry's own creative self.

If Lowry's consul is a signal casualty of the "that-thereness" of the world, Saul Bellow's Herzog, in a complementary way, is crucified in his attempt to intellectualize that materiality, to master it in a total conversion of *res extensa* into *res cogitans,* the dragon's corpse into revivified garden.

Bellow's enterprise has always been to locate meaning in the tawdry, to put the life of the cities in touch with the humanistic, philosophical traditions of which the cities are the deformed children. In *Herzog* he succeeds because his central character is so much, so familiarly, the prey of the absurdities against which he wrestles. If Geoffrey Firmin, an adept of mythology, is destroyed by history—by the inevitable ticking a way of the clock-time of his last day alive, Herzog, a student of history, is frozen to the bone by his yearning for a myth of redemption, penance, and permanence. Firmin's ruined garden is also the ruined garden in which *Herzog* begins and ends, the hero's gone-to-seed yard in the Berkshires. Herzog desperately tries to maintain an innocence in the face of his career's and civilization's wreckage, and that innocence finally succeeds because it manages to establish itself in a field of irony, of self-doubt and moral decision based upon self-doubt, which is the distinctive language of American fiction after Bellow. Here is Herzog, at once living his life and writing one of his interminable letters to the living and dead:

> I bought a gaudy vest in the Burlington Arcade last winter, and a pair of Swiss boots of the type I see now the Village fairies have adopted. Heartsore? Yes, he further wrote, and dressed-up, too. But my vanity will no longer give me much mileage and to tell you the truth I'm not even greatly impressed with my own tortured heart. It begins to seem another waste of time.

Herzog's letters are a double of, and advance over, the consul's drunken fantasies in *Under the Volcano*. For they are *writing,* even if writing in and against the void; and Herzog and Bellow, good Talmudists that they are, understand the value of scripture, even the scripture of the absurd, as the first of human technologies and last, most apocalyptic of human hopes.

Probably no author since Bellow has concentrated more obsessively upon the nature of fiction as writing than has John Barth. Nor has any author more courageously placed himself at the center of the fictive enterprise. For it is Barth's insight that the primal struggle of civilizing myth has become in our age not simply the struggle *as narrated* but the struggle *of the narrator.* With Barth the myth of the dragon ceases to be an over- or undertone of writing, and becomes the subject of the postmodern novel. We may remember here Bloom's comment about the modern poet as Oedipus and his muse as the Sphinx. For Barth's fiction has progressed, from *The Sot-Weed Factor* on, toward an admission of itself as ineluctable quotation, ineluctably inauthentic, and toward a direct treatment of the story of the hero and the dragon—eventuating, in the astounding *Chimera,* in a fiction which reestablishes the possibility of creation by asserting that man is the principle of the monstrous against which, at his most creative, he wages war.

A venture like Barth's is, of course, fraught with risks, both psychic and stylistic. And many readers predictably dismissed his penultimate book, *Lost in the Funhouse,* as a terminal failure of imagination, a reduction of his powers to the most manic degree of involution. Roughly the first half of that volume, indeed, is involved with chasing down to its last absurdity the idea of the postmodern as "play," as stories within stories for the sake of stories within stories. But Barth's real genius is to work through that progressive involution to a voice which talks about important things—life, love, death, "inspiration"—without ignoring the weight of self-consciousness our century has piled atop them. By reinventing the principle of framed narration as the very body of monstrosity, he also humanizes that monstrosity in the difficult sense that is the only sense available to us. The best tale of *Funhouse,* "Meneleiad," begins fiction all over again by assuming those quotes-within-quotes as the necessary condition of narrative, as Menelaus tries to tell the story of his fateful question to Helen—i.e., why she returned to him after the Trojan War. And Helen's response to that question, at the very center of the multiple narrations, is " ' " ' " 'Love!' " ' " ' " At that moment, with the utterance of the most fragile and civilizing of all fictions, the quotation marks begin to fall away, Menelaus begins to extricate himself from the nearly suicidal self-consciousness in which he has been trapped.

It is one of the great moments of recent fiction. "Love" in inverted commas is the subtlest delusion of the fictivized mind, but is also the first impulse of a fully human one. And the triumph of "Meneleiad" continues through *Chimera.*

The Chimera Bellerophon slew was another of the children of the dragon, another primal monster; and her name has come to signify dreams, fantasies, the irresponsible and perhaps insane freedom of the imagination. Barth's *Chimera,* with profound wit, is an exploration of that dual nature of the monstrous. The text is the monstrosity, the final and first artifice in which the self can be located and nurtured. In "Dunyazadiad," the first of the three tales, a genie who looks and talks like John Barth addresses Dunyazade, Scheherazade's younger sister, on the eve of her marriage to Scheherazade's husband's brother. His question to her is an appropriate epigraph for contemporary fiction:

> "All those nights at the foot of that bed, Dunyazade! . . . You've had the whole literary tradition transmitted to you—and the whole erotic tradition, too! . . . What are you going to do to entertain *him,* little sister? Make love in exciting ways? There are none! Tell him stories, like Scheherazade? He's heard them all! Dunyazade, Dunyazade! Who can tell your story?"

The brilliance of the passage is in the question; for to ask the question is already to tell Dunyazade's story, that difficult tale of creation and civilization *in spite of* secondarity, quotedness, the numbing sense of human inauthenticity. "The key to the treasure is the treasure," Barth gnomically reiterates throughout "Dunyazadiad": which, in terms of our history of postmodernism, maybe roughly translated as saying that our sense of loss of a creative tradition, regarded intelligently and creatively enough, can become our creative tradition.

After the overture of "Dunyazadiad," the other two tales of *Chimera,* "Perseid" and "Bellerophoniad," explore the dragon myth and its implications for the nature of writing more explicitly than any previous contemporary fictions. Perseus and Bellerophon, a major and a minor monster-slayer from the infancy of fiction, both live past their great achievements, into middle age, to find that the problems of the monstrous are not soluble by anything as simple as killing. The two tales are, among other things, *Bildungsromane:* but stories, not of the education of youths, but of the much more agonized education to be undergone by heroes, writers, and cultures like our own in the embarrassed discovery of their own finitude, their middle age. Perseus must rediscover and love his victim, the Gorgon Medusa—must learn to see the beauty and inevitability of the rockface. And Bellerophon, whose monster-victim gives a title to the book, must make the even more crucial discovery that he—his life, his obsession with "heroic patterns," with archetypes and systems—he *is,* in the profoundest way, the monster he has slain. This is the discovery that is Barth's most indelible achievement, the discovery that monster and monster-slayer, civilizing hero and the perennial entropy undermining all civilizing quests, are not contradictory but *contrary* principles, allowing us to reassert values not in spite of but upon the basis of the fictiveness, the sham which we have found to underlie all human value systems.

The novels of John Gardner carry this difficult humanism to a higher level of complexity than do Barth's. Gardner structures his work around the intimation of mortality, of the "that-thereness" of the world which may well be the only human impulse for tale telling at all. In his work, this structuring is the most fully developed "metalanguage" of those romantic visions of inescapable fictiveness whose morphology we have been tracing. From *The Resurrection* on, the central situation of Gardner's novels is this: a philosopher realizes that he is going to die. And the consequent, archetypal plot of his novels becomes the passionate debate of systems against the knowledge of death, the welter of conflicting metaphysics which, though they do not avail against the primal void, nevertheless illuminate, in their very self-contradiction, the instinctive and terrible duty of the mind to thread and humanize that void, even with lies.

In *Grendel* it is the voice of the monster himself which speaks, more human, more familiarly tormented by fear and vision than the conventional hero who, we know, will slay him. All systems are *other* to Grendel, and all—the impossibly superhuman Beowulf, the existentialist Dragon who instructs him in futility, and the ancient scop who awakens him to the melancholy of beauty—simultaneously impel him toward and clarify the abyss which is his end:

> I will fall. I seem to desire the fall, and though I fight it with all my will, I know in advance that I can't win. Standing balled, quaking with fear, three feet from the edge of a nightmare cliff, I find myself, incredibly, moving toward it. I look down, down, into bottomless blackness, feeling the dark power moving in me like an ocean current, some monster inside me, deep sea wonder, dread night monarch astir in his cave, moving me slowly to my voluntary tumble into death.

The landscape of *Grendel,* like the landscape of Barth's best fiction, is that of ventriloquized epic: the narrator assumes, and in assuming, parodies the self-confident voice we associate with the certainties of classical epic and the daemonic assertiveness of epic heroes. It is a purification of *our* fictive language, then, by the antithetical assumption of a narrative speech which implies all the powers our age so deeply lacks.

Gardner's completion and antithesis of the Blakean formula with which we began is this: we *must* create, not a system but a way of inhabiting the infinity of systems which are our birthright and our curse, or be enslaved—not by another man's system but by the paralytic consciousness of all systems as other; we must, in other words, locate a fiction which will allow us to utter words like "honor" and "courage," even though we knew that those words can never appear outside their inverted commas.

"Honor" and "courage"—and "charity," another word which Gardner reinstates—are rather old-fashioned concepts for the vortex of the contemporary imagination to reveal at its center. But that, of course, is the nature of revolutions: they return, revolve, to their point of origin, but in a clarified, more dangerous context. *Jason and Medeia* contains a number of great snakes—not just the serpent-guardian of the Golden

Fleece whom Jason and Medeia deceive, but the primal serpents, monstrous originators and annihilators of civilization, here articulated as the myth of Kadmos (Kosmos) and Harmonia, founders of Thebes whose names mean universe and music:

> King Kadmos—Kosmos, rightly—
> loved so well, old legends claim,
> that after his perfect joy in life—his faultless rule
> of soaring Thebes, great golden city where for many centuries nothing
> had stirred but the monstrous serpent Kadmos slew—
> the gods awarded him power and joy after life. Zeus filled
> his place with lightning-bolts, and the well-matched pair was changed
> to two majestic serpents, now Lady and Lord of all the Dead.

Nothing prospers but the soul, as Gardner has said. But that prosperity itself, mythicized more severely and creatively in *Jason and Medeia* than in any other contemporary fiction, is implicit with the making and unmaking, resurrection and repeated death, which is the common history of cities, languages, and stories. The serpents, once city-founders and now Lady and Lord of the Dead, who breed over the action of Gardner's epic, are complemented by his most archetypal—perhaps *the* archetypal—blind man, the Oedipus who inherited the civilization forged by Kadmos and Harmonia and destroyed it through the self-binding fire of his own lucidity.

Gardner's Jason is another monster slayer in middle age, tormented by the noonday devils of declining faith in his own rationality and the nagging sense that his great quest, the voyage of *Argo,* in fact marked the end of the heroic era and the beginning of a diminished, more difficult and dangerous age of statecraft, moral canniness, measured defeats and measured triumphs. The cataclysmic end of his love for Medeia is, above all, the end of a *marriage,* of a human world and therefore of the world; but it is also, in its very violence, a reaffirmation of the dignity, even if fictive and earth-breaking, of human love. Gardner's befuddled narrator, caught between our world and the world of myth we witness along with him, reenacts at every point in his tale the paradox of the Lord of the Dead, the serpent whose existence makes possible as it cancels our dream of human cities. And, as a book whose language presents itself as a *translation* of itself simultaneously its own voice and "another man's" system—*Jason and Medeia* becomes a metaphor for its own deepest vision. For this language, at once original and "derivative," is an icon of the ancient serpent ouroboros, the world-snake with its tail in its mouth, the cyclic history which is our perennial fall into the delusions and accomplishments of human time, human mortality, and human decency.

In the best of contemporary writers, conservative and anti-apocalyptic as it may seem, the business of writing is still the survival, within the myth of the dragon's corpse, of the myth of the City, of a human world which can absorb even our worst—clearest—visions of Last Things. That this business involves, in Barth, Pynchon, or Gardner, as much canniness and self-contradiction as it does is the sign, not of its great difficulty only, but of the ongoing vitality and necessity of the task.

Hawthorne and the Sixties: Careening on the Utmost Verge (1985)

SAMUEL COALE

What would Hawthorne have made of the "literary disruptions"[1] in the more experimental and daring fictions of the Sixties and Seventies? How would he have viewed such writers as John Barth, Thomas Pynchon, John Hawkes, Jerzy Kosinski, Kurt Vonnegut, Donald Barthelme, Robert Coover, to lump these names simplistically, for the sake of argument, as the awkwardly phrased "post-modernists"?

In his book on the writers of the Sixties, Raymond Olderman makes a strong case for linking them to the traditions of the American romance and seeing them as an extension of that tradition. They too mix fact and fiction in their "explosion of the ordinary by the fabulous." They too use "two-dimensional characters . . . and a continued hint of the mythic, allegorical, and symbolistic." They create fables, self-conscious tales about the nature of modern society, revealing "the fear of some mystery within fact itself that holds power over us."[2]

These contemporary fables differ, however, from Hawthorne's kind of romance. For one thing these writers generally employ blatant artifice in their yarn-spinning, calling attention to letters answering letters, creating narratives to be shattered and undercut, inventing games, constructing cartoons, reveling in comic-strip slapstick to display the sheer buoyant artificiality of their fiction. Such self-consciousness betrays a mannerist art in which surface action replaces reflection, the result perhaps of cinematic techniques applied to fiction. Characters appear victimized by their environment, produced by savage historical forces bearing down upon them, reduced to cartoon folk, the automatons of a behaviorist outlook and psychology. However funny, however battered, these figures reveal none of the psychological complexities of Hawthorne's characters. They react to a mad consumerism and preen and strut like television-commercial creatures, whether figures of fun or of villainy. At times the authors seem more interested in constructing their vision of a savage apocalyptic capitalism, of a sensual desire run amuck, of sheer brutal survival instincts and cliché-ridden babble than in creating more complex characters. Stick figures inhabit a terrifying landscape, puppets strung up to visions of evil militarists, collectivist societies, corrupt politics.

The post-modernist emphasis on fragmentation as form recreates a primal chaos, an open-ended arbitrary universe in which nearly every value is upended and sabotaged. "Conspiracy is both Deity and Demon"[3] in this thoroughly Manichean world, the world of Hawkes's landscapes of dream and desire, of Pynchon's blitzes and Kosinski's stark realm of survival of the fittest, of Coover's outrageously funny all-American anti-heroes. People are powerless. The individual is mauled by social mechanics. Demonic visions reign supreme, beautifully, artfully done but more one dimensional in their blackness than are Hawthorne's ambiguously resonant dark designs. Pynchon's sprocket holes, Kosinski's steps, and Vonnegut's cartoon-chapters disrupt, probe, shatter, and maim the reader's quest for connections. The visions seem so unrelievedly dark, so much the wasteland terror of Eliot's world, that one wonders if Ihab Hassan may not be right when he suggests that the post-modernists as harbingers of blight display "a radical literary imagination in the interest of essentially conservative feelings,"[4] if they are not latter-day Puritans wreaking their vengeance on a society so materialistic that their fiction will completely reproduce the density and claustrophobia of all that materialism.

The age of irony produces its black comedies. Satire, farce, parody, the picaresque, the grotesque: all are in league to distance the reader from these dark visions, in effect to make him feel superior to the stick figures that parade and are quashed before his eyes. A radical doubt disrupts all moral design. People exist only in the roles society screws them into. In attacking the trap of social convention and history, many of these writers seem to imitate that trap, creating self-enclosed, shimmering fictions that evaporate when the last page is turned. Nothing is learned. And irony protects us all, the last wedge of defense, the new sentimentality of our self-conscious materialism.

Clearly these writers produce a Manichean vision more "pure" than Hawthorne's, and for that reason their fictions, however brilliant the vision, the prose, and the artifice, seem simpler, less "real" than Hawthorne's romances. All reality remains elusive; consequently, illusion follows delusion only to reveal further levels of false selfjustification or the Freudian dark depths of sadomasochistic dreams, a lust for sex and death as the final conflagration. Olderman's connections are valuable and point clearly to the antirealistic structures of these fables as an extension of American romance, but just as clearly these fables in their dark simplicities and fragmented texts, in their Manichean starkness, do not—no matter the brilliant artifice—approach Hawthorne's moral and philosophical designs. Poe stands as godfather to these fierce fictions, especially those of Pynchon, Barth, Hawkes, and Kosinski. The spritely humor of Vonnegut, Barthelme, and Coover suggests a sourer Twain, an Ambrose Bierce in contemporary togs. The precarious balance of a Hawthorne, Faulkner, O'Connor, Gardner, Cheever vanishes. And it is that uneasy balance that may be Hawthorne's lasting legacy to the tradition of romance, that "careening on the utmost verge of a precipitous absurdity, and the skill lies in coming as close as possible, without actually tumbling over."[5]

For Hawthorne facts remained stolid, physically visible realities, the tombs of the spirit that had to be overcome, transcended. "The world has sucked me within its vortex; and I could not get back to my solitude again even if I would."[6] The attempt as a romancer was to vault that vortex, to escape becoming "covered with earthly dust . . . by rude encounters with the multitude,"[7] not to submit totally and recreate it: "How much mud and mire many pools of unclean water, how many slippery footsteps and perchance heavy tumbles, might be avoided, if we could but tread six inches above the crust of this world. Physically, we cannot do this; our bodies cannot; but it seems to me that our hearts and minds may keep themselves above moral mud-puddles, and other discomforts of the soul's pathway; and so enjoy the sunshine."[8] Surely the tension in Hawthorne's art emerges from just this confrontation, although his fascination with "moral mud-puddles" held him firm, and once he got his feet wet, he could never get into the sunshine to dry off.

Words too seemed to thwart Hawthorne, reproducing "all sorts of external things, leaving the soul's life and action to explain itself in its own way . . . [used] merely for explaining outward acts."[9] They solidified all too quickly, entrapping "spiritual realities" in the very bulk and heft that trapped them in the physically visible world of nature. Writing to Sophia as the ardent lover: "Words come like an earthly wall betwixt us. Then our minds are compelled to stand apart and make signals of our meaning."[10] Common ardent-lover remarks, and yet words like facts "compel" minds to stand apart and become only "signals," a code to break. The physical and the spiritual remain at Manichean odds; too much remains "an earth-born vision."[11] Ideas put into words run through Hawthorne's tales "like an iron rod . . . this circumstance gives the narrative a character of monotony."[12] Beyond lurks some phantasmagorical "real self," some ultimate, inviolate mystery, some soul devised of romantic aspiration in some purer state. No wonder facts and scenes, the darker the better, pressed in upon his doubly blasted allegories: at once damned by the very darkness of their vision and doomed as successful allegorical structures.

Hawthorne's invention of the American romance was both an escape from and a submission to his sense of history. He escaped into a dimmer past, where his home-feelings allowed him to undercut the bold factual realities of his earth-bound existence. That "slumbrous withdrawing of myself from the external world"[13] had to take place before his imagination could break free from the world around him. How he wanted "to make the mere words absolutely disappear into the thought,"[14] as the "real" material world disappeared into a dimmer, more shadowy past. The haunted mind conjured up spells triggered in part by the moral physical darkness of the material world, embodied in his sense of the past as shadowy veil, the aura of romance. Facts killed; the imagination, unfettered in gloomier realms, created. To Bridge he wrote:

> I would advise you not to stick too accurately to the bare fact, either in your descriptions or narrations; else your hand will be cramped, and the result will be a want of freedom, that will deprive you of a higher truth than that which you strive to attain. Allow your fancy pretty free license, and omit no heightening touches merely because they did not chance to happen before your eyes. If they did not happen, they at least ought—which is all that concerns you. This is the secret of all entertaining travelers.[15]

And, one would add, of successful romancers as well. Matters of fact must be linked to the imaginative; both battle for recognition.

And finally, in the realm of romance even facts themselves become suspect:

> Every day of my life makes me feel more and more how seldom a fact is accurately stated; how, almost invariably, when a story has passed through the mind of a third person, it becomes, so far as regards the impression that it makes in further repetitions, little better than a false

hood, and this, too, though the narrator be the most truth seeking person in existence. How marvelous the tendency is! . . . Is truth a fantasy which we are to pursue forever and never grasp?[16]

The romancer in full bloom. Faulkner would heartily approve.

Thus Hawthorne subverted historical realities for his own purposes, envisioning a world in the guise of a Manichean morality play, noble if intolerant early heroes against present-day lesser folk, sunk in dissipation and materialistic folly, revolutionary inspirations frozen into social roles and conventions as Christian parable hardened into dogma, the "new" American self in conflict with the frail old human self, guilt-ridden, prideful, sinful: in short, the human condition of the Fall recounted over and over again. The darker, grimmer, lumpier romances, *The Blithedale Romance* and *The Marble Faun,* broke beneath the weight of sin and egoism, caught up in power plays, perched on the edge of the abyss, undercutting the romancer's art almost entirely, fact become word become gloomy legacy become inert fiction or mechanical, novelistic maze. The moral and/or aesthetic equilibrium, the link in the dark design, could not hold, and if the essence of the romance became the embroidery on the "A," the labyrinthine quest for multiple meanings without a final signification, an ultimate freedom and an ultimate dread, then Manichean darkness—as in post-modernist fables—finally won. Perhaps that is why so many contemporary critics have been interested in Hawthorne's last two romances, particularly in the apparent dreamlike shape-shiftings of the faun's mythic tale.

But of course Hawthorne also submitted his romances to history. He used history, or at least the guise of history, to authenticate his own private vision. He "finds" the scarlet letter, "locates" the Pyncheon manse, mentions Brook Farm, lived in Rome: these "facts" he employs to ground his fantasies, to shape and color them. They are the ballast of his fictions, the necessary clay and soil of his neutral territories, talismans of witch craft, the objects necessary to cast the spell. Duyckinck early admired the linking of seen to unseen, of fact to imagination, when, in fact, it was just as likely that Hawthorne was linking them in the opposite manner, linking his vision to fact to make it appear historically "true" or at least as the stuff of legends passed down from generation to generation. It is this essentially conservative stance that separates Hawthorne from the post-modernists, for whom the fabulous nature of all fact is a matter of imaginative belief.

Hawthorne may also have been conscious of the sexual overtones that existed in the nineteenth century in regard to the literary work of male and female authors. As Ann Douglas suggests, popular fiction in the nineteenth century existed for the most part in "the realm of 'feminine' fantasy," whereas "the realm of 'masculine' reality" was history.[17] We know of Hawthorne's aversion to the "damn'd scribbling women" of his era. His idea of authenticating his romances with elaborate historical settings and backgrounds may have been his way of dissociating himself and his art even further from the likes of Susan Warner and Lucy Larcom.

Hawthorne would probably have understood and sympathized with the fuss over nonfiction novels and "history as a novel, the novel as history" in the Sixties. He could not have freed himself so readily from "the facts" as the fabulators appeared to do, nor would he have succumbed so readily to them as Norman Mailer and Truman Capote seemed to wish to do, or at least to look as though they were doing. So mesmerized was Mailer by the historical convolutions of the Sixties, the sheer apocalyptic fervor of them, that in describing what a novel should be he describes almost exactly what Hawthorne's definition of the romance asserts, namely, that "the novel must replace history at precisely that point where experience is sufficiently emotional, spiritual, psychical, moral, existential, or supernatural . . . that world of strange lights and intuitive speculation."[18] Mailer's novel, though he doesn't seem to realize it, is Hawthorne's romance.

In the first paragraph of *The House of the Seven Gables,* Hawthorne establishes the historical "authenticity" of his setting, at the same time throwing the shadows of the past around it, at once locating the scene of his romance on firm ground and disconnecting the reader from the ordinary events of the everyday world of the novel:

> Half-way down a by-street of one of our New England towns stands a rusty wooden house, with seven acutely peaked gables, facing towards various points of the compass, and a huge, clustered chimney in the midst. The street is Pyncheon Street; the house is the old Pyncheon House; and an elm-tree, of wide circumference, rooted before the door, is familiar to every town-born child by the title of the Pyncheon Elm. On my occasional visits to the town aforesaid, I seldom failed to turn down Pyncheon Street, for the sake of passing through the shadow of these two antiquities,—the great elm tree and the weather-beaten edifice.

The writer creates his spell. He has visited the house. Tree and house are "huge, clustered," "wide," "great." The name Pyncheon is repeated four times as if chanted, conjuring up both a name and a place, as if there were something magical in them, fraught with significance. The house is "old," "rusty," "weather-beaten," and in the second paragraph it affects the romancer "like a human countenance." And to get there one must walk halfway down a bystreet off the beaten path, "passing through the shadow of these two antiquities." The writer is drawn to the spot, the shadow, the face of the old house. And in appearing himself, he displays that attraction to the reader, connects the house, the tree, the past, old New England, and finally "a human countenance." The reader watches the writer make these connections, a man solving a mystery, conjuring up a sacred spot.

Cheever accomplishes the same thing at the beginning of *Bullet Park:* "Paint me a small railroad station then, ten minutes before dark. Beyond the platform are the waters of the Wekonsett River. . . . The setting seems in some way to be at the heart of the matter . . . this is your country—unique, mysterious and vast." The remoteness, the shadowy atmosphere, the setting as "heart of the matter": here romance begins, as it does in the first paragraph of both Wapshot books. Other examples exist in the same tradition. Here is the opening of *Set This House on Fire:* "Sambuco. . . . Aloof upon its precipice, remote and beautifully difficult of access, it is a model of invulnerability. . . ." The first two paragraphs of the novel give Sambuco's guidebook history: the facts are established. And then Styron the romancer creates his landscape. And Oates's *Belle-fleur:* "It was many years ago in that dark, chaotic, unfathomable pool of time before Germaine's birth . . . on a night in late September stirred by in numerable frenzied winds, like spirits contending with one another. . . ." The remote setting, the shadows of the past, and the Manichean vision are revealed almost at once.

How different is the opening of Thomas Pynchon's monumental *Gravity's Rainbow:*

A screaming comes across the sky. It has happened before, but there is nothing to compare it to now. It is too late. The Evacuation still proceeds, but it's all theatre. There are no lights inside the cars. No light anywhere . . . it's night. He's afraid of the way the glass will fall—soon—it will be a spectacle: the fall of a crystal palace. But coming down in total blackout, without one glint of light, only great invisible crashing.

The reader is plunged immediately into a dramatic scene, a cinematic spectacle in its play of light and shadow, a theatre of conspiracy and collapse. We don't know who "he" is. The passage is disconcerting, disconnected; chaos and turmoil thrive on the verge of some apocalyptic event. The author designs the scene but he is nowhere seen. Disconnection and fear replace Hawthorne's spell of connection and hypnotic fascination. Things are shattered and will shatter. All is darkness, including the reader's sense of exactly what is going on. This is almost an "antispell," a disorienting presentation, an almost total Manichean darkness without light. The author remains an objective, hidden observer, commenting ironically on the theatrical spectacle of the scene, distant and removed from his character's fear amidst the impending shattering of glass, the end of an era, a crystal palace "coming down in total blackout."

A similar sense of disconnection occurs at the beginning of *Slaughterhouse Five,* though Vonnegut's lighter touch, his comic distance, almost undercut the darker incidents of his remembering:

> All this happened, more or less. The war parts, anyway, are pretty much true. One guy I knew really was shot in Dresden for taking a teapot that wasn't his. Another guy I knew really did threaten to have his personal enemies killed by hired gunmen after the war. And so on. I've changed all the names.

Even the act of recounting, of telling, is served up with suspicion, the fable doubted from the very beginning, "more or less." Trivia and horror mingle with one another: murder and teapots, followed by Vonnegut's throwaway line about changing all the names. The author visibly detaches himself from his material, as if that is the only way he can confront it. Irony and distance replace Hawthorne's creation of a mesmeric spell. Facts shift and remain unreliable because the narrator is unreliable, for whatever reasons. How unlike the dreamlike openings to John Gardner's *Nickel Mountain* and *The Sunlight Dialogues.* How more like John Hawkes's opening to *Virginie*—"Mine is an impossible story. My journal burns"—or Robert Coover's to *The Public Burning:*

> On June 24, 1950, less than five years after the end of World War II, the Korean War begins, American boys are again sent off in uniforms to die for Liberty, and a few weeks later, two New York City Jews, Julius and Ethel Rosenberg, are arrested by the FBI . . . and it is on the night of their fourteenth wedding anniversary, Thursday, June 18, 1953.

(And yet Coover considered calling his encyclopedic novel, *An Historic Romance,* described Uncle Sam as reminding him of "Handsome Frank

Pierce, puzzling over the metaphysical obscurities in the books of his friend Nat Hawthorne," and at the very beginning of the book referred to one of the pronouncements of "the Divine Hawthorne": " 'There is a fatality, a feeling so irresistible and inevitable that it has the force of doom. . . !' ")

How like, too, Joseph Heller's splendid opening to *Something Happened,* the title itself almost a post-modernist proclamation of elusive facts, illusory realities, a sense of something ominous but not exactly what:

> I get the willies when I see closed doors. . . . the sight of a closed door
> is sometimes enough to make me dread that something horrible is hap-
> pening behind it, something that is going to affect me adversely . . . I
> can almost smell the disaster mounting invisibly. . . . Something must
> have happened to me sometime.

The ironies, the dread, the disconnected thoughts leading to a premonition of disaster, the uncertainty about just what has happened or is happening: post-modernist fable certainly, but not Hawthornian romance. An extension of the romance—the self at the center, the disconnection from an ordinary world, a mysterious dread or isolation, the sense of complete Manichean trap—but without Hawthorne's use of historical placement or his sense of the unending, ever present New England past of legends, generational morality plays, and quest for allegorical significances, however "mud-puddled."

Contemporary fiction reflects the Hawthornian split between novel and romance. Saul Bellow, Philip Roth, John Updike, and Paul Theroux, to name a few, write novels of character, using fairly straightforward historical and chronological narrative structures, despite the several flashbacks and juxtapositions they may create within them. Pynchon, Coover, Hawkes, and Doctorow, for example, write fables of vision in which characters are subordinated to the author's more public visions of society in general, of a world in arbitrary flux, a wasteland, a realm of ultimate conspiracy. These writers use the fragmented narrative to recreate their sense of disconnection and turmoil. The latter lies in Hawthorne's shadow more than the former, however distorted, however flattened.

And yet we find in Roth's opening of *The Ghost Writer* significant hints of romance: "It was the last daylight hour of a December afternoon more than twenty years ago. . . . when I arrived at his hideaway to meet the great man. . . . my impression was that E. I. Lonoff looked more like the local superintendent of schools than the region's most original storyteller since Melville and Hawthorne." We can recognize the fictional "region" created here, with a tip of the hat to its creator.

Paul Theroux has been heralded as a literary realist in most critical circles. "He has mastered the encounter, the scene, the techniques of blending past and present," Frederick Karl suggests, and his observations are chiefly those of a "bemused witness."[19] There are, however, several recognizable traits of the American romance that one can locate beneath or within the precise fictional realism of his novels: the descriptions of ambiguous American innocence, the Manichean confrontations, the conjuring up of dreams and possession, the exotic settings in unusual and remote places, the shadowed past emerging in gothic details, the intimations of allegorical or at least symmetrical structures in regard to characters and situations. Beyond the gothic vision of such novels as *Girls at Play* (1969) and *The Black House* (1974) and the carefully crafted observations of manners and social conventions in his short stories and in such novels as *The Family Arsenal* (1976) and *Doctor Slaughter* (1984), lies a far greater realm, the more mysterious and ultimately enigmatic moral issues that confront Jack Flowers in *Saint Jack* (1973) and Charles Fox in *The Mosquito Coast* (1982). It is as if romantic elements were submerged in novels of manners, similar perhaps to the psychologically realistic surface of an Updike novel but striking chords and creating scenes that Hawthorne could respond to. Nowhere is this more apparent than in *The Mosquito Coast* (1982).

Charlie Fox, the fourteen-year-old narrator of *The Mosquito Coast* exorcises his fascination for and the burden of his father, an adolescent ritual in which the son recognizes that the father is no longer a god. His sharp poetic eye and reportorial skills miss nothing: the shame, envy, awkward speculation, and eager eye conspire to reveal the truth, slowly and in glimpses: "I was ashamed of Father, who didn't care what anyone thought. And I envied him for being so free. . . . Selfishness had made him clever. He wanted things his way. . . . He thought of himself first!" It is Charlie who, amidst the wreckage of his father's relentless schemes, begins to see the realities of paradise ("I saw cruelty in the hanging vines and selfishness in their root systems") at the same time holding onto the glorified image of his father, despite younger brother Jerry's insistence that he is crazy, despite the mounting horror of his deeds. Slowly disillusion sets in: "It was like the slow death in dreams of being trapped and trying to scream without a voice box." It is like seeing Honduras from a distance, before the cruel reality of the place sets in: "The view from the ship had been like a picture, but now we were inside that picture." The town at night suggests "magic—the halos on old lampposts . . . the snuffle of traffic," but in the morning the town "was cracked and discolored and mobbed by people actually screaming above the braying car horns. There was no magic now." Charlie's maturation destroys his childhood faith.

Allie Fox inhabits Theroux's novel like a striding colossus with feet of clay. He is Yankee ingenuity run amock who believes that "man is God," that God created an imperfect world that he must set to rights: "Nature is crooked. I wanted right angles and straight lines." He howls and rages about an America of junk food and drug addicts, a place of scavengers and savages. He will be the God to salvage his survival, usurping the deity's role, pulling his family out of Massachusetts and floating them into the jungles of Honduras to erect his own Xanadu, his survivalist's camp. Fox turns self-reliance into obsession. "From will power alone, so it seemed, he had made the pleasant valley appear." Becoming his own derelict god, a robber baron of his sons' souls, he lusts for dominion everywhere on his own inventor's terms, a modern Ahab seeking further wilderness to conquer and cultivate: "I want a real backwater. Solitary. Uninhabited. An empty corner. That's why we're here! If it's on a map, I can't use it." Mammoth ego stalks ultimate emptiness to enjoy its full expanded powers; a rampant imperialistic nihilism lurks within the crazed compulsion to invent, reinvent, move on to darker corners. He lies, murders, drags his family up river, destroys a missionary's plane, and blows up his generator. From fire he produces ice; from his own fiery self-certainty—the mad center of the American myth—he produces destruction and devastation.

Romantic elements surface within this Manichean confrontation between the Foxes, between the idealized father and the mad inventor— "I'm Doctor Frankenstein!"—"I'm the last man!"—within the psychologically realistic disillusionment of adolescence. The Mosquito Coast itself becomes the "edge of the precipice," the ultimate void, that stark landscape of psychological confrontation and showdown. To Allie it suggests that America is everywhere: his ultimate obsession chills. That "allegorical" setting reflects the allegory of Father and Mother, the wild man and the angel in Charlie's perspective. The children build their own camp, the Acre, away from Allie's jungle sanctuary, Jeronimo. Theroux's use of doubling widens the resonances of plot. The Maywits, the family at Jeronimo named by Father (their real name is Roper, but they're too timid to tell Allie otherwise) appear to Charlie as "our reflections—shrunken shadows of us." Mr. Maywit tells Fox about the Duppy:

"Everyone got a Duppy. They is the same as yourself. But they is you other self. They got bodies of they own." The condition of the Maywits prophesies the future condition of the Foxes. At the same time, Charlie views Allie's icebox invention, Fat Boy, as a reflection of his father. Inventor and invention reflect one another: "This was Father's head, the mechanical part of his brain and the complications of his mind, as strong and huge and mysterious." And again: "I had seen Father's mind, a version of it—its riddle and slant and its hugeness—and it had scared me." Hawthorne's villain-heroes would understand the riddle and the mystery. And before Allie Fox dies, his head is all that remains alive, and then that too is ravaged, appropriately by vultures on the beach who peck away his tongue.

By far the most elaborate vision within the novel is that of the crucified scarecrow. One night in Massachusetts Charlie wakes and sees "men with torches marching at midnight across the valley fields. . . . In the fiery light of the circle of torches, I saw the cross raised up with a man on it." Searching for his father he thinks that the scarecrow is both a hallucination of his father and is in fact his father, "as if it was something I had imagined, an evil thought that had sprung out of my head." The son's immolation of the father: a gothic dream of Hawthornian romance suggesting the public disgrace and collapse of "My Kinsman, Major Molineux." That image continues to haunt Charlie: "It had been upraised like a demon and struck terror into me." The three evil soldiers of fortune who come to take possession of Jeronimo look like scarecrows, and "we had gotten used to Father looking like a live scarecrow, the wild man of the woods, and hollering." As they approach the "coastal hell" of the Mosquito Coast, Fox's image of the entire world as ultimate desolation, Fox utters a nearly final epitaph: "'Vultures,' he said, and then the terrible sentence, 'Christ is a scarecrow!'"

Allie Fox, facing down a derelict world, proclaims his Manichean faith: "That's a consequence of perfection in this world—the opposing wrath of imperfection." That wrath, of course, is his own, which comes back to destroy him. Knowing no past, viewing the present only in terms of exploitation and escape, conjuring up a future of perfect control and order which can never be, which he himself would be unable to tolerate because there would be no place in it for his self-righteous wrath and his inventor's compulsions to go, he inhabits a nihilistic no-man's-land, a place finally that his family cannot follow him into. Charlie realizes the distinctions: "Yet for me the past was the only real thing, it was my hope. . . . The future spoke to Father, but for me it was silent and blind and dark." It is at once a very un-American, a very human thing to admit.

The Mosquito Coast displays Theroux at his best. The novel resonates with the foundation elements of psychological romance, the "American" heart of Hawthorne's vision. Even its Aylmer at the center of things suggests Theroux's attachment to the great American themes. Demons and dreams and edges of precipices reveal the dark crux of a Hawthornesque world, and Allie Fox's Manichean madness illuminates that continuing fictional tradition.

Hawthorne's American romance is still with us, alive and well in its various forms and persuasions, as is the Manichean vision that created it. Paradox bred not unity but spiritual warfare unresolved, resolution hinted at only in the unending battle and the ongoing confrontation. This may indicate the very liveliness of American culture and of its literature, for resolution may breed stagnation and an ultimate complacency. The Manichean vision can lead to paralysis, as it does in several of Norman Mailer's fictions, a place where demon and deity are so equal to one another that only a stand-off remains. But for the most part conflict, in American literature at least, breeds our special "brand" of fiction, that romantic view of the world which reveals our own uncertainties and dreads, a continuing moral quest amidst fierce polarities that will not cohere. When and if they mingle, they collide and confuse, leaving darker designs in their wake.

Perhaps this results from the American myth that raises the individual self to the *sine qua non* of moral focus. The individual must exercise what he takes to be his free will. Ultimate human value demands that he choose. But in choosing he may choose evil, and in doing so may commit an action which is both good, because of the act of choice, and evil, because of what he has chosen. This basic paradox and contradiction, deeply imbedded in Western thought, spawns the Manichean clash of opposites and interpenetration of opposing forces, exaggerated in an American wilderness where the self must ultimately confront itself.

In "The Minister's Black Veil" (1836) Hawthorne spins the tale of a Calvinist clergyman who covers his eyes with black crepe and walks among his congregation as a visible emblem of Calvinist sin. He rejects the one woman who loves him and thus compounds his sin in the very act of transforming himself into a visible emblem of it. Such duplicity haunts the townspeople and himself; they are victims of their Manichean vision of a dark imprisoning world and a consciousness that knows only isolation, solitude, self-abasement and sorrow. They see nothing but that vision which traps and engulfs them.

In the story the veil, symbolizing that Manichean vision, achieves demonic powers. It possesses the people and the minister and becomes the dark idol of their devil-worship, though they insist on the guise of Christian consciousness and obeisance. What happens to that veil, how it is transformed into a demonic object of veneration and power, suggests what happens to the romance in Hawthorne's hands: it too reproduces the demonic powers of the very Manichean vision it was initially designed to transcend. The author's text becomes one more black veil, the penetration of which leads only to other veils and darker mysteries. At bottom fiction becomes the amulet, as R. P. Blackmur has suggested, to ward off a totally veil-less experience which, in Manichean terms, can only be death itself.[20] And the romancer is left to confront the saddest of all prisons, his own heart.

This dark vision lies at the heart of the American romance in its sheer bold attempts to escape from and/or submit to the world of fact that threatens and surrounds it. Perhaps this is why so many great American writers have been drawn to it, to Hawthorne's art. Such darkness may veil a vision of America too big and too terrible to contemplate and at the same time may mirror the dark interior of such an enlightened progressive democracy that fails to grapple publicly with its own doubts and deceptions. In any case the black veil has fascinated the best of our writers, and Hawthorne first drew attention to its ambiguous and mesmerizing implications.

Hawthorne was the first American writer to seize this vision in all its moral complexities, uneasy as he was with it (unlike Poe, for instance), and to create a form that suited it. The long shadow cast from that creative act haunts us still and will continue to do so as long as American fiction lasts.

NOTES

[1]See Jerome Klinkowitz, *Literary Disruptions: The Making of a Post-Contemporary American Fiction* (Urbana: University of Illinois Press, 1975); and Samuel Coale, "The Cinematic Self of Jerzy Kosinski." *Modern Fiction Studies* 20.3 (Autumn 1974), 359–70.

[2]Raymond M. Olderman, *Beyond the Wasteland: The American Novel in the Nineteen Sixties* (New Haven: Yale University Press, 1972), 5, 7, 23.

[3]Olderman, 120.

[4]Ihab Hassan, *Radical Innocence* (Princeton: Princeton University Press, 1961), 43.

[5]Nathaniel Hawthorne to J. T. Fields, Boston, Nov. 3, 1850, no. 453. *Hawthorne Papers,* Ohio State University Library, Columbus.

[6]Nathaniel Hawthorne to Sophia Peabody, Boston, Dec. 22, 1841, no. 222.

[7]Nathaniel Hawthorne to Sophia Peabody, Salem, Oct. 4, 1840, no. 173.

[8]Nathaniel Hawthorne to Sophia Peabody, Boston, Feb. 7, 1840, no. 138.

[9]Nathaniel Hawthorne to Sophia Peabody, Boston, May 19, 1840, no. 159.

[10]Nathaniel Hawthorne to Sophia Peabody, Salem, Apr. 15, 1840, no. 151.

[11]Nathaniel Hawthorne to Sophia Peabody, Brook Farm, Oct. 18, 1841, no. 216.

[12]Nathaniel Hawthorne to Charles A. Putnam, Lenox, Sept. 16, 1851, no. 512.

[13]Nathaniel Hawthorne to Sophia Peabody, Boston, June 11, 1840, no. 163.

[14]Nathaniel Hawthorne to E. A. Duyckinck, Lenox, Apr 27, 1851, no. 482.

[15]Nathaniel Hawthorne to Horatio Bridge, Concord, May 3, 1843, no. 267.

[16]Nathaniel Hawthorne to Sophia Peabody, Brook Farm, May 1, 1841, no. 194.

[17]Ann Douglas, *The Feminization of American Culture* (New York: Avon, 1977), 317.

[18]Norman Mailer, *The Armies of the Night* (New York: New American Library, 1968), 284.

[19]Frederick Karl, *American Fictions,* 520, 589.

[20]R. P. Blackmur, "Afterward," *The Celestial Railroad and Other Stories* (New York: New American Library, 1963), 293.

Realistic and Romantic Tendencies (1996)

EBERHARD ALSEN

In Toni Morrison's sixth novel, *Jazz* (1993), the central character Violet Trace says to a common-sense girl named Felice:

> "What's the world for if you can't make it up the way you want it? . . .
> Don't you want it to be something more than what it is?"
> "What's the point? I can't change it."
> "That's the point. If you don't, it will change you, and it'll be your fault
> cause you let it. I let it. And messed up my life." (208)

Violet believes that her life has been "messed up" because she accepted the world as it is rather than trying make it conform to what her imagination told her it might be. She did not try to change the world, therefore the world changed her. From that experience she has learned that we can only change the world if we imagine it as "something more than what it is."

I begin with this quotation because it illustrates a wide-spread tendency in postmodernist fiction. Many contemporary novelists entertain, embrace, or even espouse visions of life which are forms of philosophical idealism. Along with this vision of life goes a view of art which resembles that of the nineteenth-century romantics. Moreover, these postmodernists employ modes of story telling that are reminiscent of the romances of Nathaniel Hawthorne, Edgar Allan Poe, and Herman Melville.

This romantic trend has been largely ignored because the majority of critics have been preoccupied with novels and stories by authors who are trying to go beyond the innovations of the late modernists and whose vision of life—like that of the late modernists—is realistic and often nihilistic. According to this view, enshrined in the *Columbia History of the American Novel* (Hite 1991), it is the work of such writers as Kathy Acker and Robert Coover which forms the mainstream of postmodernist fiction.

I question this majority view for two reasons. One is that much of the fiction which critics celebrate as the postmodernist mainstream is so difficult that very few people enjoy reading it, and the other is that the emphasis on this kind of fiction marginalizes the work of more widely read authors such as the Nobel laureates Saul Bellow and Toni Morrison.

As an alternative to the majority view, I propose the hypothesis that there are two major trends in postmodernist fiction, a realistic and a romantic one. The realistic one is often disjunctive in its form, and its vision of life is grounded in philosophical materialism. The romantic one revives the form of the nineteenth century romance, and its vision of life is grounded in philosophical idealism.

I believe that it is the romantic trend which is the mainstream because it better reflects the spirit of the Age of Postmodernism. I base this opinion on a cyclical view of literary change that I derive—with a few alterations—from the oscillation theories of the linguist Roman Jakobson and the historian Hayden White.

In the 1956 study, *Fundamentals of Language,* Roman Jakobson makes this observation:

> The primacy of the metaphoric process in the literary schools of romanticism and symbolism has been repeatedly acknowledged, but it is still insufficiently realized that it is the predominance of metonymy which underlies and actually predetermines the so-called 'realistic' trend. . . .
>
> The alternative predominance of one or the other of these two processes is by no means confined to verbal art. The same oscillation occurs in sign systems other than language. A salient example from the history of painting is the manifestly metonymical orientation of cubism, where the object is transformed into a set of synecdoches; the surrealist painters responded with a patently metaphorical attitude. (91–92)

Although Jakobson was more concerned with sign systems than with literary history, he made observations about the nature of literary change which can help us understand the shift from Modernism to Postmodernism. I will elaborate on three of his ideas which I find useful, and I will modify two others which I find questionable.

The first one of Jakobson's ideas that I want to adopt is that the succession of major periods in literary history reveals an alternating predominance of realistic and romantic tendencies. Variations of that idea have been advanced by Robert Spiller, David Lodge, and Northrop Frye.[1]

A second idea of Jakobson's that I agree with wholeheartedly is the notion that an artist's ideology or basic philosophy shapes the form of his work and that therefore the form of a romantic work of art will be very different from the form of a realistic one.

And the third of Jakobson's ideas about literary change that I find useful is his assertion that the romantic outlook reveals itself in metaphoric processes of expression while the realistic outlook reveals itself in metonymic ones. When Jakobson says that "romanticism is closely linked with metaphor" while there are "equally intimate ties of realism with metonymy" (95), he uses the terms metaphor and metonymy to designate two attitudes rather than two specific uses of figurative language. This becomes apparent in his comments on the "manifestly metonymical orientation of cubism" and the "patently metaphoric attitude" of surrealism. Jakobson here suggests that the two movements express opposite visions of life.

These opposites become apparent when we compare two paintings. Pablo Picasso's *Three Musicians* (Fig. 1) illustrates what Jakobson calls the "manifestly metonymical orientation of cubism." As we can see in Picasso's painting, the human figures have been broken up into quasi-geometric parts that stress the feeling of fragmentation.

By contrast, Salvador Dalí's painting Sleep (Fig. 2) illustrates Jakobson's point that to the fragmentation that is characteristic of cubism, "the surrealist painters responded with a patently metaphorical attitude." Thus in Dalí's painting we see wholeness rather than fragmentation. This sense of wholeness in surrealist paintings is due the fact that they are usually dominated by what Dalí calls a "psychic anamorph" (Alexandrian 103), a central image that springs from the artist's subconscious or from his dreams.

Realism and fragmentation, romanticism and wholeness: These antinomies point to a more fundamental one which Ralph Waldo Emerson expressed when he said that

mankind have ever been divided into two sects, Materialists and Idealists. (Transcendentalist 87)

Fig. 1: Pablo Picasso, *Three Musicians* (1924)

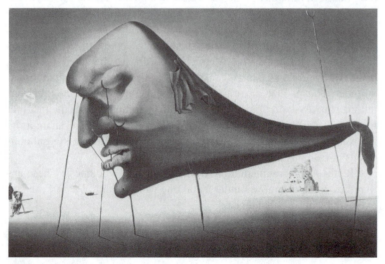

Fig. 2: Salvador Dalí, *Sleep* (1937)

And then Emerson goes on to explain: "The materialist insists on facts, on history, on the force of circumstances, and the animal wants of man; the idealist on the power of Thought and of Will, on inspiration, on miracle, on individual culture" (87). It seems to me that this fundamental distinction between the materialist and idealist outlook is implicit in Jakobson's oscillation theory. Jakobson suggests that the mainstream of literature during a romantic period consists of works that express an idealist vision of life and that the mainstream of literature during a realist period consists of works that express a materialist outlook. This proposition is the most important idea I derive from Jakobson.

The two aspects of Jakobson's oscillation theory that I would like to modify are the notion that major literary change occurs at regular intervals and that it occurs about every twenty years or so. The first of these ideas is implied in Jakobson's use of the term oscillation. This term suggest a mechanical back-and-forth movement as in the swing of a pendulum. Such a view of literary change not only implies radical changes in direction but also regular intervals. Both are notions that are contradicted by empirical observation of how literary change takes place. Moreover, the oscillation metaphor does not do justice to the fact that literature is created by living creatures and not by machines.

Instead of the oscillation metaphor to describe literary change, I would like to propose that of the spiral. This is a metaphor which I borrow from the historian Arthur Schlesinger who used it to describe the "cycles of American history" (24). Schlesinger in turn borrowed it from Ralph Waldo Emerson who compared the tendencies of the human mind to the "spiral tendency of vegetation" (Beauty 281). I like the spiraling metaphor better than that of oscillation because it takes into account that transitions from one period to the next are fluid and may happen at irregular intervals. Moreover, the upward movement of the spiral expresses something that the oscillation metaphor cannot, the dialectical nature of the development of intellectual and literary history, the fact that each new romantic or realistic period comes into being as a synthesis of what has gone before (Fig. 3).

If we combine this spiral theory of literary history with Jakobson's notion of the alternating predominance of romantic and realistic tendencies, then we can describe literary change in this way: As the romantic outlook of a period loses vitality, it is challenged and replaced by its opposite, the realistic outlook. With time, the realistic outlook weakens, is challenged, and is replaced by a new romantic outlook, and so on. In this way, each new romantic period or each new realistic period is a synthesis of old and new ideas. This modification of Jakobson's oscillation theory stresses the

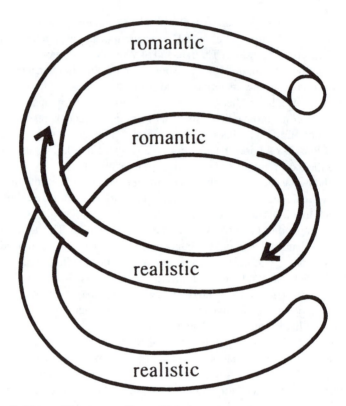

Fig. 3: Literary History as an Upward Spiral

presence of realistic trends during periods that are essentially romantic and of romantic trends during periods that are essentially realistic.

A more radical modification of Jakobson's theory that I want to propose concerns the duration of literary periods. Jakobson doesn't actually spell out how long he thinks major eras in literary or intellectual history last, but he speaks of Symbolism as a major literary period in European literature and of Cubism and Surrealism as major periods in art history. None of these movements lasted longer than 20 years.

It is my opinion that major literary periods last much longer than Jakobson envisioned, at least 50 years and more often around 100 years. This opinion is supported by the historian Hayden White. In a 1975 essay entitled "The Problem of Change in Literary History," White says that

> *historically significant literary innovation* is possible only at those
> times in which the potential audience for a given form of literary work
> have been so constituted as to render unintelligible or banal both the
> messages and the modes of contact that prevailed in some preceding
> era [White's emphasis]. (108)

White doesn't spell out at what intervals he thinks major changes occur
in literary history, but it seems to me that it would take a good deal longer
than a mere 20 years until the ideas of a literary movement become "unintelligible or banal."

If we accept the modifications of Jakobson's oscillation theory that
I am proposing, then we get a view of American literary history that
differs somewhat from the currently accepted outline. First of all, it de-
emphasizes the linearity of literary history and stresses the equitemporal-
ity or overlapping of literary periods, and secondly it assigns around a
hundred years to each major period.

According to this view, the first romantic period, that is, the first period in which the dominant vision of life was basically idealist rather
than materialist, is the Puritan Age. When writers begin to react against
the otherworldliness of Puritanism, we get the first realistic era, the Age
of Reason, and when writers rebel against the rationalism of that period,
we get the Romantic Age. So far my outline of literary history does not
differ from the traditional view.

However, when we come to the periods called Realism, Naturalism,
and Modernism, my outline departs from the traditional view because I
agree with Hayden White that historically significant literary change
does not occur until the majority of readers consider the forms and ideas
of a previous period "unintelligible or banal." Seen that way, the shift
from Realism to Naturalism and the shift from Naturalism to Modernism
were not major changes. Moreover, since the vision of life in most of the
major works of Realism, Naturalism, and Modernism is grounded in
philosophical materialism, I propose that we consider these three literary
trends one major period. That period, which we might call Early, Middle
and Late Modernism, lasts from about 1850 to about 1950.

And this brings me to the crux of my spiral theory of literary history.
If the spirit of the Age of Modernism is materialist and realist, then it follows that the spirit of the Age of Postmodernism is idealist and romantic.

The cyclical view of literary history that I am proposing explains not
only why the spirit of the Postmodern Age is basically romantic but also

why we get both realistic and romantic tendencies in the literature of the second half of the twentieth century. Before I develop my definition of the distinctive traits of romantic postmodernism, I will explain what the realistic trend is like which the majority of critics consider to be the mainstream of postmodernist fiction.

First off, a note on terminology: I call this trend realistic postmodernism or neo-modernism because its vision of life, like that of most modernist fiction, is grounded in the belief that only that part of reality exists which can be empirically known. This fiction is realistic in its basic outlook but often nonmimetic in its representation of reality. Almost everyone who has written about realistic postmodernism agrees that its most notable trait is its iconoclastic and disjunctive character. That notion has its origin in the early seventies when the term postmodernism first became fashionable among literary critics. At that time, the term was used exclusively to designate experimental writing. In recent years, however, many critics have come to use it as a period term for all writing after the Age of Modernism. Therefore, distinctions are now being made among various forms of postmodernist fiction. Most of those classifications distinguish between mainstream and marginal writing, and those distinctions are generally made on the basis of the form of the works rather than on the basis of their vision of life.

These points are illustrated in an essay entitled "On Reading 300 American Novels" that the novelist and short story writer Robert Coover wrote for the *New York Times Book Review.* In that essay, Coover admits that the voice of writers like himself "is often thought of as disruptive, eccentric, even inaccessible," but he says,

> It could easily be argued that it is true mainstream fiction, emerging from the very core of the evolving form, peculiarly alert to the decay in the social forms that embrace it, early signals of larger mutations to follow. (38)

Coover's paradoxical idea that the typical mainstream author is "the rebel, the iconoclast, the transformer," is endorsed in the *Columbia History of the American Novel.;* Molly Hite, the author of the chapter on "Postmodern Fiction," echoes Coover when she says that "the postmodern novel is the mainstream avant-garde novel of the contemporary period" (698).

Hite describes the postmodernist mainstream in terms of the following seven criteria that all have to do with the authors' efforts to go beyond modernist innovations in language, structure, and narrative technique:

1.	"The undermining of established narrative conventions" (700).
2.	A belief in "literary language as inseparable from the discourses of praxis and power," i.e., in the inability of literature to be politically "disinterested and value-neutral" (700).
3.	"Metafictional strategies" that break up the fictionality of the text, as when the author interrupts the narrative to discuss his or her story telling techniques (702).
4.	A tendency to "fuzz the border between high and low culture" (704).
5.	An emphasis on "plot rather than character" (705).
6.	"Characters [who] are often stereotypes," who are "passive," and who "are rarely agents of their own destinies" (705-706).
7.	A style that is often "wrenched to the point of non-communication or into a kind of sublime clunkiness" because style is not seen as an expression of the author's identity but tends to be manipulated for the purposes of parody or subversion (706).

According to Hite, this mainstream consists of the work of these twelve experimentalist authors:

Kathy Acker	Samuel Delaney	Thomas Pynchon
John Barth	Don DeLillo	Ishmael Reed
Donald Barthelme	John Hawkes	Joanna Russ
Robert Coover	Vladimir Nabokov	Kurt Vonnegut

Like much that has recently been written about postmodernist fiction, Hite's definition is fashionably indebted to the ideas of the French critics Jacques Derrida, Michel Foucault, and Francois Lyotard.

From Jacques Derrida comes the opposition, on the part of Hite and many other critics, to the "totalizing" concepts of unity and closure in literature, because—so their argument runs—these concepts are used consciously or unconsciously to perpetuate the notion of a "transcendental signified," that is, of the existence of an illusory metaphysical reality. Another important idea of Derrida's that appears in Hite's definition is the notion that we cannot ever be sure what a given text means because language is basically Nietzschean "play" and states presence but implies absence. Therefore each statement contains within itself the "trace" of its opposite (Structure 1125).

From Michel Foucault comes the idea that postmodernists try to subvert language so as to unmask as falsehoods the pseudo-truths that ruling classes try to perpetuate in order to retain their power. Thus for Foucault the task of literature should be that of "detaching the power of truth from the forms of hegemony, social, economic, and cultural, within which it operates at the present time" (Truth 1145).

And from Francois Lyotard comes the notion—similar to Derrida's belief that there are no centers of meaning and no unities—that an important part of the "postmodern condition" is a Nietzschean "lack of reality" (Condition 77) and a universal awareness of processes of "unmaking" in which unities break up into diversities (Condition 32).

Many critics have made the connection between the tendency toward disjunction and fragmentation in American postmodernist fiction and the disbelief in centers or unities that comes from French critical thought. Nevertheless, as Hans Bertens has pointed out, critics do not seem to believe that there is a common world view in postmodernist fiction. Bertens draws this conclusion from an examination of over 50 critical articles and book chapters on postmodernism. However, Bertens does conclude that

> in practically all recent concepts of Postmodernism the matter of ontological uncertainty is absolutely central. It is the awareness of the absence of centers, of privileged languages, higher discourses, that is seen as the most striking difference with Modernism. (46)

In passing, Bertens notes that the name of Nietzsche comes up frequently in discussions of the ideology of postmodernist literature. Nietzsche is also frequently cited in the writings of Derrida, Foucault, and Lyotard. These references to Nietzsche are signals of a vision of life that is grounded in philosophical materialism in general and in nihilism in particular.

The vision of life that underlies many of the stories and novels by the authors who are considered to belong to the mainstream of postmodernist fiction is clearly a nihilistic one. In a John Barth story named "Title," the main character—who is a writer—makes this paradigmatic statement:

> Everything leads to nothing. . . . The final question is, Can nothing be made meaningful? (102)

It seems to me that this nihilism is essentially an extreme form of realism. At the core of this outlook lies the determination to deal only with empirically verifiable facts, and such facts suggest the entropic notion that eventually everything will come to nothing.

While critics such as Irving Howe, Frank Kermode, and Gerald Graff have noted the nihilist tendencies in postmodernist fiction, very few have commented on its essentially realistic attitude.[2] Allan Lloyd Smith, however, points out that despite its non-mimetic character, much disjunctive fiction is profoundly concerned with reality, and he cites Ronald Sukenick's famous statement that what he wants to do in his fiction is "to 'bang' the readers with reality" (42).

But it is not in the representation of reality but in the form of the fiction that the realistic attitude of the disjunctive writers manifests itself. Raymond Federman, for example, believes that the only connection between fiction and reality should lie in the structure of the texts which should be as disjointed as the world itself. Otherwise fiction should be non-representational, and writers should stress this quality of their texts by using difficult, irrational language. Federman explains, "by rendering language somewhat irrational and seemingly unreadable, the new fiction writers . . . neutralize the fiasco of reality and the imposture of history. By confronting the unreality of reality they come closer to the truth of the world today" (16). Likewise, Robert Coover has expressed the notion that his non-representational texts are actually more realistic than conventional fiction. During an interview, Coover reflected: "Maybe I think that all my fiction is realistic, and that so far it has simply been misunderstood as otherwise" (LeClair 67). Similarly, despite its extreme subjectivity and its expressionist departures from representational realism, late modernist fiction remained essentially realistic because its vision of life was grounded in philosophical materialism.

It seems to me that the attempts of the disjunctive postmodernists to innovate storytelling do not go significantly beyond experiments by such modernist authors as Franz Kafka, James Joyce, and Samuel Beckett. I am not the only one who holds this opinion. Back in 1968, Frank Kermode made the same point. Refusing to call the contemporary iconoclastic writers postmodernists, he called them "neo-modernists" and observed that as far as their "theoretical bases" are concerned, "they are not 'revolutionary.' They are marginal developments of older modernism" (23). More recently, in 1989, another famous critic, Leslie Fiedler, said during a symposium that "Postmodernism turns out to be merely late modernism" (Scholes 235). During that same symposium, the novelist William Gass, who is usually labeled a postmodernist, rejected that label and said that he sees himself as "a very old, or late modernist." And then Gass went on to say: "I do not see in my work any basic divergence from the great modernist people" (Scholes 250).

One of the effects of the high regard that realistic postmodernists have for such infamous works of modernism as James Joyce's *Finnegan's Wake* (1935) or Samuel Beckett's *Murphy* (1938) is that their own fiction is often just as difficult to read. Some realistic postmodernists even take pride in the difficulty of their work. Raymond Federman, for instance, makes an important point about disjunctive fiction when he says that much of it is "seemingly unreadable"(16). This brings us back to an important part of the definition of mainstream postmodernist fiction in the *Columbia History of the American Novel*. In that definition, Molly Hite describes the style of much disjunctive fiction as being "wrenched to the point of noncommunication" (706). This near-unreadability is the major reason why it does not make sense to say that the work of the disjunctive writers represents the mainstream of postmodernist fiction. How can we consider these texts the mainstream when only very few people outside of the universities actually read them?

By the early eighties, a number of the more disjunctive among the realistic postmodernists had apparently become discontent with writing for such a small audience, or else they realized that their work was being outsold by the more readable fiction of romantic postmodernist such as Toni Morrison and William Kennedy or of minimalists such as Raymond Carver and Ann Beattie. At any rate, we can see that several major realistic postmodernists, among them John Barth, Donald Barthelme, and Robert Coover, moved away from their earlier disjunctive styles and began to write more conventional fiction. With Barth, this change of style seems to have been a result of a change of heart but with Barthelme and Coover it was only a superficial change, for even though Barthelme's novel *Paradise* (1986) and Coover's novel *Gerald's Party* (1987) are more conventionally structured than their earlier work, the vision of life in these novels continues to be nihilistic. Thus, despite their more conventional form, these novels cannot possibly be mistaken for works of romantic postmodernism.

Before I begin to deal with romantic postmodernism, I want to comment briefly on another realistic trend in contemporary literature. This trend has been variously called Minimalism, K-Mart Realism, or Neo-

Realism. Representative writers are Ann Beattie, the late Raymond Carver, Bobbie Ann Mason, and Frederick Barthelme.[3] The trend is called Minimalism because it is marked by a sparse, laconic style reminiscent of that of Ernest Hemingway. Sometimes it is also called K-Mart Realism because it tends to deal chiefly with the working class people who form the clientele of the K-Mart department stores. And it is sometimes called Neo-Realism because some critics see this trend as the avant garde of a new realistic era in American literature.[4]

The minimalists' concern with sociological themes, their focus on representative rather than extraordinary characters, and the absence of the fantastic or supernatural in their of fiction links it more strongly with the realistic impulse of Modernism than the romantic one of Postmodernism. I am therefore inclined to agree with those scholars who believe that the heyday of Postmodernism is over and that we are on the brink of a new Age of Realism.[5]

The vision of life and the view of art in typical works of romantic postmodernism are the opposite of what we find in realistic postmodernism. Instead of a nihilist vision of life, we get an idealist one, and instead of an aesthetics of disjunction we get an aesthetics of organicism. And while much of the fiction of the realistic postmodernists attempts to develop further the forms and techniques of their modernist forebears, the fiction of the romantic postmodernists picks up where the nineteenth-century romantics left off and develops further the form of the romance.

The essential difference that distinguishes romantic from realistic postmodernism is its idealist vision of life. This idealist ideology is the most important trait that the contemporary romantics have in common with their nineteenth-century ancestors. For most definitions of Romanticism agree that the world view of major romantic writers such as Rousseau, Goethe, Wordsworth, and Emerson was shaped by their reaction against eighteenth-century rationalism and by the revival of idealist philosophy. As René Wellek puts it:

> This new view emphasizes the totality of man's forces, not reason alone, nor sentiment alone, but rather intuition, "intellectual intuition," imagination. It is a revival of Neoplatonism, a pantheism (whatever its concessions to orthodoxy), a monism which arrived at identification of God and the world, soul and body, subject and object. The propounders of these ideas were always conscious of the precariousness

and difficulty of these views, which frequently appeared to them only
as distant ideals. . . . (48)

However, not all romantics held the neo-platonic views of Rousseau,
Goethe, Wordsworth, or Emerson. Edgar Allan Poe, Nathaniel
Hawthorne, and Herman Melville had serious reservations about such
central assumptions as the monist identification of God and the world or
of the soul and the body. However, all romantics either embraced or en-
tertained the basic idealist belief that the physical world is only temporal
and hence less real than the eternal world of the spirit. And the romantic
postmodernists agree with their nineteenth century forebears that spirit
and not matter is the ultimate reality because essence both precedes and
outlasts existence.

A second attitude that the romantics of the nineteenth and twentieth
century share is their organic view of art. There is widespread agreement
among critics that the core of romantic aesthetics is the notion of organicism.[6] At the core of the organic view of art, so Morse Peckham has suggested, lies the notion that "the history of the universe is the history of
God creating himself" (237). In short, everything that grows, has its origin in God, and that includes works of art. Thus an artist is actually
God's instrument, linked to God via inspiration. Once God has inspired
the artist, the content and shape of the work grow organically.

As I describe it here, this organic view of art is an ideal construct, a
notion that only some nineteenth century romantics and some romantic
postmodernists agree with. However, since all romantic postmodernists
accept at least some aspects of this view and since this view is radically
different from the mechanistic aesthetics held by most realistic postmodernists, I will develop it in some detail.

The notion of inspiration as the source of art was first expressed by
Plato. In the dialogue entitled "Ion," Plato has Socrates say to Ion, the ancestor of all literary critics:

> The gift which you possess of speaking excellently about Homer is not
> an art, but . . . an inspiration; there is a divinity moving you, like that
> contained in the stone which Euripides calls a magnet, but which is com-
> monly known as the stone of Heraclea. This stone not only attracts iron
> rings, but also imparts to them a similar power of attracting other rings;
> and sometimes you may see a number of pieces of iron and rings sus-
> pended from one another so as to form quite a long chain: and all of them
> derive their power of suspension from the original stone. In a like man-

ner the Muse first of all inspires men herself; and from these inspired persons a chain of other persons is suspended, who take the inspiration. For all good poets, epic as well as lyric, compose their beautiful poems not by art but because they are inspired and possessed. (14)

Ralph Waldo Emerson developed Plato's ideas further when he combined the notion of divine inspiration with the idea that the ideal poem pre-exists in the mind of God. In the essay "The Poet" (1844), Emerson says that

poetry was all written before time was, and whenever we are so finely organized that we can penetrate into that region where the air is music, we hear those primal warblings and attempt to write them down, but we lose ever and anon a word or a verse and substitute something of our own, and thus miswrite the poem. The men of more delicate ear write down these cadences more faithfully, and these transcripts, though imperfect, become the songs of the nations. (322)

Even if Emerson overstates the importance of inspiration, his comments imply a principle that most romantic postmodernists subscribe to. Emerson spells this principle out when he says that "the thought and the form are equal in the order of time, but in the order of genesis the thought is prior to the form" because the origin of the poem lies in "a thought so passionate and alive that like the spirit of a plant or an animal it has an architecture of its own, and adorns nature as with a new thing" (Poet 323). In other words, it is the thought of a poem that shapes its form and not the other way around, and this shaping is a process that is as natural as the growth of a plant out of a seed.

That the form of a work of art should not be mechanically imposed but grow organically is an idea that was also expressed by Emerson's friend Henry David Thoreau. In "A Week on the Concord and Merrimack Rivers" (1849), Thoreau writes:

As naturally as the oak bears an acorn, and the vine a gourd, man bears a poem, either spoken or done. The poet sings how the blood flows in his veins. He performs his functions so well that he needs such stimulus to sing only as plants to put forth leaves and blossoms. He would strive in vain to modulate the remote and transient music which he sometimes hears, since his song is a vital function like breathing, and an integral result like weight. (345)

These ideas were not original with Emerson and Thoreau. Very similar notions had been developed earlier by the British poet and critic Samuel Taylor Coleridge and before Coleridge by the German scholar August Wilhelm Schlegel. In Coleridge's essay "Shakespeare's Judgement Equal to His Genius" (1836), there occurs a famous passage which he translated almost word for word from an 1809 lecture of Schlegel's:[7]

> The form is mechanic, when on any given material we impress a predetermined form, not necessarily arising out of the properties of the material; as when to a mass of wet clay we give whatever shape we wish it to retain when hardened. The organic form, on the other hand, is innate; it shapes, as it develops, itself from within, and the fullness of its development is one and the same with the perfection of its outward form. Such as the life is, such is the form. Nature, the prime genial artist, inexhaustible in diverse powers, is equally inexhaustible in forms. . . . (471)

Taking this passage out of context, Coleridge suggests—as does Emerson later on—that the artist does not have to do anything to shape the poem because the poem shapes itself. This is not quite how Schlegel described the creative process.

In his earlier "Vorlesungen über schöne Litteratur und Kunst" (1804), Schlegel expresses the opinion that the writing of poetry involves more than merely taking dictation from one's Muse. Schlegel affirms that the impetus of all works of art comes from a "universal creative power." This creative power is inherent in external Nature but also in man himself because man is a microcosm of the natural universe. According to Schlegel, "the artist should create living works in the same manner as Nature, that is, in a structured and structuring manner, and these works should not be set in motion by an outside mechanism, as is the case with a pendulum clock, but they should be set in motion by an indwelling force, as is the case with the solar system" (102). However, Schlegel also says that true works of art are the result of the "most intimate union of conscious and unconscious activity in the human spirit," a union "of instinct and purpose, of freedom and necessity" [my own translation] (83). In short, according to Schlegel, great works of art have their origin in inspiration and are organic in shape, but that shape has to be created by a conscious effort on the part of the artist. And it is this kind of organicism, this balanced view of the work of art as the result of both unconscious and conscious activity, that we find most often among the romantic postmodernists.

While not all romantic postmodernists embrace the view of art that I have just outlined, some of them clearly do, as we can see from statements that they or their fictional characters have made. The most striking expression of the romantic view of artistic creation by a postmodernist occurs in a 1973 interview with Kurt Vonnegut. Commenting on how he wrote his novel *Slaughterhouse-Five* (1969), Vonnegut said:

> I suppose that flowers, when they're through blooming, have some sort of awareness of some purpose having been served. Flowers didn't ask to be flowers and I didn't ask to be me. At the end of *Slaughterhouse-Five* I had the feeling that I had produced this blossom. So I had a shutting-off feeling, you know, that I had done what I was supposed to and that everything was o.k. (Allen 107)

Similar statements about the role of inspiration and the organic nature of their art can be found in interviews with Saul Bellow, Toni Morrison, Alice Walker, and Paul Auster. But even those romantic postmodernists who never made statements that reveal a commitment to an organic view of art still produce works whose form has more in common with the fiction of the nineteenth-century romantics than with that of the twentieth-century modernists.

At this point I want to reiterate that the organic union of content and form that is the ideal of romantic aesthetics is just that, an ideal that is not realized very often. For instance, many of the works of early nineteenth-century romantics such as Washington Irving, William Cullen Bryant, Edgar Allan Poe, and Ralph Waldo Emerson still use some of the rigid forms characteristic of the Age of Reason. Thus, none of the standard definitions of Romanticism fit all of the major works of the nineteenth century romantics. The same is true for the definitions and the major works of other literary periods. Nevertheless, it is still useful to set up a working definition of the traits that distinguish the fiction of the romantic postmodernists, to apply this definition to a number of novels and stories, and to modify it as necessary.

The heart of the definition I shall propose is that the vision of life in works of romantic postmodernism is grounded in philosophical idealism, in the belief that spirit and not matter is the ultimate reality. From this ideological core grow all the other traits that distinguish works of romantic postmodernism, the view of art, the content, the structure, and the form.

The idealist vision of life first of all determines the view of art implicit in neo-romantic fiction. This view of art consists of two components, the belief in inspiration and the belief in the organic nature of art. These beliefs determine both the content and the form in the fiction of most romantic postmodernists. This organic view of art was first formulated by the early romantics of the late eighteenth century. In my literature classes, I illustrate it with the following graphic representation which my students have come to call "Alsen's Apple" (Fig. 4).

The vision of life that forms the core of all works of romantic postmodernism is most clearly reflected in the themes which tend to be metaphysical or even religious rather than sociological or economic ones.[8] Pervasive themes concern the nature and purpose of human beings, the nature of God and the nature of evil, and—above all—the quest for proofs of transcendence, that is, for proofs that the universe is ordered by some metaphysical force.

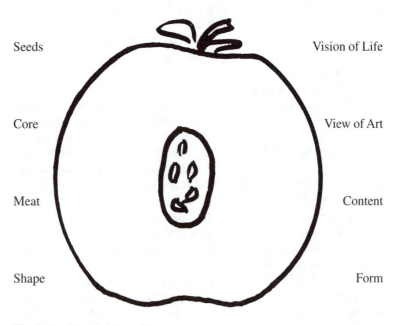

Seeds   Vision of Life

Core   View of Art

Meat   Content

Shape   Form

Fig. 4: The Organic View of Art

The organic view of art is reflected in relatively simple narrative structures that have unity and closure, structures that seem to have grown organically rather than having been consciously contrived. This is also why we get mostly single and thus subjective points of view, rather than multiple and objective ones, and why—more often than not—we get a readerly or rather "speakerly" style that tends toward the simplicity of oral narrative.

Moreover, the romantic view of art held by most romantic postmodernists also explains why we find elements of the nineteenth-century romance in their fiction. A number of scholars have commented on the resurgence of the romance in contemporary fiction, but because of widely divergent definitions of the genre, there has been much disagreement on this topic. Rather than review the controversy, I will present my own opinion on what elements of the nineteenth-century romance reappear in postmodernist fiction.

Because Nathaniel Hawthorne was the most important nineteenth-century romancer and because it is with Hawthorne's romances that the novels and stories of the romantic postmodernists have the greatest affinities, I derive several criteria of my working definition of neo-romantic fiction from Hawthorne's view of the romance and from his practice as a storyteller.

In my opinion, Hawthorne's view of art—and thus his definition of the romance—was shaped decisively by Emersonian idealism. In the "Custom House" introduction to *The Scarlet Letter,* Hawthorne makes it a point to mention that he lived for "years within the subtile influence of an intellect like Emerson's" (98). But while Hawthorne admired Emerson's poetry, he was skeptical about Emerson's philosophy and its lack of a vision of evil. After all, the nature of evil was one of Hawthorne's preoccupations. However, as we can see in Hawthorne's use of symbolism, he accepted Emerson's belief that "Nature [or matter] is the symbol of spirit" (Nature 14), and he also accepted Emerson's organic view of art.[9] After all, he constantly juxtaposed organic and mechanical metaphors. Moreover, one of the key elements of Hawthorne's definition of the romance, his ideas concerning the "Marvelous," that is, the supernatural, derives from Emerson's belief that "[p]articular natural facts are symbols of particular spiritual facts" (Nature 14). In short, the supernatural in Hawthorne's fiction is an indication of his belief in the existence of a spiritual world beyond the world of physical objects.[10]

As in Hawthorne's romances, the supernatural in the fiction of the romantic postmodernists usually points to some spiritual truth. The first generation of romantic postmodernists—writers such as Saul Bellow, Norman Mailer, and Flannery O'Connor—seem to have followed Hawthorne's advice in the "Preface" to *The House of the Seven Gables,* "to mingle the Marvelous rather as slight, delicate, and evanescent flavor, than any portion of the actual substance of the dish offered to the public" (243). But second generation romantic postmodernists such as Thomas Pynchon, Toni Morrison, and William Kennedy give the supernatural a more important role.

What the fiction of all romantic postmodernists has in common with the romances of Nathaniel Hawthorne is that, in a number of ways, it mingles fact and fiction, the ordinary and the extraordinary. In the best know part of Hawthorne's definition of the romance, in the "Custom House" introduction to *The Scarlet Letter,* Hawthorne says that the romance differs from the novel because it stakes out for itself, "a neutral territory, somewhere between the real world and fairy-land, where the Actual and the Imaginary may meet, and each imbue itself with the nature of the other" (105). This statement has two important implications for both Hawthorne's romances and for the fiction of his postmodernist descendants, an ideological one relating to the underlying vision of life and a practical one relating to the craft of story telling. For one thing, the action in the romances of Hawthorne and the fiction of the romantic postmodernists hovers in the neutral territory between the physical and the spiritual world and thus suggests that the authors believe in a spiritual reality beyond that of the object world. For another, this kind of story telling mingles the probable and the improbable in terms of settings, events, and characters.

Finally, I want to give special attention to the role of the characters in the fiction of the romantic postmodernists. Here, too, we get a mingling of the actual and the imaginary, a mingling of historical figures and imaginary characters. But above all, the major characters in contemporary romances are extraordinary individuals. For while the realist storyteller tends to develop protagonists who are representative, the romantic storyteller tends to develop protagonists who are unusual. The realist shows us what human beings really are; the romantic shows us what human beings can ideally be. But despite this tendency toward the extraordinary, the romantic postmodernists—like Hawthorne—always stick to psychological probability in characterization. As Hawthorne says in the "Preface" to the *House of the Seven Gables,* the romance "sins unpardonably so far as it may swerve aside from he truth of the human heart" (243). In fact, in both the romances of Hawthorne and the fiction of the romantic postmodernists, the emphasis is not on action but on character. This is why I emphatically disagree with the famous definition of the difference between the novel and the romance that Richard Chase advanced in his book *The American Novel and Its Tradition*. According to Chase, "the romance prefers action over character," and it doesn't provide "much intricacy of relation" (13). Moreover, the characters in the romance are supposedly "two-dimensional types" who are "not complexly related to each other or to society or to the past" (13). As I see it, both Hawthorne's romances and the fiction of his postmodernists descendants prefer character over action and provide much "intricacy of relation." Moreover, the characters are almost always developed in great depth and are "complexly related" to each other, to society, and to the past.

Twelve representative authors whose work illustrates many of the romantic ideas I have been discussing are the following:[11]

Paul Auster	Norman Mailer	Philip Roth
The later John Barth	Toni Morrison	J.D. Salinger
Saul Bellow	Flannery O'Connor	Kurt Vonnegut
William Kennedy	Thomas Pynchon	Alice Walker

I will conclude this introduction with a ten-point working definition of the major traits that distinguish works of romantic postmodernism. Only a few novels written since 1950 have all of the ten traits that I list. But there are scores of novels that have the most important trait, a vision of life grounded in philosophical idealism, plus several of the other nine.

In the body of this book [*Romantic Postmodernism in American Fiction*], I will test this working definition by analyzing the following novels: Saul Bellow, *Henderson the Rain King* (1958); Flannery O'Connor, *The Violent Bear It Away* (1960); J. D. Salinger, *Franny and Zooey* (1961); Norman Mailer, *An American Dream* (1963); Kurt Vonnegut, *Breakfast of Champions* (1972); Philip Roth, *The Breast* (1972); Thomas Pynchon, *Gravity's Rainbow* (1973), Toni Morrison, *Song of Solomon* (1977), John Barth, *Sabbatical: A Romance* (1982); Alice Walker, *The Color Purple* (1982); William Kennedy, *Ironweed* (1983); Paul Auster, *Ghosts* (1986) and *Mr. Vertigo* (1994).

Working Definition of Romantic Postmodernism

1. The vision of life is a form of philosophical idealism, that is, a belief that the ultimate reality is that of ideas rather than of matter, and that essence precedes existence.
2. The view of art has two components. One is a belief in inspiration that goes back to Plato. The other is an organic conception of art that was first formulated by the early romantics at the end of the eighteenth century.
3. The major themes are philosophical or even religious ones, some of them familiar from nineteenth century romanticism. A typical theme is the quest for proofs of transcendence or for proofs that there is some pattern of order in the universe.
4. Ideas are occasionally illustrated with references or allusions to—or even quotations from—works by nineteenth century romantics.
5. Representation of reality is generally mimetic but combines the "Actual and the Imaginary," that is, the plausible and the fantastic. The fantastic consists of such things as bizarre characters, unusual locations, and supernatural incidents.
6. Narrative development is usually simple rather than complex, often giving the impression of oral narrative and tending toward unity and closure.
7. Point of view is mostly subjective, that is, first person or third person center of consciousness. Omniscient narrators and multiple points of view are rare.
8. Characterization concentrates on "the truth of the human heart," the thoughts and feelings of the characters rather than on their appearance and belongings. The central characters are extraordinary individuals rather than representative types.
9. Style varies greatly but tends to be more readerly than writerly, closer to the simplicity of Hemingway than the complexity of Faulkner.
10. Imagery is dominated by organic rather than mechanistic tropes, and there is a general preference for metaphor over metonymy.

NOTES

[1]Robert Spiller, *The Third Dimension: Studies in Literary History* (New York: Collier, 1965); David Lodge, *Modes of Modern Writing* (Ithaca, N.Y.: Cor-

nell University Press, 1977); and Northrop Frye, *The Secular Scripture: A Study of the Structure of Romance* (Cambridge: Harvard University Press, 1979).

[2]Irving Howe, *The Idea of the Modern in Literature and the Arts* (New York: Oxford University Press, 1967), 29; Frank Kermode, *Continuities* (London: Routledge, 1968), 21; Gerald Graff, "The Myth of the Postmodernist Breakthrough." *Tri-Quarterly* 16 (1973), 403.

[3]The following are representative collections of minimalist short stories: Ann Beattie, *Secrets and Surprises* (New York: Collier, 1978); Raymond Carver, *What We Talk About When We Talk About Love* (New York: Knopf, 1981); Bobbie Ann Mason, *Shiloh and Other Stories* (New York: Harper, 1985); Frederick Barthelme, *Chroma* (New York: Simon Schuster, 1987).

[4]For opposite opinions on whether or not the new realism marks the end of the Age of Postmodernism, see Kim Herzinger, "Minimalism as a Postmodernism: Some Introductory Notes." *New Orleans Review* 16 (1989), 73–81, and Winfried Fluck, "Surface Knowledge and 'Deep' Knowledge: The New Realism in American Fiction." In *Neo-Realism in Contemporary American Fiction.* Ed. Kristiaan Versluys (Amsterdam & Atlanta: Rodopi, 1992).

[5]In a recent study, Melvin Bukiet has pointed out yet another manifestation of the realistic impulse in contemporary American fiction. Borrowing a term from Richard Powers' novel *The Prisoner's Dilemma,* Bukiet calls this new trend "Crackpot Realism." See "Crackpot Realism: Fiction of the Forthcoming Millenium," *Review of Contemporary Fiction* 16 (Spring 1996), 13–22. Other "crackpot realists" whom Bukiet mentions are Steve Erickson, Jonathan Franzen, and Dennis Johnson.

[6]See Arthur Lovejoy, "The Meaning of Romanticism for the History of Ideas," *Journal of the History of Ideas* 2 (June 1941), 257–278; René Wellek, "The Concept of 'Romanticism' in Literary History," *Comparative Literature* 1/2 (1949), 1–23; 147–172; and Morse Peckham, "Toward a Theory of Romanticism," *PMLA* 66 (1951), 5–23.

[7]The passage that Coleridge translated almost word for word occurs in August Wilhelm Schlegel, "Vorlesungen über dramatische Kunst und Litteratur." In *Sämtliche Werke.* Vol 6. Ed. Eduard Böcking (Leipzig: Weidmann, 1846), 157.

[8]Most critics who have written about postmodernism agree with Fredric Jameson's pronouncement that "spirituality no longer exists" and that the absence of a spiritual dimension is the crux of the definition of postmodernism. (Postmodernism 387). Recently, however, this notion has come under attack. For example, John McClure has pointed out that "many postmodern texts are shot through with and even shaped by spiritual concerns (Postmodern/Post-Secular 143).

[9]See Roy Male, "'From the Innermost Germ': The Organic Principle in Hawthorne's Fiction," *Journal of English Literary History* 20 (Sep 1953), 218–236.

[10]For analyses of Hawthorne's vision of life that are radically different from mine, see Michael D. Bell, *The Development of American Romance* (Chicago: University of Chicago Press, 1980), and Samuel Coale, *In Hawthorne's Shadow: American Romance from Melville to Mailer* (Lexington: University Press of Kentucky, 1985). Bell describes Hawthorne as a nihilist when he says: "In his fiction, Hawthorne simply assumes as a given what so horrified Melville as a possibility—that 'there's naught beyond'" (152). And Coale dubs Hawthorne a Manichean, explaining: "To the Manichean mind the world remains a prison, created in a demonic cosmos by someone other than God, some Demiurge or evil Jehovah sprung from the hosts of darkness" (4).

[11]Three of these twelve authors—Vonnegut, Pynchon, and Barth—also appear on the list of disjunctive postmodernists in the *Columbia History of the American Novel*. I include Vonnegut and Pynchon in my analyses because their work is romantic in its vision of life even though it is disjunctive in its form. And I include John Barth because although his early work was nihilistic and deliberately fragmented, the novel *Sabbatical: A Romance* (1982) marks a shift toward a neo-platonic ideology and toward romantic modes of story telling.

WORKS CITED

Alexandrian, Sarane. *Surrealist Art.* Trans. Gordon Clough. New York: Praeger, 1970.

Allen, William R., ed. *Conversations with Kurt Vonnegut.* Jackson: University of Mississippi Press, 1987.

Barth, John. "Title" [1968]. In *Lost in the Funhouse.* New York: Bantam, 1969.

Bell, Michael D. *The Development of American Romance.* Chicago: University of Chicago Press, 1980.

Bertens, Hans. "The Postmodern *Weltanschauung* and its Relation with Modernism: An Introductory Survey." In *Approaching Postmodernism.* Eds. Hans Bertens and Douwe Fokkema. Amsterdam: Benjamins, 1986.

Bukiet, Melvin Jules. "Crackpot Realism: Fiction for the Forthcoming Millennium." *Review of Contemporary Fiction,* 16 (Spring 1996): 13–22.

Chase, Richard. *The American Novel and Its Tradition.* Garden City, N.Y.: Doubleday, 1957.

Coale, Samuel. *In Hawthorne's Shadow: American Romance from Melville to Mailer.* Lexington: University Press of Kentucky, 1985.

Coleridge, Samuel Taylor. "Shakespeare's Judgement Equal to His Genius" [1836]. In *Critical Theory Since Plato.* Ed. Hazard Adams. Rev. ed. New York: Harcourt Brace, 1991.

Coover, Robert. "On Reading 300 American Novels." *New York Times Book Review,* 18 Mar 84, pp. 1, 37–38.

Derrida, Jacques. "Structure, Sign, and Play." In *Critical Theory Since Plato.* Ed. Hazard Adams. Rev. ed. New York: Harcourt Brace, 1991.

Emerson, Ralph Waldo. "Beauty." In *The Complete Works of Ralph Waldo Emerson.* Vol. 6. Boston: Houghton Mifflin, 1904.

———. "The Transcendentalist," "The Poet." In *The Selected Writings of Ralph Waldo Emerson.* Ed. Brooks Atkinson. New York: Random House, 1950.

Federman, Raymond. "Fiction in America Today or the Unreality of Reality." *Indian Journal of American Studies,* 14 (Jan 1984): 5–16.

Fluck, Winfried. "Surface Knowledge and 'Deep' Knowledge: The New Realism in American Fiction." In *Neo-Realism in Contemporary American Fiction.* Ed. Kristiaan Versluys. Amsterdam: Rodopi, 1992.

Foucault, Michel. "Truth and Power." In *Critical Theory Since Plato.* Ed. Hazard Adams. Rev. ed. New York: Harcourt Brace, 1991.

Frye, Northrop. *The Secular Scripture: A Study of the Structure of Romance.* Cambridge: Harvard University Press, 1976.

Graff, Gerald. "The Myth of the Postmodernist Breakthrough." *Tri-Quarterly,* 26 (1973): 383–417.

Hawthorne, Nathaniel. *The Complete Novels and Selected Tales.* Ed. Norman Holmes Pearson. New York: Modern Library, 1965.

Herzinger, Kim. "Minimalism as a Postmodernism: Some Introductory Notes." *New Orleans Review,* 16 (1989): 72–81.

Hite, Molly. "Postmodern Fiction." In *The Columbia History of the American Novel.* Ed. Elliott Emory. New York: Columbia University Press, 1991.

Howe, Irving. *The Idea of the Modern in Literature and the Arts.* New York: Oxford University Press, 1967.

Jakobson, Roman and Morris Halle. *Fundamentals of Language.* Den Haag: Mouton, 1956.

Jameson, Fredric. *Postmodernism; or, The Cultural Logic of Late Capitalism.* Durham: Duke University Press, 1991.

Kermode, Frank. *Continuities.* London: Routledge, 1968.

LeClair, Tom and Larry McCaffery, eds. *Anything Can Happen: Interviews With Contemporary American Novelists.* Urbana: University of Illinois Press, 1983.

Lodge, David. *The Modes of Modern Writing.* Ithaca, N.Y.: Cornell University Press, 1977.

Lyotard, Francois. *The Postmodern Condition: A Report on Knowledge.* Trans. Geoff Bennington and Brian Massumi. Minneapolis: University of Minnesota Press, 1984.

Lovejoy, Arthur. "The Meaning of Romanticism for the History of Ideas." *Journal of the History of Ideas* (June 1941): 257–278.

Male, Roy R. " 'From the Innermost Germ': The Organic Principle in Hawthorne's Fiction." *Journal of English Literary History,* 20 (Sep 1953): 218–236.

McClure, John A. "Postmodern/Post-Secular: Contemporary Fiction and Spirituality." *Modern Fiction Studies,* 41 (Spring 1995): 141–163.

Mizener, Arthur. "The New Romance." *Southern Review,* 8 (1972): 106–117.

Morrison, Toni. *Jazz.* New York: Knopf, 1992.

Peckham, Morse. "Toward a Theory of Romanticism." *PMLA,* 66 (1951): 5–23.

Plato, "Ion." In *The Dialogues of Plato.* Vol. 1. Trans. Benjamin Jowett. New York: Random House, 1937.

Schlegel, August Wilhelm. "Vorlesungen über dramatische Kunst und Litteratur" [1809]. In *Sämtliche Werke.* Vol. 6. Ed. Eduard Böcking. Leipzig: Weidmann, 1846.

———. "Vorlesungen über schöne Litteratur und Kunst" [1804]. In *Deutsche Litteraturdenkmale des 18. und 19. Jahrhunderts.* Vol. 17. Ed. Bernhard Seuffert. Heilbronn: Behr, 1884.

Schlesinger, Arthur M. *The Cycles of American History.* London: André Deutsch, 1986.

Scholes, Robert. "Postmodernism: The Uninhabited Word: Critics' Symposium." *Critique,* 31 (Summer 1990): 256–275.

Smith, Allan Lloyd. "Brain Damage: The Word and the World in Postmodern Writing." In *Contemporary American Fiction.* Ed. Malcolm Bradbury and Sigmund Ro. London: Arnold, 1987.

Spiller, Robert. *The Third Dimension: Studies in Literary History.* New York: Collier, 1965.

Thoreau, Henry David. "A Week on the Concord and Merrimack Rivers" [1849]. In *Walden and Other Writings by Henry David Thoreau.* Ed. Brooks Atkinson. New York: Random House, 1950.

Wellek, René. "The Concept of 'Romanticism' in Literary History." *Comparative Literature,* 1/2 (1949): 1–23; 147–172.

White, Hayden. "The Problem of Change in Literary History." *New Literary History,* 7 (Autumn 1975): 97–111.

PART IV
Bibliography

Bibliography

NOTE #1:   This checklist is not meant to be comprehensive. It represents only the tip of the iceberg because I did not look much further than he on-line bibliography of the MLA.

NOTE #2:   A number of novelists who appear in this checklist espouse a realistic rather than a romantic vision of life and use romantic ideas in their works only to disparage them.

I. CONTEMPORARY NOVELISTS ON ROMANTICS AND ROMANTICISM

Barth, John. "The Arabesque" [On German Romanticism and Postmodernist Aesthetics]. In *Further Fridays: Essays, Lectures, and Other Non-Fiction: 1984–1994.* New York: Little, Brown, 1995, 276–348.

———. " 'Still Farther South': Some Notes on Poe's *Pym.*" In *Poe's Pym: Critical Explorations.* Ed. Richard Kopley. Durham, NC: Duke University Press, 1992, 217–230.

Bellow, Saul. "A World Too Much with Us." *Critical Inquiry,* 2 (Autumn 1975): 1–9.

Gardner, John. "Bartleby: Art and Social Commitment." *Philological Quarterly,* 43 (1964): 87–98.

Gass, William. "Emerson and the Essay." In *Habitations of the Word.* New York: Simon-Schuster, 1983. 50–56.

Morrison, Toni. "Romancing the Shadow." In *Playing in the Dark: Whiteness and the Literary Imagination.* Cambridge: Harvard University Press, 1992, 29–59.

Nabokov, Vladimir. "Romanticism." In *Eugene Onegin: A Novel in Verse by Aleksandr Pushkin, Translated from the Russian, With Commentary.* Vol. 3. New York: Pantheon, 1964, 32–37.

Oates, Joyce Carol. "Melville and the Tragedy of Nihilism." In *The Edge of Impossibility: Tragic Forms in Literature.* New York: Vanguard, 1972, 61–83.

———. "The Mysterious Mr. Thoreau." *New York Times Book Review,* 1 May 1988, pp. 1, 31–33.

Percy, Walker. "Herman Melville." *The New Criterion,* 13 (Nov 1983): 41.

Pynchon, Thomas. "Is It O.K. to Be a Luddite?" *New York Times Book Review,* 28 Oct 84, pp. 1, 40–41.

Updike, John. "Emersonianism." In *Odd Jobs: Essays and Criticism.* New York: Knopf, 1991, 148–168.

———. "Hawthorne's Creed." In *Hugging the Shore: Essays and Criticism.* New York: Knopf, 1983, 73–80.

———. "On Hawthorne's Mind." *New York Review of Books,* 19 Mar 1981, pp. 41–42.

———. "Melville's Withdrawal." In *Hugging the Shore,* 80–106.

———. "Whitman's Egotheism." In *Hugging the Shore,* 106–117.

II. CRITICISM ON CONTEMPORARY NOVELISTS

Kathy Acker

Phillips, Rod. "Purloined Letters: *The Scarlet Letter* in Kathy Acker's *Blood and Guts in High School.*" *Critique,* 35.3 (Spring 1994): 173–180.

Conrad Aiken

Cowley, Malcolm. "Conrad Aiken: From Savannah to Emerson." *The Southern Review,* 11 (1975): 245–259.

Robillard, Douglas. "Conrad Aiken and Herman Melville." In *Conrad Aiken: A Priest of Consciousness.* Ed. Ted Spivey and Arthur Waterman. New York: AMS, 1989, 191–204.

Paul Auster

Alsen, Eberhard. "Paul Auster's *Ghosts* and *Mr. Vertigo:* Homage to the Romantics." In *Romantic Postmodernism in American Fiction.* Amsterdam & Atlanta: Rodopi, 1996, 240–257.

Marling, William. "Paul Auster and the American Romantics." *Lit,* 7.4 (1997): 302–310.

Rudman, Mark. "Paul Auster: Some 'Elective Affinities'" [On Auster and Goethe]. *Review of Contemporary Fiction,* 14.1 (Spring 1994): 4–45.

John Barth

Alsen, Eberhard. "John Barth's 'Night Sea Journey' and *Sabbatical: A Romance:* From Exhaustion to Replenishment." In *Romantic Postmodernism in American Fiction.* Amsterdam & Atlanta: Rodopi, 1996, 153–170.

Bottroff, William K. "Thoreau and Walden, Ebenezer Cooke and Malden: Barth's Ribald Allusion." *Thoreau Society Bulletin,* 152 (1980): 8.

Carmichael, Thomas. "A Postmodern Genealogy: John Barth's *Sabbatical* and [Edgar Allan Poe's] *The Narrative of Arthur Gordon Pym.*" *University of Toronto Quarterly,* 60.3 (Spring 1991): 389–401.

Green Daniel. "Metafiction and Romance" [On Barth's *Sabbatical: A Romance*]. *Studies in American Fiction,* 19.2 (Autumn 1991): 229–242.

Oggle, L. Terry. "Twin Tongues of Flame: Hawthorne's Pearl and Barth's Jeannine as the Morally Redemptive Child." *Nassau Review,* 4.1 (1980): 41–49.

Scharnhorst, Gary. "Another 'Night-Sea Journey': Poe's 'Ms. Found in a Bottle'." *Studies in Short Fiction,* 22.2 (Spring 1985): 203–208.

Shimura, Masao. "John Barth, *The End of the Road,* and the Tradition of American Fiction" [On Hawthorne and Barth]. *Studies in English Literature,* 162 (1971): 73–87.

Saul Bellow

Alsen, Eberhard. "Saul Bellow's *Henderson the Rain King:* A Romantic Manifesto." In *Romantic Postmodernism in American Fiction.* Amsterdam & Atlanta: Rodopi, 1996, 41–57.

———. "The Beginnings of Postmodernism in American Fiction." In *Romantic Postmodernism in American Fiction.* Amsterdam & Atlanta: Rodopi, 1996, 25–36.

Campbell, Jeff H. "Bellow's Intimations of Immorality: *Henderson the Rain King*" [On Bellow and Wordsworth]. *Studies in the Novel,* 1 (1969): 323–333.

Chapman, Sara S. "Melville and Bellow in the Real World: Pierre and Augie March." *West Virginia University Philological Papers,* 18 (1971): 51–57.

Chavkin, Allan, "The Romantic Imagination of Saul Bellow." In *English Romanticism and Modern Fiction.* Ed. Allan Chavkin. New York: AMS, 1993, 113–138.

————. "Bellow and English Romanticism." *Studies in the Literary Imagination*, 17.2 (Fall 1984): 7–18.

————. "Bellow's Alternative to the Wasteland: Romantic Theme and Form in *Herzog*." *Studies in the Novel*, 11 (1979): 326–337.

————. "Humboldt's Gift and the Romantic Imagination." *Philological Quarterly*, 62.1 (Winter 1983): 1–19.

————. "*The Dean's December* and Blake's 'The Ghost of Abel'," *Saul Bellow Journal*, 13.1 (Winter 1995): 22–26.

————. "Wordsworth's 'Ode' and Bellow's *Seize the Day*." *American Notes and Queries*, 3.3 (July 1990): 121–124.

Gold, R. Michael. "The Influence of Emerson, Thoreau, and Whitman on the Novels of Saul Bellow." *DAI* 40 (1980): 5055A–5056A.

Knight, Karl F. "Bellow's Henderson and Melville's Ishmael: Their Mingled Worlds." *Studies in American Fiction*, 12.1 (Spring 1984): 91–98.

Majdiak, Daniel. "The Romantic Self and *Henderson and Rain King*" [On Bellow and Wordsworth]. *Bucknell Review*, 19.2 (1971): 125–146.

Marovitz, Sanford E. "The Emersonian Lesson of *Humboldt's Gift*." *Saul Bellow Journal*, 14.1 (Winter 1996): 84–95.

May, John R. "Myth and Parable in American Fiction" [On Cooper, Hawthorne, Melville and *Mr. Sammler's Planet*]. *Thought*, 57 (Mar 1982): 51–61.

Mowat, John. "*Humboldt's Gift:* Bellow's 'Dejection' Ode" [On Bellow and Coledridge]. *Dutch Quarterly Review of Anglo-American Letters*, 8 (1978): 184–211.

Nilsen, Helge N. "Saul Bellow and Transcendentalism: From *The Victim* to *Herzog*." *CLA Journal*, 30.3 (Mar 1987): 307–327.

Pinsker, Sanford. "Saul Bellow, Going Everywhere: History, American Letters, and the Transcendental Itch." *Saul Bellow Journal*, 3.2 (Spring-Summer 1984): 47–52.

Pollin, Burton R. "Poe and Bellow: A Literary Connection." *Saul Bellow Journal*, 7.1 (Winter 1988): 15–26.

Porter, M. Gilbert. "*Herzog:* A Transcendental Solution to an Existential Problem." *Forum*, 7.2 (1969): 32–36.

————. "*Herzog:* Law of the Heart." In *Whence the Power: The Artistry and Humanity of Saul Bellow*. Columbia, MO: University of Missouri Press, 1974, 146–159.

————. "Hitch Your Agony to a Star: Bellow's Transcendental Vision." In *Saul Bellow and His Work*. Ed. Edmond Schraepen and Tony Tanner. Brussels: University of Brussels Press, 1978, 73–88.

————. "Is Going Up Worth the Coming Down? Transcendental Dualism in Bellow's Fiction." *Studies in the Literary Imagination*, 17.2 (Fall 1984): 19–37.

Quayum, M. A. "Adopting Emerson's Vision of Equilibrium: Citrine and the Two Opposite Poles of Twentieth-Century Consciousness in *Humboldt's Gift.*" *Studies in American Jewish Literature,* 10.1 (Spring 1991): 8–23.

————. "An 'Arbiter of the Diverse': Bellow's Philosophical Affinity with Emerson and Whitman in *Henderson the Rain King.*" *Saul Bellow Journal,* 10.2 (Winter 1992): 42–64.

————. "Emerson's 'Humboldt': A Probable Source for Bellow's Von Humboldt Fleisher in *Humboldt's Gift.*" *Notes on Contemporary Literature,* 22.4 (Sep 1992): 7–8.

————. "Finding the Middle Ground: Bellow's Philosophical Affinity with Emerson in *Mr. Sammler's Planet.*" *Saul Bellow Journal,* 8.2 (Summer 1989): 24–38.

————. "Quest for Equilibrium: Transcendental Ideas in Bellow's *Herzog.*" *Saul Bellow Journal,* 14.2 (Fall 1996): 43–69.

Schulz, Dieter. "The Poe Connection in Bellow's *More Die of Heartbreak.*" *Saul Bellow Journal,* 11.1 (Fall 1992): 41–51.

Stanger, James. "The Power of Vision: Blake's System and Bellow's Project in *Mr. Sammler's Planet.*" *Saul Bellow Journal,* 12.2 (Fall 1994): 17–36.

Sullivan, Quentin M. "The Downward Transcendence of Moses Herzog." *Gypsy Scholar,* 3 (1975): 44–50.

Van Egmond, Peter G. "Herzog's Quotation of Walt Whitman." *Walt Whitman Review,* 13 (1967): 54–56.

Yetman, Michael G. "Who Would Not Sing For Humboldt?" *English Literary History,* 48 (Winter 1981): 935–951.

Paul Bowles

Pounds, Wayne. "Paul Bowles and Edgar Allan Poe: The Disintegration of Personality." *Twentieth Century Literature,* 32.3–4 (Fall-Winter 1986): 424–439.

Rainwater, Catherine. "'Sinister Overtones,' 'Terrible Phrases': Poe's Influence on the Writings of Paul Bowles." *Essays In Literature,* 11.2 (Fall 1984): 253–266.

Richard Brautigan

Hackenberry, Charles. "Romance and Parody in Brautigan's *The Abortion.*" *Critique,* 23.2 (Winter 1981–1982): 24–36.

————. "*Walden* Reworked [On Brautigan's *So the Wind Won't Blow It All Away*]." *Thoreau Society Bulletin,* 65 (Fall 1983): 3.

Hayden, Brad. "Echoes of *Walden* in *Trout Fishing in America.*" *Thoreau Journal Quarterly,* 8.3 (1976): 21–26.

Way, Brian T. "The Fiction of Fishing: Richard Brautigan's Metafictional Romance." *DAI* 53.11 (May 1993): 3914A–3915A.

Truman Capote

Freese, Peter. "Das Motiv des Doppelgängers in Truman Capotes 'Shut a Final Door' und E.A. Poes 'William Wilson'." *Literatur in Wissenschaft und Unterricht,* 1 (1968): 40–48.

John Cheever

Bidney, Martin. "'The Common Day' and the Immortality Ode: Cheever's Wordsworthian Craft." *Studies in Short Fiction,* 23.2 (Spring 1986): 139–151.

Chesnik, Eugene. "John Cheever's Domesticated Stroke" [On Cheever, Emerson and Thoreau]. *New England Quarterly,* 44.4 (Dec 1971): 531–552.

Coale, Samuel. "Cheever and Hawthorne: The American Romancer's Art." In *Critical Essays on John Cheever.* Ed. Robert G. Collins. Boston: G.H. Hall, 1982. 193–209.

Harmsel, Henrietta. "[Hawthorne's] 'Young Goodman Brown' and 'The Enormous Radio'." *Studies in Short Fiction,* 9 (1972): 407–408.

Wemhöner, Annegret. *"The Deepest Levels of Life and the Sense of Time and Place": John Cheevers Romanwerk zwischen Romance und Novel of Manners.* Amsterdam: Grüner, 1988.

Don De Lillo

Caton, Lou F. "Romanticism and the Postmodern Novel: Three Scenes From Don DeLillo's *White Noise." English Language Notes,* 35.1 (Sep 1997): 38–48.

Maltby, Paul. "The Romantic Metaphysics of Don DeLillo." *Contemporary Literature,* 37.2 (Summer 1996): 258–277.

McClure, John A, "Postmodern Romance: Don DeLillo and the Age of Conspiracy." In *Introducing Don DeLillo.* Ed. Frank Lentriccia. Durham, NC: Duke University Press, 1991, 99–115.

Oriard, Michael. "Don DeLillo's Search for Walden Pond." *Critique,* 20.1 (1978): 5–24.

Joan Didion

Coale, Samuel. "Joan Didion: Witnessing the Abyss." In *In Hawthorne's Shadow: American Romance from Melville to Mailer.* Lexingon: University Press of Kentucky, 1985, 180–202.

Wolff, Cynthia Griffin. "*Play It As It Lays:* Didion and the Diver Heroine" [On Didion and Melville]. *Contemporary Literature,* 24.4 (Winter 1983): 480–495.

E. L. Doctorow

Budick, Emily Miller. "Seeking the Shores of Self: E. L. Doctorow's *Ragtime* and the Moral Fiction of History" [On *Ragtime* as a Romance]. In *Fiction and Historical Consciousness: The American Romance Tradition.* New Haven, CT: Yale University Press, 1989, 185–207.

Faber, Marion. "Michael Kohlhaas in New York: Kleist and E. L. Doctorow's *Ragtime.*" In *Heinrich von Kleist Studies.* Ed. Alexej Ugrinsky et al. New York: AMS, 1980, 147–156.

Kurth-Voigt, Liselotte. "Kleistian Overtones in E. L. Doctorow's *Ragtime.*" *Monatshefte,* 69 (1977): 404–414.

Neumeyer, Peter F. "E. L. Doctorow, Kleist, and the Ascendancy of Things." *CEA Critic,* 39.4 (1977): 17–21.

Strout, Cushing. "Historizing Fiction and Fictionalizing History: The Case of E. L. Doctorow" [On Doctorow and Hawthorne]. *Prospects,* 5 (1980): 423–437.

Wagner-Martin, Linda. "*Billy Bathgate* and [Melville's] *Billy Budd:* Some Recognitions." *Notes on Contemporary Literature,* 20.1 (Jan 1990): 4–7.

Ralph Ellison

Brown, Alan. "Ellison's *Invisible Man*" [and Edgar Allan Poe]. *Explicator,* 48.1 (Fall 1989): 59–61.

Deutsch, Leonard J. "Ralph Waldo Ellison and Ralph Waldo Emerson: A Shared Moral Vision." *CLA Journal,* 16 (1972): 159–178.

Gray, Valerie Bonita. *Invisible Man's Literary Heritage: [Melville's] Benito Cereno.* Amsterdam: Rodopi, 1978.

Lee, Kun Jong. "Reading Race in(to) the American Renaissance: A Study of Race in Emerson, Whitman, Melville, and Ellison." *DAI* 53.8 (Feb 1993): 2815A.

———. "Ellison's *Invisible Man:* Emersonianism Revisited." *PMLA,* 107.2 (Mar 1992): 331–344.

Lyons, Eleanor. "Ellison and the Twentieth Century American Scholar." *Studies in American Fiction,* 17.1 (Spring 1989): 93–106.

Mengeling, Marvin E. "Whitman and Ellison: Older Symbols in a Modern Mainstream." *Walt Whitman Review,* 12 (1966): 67–70.

Nichols, William W. "Ralph Ellison's Black American Scholar." *Phylon,* 31 (1970): 70–75.

Omans, Stuart E. "The Variations on a Masked Leader: A Study of the Literary Relationship of Ralph Ellison and Herman Melville." *South Atlantic Bulletin,* 40.2 (1975): 15–23.

Schultz, Elizabeth A. "The Illumination of Darkness: Affinities between *Moby Dick* and *Invisible Man.*" *CLA Journal,* 32.2 (Dec 1988): 170–200.

Selke, Hartmut K. "'The Education at College of Fools': References to Emerson's 'Self-Reliance' in *Invisible Man.*" *Notes on Contemporary Literature,* 4.1 (1974): 13–15.

Sidney, Mary F. "The Power and the Horror of Whiteness: Wright and Ellison Respond to Poe." *CLA Journal,* 29.1 (Sep 1985): 82–90.

Louise Erdrich

Matchie, Thomas. "Louise Erdrich's *Scarlet Letter:* Literary Continuity in Tales of Burning Love." *North Dakota Quarterly,* 63.4 (Fall 1986): 113–123.

———. "*Love Medicine:* A Female *Moby Dick.*" *Midwest Quarterly,* 30.4 (Summer 1989): 478–491.

McKay, Mary A. "Cooper's Indians and Erdrich's Native Americans." In *Global Perspectives on Teaching.* Ed. Sandra Lott Ward et al. Urbana, IL: National Council of Teachers, 1993, 152–167.

John Gardner

Ackland, Michael. "Blakean Sources in John Gardner's *Grendel.*" *Critique,* 23.1 (1981): 57–66.

Billy, Ted. "'The King's Indian': Gardner's Imp of the Poeverse." *Notes on Modern American Literature,* 5 (1980): Item 2.

Coale, Samuel. "'Into the Farther Darkness': The Manichean Pastoralism of John Gardner." In *John Gardner: Critical Perspectives.* Ed. Robert A. Morace and Kathryn Van Spanckeren. Carbondale: Southern Illinois University Press, 1982, 15–27.

Ellis, Helen B. and Warren Ober. "*Grendel* and Blake: The Contraries of Existence." *English Studies in Canada,* 3 (1977): 87–102.

Fenlon, Katherine Feeney. "John Gardner's 'The Ravages of Spring' as Re-Creation of 'The Fall of the House of Usher'." *Studies in Short Fiction,* 31.3 (Summer 1994): 481–487.

Fitzpatrick, W. P. "Down and Down I Go: A Note on Shelley's *Prometheus Unbound* and Gardner's *Grendel.*" *Notes on Contemporary Literature,* 7.1 (1977): 2–5.

Foor-Pessin, Michael. "The New Romance of 'The King's Indian': John Gardner's Step Away from the Abyss." Master's Thesis, SUNY Cortland, 1986.

Howell, John M. "The Wound and the Albatross: John Gardner's Apprenticeship" [On Gardner and Coleridge]. In *Thor's Hammer: Essays on John Gardner.* Ed. Jeff Henderson et al. Conway: University of Central Arkansas Press, 1985, 1–16.

Morris, Gregory. "*The King's Indian: Stories and Tales*" [On Gardner, Poe, and Melville]. In *A World of Order and Light: The Fiction of John Gardner.* Athens: University of Georgia Press, 1984, 116–142, 243–244.

William Gass

Schneider, Richard J. "Rejecting the Stone: William Gass and Emersonian Transcendence." *Review of Contemporary Fiction,* 11.3 (Fall 1991): 115–23.

Stewart, Susan. "An American Faust" [On Goethe and Gass' *The Tunnel*]. *American Literature,* 69.2 (June 1977): 399–416.

William Gibson

Glazer, Miriyam. "'What Is Within Now Seen Without': Romanticism, Neuromanticism, and the Death of the Imagination in William Gibson's Fictive World." *Journal of Popular Culture,* 23.3 (Winter 1989): 155–164.

McGuirk, Carol. "The 'New' Romances: Science Fiction Innovators from Gernsback to Gibson." In *Fiction 200: Cyberpunk and the Future of Narrative.* Ed George Slusser and Thomas Shippey. Athens: Georgia University Press, 1992, 108–129.

Schroeder, Randy. "Determinacy, Indeterminacy, and the Romantic in William Gibson." *Science-Fiction Studies,* 21 (1994): 155–163.

Voller, Jack G. "Neuromanticism: Cyberspace and the Sublime." *Extrapolation,* 34.1 (1994): 18–29.

John Hawkes

Berryman, Charles. "Hawkes and Poe: *Travesty.*" *Modern Fiction Studies,* 29.4 (Winter 1983): 643–654.

Cantrell, Carol Halmstetter. "John Hawkes's *Second Skin:* The Dead Reckoning of a Northrop Frye Romance." *Bulletin of the Rocky Mountain Modern Language Association,* 35.4 (1981): 281–290.

Warner, John M. "The 'Internalized Quest Romance' in Hawkes' *The Lime Twig.*" *Modern Fiction Studies,* 19 (1973): 89–95.

Wineapple, Brenda. "*Second Skin* and the Dead Reckoning of Romance." *CLA Journal,* 25.4 (June 1982): 468–475.

Joseph Heller

Gordon, Andrew. "Dead Letter Offices: Joseph Heller's *Something Happened* and Herman Melville's 'Bartleby the Scrivener'." *Notes on Contemporary Literature,* 12.5 (Nov 1982): 2–4.

Gayl Jones

Byerman, Keith. "Black Vortex: The Gothic Structure of [Gayl Jones'] *Eva's Man." MELUS,* 7.4 (1980): 93–101.

Kalfopopulou, Adrianne. "Gendered Silences and the Problem of Desire in Nathaniel Hawthorne's *The Scarlet Letter,* Gertrude's Stein's "Melanctha," and Gayl Jones' *Corregidora."* In *Nationalism and Sexuality; Crises of Identity.* Ed. Yiorgos Kalogeras and Domna Patourmatzi. Thessaloniki: Aristotle University Press, 1996, 115–123.

William H. Kelley

Bruck. Peter. "The Romance as an Epistemological Design: William Melvin Kelley's *A Different Drummer."* In *The Afro-American Novel Since 1960.* Ed. Peter Bruck and Wolfgang Karrer. Amsterdam: Grüner, 1982, 103–122.

Davis, Charles E. "W.M. Kelley and H.D. Thoreau: The Music Within." *Obsidian II,* 2.1 (Spring 1987): 2–13.

William Kennedy

Alsen, Eberhard. "Sin and the Supernatural in William Kennedy's *Ironweed."* In *Romantic Postmodernism in American Fiction.* Amsterdam & Atlanta: Rodopi, 1996, 223–239.

Yetman, Michael G. *"Ironweed:* The Perils and Purgatories of Male Romanticism." *Papers on Language and Literature,* 27.1 (Winter 1991): 84–104.

Jack Kerouac

D'Orso, Michael. "Man Out of Time: Kerouac, Spengler, and the 'Faustian Soul' " [On Kerouac and Goethe]. *Studies in American Fiction,* 11.1 (Spring 1983): 19–30.

Hipkiss, Robert A. *Jack Kerouac: Prophet of the New Romanticism.* Lawrence, KS: Regents Press, 1976.

Panish, Jon. "Kerouac's *The Subterraneans:* A Study of 'Romantic Primitivism'." *MELUS,* 19.3 (Fall 1994): 107–123.

Rideout, George. "[Kerouac's] Duloz and [Goethe's] Faust." *Review of Contemporary Fiction,* 3.2 (Summer 1983): 46–50.

Ken Kesey

Baurecht, William Carl. "Romantic Deviance and the Messianic Impulse in American Masculinity: Case Studies of *Moby-Dick, One Flew Over the Cuckoo's Nest,* and *Sometimes a Great Notion.*" *DAI* 39 (1979): 7343A–7344A.

Hipkiss, Robert, "Ken Kesey." In *Jack Kerouac: Prophet of the New Romanticism.* Lawrence, KS: Regents Press, 1976, 121–129.

Marsden, James Douglas. "Modern Echoes of Transcendentalism: Kesey, Snyder, and Other Countercultural Authors." *DAI* 38 (1978): 4830A– 4831A.

Stone, Edward. "[Kesey's] *Cuckoo's Nest* and [Melville's] *Moby-Dick.*" *Melville Society Extracts,* 38 (1979): 11–12.

Maxine Hong Kingston

Tanner, James F. "Walt Whitman's Presence in Maxine Hong Kingston's *Tripmaster Monkey: His Fake Book.*" *MELUS,* 10.4 (Winter 1995): 61–74.

John Knowles

Hipkiss, Robert. "John Knowles." In *Jack Kerouac: Prophet of the New Romanticism.* Lawrence, KS: Regents Press, 1976, 112–121.

Jerzy Kosinski

Gladsky, Thomas S. "Jerzy Kosinski: The Polish Cooper." *Notes on Contemporary Literature,* 19.2 (Mar 1989): 11–12.

McGinnis, Wayne. "Transcendence and Primitive Sympathy in Kosinski's *The Painted Bird.*" *Studies in the Humanities,* 8.1 (1980): 22–27.

Norman Mailer

Alsen, Eberhard. "The Manichean Pessimism of Norman Mailer's *An American Dream.*" In *Romantic Postmodernism in American Fiction.* Amsterdam & Atlanta: Rodopi, 1996, 73–89.

Busch, Frederick. "The Whale as a Shaggy Dog: Melville and 'The Man Who Studied Yoga'." *Modern Fiction Studies,* 19 (1973): 193–206.

Coale, Samuel. "Melville to Mailer: Manichean Manacles." In *In Hawthorne's Shadow: The American Romance from Melville to Mailer.* Lexington, KY: University Press of Kentucky, 1985, 22–45.

Horn, Bernard. "Ahab and Ishmael at War: The Presence of *Moby Dick* in *The Naked and the Dead.*" *American Quarterly,* 34.4 (Fall 1982): 379–395.

Marks, Barry A. "Civil Disobedience in Retrospect: Henry David Thoreau and Norman Mailer." *Soundings,* 62 (1979): 144–165.

Monteiro, George. *"Moby Dick* and *The Naked and the Dead* Reviewed in the *Fourth International." Melville Society Extracts,* 106 (Sep 1996): 15–16.

Ross, Morton L. "Thoreau and Mailer: The Mission of the Rooster." *Western Humanities Review,* 25 (1971): 47–56.

Bernard Malamud

Eigner, Edwin M. "Malamud's Use of the Quest Romance." *Genre,* 1 (1968): 55–75.

Freese, Peter. "Bernard Malamud: 'The Last Mohican'." In *Die amerikanische Short Story der Gegenwart: Interpretationen.* Ed. Peter Freese. Berlin: Schmidt, 1976, 205–214.

Hoyt, Charles A. "Bernard Malamud and the New Romanticism." In *Contemporary American Novelists.* Ed. Harry T. Moore. Carbondale: Southern Illinois University Press, 1964, 65–79.

Kennedy, J. Gerald. "Parody as Exorcism: [Poe's] 'The Raven' and 'The Jewbird'." *Genre,* 13 (1980): 161–169.

Shipman, Barry Mark. "Wordsworthian Romanticism in the Fiction of Bernard Malamud." *DAI* 55.4 (Oct 1994): 967A.

Winn, H. Harbour, III. "Malamud's Uncas: 'Last Mohican'." *Notes on Contemporary Literature,* 5.2 (1975): 13–14.

Carson McCullers

Budick, Emily Miller. "The Mother Tongue: Carson McCullers." In *Engendering Romance: Women Writers and the Hawthorne Tradition 1850–1990.* New Haven: Yale University Press, 1994, 143–161.

Clark, Charlene Kerne. "Carson McCullers and the Tradition of Romance." *DAI* 35 (1975): 5319A.

Fletcher, Mary Dell. "Carson McCullers' 'Ancient Mariner' " [On McCullers and Coleridge]. *South Central Bulletin,* 35 (1975): 123–125.

Henry Miller

Daugherty, Francis L. "Henry Miller and the Heterocosm: The General and Applied Literary Theory of an American Neo-Romantic." *DAI* 32 (1971): 423A.

Gordon. William Alexander. "Henry Miller and the Romantic Tradition." DAI 24 (1964): 3335–3336.

Hoffman, Michael J. "Miller's Debt to Emerson, Thoreau et al.; Miller and the Apocalypse of Transcendentalism." *Lost Generation Journal,* 4.3 (1976–77): 18–21.

Jackson, Paul R. "Henry Miller, Emerson, and the Divided Self." *American Literature,* 43 (1971): 231–241.

McCarthy, Harold. "Henry Miller's Democratic Vistas" [On Miller and Whitman]. *American Quarterly,* 23 (1971): 221–235.

Rose, Edward J. "The Aesthetics of Civil Disobedience: Henry Miller, Twentieth Century Transcendentalist." *Edge,* 1.1 (Fall 1965): 5–16.

Smithline, Arnold. "Henry Miller and the Transcendental Spirit." *Emerson Society Quarterly,* 43 (1966): 50–56.

Toni Morrison

Alsen, Eberhard. "Toni Morrison's *Song of Solomon* and the Secret of Spiritual Flight." In *Romantic Postmodernism in American Fiction.* Amsterdam & Atlanta: Rodopi, 1996, 189–206.

Britton, Wesley. "The Puritan Past and Black Gothic: The Haunting of Toni Morrison's *Beloved* in Light of Hawthorne's *The House of the Seven Gables.*" *Nathaniel Hawthorne Review,* 21.2 (Fall 1995): 7–23.

Budick, Emily Miller. "Absence, Loss, and the Space of History in Toni Morrison's *Beloved.*" In *Engendering Romance: Women Writers and the Hawthorne Tradition 1850–1990.* New Haven: Yale University Press, 1994, 181–218.

Cocalis, Jane. "The 'Dark and Abiding Presence' in Nathaniel Hawthorne's *The Scarlet Letter* and Toni Morrison's *Beloved.*" In *The Calvinist Roots of the Modern Era.* Ed. Aliki Barnstone et al. Hanover, NH: University Press of New England, 1997, 250–262.

Gravett, Sharon L. "Toni Morrison's *The Bluest Eye:* An Inverted *Walden?*" *West Virginia University Philological Papers,* 38 (1992): 201–211.

Lewis, Charles. "The Ironic Romance of New Historicism: *The Scarlet Letter* and *Beloved* Standing in Side by Side." *Arizona Quarterly,* 51.1 (Spring 1995): 32–60.

Steiner, Annie Delores. "Reading Blake, Reading Morrison: A Blakean Reading of Toni Morrison." *DAI* 56.1 (July 1995): 195A.

Stryz, Jan. "Memorial Pictures: Visual Representation in the American Romance" [on Hawthorne, James, Faulkner, and Morrison]. *DAI* 57.7 (January 1992): 2557A.

———. "The Other Ghost in *Beloved:* The Specter of *The Scarlet Letter.*" *Genre,* 24 (Winter 1991): 417–434.

Woidat, Caroline M. "Talking Back to Schoolteacher: Morrison's Confrontation with Hawthorne in *Beloved.*" *Modern Fiction Studies,* 39.3–4 (Fall–Winter 1993): 527–546.

Vladimir Nabokov

Banta, Martha. "Benjamin, Edgar, Humbert and Jay: Franklinian Fable and Poesque Dream in *Gatsby* and *Lolita.*" *Yale Review,* 60 (1971): 532–549.

Barabtarlo, Gene. "Pushkin Embedded [in Nabokov's fiction]." *Vladimir Nabokov Research Newsletter,* 8 (Spring 1982): 28–31.

Bouazza, A. "Lord Byron's Pack" [Byron Allusions in *Lolita*]. *Nabokovian,* 33 (Fall 1994): 15–16.

Brown, Clarence. "Nabokov's Pushkin and Nabokov's Nabokov." *Wisconsin Studies in Contemporary Literature,* 8.2 (Spring 1967): 280–293.

Clark, George P. "A Further Word on Poe and *Lolita.*" *Poe Newsletter,* 3 (1971): 39.

Davydov, Sergej. "Nabokov and Pushkin." In *The Garland Companion to Vladimir Nabokov.* Ed. Vladimir E. Alexandrov. New York: Garland, 1995, 482–496.

Delizia, Michael. "Dr. Nabokov and Mr. Thoreau." *Thoreau Society Bulletin,* 142 (1977): 1–2.

DuBois, Arthur E. "Poe and *Lolita.*" *CEA Critic,* 26.6 (1964): 1, 7.

Godshalk, William L. "Nabokov's Byronic *Ada:* A Note." *Notes on Contemporary Literature,* 2.2 (1972): 2–4.

Goldhurst, William, Alfred Appel, Jr., and George P. Clark. "Three Observations on [Poe's] 'Amontillado' and [Nabokov's] *Lolita.*" *Poe Studies,* 5.2 (1972): 51.

Greenleaf, Monika. "Fathers, Sons and Impostors: Pushkin's Trace in 'The Gift'." *Slavic Review,* 53.1 (Spring 1994): 140–158.

Johnson, D. Barton. "Nabokov's *Ada* and Pushkin's *Eugene Onegin.*" *Slavic and East European Journal,* 15 (1971): 316–323.

LeClair, Thomas. "Poe's *Pym* and Nabokov's *Pale Fire.*" *Notes on Contemporary Literature,* 3.2 (1973): 2–3.

Link, Franz H. "Nabokov's *Lolita* and Aesthetic Romanticism." *Literatur in Wissenschaft und Unterricht,* 9 (1976): 37–48.

Madden, David W. "'We Poets': Humbert and Keats." *Notes on Contemporary Literature,* 10.3 (1980): 5–6.

Maddox, Lucy B. "Necrophilia in *Lolita*" [On Nabokov and Poe]. *Centennial Review,* 26.4 (Fall 1982): 361–374.

Meyer, Priscilla. "Nabokov's Lolita and Pushkin's Onegin: McAdam, McEve and McFate." In *The Achievements of Vladimir Nabokov.* Ed. George Gibian and Stephen Parker. Ithaca: Cornell University Press, 1984, 179–211.

Mroz, Edith Maria Fay. "Vladimir Nabokov and Romantic Irony." *DAI* 49.12 (June 1989): 3734A.

Naumann, Marina Turkevich. "Nabokov and Pushkin's Tuning Fork." *Russian, Croatian and Serbian, Czech and Slovak, Polish Literature,* 29.2 (15 Feb 1991): 229–242.

Novak, Frank G. Jr. "Ambiguity and Incest: An Allusion to Melville in Nabokov's *Lolita.*" *Notes on Contemporary Literature,* 11.5 (Nov 1981): 10.

Peterson, Dale E. "Nabokov and Poe." In *The Garland Companion to Vladimir Nabokov.* Ed. Vladimir Alexandrov. New York: Garland, 1995, 463–472.

———. "Nabokov and the Poe-etics of Composition." *Slavic and East European Journal,* 33.1 (Spring 1989): 95–107.

Petty, Chapel Louise. "A Comparison of Hawthorne's 'Wakefield' and Nabokov's 'The Leonardo': Narrative Commentary and the Struggle of the Literary Artist." *Modern Fiction Studies,* 25 (1979): 499–507.

Pultorak, Jake. "Goethe in Humberland [*Elective Affinities* and *Lolita*]." *Nabokovian,* 30 (Spring 1993): 49–53.

Rennert, Hal H. "Literary Revenge: Nabokov's 'Mademoiselle O' and Kleist's 'Die Marquise von O'." *Germano-Slavica,* 4.6 (Fall 1984): 331–337.

Sweeney, S. E. "Purloined Letters: Poe, Doyle, Nabokov." *Russian Literature Triquarterly,* 24 (1990): 213–237.

Tammi, Pekka. "Nabokov's Symbolic Cards and Pushkin's 'The Queen of Spades'." *Nabokovian,* 13 (Fall 1984): 31–32.

Gloria Naylor

Berg, Christine G. " 'Giving Sound To The Bruised Places in Their Hearts': Gloria Naylor and Walt Whitman." In *Critical Responses to Gloria Naylor.* Ed. Sharon Felton and Michelle Loris. Westport, CT: Greenwood, 1997, 98–111.

Sandiford, K.A. "Gothic and Intertextual Constructions in *Linden Hills.*" *Arizona Quarterly,* 47.3 (Autumn 1991): 117–139.

Joyce Carol Oates

Coale, Samuel. "Joyce Carol Oates: On Contending Spirits." In *In Hawthorne's Shadow: American Romance from Melville to Mailer.* Lexington, KY: University Press of Kentucky, 1985, 161–179.

Egan, James. " 'Romance of a Darksome Type': Versions of the Fantastic in the Novels of Joyce Carol Oates." *Studies in Weird Fiction,* 7 (Spring 1990): 12–21.

Keyser, Elizabeth Lennox. "*A Bloodsmoor Romance:* Joyce Carol Oates's *Little Women.*" *Women's Studies,* 14.3 (1988): 211–223.

Winslow, Joan D. "The Stranger Within: Two Stories by Oates and Hawthorne." *Studies in Short Fiction,* 17 (1980): 263–268.

Flannery O'Connor

Allen, William Rodney. "Mr. Head and Hawthorne: Allusion and Conversion in Flannery O'Connor's 'The Artificial Nigger'." *Studies in Short Fiction,* 21.1 (Winter 1984): 17–23.

Alsen, Eberhard. "The Figure of the Devil in Flannery O'Connor's *The Violent Bear It Away* and 'The Lame Shall Enter First'." In *Romantic Postmodernism in American Fiction.* Amsterdam & Atlanta: Rodopi, 1996, 90–109.

Asals, Fredrick J., Jr. "Hawthorne, Mary Ann, and "The Lame Shall Enter First'." *Flannery O'Connor Bulletin,* 2 (1973): 3–18.

Budick, Emily Miller. "Art and the Female Spirit: Flannery O'Connor." In *Engendering Romance: Women Writers and the Hawthorne Tradition 1850–1990.* New Haven: Yale University Press, 1994, 162–180.

Burt, John Davies "American Romance and the Bounds of Sense" [On Hawthorne, Poe, and O'Connor]. *DAI* 45.2 (Aug 1984): 519A–520A.

Emerick, Ronald. "Hawthorne and O'Connor: A Literary Kinship." *The Flannery O'Connor Bulletin,* 18 (1989): 46–54.

————. "Romance, Allegory, Vision: The Influence of Hawthorne on Flannery O'Connor." *DAI* 36 (1976): 4485A–4486A.

————. "*Wise Blood:* O'Connor's Romance of Alienation." *Literature and Belief,* 12 (1992): 27–38.

Farley, Blanche. " 'Echoes of Poe, in [O'Connor's] 'Sawmill and Loft'." *Flannery O'Connor Bulletin,* 14 (1985): 14–24.

Gatta, John. "*The Scarlet Letter* as Pre-Text for Flannery O'Connor's 'Good Country People'." *Nathaniel Hawthorne Review,* 16.2 (Fall 1990): 6–9.

Knutson, Roslyn Lander. "A Faust in Eastrod, Tennessee?" [On Goethe and O'Connor]. *Publications of the Arkansas Philological Association,* 5.2–3 (1979): 16–22.

Meyer, William E. H., Jr. "Melville and O'Connor: The Hypervisual Crisis." *Stanford Literature Review,* 4.2 (Fall 1987): 211–229.

Montgomery, Marion. "The Artist as 'A Very Doubtful Jacob': A Reflection on Hawthorne and O'Connor." *Southern Quarterly,* 16 (1978): 95–103.

Walsh, Thomas F. "The Devils of Hawthorne and Flannery O'Connor." *Xavier Review,* 5 (1966): 117–122.

Grace Paley

Budick, Emily Miller. "The Graceful Art of Conversation: Grace Paley." In *Engendering Romance: Women Writers and the Hawthorne Tradition 1850–1990*. New Haven: Yale University Press, 1994, 219–245.

Walker Percy

Johnson, Mark. "*Lancelot:* Percy's Romance" [On Percy and Hawthorne]. *Southern Literary Journal,* 15.2 (Spring 1983): 19–30.
Lawson, Lewis A. "'English Romanticism . . . and 1930 Science' in *The Moviegoer.*" *Rocky Mountain Review of Language and Literature,* 38.1–2 (1984): 70–84.
Lawson, Lewis A. "The Fall of the House of Lamar" [On Percy and Poe]. In *The Art of Walker Percy. Stratagems for Being.* Ed. Panthea Reid Broughton. Baton Rouge: Louisiana State University Press, 1979, 219–245.
Olesky, Elzbieta H. "Walker Percy's Demonic Vision" [On Percy and Melville]. In *Walker Percy: Novelist and Philosopher.* Ed. Jan Nordby Gretlund and Karl-Heinz Westarp. Jackson: University Press of Mississippi, 1991, 199–209.
Olesky, Elzbieta. *Plight in Common: Hawthorne and Percy.* New York: Peter Lang, 1993.
Samway, Patrick, S.J. "Another Case of the Purloined Letter" (In *Lancelot*). *New Orleans Review,* 16.4 (Winter 1989): 37–44.
Stephenson, Will and Mimosa Stephenson. "A Keats Allusion in Walker Percy's *The Last Gentleman.*" *Notes on Contemporary Literature,* 22.3 (May 1992): 3–4.

James Purdy

Hipkiss, Robert. "James Purdy." In *Jack Kerouac: Prophet of the New Romanticism.* Lawrence, KS: Regents Press, 1976, 105–112.

Thomas Pynchon

Alsen, Eberhard. "'Transcendent Doings' in Thomas Pynchon's *Gravity's Rainbow.*" In *Romantic Postmodernism in American Fiction.* Amsterdam & Atlanta: Rodopi, 1996, 71–188.
Bakker, Jan. "From Leatherstocking to Rocketman: Cooper's Leatherstocking Tales and Pynchon's *Gravity's Rainbow* Reconsidered." In *James Fenimore Cooper: New Historical and Literary Contexts.* Ed. W. M. Verhoeven. Amsterdam & Atlanta: Rodopi, 1993, 161–176.

Banta, Martha. "About America's 'White Terror': James, Poe, Pynchon, and Others." In *Literature and the Occult: Essays in Comparative Literature.* Ed. Luanne Frank. Arlington, TX: University of Texas Press, 1977, 31–53.

Benoit, Robert. "Slothrop Unbound: Shelley's Prometheus and *Gravity's Rainbow.*" *Pynchon Notes,* 30–31 (Spring/Fall 1992): 188–191.

Berressem, Hanjo. "Godolphin, Goodol'phin, Goodol'Pyn, Good ol' Pyn: A Question of Integration" [On Poe's *Pym* and Pynchon's *V.*]. *Pynchon Notes,* 10 (1982): 3–17.

Black, Joel D. "Probing a Post-Romantic Paleontology: Thomas Pynchon's *Gravity's Rainbow.*" *Boundary 2,* 8.2 (1980): 229–254.

Campbell, Elizabeth. "Metaphor and *V.:* Metaphysics in the Mirror" [On *V.* and *Moby Dick*]. *Pynchon Notes,* 22–23 (Spring/Fall 1988): 57–70.

Chaffee, Patricia. "The Whale and the Rocket: Theology as a Sacred Symbol" [On Pynchon and Melville]. *Renascence,* 33 (1980): 146–151.

Cox, Stephen D. "Berkeley, Blake, and the Apocalypse of Pynchon's *The Crying of Lot 49.*" *Essays in Literature,* 7 (1980): 91–99.

Daw, Lawrence. "The Apocalyptic Milieu of Pynchon's *Gravity's Rainbow.*" In *Apocalyptic Visions Past and Present.* Ed JoAnn James and William J. Cloonan. Tallahassee: Florida Sate University Press, 1988, 91–98.

Hans, James S. "Emptiness and Plenitude in 'Bartleby the Scrivener' and *The Crying of Lot 49.*" *Essays in Literature,* 22.2 (Fall 1995): 285–299.

Hume, Beverly Ann. "The Framing of Evil: Romantic Visions and Revisions in American Fiction" [On Hawthorne, Poe, Melville, and Pynchon]. *DAI* 44.12 (June 1984): 3685A.

Kopcewicz, Andrzej. "The Rocket and the Whale: Thomas Pynchon's *Gravity's Rainbow* and *Moby Dick.*" In *Proceedings of a Symposium on American Literature.* Ed. Marta Sienicka. Poznan: Poznan University Press, 1979, 145–150.

Krafft, John M. "Anarcho-Romanticism and the Metaphysics of Counterforce: Alex Comfort and Thomas Pynchon." *Paunch,* 40–41 (1975): 78–107.

Limon, John. "How to Place Poe's Arthur Gordon Pym in Science-Dominated Intellectual History and How to Extract It Again" [On Poe and Pynchon]. *North Dakota Quarterly,* 51.1 (Winter 1983): 31–47.

Link, Eric Carl. "Luddism in 'Under the Rose'." *Pynchon Notes,* 30–31 (Spring/Fall 1992): 157–64.

Mattessich, Stefan N. "Blake and Pynchon: A Study in Discursive Time." *DAI* 57.11 (May 1997): 4736A.

Mizener, Arthur. "The New Romance." *Southern Review,* 8 (1972): 106–117.

Salazar, Rothman. "Historicizing Phrenology: Wordsworth, Pynchon, and the Discursive Economy of the Cranial Text." *Raritan,* 8.1 (Summer 1988): 80–91.

Thompson, Gary Lee. "Fictive Models: Carlyle's *Sartor Resartus,* Melville's *The Confidence-Man,* Gaddis' *The Recognitions,* and Pynchon's *Gravity's Rainbow.*" *DAI* 40 (1979): 1462A–1463A.

Ishmael Reed

Hardack, Richard. "'Swing to the White, Back to the Black': Writing and 'Sourcery' in Ishmael Reed's *Mumbo Jumbo*" [On Reed and Emerson]. *Arizona Quarterly,* 49.4 (Winter 1993): 117–138.

Weixlman, Joe. "Ishmael Reed's Raven" [On Reed and Poe]. *Review of Contemporary Fiction,* 4.2 (Summer 1984): 205–208.

Marilynne Robinson

Liscio, Lorraine. "Marilynne Robinson's *Housekeeping:* Misreading [Wordsworth's] *The Prelude.*" In *English Romanticism and Modern Fiction.* Ed. Allan Chavkin. New York: AMS, 1993, 139–162.

Newman, Judie. "Solitary Sojourners in Nature: Revisionary Transcendentalism in Alison Lurie's *Love and Friendship* and Marilynne Robinson's *Housekeeping.*" In *The Insular Dream: Obsession and Resistance.* Ed. Kristiaan Versluys. Amsterdam: Vrij University Press, 1995, 303–323.

Philip Roth

Alsen, Eberhard. "The Fantastic in Philip Roth's *The Breast* and Donald Barthelme's *The Dead Father.*" In *Romantic Postmodernism in American Fiction.* Amsterdam & Atlanta: Rodopi, 1996, 133–152.

Noble, Donald R. "Dickinson to Roth." *American Notes and Queries,* 9 (1971): 150–151.

J. D. Salinger

Alsen, Eberhard. "Epilog: Salinger as a Neo-Romantic Writer." In *Salinger's Glass Stories as a Composite Novel.* Troy, NY: Whiston, 1983, 248–254.

———. "J.D. Salinger's *Franny and Zooey* and the Teachings of the *Bhagavad Gita.*" In *Romantic Postmodernism in American Fiction.* Amsterdam & Atlanta: Rodopi, 1996, 58–72.

Gale, Robert L. "[Melville's] Redburn and [Salinger's] Holden—Half-Brothers One Century Removed." *Forum,* 3.12 (1963): 32–36.

Gunter, Bernd. "Holden Caulfield: Sentimentaler oder sentimentalischer Idealist?" *Die Neueren Sprachen,* 21 (1972): 728–738.

Hipkiss, Robert. "J.D. Salinger." In *Jack Kerouac: Prophet of the New Romanticism.* Lawrence, KS: Regents Press, 1976, 97–105.

Karlstetter, Karl. "J.D. Salinger, R.W. Emerson and the Perennial Philosophy." *Moderna Sprak,* 63 (1969): 244–236.

Luedtke, Luther S. "J.D. Salinger and Robert Burns: *The Catcher in the Rye.*" *Modern Fiction Studies,* 16 (1970): 198–201.

Lyons, John O. "The Romantic Style of 'Seymour: An Introduction'." *Wisconsin Studies in Contemporary Literature,* 4.1 (1963): 62–69.

Strauch, Carl F. "Salinger: The Romantic Background." *Wisconsin Studies in Contemporary Literature,* 4 (Winter 1963): 31–40.

Tsuchida, Kuniyasu. "Jerome David Salinger no Sakuhin ni Mirareru Ralph Waldo Emerson no Shiso." In *J. D. Salinger Bungaku no Kenkyu.* Ed Hisashi Shigeo and Ayako Sato. Tokyo: Tokyo Shirakawa Shoin, 1983, 185–196.

Isaac Bashevis Singer

Gottlieb, Elaine. "Singer and Hawthorne: A Prevalence of Satan." *Southern Review,* 8 (1972): 359–370.

Rubinstein, Esther Levin. "The Grotesque: Aesthetics of Pictorial Disorder in the Writings of Edgar Allan Poe and Isaac Bashevis Singer." *DAI* 45.3 (Oct 1984): 1116A.

William Styron

Coale, Samuel. "Styron's Choice: Hawthorne's Guilt in Poe's Palaces." *Papers on Language and Literature,* 23.4 (Fall 1987): 514–522.

Pearce, Richard. "William Styron" [and Herman Melville]. In *The Critical Response to William Styron.* Westport, CT: Greenwood, 1995, 83–86.

Paul Theroux

Coale Samuel. "Hawthorne and the Sixties: Careening on the Utmost Verge." In *In the Shadow of Hawthorne: American Romance from Melville to Mailer.* Lexington, KY: University Press of Kentucky, 1985, 203–217.

Lyons, Paul. "From Man Eaters to Spam Eaters: Literary Tourism and the Discourse of Cannibalism from Herman Melville to Paul Theroux." *Arizona Quarterly,* 51.2 (Summer 1995): 33–62.

John Updike

Brenner, Gerry. "*Rabbit, Run:* John Updike's Criticism of the 'Return to Nature'." *Twentieth Century Literature,* 12 (1966): 3–14.

Budick, Emily Miller. "A Note on John Updike's *Rabbit is Rich.*" In *Fiction and Historical Consciousness: The American Romance Tradition.* New Haven, CT: Yale University Press, 1989, 207–215.

Coale, Samuel. "John Updike: The Beauty of Duality." In *In Hawthorne's Shadow: American Romance from Melville to Mailer.* Lexington: University Press of Kentucky, 1985, 123–146.

Duvall, John N. "The Pleasure of the Textual/Sexual Wrestling: Pornography and Heresy in *Roger's Version.*" *Modern Fiction Studies,* 37 (1991): 81–95.

Greiner, Donald J. *Adultery in the American Novel: Updike, James, and Hawthorne.* Columbia: University of South Carolina Press, 1985.

————. "Body and Soul: John Updike and *The Scarlet Letter.*" *Journal of Modern Literature,* 15.4 (Spring 1989): 475–449.

Iannone, Carol. "Adultery from Hawthorne to Updike." *Commentary,* 86.4 (Oct 1988): 55–59.

Kesterson, David B. "Updike and Hawthorne: Not So Strange Bedfellows." *Notes on Modern American Literature,* 3 (1979): Item 1.

Matthews, John T. "The Word as Scandal: Updike's *Month of Sundays*" [compared to *The Scarlet Letter*]. *Arizona Quarterly,* 39.4 (Winter 1983): 351–380.

Porter, M. Gilbert. "John Updike's 'A & P': The Establishment and an Emersonian Cashier." *English Journal,* 61 (1972): 155–158.

Schiff, James A. "Updike's *Roger's Version:* Revisualizing *The Scarlet Letter.*" *South Atlantic Review,* 57.4 (Nov 1992): 59–76.

————. "Updike's *Scarlet Letter* Trilogy: Recasting an American Myth." *Studies in American Fiction,* 20.1 (Spring 1992): 17–31.

————. *Updike's Version: Rewriting Hawthorne's The Scarlet Letter.* Columbia: University of Missouri Press, 1993.

Shaw, Patrick W. "Checking Out Faith and Lust: Hawthorne's 'Young Goodman Brown' and Updike's 'A & P'." *Studies in Short Fiction,* 23.3 (Summer 1986): 321–323.

Thomas, Lloyd Spencer. "Scarlet Sundays: Updike vs. Hawthorne." *CEA Critic,* 39.3 (1977): 16–17.

Wilson, Raymond III. "*Roger's Version:* Updike's Negative-Solid Model of *The Scarlet Letter.*" *Modern Fiction Studies,* 35 (1989): 241–250.

Kurt Vonnegut

Alsen, Eberhard. "*Breakfast of Champions:* Kurt Vonnegut on the Nature of Man and God." In *Romantic Postmodernism in American Fiction.* Amsterdam & Atlanta: Rodopi, 1996, 110–132.

Cooley, John. "The Garden in the Machine: Three Postmodern Pastorals" [On Thoreau and Vonnegut]. *Michigan Academician*, 13.4 (Spring 1987): 405–420.

Alice Walker

Alsen, Eberhard. "Alice Walker's *The Color Purple* as a Transcendentalist Romance." In *Romantic Postmodernism in American Fiction*. Amsterdam: & Atlanta: Rodopi: 1996, 207–222.

Curtis-Webber, Amy J. "Re-Envisioning an American Metaphor: Incest in the Novel from Melville to Walker." *DAI* 57.7 (Jan 1997): 3017A.

Morgan, Winifred. "Alice Walker: *The Color Purple* as Allegory." In *Southern Writers at Century's End*. Ed Jeffrey Folks et al. Lexington: University Press of Kentucky, 1997, 177–184.

Eudora Welty

Carson, Gary. "The Romantic Tradition in Eudora Welty's 'A Curtain of Green'." *Notes on Mississippi Writers*, 9 (1976): 97–100.

Givner, Joan. "Katherine Anne Porter, Eudora Welty, and [Hawthorne's] 'Ethan Brand'." *International Fiction Review*, 1 (1974): 32–37.

Jolly, John. "The Schillerian Dialectic and Eudora Welty's 'A Still Moment'." *Notes on Mississippi Writers*, 15.2 (1983): 65–71.

McGinnis, Wayne D. "Welty's 'Death of a Traveling Salesman' and William Blake Once Again." *Notes on Mississippi Writers*, 11 (1979): 52–54.

Travis, Mildred K. "A Note on [Hawthorne's] 'Wakefield' and [Eudora Welty's] 'Old Mr. Marblehall'." *Notes on Contemporary Literature*, 4.3 (1974): 9–10.

Tom Wolfe

Hurd, Myles Raymond. " 'The Masque of the Read Death' in Wolfe's *The Bonfire of the Vanities*." *Notes on Contemporary Literature*, 20.3 (May 1990): 4–5.

III. OVERVIEWS

Alsen, Eberhard. "Realistic and Romantic Tendencies" and "Chaos Science and the Spirit of the Age of Postmodernism." In *Romantic Postmodernism in American Fiction*. Amsterdam & Atlanta: Rodopi, 1996, 1–24, 263–277.

Brier, Peter A. "Caliban Reigns: Romantic Theory and Some Contemporary Fantasists." *Denver Quarterly*, 13.1 (Spring 1978): 38–51.

Budick, Emily Miller. "Introduction." In *Engendering Romance: Women Writers and the Hawthorne Tradition 1850–1990.* New Haven: Yale University Press, 1994, 1–9.

Caramello, James. "*Moby Dick* and the Postmodern Turn." In *Silverless Mirrors: Book, Self & Postmodern American Fiction.* Tallahassee: University Press of Florida, 1983, 54–93.

Caton, Louis Freitas. "'. . . Such Was the Paradise That I Lived': Multi-culturalism, Romantic Theory, and the Contemporary American Novel." *DAI* 57.1 (July 1996): 212A.

Coale, Samuel. "Hawthorne and the Sixties: Careening on the Utmost Verge." In *In Hawthorne's Shadow: American Romance from Melville to Mailer.* Lexington: University Press of Kentucky, 1985, 203–217.

Davis, Ronald L. "*All the New Vibrations:* Romanticism in 20th-Century America." *Southwest Review,* 54 (1969): 256–270.

Graff, Gerald. "The Myth of the Postmodernist 'Breakthrough'." *Tri-Quarterly,* 26 (1973): 383–417.

Hipkiss, Robert. "The New Romanticism." In *Jack Kerouac: Prophet of the New Romanticism.* Lawrence: Regents Press of Kansas, 1976, 95–129.

Kobler, Sheila Frazier. "Postmodern Narrative Techniques in the Works of Nathaniel Hawthorne: Metafiction, Fabulation and Hermeneutical Semiosis." *DAI* 54.8 (Feb 1994): 3030A–3031A.

Knoke, Paul D. "The Allegorical Mode in the Contemporary American Novel of Romance." *DAI* 32 (1971): 2695A.

McConnell, Frank. "The Corpse of the Dragon: Notes on Postromantic Fiction." *Tri-Quarterly,* 33 (Spring 1975): 273–303.

Miura, Shoko Yoshimoto. "The Trickster Archetype: His Function in Contemporary Fiction" [Melville's *Confidence Man* and Contemporary Writers]. *DAI* 43.7 (Jan 1983): 2345A.

Olderman, Raymond. "The Problem of Reality and the New Rationale for Romance." In *Beyond the Wasteland: The American Novel in the Nineteen Sixties.* New Haven: Yale University Press, 1972, 1–29.

Remak, Henry H. "European Romanticism and Contemporary American Counterculture." In *Romanticism and Culture.* Ed. H.W. Matalene. New York: Camden House, 1984, 71–95.

Wineapple, Brenda. "Neo-Romanticism in Contemporary American Fiction." *DAI* 37 (1977): 5133A.

Index

Acker, Kathy, 278, 285, 306
Ahab, Captain, 8, 111, 271
Aiken, Conrad, 306
Allegory, 27, 129, 131, 132, 135, 271
"The American Scholar" (Ralph Waldo Emerson), 56, 178, 193
The American Scholar (Ralph Ellison), 193
An American Dream (Norman Mailer), 119
The Assistant (Bernard Malamud), 3
Auster, Paul, 293, 297, 306–307

Barth, John, 24, 25, 26, 80, 92, 235, 238, 240, 241, 243, 248, 252, 255–258, 260, 261, 263, 285, 286, 288, 297, 305, 307
Barth, Karl, 165, 172
Barzun, Jacques, 220
Bellow, Saul, xi, 10, 11, 12, 13, 16, 17, 24, 26, 31–40, 67, 113–126, 235, 237, 238, 252, 254–255 , 278, 293, 296, 297, 307–309
Berryman, John, 33, 122, 138, 235

"The Birthmark" (Nathaniel Hawthorne), 128
Blake, William, xii, 14, 15, 17, 24, 46, 116, 121, 122, 124, 233, 234, 235, 237, 238, 239, 242, 244, 245, 246, 247, 249, 250, 251, 258
The Blithedale Romance (Nathaniel Hawthorne), 168, 169, 265
Bloom, Harold, 24, 128, 153, 155–156, 233, 236, 241, 242, 255
Bowles, Paul, 309
Brautigan, Richard, 309–310
Byron, Lord, George Gordon, vii, 5, 6, 8, 13, 21, 44, 49, 72, 74, 75, 78 79, 105, 233, 237, 242, 250–251

Capote, Truman, 310
The Castle of Otranto (Horace Walpole), 45, 46
Catch-22 (Joseph Heller), 23, 225
The Catcher in the Rye (J.D. Salinger), 3, 23, 75, 226

Chase, Richard, 12, 13, 28, 91, 92, 297

Cheever, John, 25, 263, 267, 310

Chomsky, Noam, 238, 239, 248, 249

"Christabel" (Samuel Taylor Coleridge), 24, 245

Clarel (Herman Melville), 15, 110

Coleridge, Samuel Taylor, 15, 17, 24, 73, 79, 105, 106, 116, 122, 234, 238, 239, 245, 292

Conrad, Joseph, 33, 71, 72, 116, 127

"The Conversation of Eiros and Charmion" (Edgar Allan Poe), 211

Coover, Robert, 25, 261, 262, 263, 268–269, 278–279, 284, 285, 287, 288

The Crying of Lot 49 (Thomas Pynchon), 14, 80, 83–84, 86, 252

"The Custom House" (Nathaniel Hawthorne), 101, 130, 146, 295, 296

The Deer Park (Norman Mailer), 3

DeLillo, Don, 285, 310

Derrida, Jacques, 285–286

Didion, Joan, 25, 310–311

Doctorow, E. L., 269, 311

Don Juan, (Lord Byron), 74, 75, 78, 163

Ellison, Ralph, xi, 13, 20–21, 177–201, 311–312

Emerson, Ralph Waldo, xii, 3, 5, 7–8, 16, 20–21, 27, 56, 61, 161, 177–201, 279, 281, 289, 290, 291, 292, 293, 295, 305, 306

Endymion (Percy Bysshe Shelley), 118

The English Notebooks (Nathaniel Hawthorne), 8

"Entropy" (Thomas Pynchon), 14, 80–89, 247

"The Eolian Harp" (Samuel Taylor Coleridge), 234

Erdrich, Louise, 312

"Ethan Brand" (Nathaniel Hawthorne), 15, 94–96, 98, 100

Evil, 5, 6, 7, 15, 27, 55, 67, 02, 93, 96–100, 129, 131, 162, 225, 226, 244, 245, 272, 273, 294, 295

Fabulation and Metafiction (Robert Scholes), 92

The Fantastic (*See also* Magic/the Marvelous/Mystery/the Supernatural), 1, 26, 67, 92, 106, 148–149, 211, 227, 242, 253, 265, 289, 298

Faust (the character), 5, 7, 107, 118, 120, 251, 253

Federman, Raymond, 287–288

Feidelson, Charles, 3

Fiedler, Leslie, 135, 251, 287

Fitzgerald, F. Scott, 2, 81, 82, 211, 222

Foerster, Norman, 4–5

Foucault, Michel, 285–286

Frankenstein (Mary Shelley), 12, 45, 46, 47, 243, 271

Franny and Zooey (J.D. Salinger), 71, 297

Gardner, John, xi, 13, 15, 16, 24, 25, 100, 101, 105–112, 235, 238, 242, 243, 252, 257, 258, 259, 260, 305, 312–313

Gass, William, 288, 305, 313

Gibson, William, 313

God, 3, 4, 5, 6, 8, 27, 46, 53, 93, 98, 99, 105–106, 107, 109,

119–120, 121, 132, 133, 134, 167, 233–234, 248, 249, 254, 271, 289, 290, 291, 294,

Goethe, Johann Wolfgang, 2, 17, 21, 34, 193, 251, 289–290

"The Gold Bug" (Edgar Allan Poe), 66

Graff, Gerald, 240, 241, 287

Grendel (John Gardner), 24, 242, 243, 258

Grunwald, Henry Anatole, 13, 227

Gravity's Rainbow (Thomas Pynchon), 24, 243–244, 267–268, 297

Hawkes, John, 128–129, 261, 262, 263, 268. 269, 285, 313–314

Hawthorne, Nathaniel, xii, 5, 8, 14, 15, 17, 18, 19, 20, 24, 25, 26, 27, 28, 63, 91–101, 127–136, 141, 144–149, 151, 152, 155, 159–175, 261–266, 269, 272–275, 277, 290, 295–297, 306

Heller, Joseph, 23, 80, 225, 269, 314

Henderson The Rain King (Saul Bellow), 3, 16, 17, 67, 116, 117, 119, 297

Herzog (Saul Bellow), 16, 17, 24, 117–119, 122, 254–255

Hite, Molly, 285, 288

The House of the Seven Gables (Nathaniel Hawthorne), 129, 266, 296–297

"How to Write a Blackwood Article" (Edgar Allan Poe), 66

Hoyt, Charles, 9–10

Humboldt's Gift (Saul Bellow), 16, 17, 121–123

Hume, Robert, 6–7, 235

Idealism, philosophical, 7, 8, 22, 24, 26, 118, 119, 123, 277, 278, 293, 294, 295, 297, 298

"Immortality Ode" (Wordsworth), 17, 116, 119, 122, 123

Inspiration, 22, 26, 74, 206, 212, 236, 256, 265, 277, 281, 290–294, 298

"Ion" (Plato), 290

Jakobson, Roman, 26, 278–279, 281–283

Jason and Medeia (John Gardner), 109–110, 259

Jazz (Toni Morrison), 277

Jones, Gayl, 314

Kant, Immanuel, 38, 39

Keats, John, 17, 21, 118, 119, 122, 124

Kelley, William H., 314

Kennedy, William, 26, 288, 296, 297, 314

Kermode, Frank, 287

Kerouac, Jack, 3, 10, 160, 228, 314

Kesey, Ken, 315

Kingston, Maxine Hong, 315

Knowles, John, 315

Kosinski, Jerzy, 216, 262, 263, 315

The Last Gentleman (Walker Percy), 98, 101

Levin, Harry, 3

"Ligeia" (Edgar Allan Poe), 111, 210

Lolita (Vladimir Nabokov), 21, 22, 204–205, 210

Love in the Ruins (Walker Percy), 98, 99

Lovejoy, Arthur, 3, 253

Lyotard, Francois, 286

Magic (*See also* the Fantastic/the Marvelous/Mystery/the Supernatural), 2, 45, 46, 110, 140, 253, 271

Mailer, Norman, 3, 10, 25, 26, 119–120, 252, 266, 273, 296, 297, 315–316

Malamud, Bernard, 3, 9–10, 316

Manicheanism, 7, 8, 25, 92, 98–100, 245, 262–266

The Man of La Mancha, 3, 230

Marx, Karl, 31, 34, 49, 205

The Marvelous (*See also* the Fantastic/Magic/Mystery/the Supernatural), 38, 295–296, 298

Matthiessen, Francis O., 3

Maturin, Charles, 7

McCullers, Carson, 316

Melmoth, the Wanderer (Charles Maturin), 7

Melville, Herman, vii, 5, 7, 8, 14, 15, 16, 20–21, 25, 27, 28, 55, 63, 99, 100, 105, 109, 110, 111, 137, 161, 185, 186, 197, 269–270, 306

Miller, Henry, 85, 316–317

"Milton" (William Blake), 235, 250

Minimalism, 288–289

"The Minister's Black Veil" (Nathaniel Hawthorne), 273

Moby Dick (Herman Melville), 7, 8, 15, 40, 55, 110, 111

A Month of Sundays (John Updike), 19, 159, 163–166

Morrison, Toni, xi, 10, 12–13, 18–19, 26, 51–67, 137–157, 277, 278, 288, 293, 296, 297, 317–318

The Mosquito Coast (Paul Theroux), 270–273

Mr. Sammler's Planet (Saul Bellow), 17, 119, 120, 121, 237

"My Kinsman Major Molineux" (Nathaniel Hawthorne), 272

Mystery (*See also* the Fantastic/Magic/the Marvelous/The Supernatural), 5, 7, 8, 14, 18, 72, 73, 76, 94, 98, 108, 130, 145, 166, 206, 210, 261, 264, 272, 274

Mystery and Manners (Flannery O'Connor), 131, 132, 133

Myth 4, 7, 24, 27, 71, 72, 152, 153, 160, 162, 163, 236–260, 261, 265, 271, 273

Nabokov, Vladimir, xi, 13, 14, 21–22, 166, 203–215, 236, 285, 306, 318–319

The Narrative of Arthur Gordon Pym (E. A. Poe), 15, 16, 51–52, 63, 66, 111–112

Nature, 4, 5, 11, 16, 27, 32, 36, 54, 55, 130, 271, 292

"Nature" (Ralph Waldo Emerson), 8, 295

Naylor, Gloria, 138, 142, 143, 319

Neoplatonism, 3, 289

Negative Romanticism, xii, 5–7, 8, 23–24, 233–234, 274

Nihilism, 6, 8, 119, 120, 134, 231, 271, 272, 278, 286, 287, 288, 289

Nietzsche, Friedrich, 285–286

Noyes, Russell, 2

Oates, Joyce Carol, 25, 262, 319–320

O'Connor, Flannery, xi, 13, 14, 17–18, 19, 25, 26, 91, 100, 101, 127–136, 263, 296, 297, 320

Olderman, Raymond, 261, 263

On the Road (Jack Kerouac), 3, 160

Organic View of Art, 4, 6, 14, 26, 72, 74, 289, 290, 291, 292–295

Paley, Grace, 321

Peckham, Morse, 3, 6, 290

Percy, Walker, xi, 13, 14–15, 91–103, 306, 321

"The Philosophy of Composition" (Edgar Allan Poe), 22, 206

Pieper, Joseph, 38–39

Plato, 22, 33, 35, 39, 105, 193, 206, 207, 208, 210, 212, 290–291, 298

Poe, Edgar Allan, xii, 5, 12, 14, 15, 16, 17, 21, 22, 26, 28, 51, 52 , 66, 105, 106, 109, 111–112, 127, 128, 165, 203–215, 263, 274, 277, 290, 293

"The Poet" (Ralph Waldo Emerson), 291

"The Poetic Principle" (Edgar Allan Poe), 22, 206

Positive Romanticism, xii, 3–5, 233

Praz, Mario, 1–2, 5–6

Prometheus Unbound (Percy Bysshe Shelley), 245

Purdy, James, 321

Pynchon, Thomas, xi, 10, 11–12, 13, 14, 24, 25, 26, 27, 79–89, 235, 241, 243–245, 247, 252, 260, 261, 262, 263, 267–268, 269, 297, 321–323

Reed, Ishmael, 285, 323

Robinson, Marilynne, 323

Roger's Version (John Updike), 20, 159, 161, 163, 166–169

Romance, xii, 1, 7, 12, 13, 14, 15, 17, 18, 19, 25, 26, 27, 47, 54, 55, 64, 65, 79–89. 91, 92, 93, 97, 100, 101, 102, 128, 129, 130, 131, 135, 140, 146, 153, 207, 261, 262–263, 264. 265, 266, 267, 269, 270, 273, 274, 277, 278, 289, 295–297

The Romantic Agony (Mario Praz), 1–2, 5–6

Rosenberg, Harold, 31

Roth, Philip, 26, 269, 297, 323

Rousseau, Jean Jacques, 1–2, 251, 289

S. (John Updike), 20, 159, 163, 169–171

Sade, Donatien A. F., Marquis de, 79

Salinger, J. D., xi, 3, 10, 13, 14, 23, 26, 71–78, 226–227, 297, 323–324

Sartre, Jean Paul, 34–35, 248

The Scarlet Letter (Nathaniel Hawthorne), xii, 18, 19, 20, 93, 94, 96, 101, 130, 137–157, 159–175, 295, 296

Schlegel, August Wilhelm, 239, 292

Scholes, Robert, 92, 287–288

Shelley, Mary, 12, 45, 47

Shelley, William Bysshe, 14, 15, 17, 24, 116, 121, 124, 238, 242, 245, 253

Singer, Isaac Bashevis, 324

Smith, Allan Lloyd, 287

Song of Solomon (Toni Morrison), 18, 140, 144, 145, 146, 153, 154, 297

Star Wars (George Lucas), 3, 46

Steiner, Rudolf, 113, 121

Sterne, Lawrence, 72, 74

Styron, Willam, 25, 67, 267, 324

Sukenick, Ronald, 287

The Supernatural (*See also* the
Fantastic/Magic/the Marvelous,
Mystery), 7, 8, 18, 26, 27, 46,
73, 130, 266, 289, 295–296, 298

Theroux, Paul, 25, 270–273, 324
Thompson, G. R., 7
Thoreau, Henry D., 12, 61, 72, 74,
75–76, 78, 85, 291, 293, 306
Transcendence, 8, 12, 14, 17, 24,
26, 28, 47, 79, 80, 121, 130,
141, 183, 188, 195, 245, 285,
294, 298
Transcendentalism, 20, 27, 178,
308–309

Updike, John, xi, 13, 17, 19–20,
25, 71, 159–175, 269, 270,
324–325

Vonnegut, Kurt, 26, 261, 262, 263,
268, 285, 293, 297, 325–326

Walden (Henry David Thoreau),
76, 78
Walker, Alice, 26, 139, 293, 297,
326
Walpole, Horace, 45, 46
"A Week on the Concord and
Merrimack Rivers" (H. D.
Thoreau), 291
Wellek, René, 3–4, 5, 162,
289–290
Welty, Eudora, 326
White, Hayden, 282–283
Whitman, Walt, 21, 161, 185,
306
Wimsatt, William K., 238–240
Wolfe, Tom, 326
Wordsworth, William, xii, 2, 4, 5,
10, 13, 14, 17, 27, 31, 32, 33,
40, 72, 73, 74, 76, 114–115,
116, 117, 118, 119, 120,
121–122, 123, 124, 233, 237,
251, 289